CIMETIÈRE DE MONTMARTRE
MONTMARTRE
Basilique du Sacré-Cœur
St-Pierre
Bd Barbès
Av. de Clichy
R. Caulaincourt
Moulin Rouge
Rue des Abbesses
St-Jean
Boulevard de Clichy
Place de Clichy
Boulevard de Rochechouart
Pl. Pigalle
page 160
Rue Notre-Dame-de-Lorette
Rue La Bruyère
Rue d'Amsterdam
Rue de Clichy
Rue Blanche
Rue des Martyrs
Rue Rodier
Rue de Londres
Rue St-Lazare
Rue de Châteaudin
St-Lazare
Rue la Fayette
R. de la Chaussée
Rue de Provence
Rue Haussmann
Folies Bergère
Rue Richer
R. Drouot
Palais Garnier
R. Tronchet
Bd des Italiens
-Marie-de-la-Madeleine
Bd des Capucines
Th. des Capucines
Rue du Quatre-Septembre
R. de la Paix
Place Vendôme
Rue Cambon
Av. de l'Opéra
R. des Petits Champs
page 76
La Bourse
Bibliothèque Nationale-Richelieu
Rue N.D. des Victoires
Rue Montmartre
Bd Poissonnière
Rue Réaumur
Rue Montorgueil
Rue Poissonnière
Rue de Cléry
St-Roch
Rue St-Honoré
Jeu de Paume
JARDIN DU PALAIS ROYAL
Comédie Française
Palais Royal
JARDIN DES TUILERIES
JARDIN DU CARROUSEL
Quai des Tuileries
Seine
Musée du Louvre
Quai Fr.-Mitterrand
Pont Royal
Musée d'Orsay
Pont du Carrousel
Rue de Lille
Rue du Bac
Bourse de Commerce
St-Eustache
Rue du Louvre
Rue Étienne-Marcel
Forum des Halles
Rue Berger
Rue de Rivoli
Pont Neuf
Quai de Conti
École Nationale Supérieure des Beaux-Arts
Institut de France
Rue Bonaparte
R. Mazarine
Rue Dauphine
Saints Pères
R. de l'Université
Palais de Justice
Ste-Chapelle
Bd du Palais
Quai d. Grands Augustins
St-Germain-des-Prés
Boulevard St-Germain
R. St-André-des-Arts
Rue de Seine
Rue du Four
St-Sulpice
R. St-Sulpice
Théâtre National de l'Odeon
Rue Madame
Rue de Vaugirard
Palais du Luxembourg
JARDIN DU LUXEMBOURG
Rue Guynemer
Rue A.-Comte
Rue d'Assas
Musée Zadkine
Boulevard Raspail
Rue de Rennes
Rue du Midi
Rue de Grenelle
Boulevard St-Michel
La Sorbonne
Rue St-Jacques
R. Soufflot
R. Cujas
Panthéon
Rue Clovis
Rue Gay-Lussac
Rue Lhomond
Rue des Écoles
Rue Monge
St-Julien-le-Pauvre
Notre-Dame
Île de la Cité
Quai de la Tournelle
Rue de la Cité
Hôtel de Ville
Quai de l'Hotel de Ville
St-Merri
Centre Georges Pompidou
Rue Rambuteau
Rue du Temple
Rue St-Martin
Rue St-Denis
Boulevard de Sébastopol
Rue Beaubourg
MARAIS
Rue de Turbigo
Musée des Arts et Métiers
Rue de Réaumur
Boulevard de Strasbourg
Rue du Faubourg St-Denis
Rue du Faubourg St-Martin
Bd de Bonne Nouvelle
Bd St-Martin
R. des Petites Écuries
Rue d'Hauteville
Rue de Paradis
Rue de Chabrol
Rue de Maubeuge
Rue de Magenta
Gare du Nord
Gare de l'Est
Rue du Faubourg St-Denis
Rue de la Chapelle
Bd de la Chapelle
Rue de l'Aqueduc
Rue la Fayette
Rue du Faubourg St-Martin
Quai de Valmy
Quai de Jemmapes
Canal St-Martin
Rue de la Grange
Pl. du Colonel-Fabien
Avenue Claude-Vellefaux
Bd de la Villette
page 179
Rue du Château d'Eau
Rue de Magenta
Rue du Faubourg-du-Temple
Pl. de la République
Av. de la République
Boulevard Voltaire
Bd du Temple
R. de Bretagne
Rue Charlot
Rue de Turenne
Rue des Archives
Musée de l'Histoire de France
Musée National Picasso
Musée Carnavalet
page 190
Rue des Francs-Bourgeois
Rue Vieille du Temple
Bd des Filles du Calvaire
Boulevard Beaumarchais
Pl. des Vosges
Maison de Victor Hugo
Rue St-Antoine
Place de la Bastille
Hôtel d'Aumont
Hôtel de Sens
R. des Deux Ponts
Île St-Louis
Pont de Sully
Bd Henri IV
Bd Morland
Quai Henri IV
Quai St-Bernard
Institut de Mode Arabe
Rue Jussieu
Rue Cuvier
JARDIN DES PLANTES
JARDIN TINO ROSSI
Pont d'Austerlitz
Quai de la Rapée
Bd Bourdon
Bd de la Bastille
Rue de Lyon
Bd de l'Hôpital
Gare d'Austerlitz

INSIGHT GUIDES

PARIS

APA PUBLICATIONS
Part of the Langenscheidt Publishing Group

INSIGHT GUIDES
PARIS

Series Editor
Rachel Lawrence
Picture Editor
Steven Lawrence
Art Director
Ian Spick
Cartography Editor
Zoë Goodwin
Series Publishing Manager
Rachel Fox

Distribution

UK & Ireland
GeoCenter International Ltd
Meridian House, Churchill Way West, Basingstoke, Hampshire, RG21 6YR
sales@geocenter.co.uk
United States
Langenscheidt Publishers, Inc.
36–36 33rd Street 4th Floor
Long Island City, NY 11106
orders@langenscheidt.com
Australia
Universal Publishers
1 Waterloo Road
Macquarie Park, NSW 2113
sales@universalpublishers.com.au
New Zealand
Hema Maps New Zealand Ltd (HNZ)
Unit 2, 10 Cryers Road
East Tamaki, Auckland 2013
sales.hema@clear.net.nz
Worldwide
Apa Publications GmbH & Co. Verlag KG (Singapore branch)
38 Joo Koon Road, Singapore 628990
Tel: (65) 6865-1600.
apasin@singnet.com.sg

Printing

Insight Print Services (Pte) Ltd
38 Joo Koon Road, Singapore 628990
Tel: (65) 6865-1600.

First Edition 1988
Twelfth Edition 2010

www.insightguides.com

ABOUT THIS BOOK

What makes an Insight Guide different? Since our first book pioneered the use of creative full-colour photography in travel guides in 1970, we have aimed to provide not only reliable information but also the key to a real understanding of a destination and its people.

Now, when the internet can supply inexhaustible (but not always reliable) facts, our books marry text and pictures to provide that more elusive quality: knowledge. To achieve this, they rely on the authority of locally based writers and photographers.

Paris abundantly supplies the things visitors expect from the capital of fashion, fine dining, arts and romance; but it also works hard to keep itself new. Many major museums have been revamped and exciting newcomers like the Musée du Quai Branly have joined the throng. The shopping scene is booming; the nightlife is newly revitalised, some world-class hotels have opened, and all in all, Paris is in better shape than ever. *Insight Guide: Paris* takes you to the best of it.

CONTACTING THE EDITORS

We would appreciate it if readers would alert us to errors or outdated information by writing to:

Insight Guides, P.O. Box 7910, London SE1 1WE, England.
insight@apaguide.co.uk

THE CONTRIBUTORS TO THIS BOOK

This edition of *City Guide: Paris* was commissioned and edited by **Rachel Lawrence**, Series Editor for City Guides in Insight's London editorial office.

This new edition has been thoroughly updated by **Fabienne Gondrand**, a freelance translator and writer based in the historic district of Montmartre. Bilingual Gondrand has been a Paris resident for over ten years, but has always loved to travel; prior to settling in Paris, she lived in England and in the USA.

This edition of the book builds on previous editions produced by **Carine Tracanelli**, **Nick Rider**, **Andrew Eames**, **Caroline Radula-Scott**, **Clare Griffiths**, **Natasha Edwards** and **Cathy Muscat**. Past contributors whose work is still evident here include **Simon Cropper** (Chic Shopping and Paris After Dark chapters, and the essay on Parisian suburbs, The Outsiders), **Patrick Welch** (accommodation and restaurant listings), **Marton Radkai** (history chaptesr), **Susan Bell** (one-page features on Café Life, The Métro and Paris Schooling), **Philippe Artru** (architecture), **Brent Gregston** (Parisiens, Parisiennes), and Paris-based food writer **Laura Calder** (Paris on a Plate).

The design was created by **Klaus Geisler** and implemented by **Corrie Wingate**. The principal photographers were Insight regulars **Ilpo Musto**, **Kevin Cummings**, **Jerry Dennis** and **Britta Jaschinski**.

The book was proof-read by **Neil Titman** and indexed by **Helen Peters**. Additional help was provided by Editorial Assistant **Catherine Dreghorn**.

The Guide at a Glance

The book is carefully structured both to convey an understanding of the city and its culture and to guide readers through its attractions and activities:

◆ The Best Of section at the front of the book helps you to prioritise. The first spread contains all the Top Sights, while Editor's Choice details unique experiences, the best buys or other recommendations.

◆ To understand Paris, you need to know something of its past. The city's history and culture are described in authoritative essays written by specialists in their fields who have lived in and documented Paris for many years.

◆ The Places section details all the attractions worth seeing. The main places of interest are coordinated by number with the maps.

◆ A list of recommended restaurants, bars and cafés is printed at the end of each chapter.

◆ Photographs throughout the book are chosen not only to illustrate geography and buildings, but also to convey the moods of the city and the life of its people.

◆ The Travel Tips section includes all the practical information you will need, divided into five key sections: transport, accommodation, activities (including nightlife, events, tours and sports), shopping, and an A–Z of practical tips. Information may be located quickly by using the index on the back cover flap of the book.

◆ Two detailed street atlases are included at the back of the book, complete with a full index. On the second one, you will find all the restaurants and hotels plotted for your convenience.

Places & Sights

Colour-coding at the top of every page makes it easy to find each area in the book. These are coordinated by specific area on the orientation map on pages 70–1.

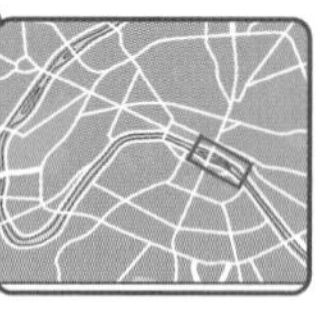

A locator map pinpoints the specific area covered in each chapter. The page reference at the top indicates where to find a detailed map of the area highlighted in red.

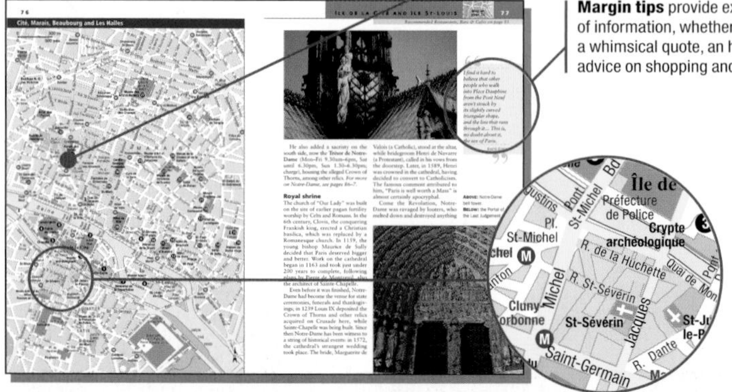

Margin tips provide extra little snippets of information, whether it's a practical tip, a whimsical quote, an historical fact or advice on shopping and eating.

A four-colour map provides a bird's-eye view of the area covered in the chapter, with the main attractions co-ordinated by number with the main text.

PHOTO FEATURES

Picture stories offer visual coverage of major sights or unusual attractions. The map shows where it is, while vital statistics convey practical information: address, contact details, website, opening times, and if there's a charge.

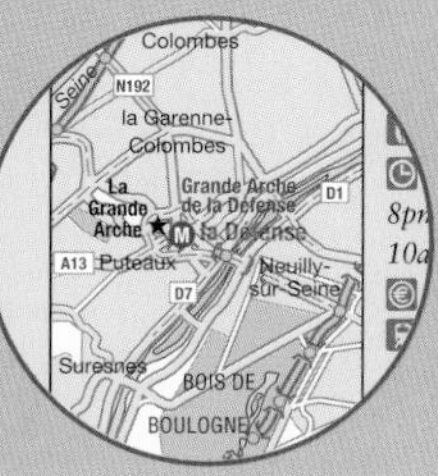

RESTAURANT LISTINGS

Restaurant listings feature the best establishments within each area, giving the address, phone number, opening times and price category followed by a useful review. The grid reference refers to the atlas at the back of the book.

Le Pamphlet
38 rue Debelleyne, 3rd
☎ 01 42 72 39 24 Ⓒ L
Tue–Fri, D Mon–Sat. €€
[p339, D1]
You'll find very fine cooking and a remarkably good-value menu at this discreet and

TRAVEL TIPS

Rail
The fast, frequent train service from London St Pancras to Paris (Gare du Nord), runs about 16 times a day, and takes 2 hours 25 minutes. Some trains stop at Ashford in Kent (two hours from Paris). For reservations, contact Eurostar, tel: 0870 518 6186 (UK) or 01 70 70 99 49 (France) or www.eurostar.com. There are frequent fare offers, and lower fares for children aged 4–11; those under 3 travel free but are not guaranteed a seat.

Advice-packed Travel Tips provide all the practical knowledge you'll need before and during your trip: how to get there, getting around, where to stay and what to do. The A–Z section is a handy summary of practical information, arranged alphabetically.

Contents

Best of Paris

Introduction

History

Features

Insights

Places

Restaurants & Bars

Travel Tips

Maps

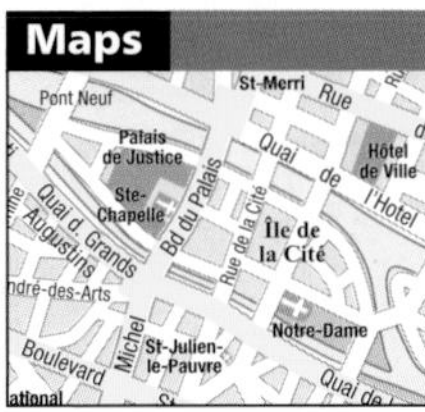

The Best of Paris: Top Sights

At a glance, everything you can't afford to miss in Paris, from the emblematic Eiffel Tower and Arc de Triomphe to the world-class museums and the cutting-edge architecture of what is a thoroughly modern city.

▽ The **Eiffel Tower** was built for the centenary of the Revolution, and the city authorities originally planned to take it down after a few years. The tower is the city's number one visitor attraction, and a global icon. *See pages 234–5*

▷ West of the city, the business district's centrepiece is the **Grande Arche de la Défense** – so large, Notre-Dame cathedral could fit underneath it. *See pages 252–3*

△ A palace fit for a king: the **Château de Versailles** is an awe-inspiring confection of gilt, paintings, mirrors, lavish fabrics, stunning architecture and landscaped gardens. As extensive restoration work progresses it is becoming more gorgeous. *See pages 272–5*

◁ The **Arc de Triomphe** honours Napoleon's armies, and is the focus of national celebrations in France. The view from the top is breathtaking. *See pages 156–7*

▷ Once a railway station, the **Musée d'Orsay** is now one of the world's finest museums of Impressionist art. *See pages 236–9*

▽ **St-Germain-des-Prés** still evokes memories of its 1950s heyday of intellectual prowess and easy-going chic – though these days fashion has largely replaced philosophy. *See pages 203–5*

◁ The **Centre Pompidou** is an international icon of inside-out high-tech and is as much of an attraction as its contents, which include the Musée National d'Art Moderne. *See pages 114–5*

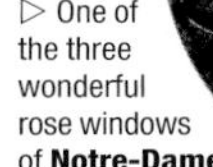

▷ One of the three wonderful rose windows of **Notre-Dame** cathedral, the best-known sacred building in Europe. *See pages 86–7*

◁ The Moulin Rouge keeps the spirit of cabaret **Montmartre** alive. *See pages 159–75*

△ The Fontaine de l'Observatoire, at the lovely **Jardin du Luxembourg**, which is full of fine sculptures of famous artists, historic figures and animals. *See pages 208–9*

▷ The glass-and-steel pyramid is an inspired addition to the venerable architecture of the **Louvre**, the best museum in the world. *See pages 136–41*

The Best of Paris: Editor's Choice

Unique attractions, festivals and events, top cafés and shops, family outings and money-saving tips personally selected by our editor

Only In Paris

- The view from the top of the Eiffel Tower one hour before sunset, and the tower's shimmering costume of light after dark. *See pages 234–5*
- The view of the city, as night falls, from the steps in front of Sacré-Cœur. *See page 162*
- The lift ride to the top of the Grande Arche de la Défense, and the view across the Bois de Boulogne. *See pages 252–3*
- The *Mona Lisa*'s enigmatic smile at the Louvre. *See page 122*
- The Impressionists at the Musée d'Orsay. *See pages 236–9*
- Rodin's beautiful sculpture garden. *See pages 228–9*
- Picasso's legacy to the French state. *See page 96*
- The 19th-century shopping arcades around the Palais Royal. *See page 132*
- The elegant mansions of the Marais and its glorious centrepiece, the Place des Vosges. *See page 92*
- The offbeat boutiques and hip cafés of Bastille. *See pages 178–9*
- The quiet backstreets, arty shops and bars of Montmartre. *See page 166*
- Napoleon's tomb in Hôtel des Invalides. *See page 227*
- The famous graves of Père Lachaise cemetery. *See page 182*
- Subterranean passages, packed with skulls and bones in the catacombs. *See page 212*
- Enjoy a coffee and a croissant in a literary café and browse through the boutiques of St-Germain-des-Prés. *See page 203*
- Mint tea in the Paris Mosque. *See page 198*
- Evening picnic with wine, on the Pont des Arts. *See page 204*
- Late-night contemporary art at the Palais de Tokyo. *See page 222*
- Open-air swimming followed by drinks on the terrace at the floating pool on the Seine. *See page 213*
- The stunning Cinémathèque Française. *See page 185*
- The two MK2 cinemas on opposite banks of the Canal St-Martin, linked by a nifty little ferry. *See page 214*
- A 21st-century take on public transport: the driverless trains on Métro line 14. *See page 281*

BEST MUSEUMS AND MONUMENTS

- **Centre Pompidou** Masterpieces of modern and contemporary art in an icon of high-tech architecture. *See pages 114–5*
- **Les Invalides** Testament to the imperial ambitions of Louis XIV and Napoleon. *See page 227*
- **Musée des Arts Forains** A magical collection of old fairground rides, all in working order. *See page 184*
- **Musée Guimet** Buddhist sculptures from Angkor and other treasures from the Orient. *See page 223*
- **Musée du Quai Branly** Tribal art housed in one of the city's most dynamic buildings. *See page 224*
- **Musée du Louvre** The *Mona Lisa*, *Venus de Milo*, *Raft of the Medusa* and much, much more – all in palatial surroundings. *See pages 136–41*
- **Musée de l'Orangerie** A refurbished Monet showcase. *See page 127*
- **Musée d'Orsay** A treasure trove of Impressionist masterpieces. *See pages 236–9*
- **Musée Zadkine** An intimate glimpse of the artistic past of Montparnasse. *See page 211*
- **Notre-Dame** and **Sainte-Chapelle** Two of the finest Gothic churches in the world. *See pages 75, 86–7 and 80*
- **Palais Garnier** Opulence at the opera in the grand staircase and magnificent foyer. *See page 145*

BEST SHOPPING

- **Au Printemps** The department store that tops them all: six floors of fashion. *See pages 57, 146, 303*
- **The Champs-Elysées** Fashionable again with a slew of swanky concept stores. *See page 148*
- **Colette** Pioneering concept store that picks the best of what's stylish and innovative. *See pages 57 and 128*
- **Galerie Vivienne** The best preserved of the capital's 19th-century shopping galleries, elegant precursors of the department store. *See page 132*
- **La Hune** A quintessential Left Bank bookstore. *See page 204*
- **Le Bon Marché** The oldest, and still the most chic department store in Paris. *See page 302*
- **Les Caves Taillevent** A dazzling array of wines. *See page 306*
- **Marché aux Puces de St-Ouen** Wander among the bric-a-brac stalls of this huge flea market. *See page 59*

LEFT: Art Nouveau Métro station. **ABOVE:** behind the Musée d'Orsay clock. **RIGHT:** fashion emporium Au Printemps.

PARIS FOR FAMILIES

- **Aquarium Tropical** Catch up with the crocs and tropical fish at the Palais de la Porte Dorée. *See page 249*
- **Bois de Boulogne** The Parisian's favourite Sunday afternoon playground, with woods, gardens, lakes and cycling tracks, an amusement park for children and even a folk museum. *See page 243*
- **Canal St-Martin** With its nine locks, the tranquil canal makes for an attractive boat trip, starting from Bastille. *See page 180*
- **Disneyland Paris** The most popular tourist attraction in Europe. *See pages 254–9*
- **Grande Galerie de l'Evolution** Revamped natural history museum with a truly impressive collection of stuffed animals. *See page 200*
- **Jardin du Luxembourg** Puppet shows, tennis courts, model boats, playgrounds, chess tables and honey bees in the quintessential Parisian park. *See pages 208–9*
- **Jardins des Tuileries** The well-manicured gardens adjacent to the Louvre are the perfect pleasure park: avenues of trees, statues, pony rides, toy boats, cafés and children's trampolines, as well as a giant Ferris wheel at Christmas and Easter. *See page 125*
- **Musée Grévin** A fun waxworks museum, full of cheerfully incompatible figures from Marie-Antoinette to Spiderman. *See page 144*
- **Notre-Dame** Kids love climbing steps: ascend the towers of Notre-Dame for a bird's-eye view of the gargoyles. *See page 79*
- **Parc des Buttes-Chaumont** Ice-skating, a boating lake, a fake mountain and waterfall, puppet shows and donkey rides. *See page 248*
- **Parc de la Villette** Science museum, music and dance conservatory, a giant IMAX screen and children's museum, all set in futuristic gardens. *See page 246*

GOURMET PARIS

- **Berthillon ice-cream** on the Ile St-Louis. *See page 82*
- **Chez René** Timeless bistro atmosphere and the perfect *coq au vin*. *See page 206*
- **Drouant** A revamped classic that puts a new spin on the hors d'oeuvre concept. *See page 154*
- **Fauchon** and **Hédiard** Famous delicatessens brimming with visually stunning and mouth-watering delicacies. *See page 146*
- **Guy Savoy** Light and sophisticated dishes: a gastronomic treat. *See page 154*
- **La Coupole** For an oyster feast and classic brasserie experience. *See page 217*
- **Ladurée** This elegant *salon de thé* is a Paris institution, famous for its melt-in-the-mouth macaroons. *See page 154*
- **Le Comptoir** Yves Camdeborde's no-choice set meal is the talk of the town – but you'll need to book for it months ahead. *See page 206*
- **Le Meurice** Yannick Alléno's wonderful cooking in the splendorous dining room of a grand hotel. *See page 129*
- **L'Ourcine** Run by one of a new generation of young chefs revisiting bistro cuisine. *See page 207*
- **Marché d'Aligre** Sells some of the best and cheapest produce in Paris. *See page 183*
- **Marché Biologique** Organic food and veg at the Sunday morning market on Boulevard Raspail. *See page 203*
- **Pierre Hermé** Ogle the exquisite cakes at one of the city's most celebrated patisseries. *See page 201*

ABOVE AND BELOW: French cuisine – haute or otherwise – has an unrivalled reputation across the globe.

BEST EVENTS & FESTIVALS

- **Feb–Mar**: *Salon de l'Agriculture*. A festival of regional food.
- **Apr–May**: *Foire du Trône*. A huge funfair comes to town.
- **May–July**: Open-air jazz in the Parc de Vincennes.
- **21 June**: *Fête de la Musique*. Free street concerts and dancing.
- **Mid-June**: Gay Pride.
- **July**: Bastille Day. Street party on the night of 13 July at Place de la Bastille. On 14 July, a military parade and fireworks.
- **July–Aug**: *Paris Plage*. The seaside comes to the Seine.
- **Sept**: *Festival d'Automne*. Modern theatre and dance.
- **Oct**: *FIAC*. International modern art fair.
- **Oct**: *La Nuit Blanche*. Museums, monuments, cinemas open all night.

BEST CAFÉS

- **Café Beaubourg** Terraced designer café by the Centre Pompidou with a chic clientele. *See page 113*
- **Café Charbon** A coal shop turned café that's a neighbourhood fixture. *See page 187*
- **Café de Flore** The Left Bank literary café still retains something of the charm of its intellectual heyday. *See page 207*
- **Café de la Ville** Trendy new hangout on the Grands Boulevards. *See page 155*
- **Café du Marché** Classic neighbourhood café with a good menu of market-inspired food. *See page 233*
- **Café Marly** The Louvre's classiest café, with a superb terrace looking onto the Pyramid. *See page 135*
- **Chez Prune** A cornerstone of the trendy Canal St-Martin area. *See page 186*
- **Le Procope** The oldest café in Paris, established in 1686. *See page 207*
- **Le Sancerre** One of the best cafés in Montmartre, drawing an eclectic, young, arty crowd. *See page 173*

ABOVE: the *Fête de la Musique* is a huge street festival, with free concerts and dancing everywhere.

MONEY-SAVING TIPS

Paris Museum Pass (sold at museums, tourist offices, FNAC and Métro stations) gives you priority entrance at the Louvre and enables you to skip the queues while saving money.

Tickets to Ride A *carnet* of 10 tickets (available from bus or Métro stations) gives reduced fares on public transport. The Paris Visite card is valid for one, two, three or five consecutive days on the Métro, bus and railway.

Kiosques Theatre (15 place de la Madeleine and Montparnasse Square) sell half-price theatre tickets from 12.30pm for performances that day.

The sales Traditionally the sales *(soldes)* are held in July and early January but many shops offer mid-season reductions.

Free museums Entry to the permanent collections of ten Paris museums is free, including the Musée Carnavalet, Musée d'Art Moderne, Musée Cognacq-Jay, Musée Zadkine, Musée de la Vie Romantique, Musée Bourdelle, Musée Jean-Moulin, Maison de Victor Hugo and Maison de Balzac. See www.paris.fr/musees for details. All Réunion des Musées Nationaux (RMN) museums are free on the first Sunday of the month.

Free concerts In the Jardin du Luxembourg bandstand in summer, and on Sundays at 5pm in St-Eustache church.

Salades Composées
Salade Niçoise 9.00
Salade Parisienne 9.00
Salade aux Crevettes 9.00
Salade Périgourdine 10.50
Salade de Crottin Chèvre 9.00
"Chaud"
Salade Nordique 10.50
Tartines
"au Pain Poilâne"
Frites & Salades
Tartine Parisienne 8.50
Tartine 3 Fromages 8.50
Tartine Italienne 8.50
Spécialités
"de la maison"
Fondue Bourguignonne
Servie 2 Fois
Entrecôte "XXL"
Côte de Boeuf "pour 2 Personnes"
Entrecôte "Sauce Béarnaise"
Viandes & Plats
Garnis
Pavé au Poivre 12.00
Travers de Porc Caramelisé 11.00
Magret de Canard "au Poivre ou Miel" 12.00
Escalope de Veau "Normande" 12.00
Poulet Rôti 10.00
Steack Tartare "à la Commande" 12.00
Cheddar

PARISIENS, PARISIENNES

Everyone knows something about Paris, even without ever having visited. But the legends and stereotypes have more truth to them than you might think, and there are many exceptions that confound the rules

Paris is divided by the Seine into two lobes that look vaguely like the hemispheres of a brain, with the Ile de la Cité and Ile St-Louis in the centre. According to an old saying, the Left Bank was where you did your thinking – the Sorbonne University has been located there since the Middle Ages – and the Right Bank was the place to spend money. Over time, the city was organised into *arrondissements* (districts), running outwards in a clockwise spiral from the Ile de France (1st *arrondissement*) to the north-east (20th *arrondissement*), all contained within the *Périphérique* (ringroad).

Within the various *arrondissements* there are recognised *quartiers*, or neighbourhoods, often worlds apart though linked by a short Métro ride. Each has its own shops, markets, cafés and local eccentricities. Parisians develop lifetime attachments to their *quartier*. Although supermarket chains are ubiquitous, residents still support local merchants and shop in specialist shops and local markets. Thus, each *quartier* develops a village atmosphere in which residents are known by sight and often by name.

When Parisians talk about where they live, whether they're at the tax office or at a party, they give the number of their arrondissement.

PRECEDING PAGES: street entertainer by the Sacré-Coeur; the glass pyramid entrance to the Louvre.
LEFT AND RIGHT: café life.

The east-west divide

The most important unofficial division in Paris is between the traditionally working-class east end and the mostly bourgeois west. In general, the further east you go, the further left you'll find its inhabitants on the political spectrum. Rents are exorbitant in the western *arrondissements*, but there's a substantial reservoir of affordable real estate in the east. City planners have been struggling for decades to improve the balance, hence the massive urban renewal projects at Bercy and the "new" Left Bank in the southeast.

The east-west dichotomy is rooted in recent history. When Baron Haussmann began to demolish the city's medieval slums in 1860, the

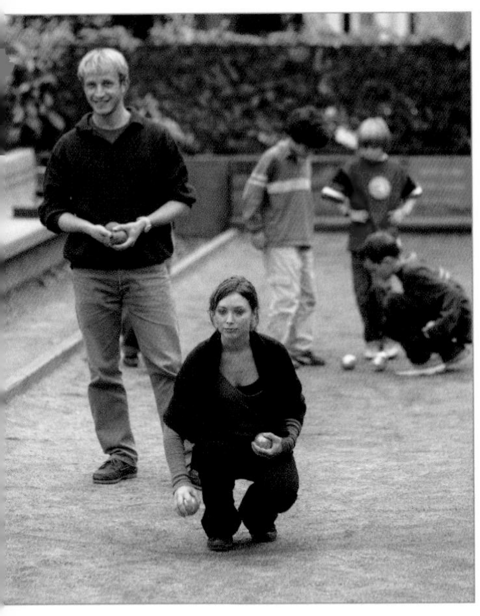

middle classes tended to relocate to the west, whereas the working class moved east. The following decade was one of the most turbulent in the history of Paris and ended in the terrible events of the Commune *(see pages 32–3)*.

Immigrants live on both sides of the Seine, east and west, from Chinatown in the 13th to the predominantly African Goutte d'Or in the 18th. However, the most diverse community of all is probably in the 19th *arrondissement*; in some schools half of the children speak Arabic as a first language, and there are nearly seventy other ethnic groups. The neighbourhood is dotted with mosques, synagogues, and churches of different denominations.

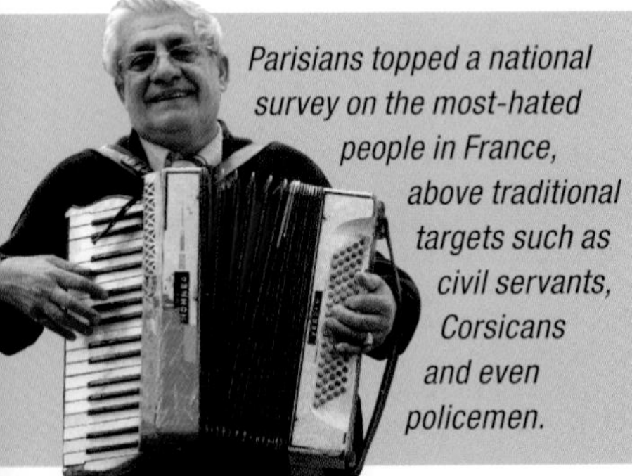

Parisians topped a national survey on the most-hated people in France, above traditional targets such as civil servants, Corsicans and even policemen.

Although the iconic *rive gauche* (Left Bank) still pulls millions of tourists south of the Seine in search of the literary vibe, there have been huge changes in the social geography of Paris since the days of Sartre and de Beauvoir. The Left Bank's Latin Quarter is one of the city's most expensive neighbourhoods, more notable for designer boutiques than it is for literary activity and bohemian lifestyles.

So, where do you go in Paris if you're young and adventurous? From the 1980s up until recently, the simple answer was Bastille. The labyrinth of cobbled backstreets around Place de la Bastille still has a great bar scene, trendy art galleries and cabaret theatre. However, nearby Rue Oberkampf and Rue Ménilmontant are now much cooler, particularly for clubbing. Belleville is also on the map, and for gay or lesbian hotspots, head straight for the Marais.

Outside the *Périphérique*

Paris proper has few ghettos to speak of. For the most part, they're beyond the *Périphérique* where many of the poor are housed in the *cités* (housing estates) of the *banlieue* (suburbs). Until recently, Paris seems to have turned a blind eye to the problems of its poorer suburbs, and most Parisians were rarely confronted with ghetto life unless they wanted to be.

The *cités* in the French suburbs were built in response to the housing shortage after World War II. Row upon row of ugly, grey rectangular high-rises were built to house French workers. Immigrants, encouraged to come to France during the economic boom of the 1960s, moved in later. With the oil crisis and recession of the 1970s, there was less and less employment. Crime and drug use soared *(see box, page 37)*.

Culture and multiculture

Paris considers itself to be the capital of everything French. Despite an official effort to promote regional development, there's still a lot of one-way traffic to Paris for the best and the brightest provincials in almost every field of human endeavour. The tendency of the capital has long been to look down on the provinces. In return, many French people who live outside Paris are disdainful of its inhabitants: "*Parigot, tête de veau*" (which means "the Parisian is pig-headed" – or, literally, calf-headed).

But, as France moves gradually away from its rigidly centralised history, attitudes about the provinces are changing. The Paris press is full of stories about stressed-out Parisians who escape to a better life in the countryside. Regional development programmes are pumping a great deal of capital into cities like Bordeaux and Toulouse. And the new high-speed trains, that zap south in a flash, are worshipped not so much by provincials, but by Parisians who, much as they love their city, can't get out of it fast enough.

FAR LEFT: *boules* is a game loved by French people of all generations. **TOP LEFT:** timeless elegance. **ABOVE:** the international language of graffiti.

Aside from the provinces, the largest contributors to the Parisian cultural and racial *pot au feu* are the former colonies of West and North Africa. Other, earlier waves of immigration have brought an influx of Chinese, Vietnamese, Poles, Russians, Bosnians, Serbs, Armenians, Turks and Greeks. France has the largest Muslim population in Europe and its largest Jewish minority outside of Russia. If Paris on the whole displays genuine tolerance of other races and religions, "immigration" is still used as a code word – particularly by right-wing extremists – to express their fear of foreigners. Legislation has been passed in recent years to beef up the country's security, expand the police force and make it harder for foreigners to move to the country.

The people who live here

Incredibly, Paris is more densely populated than Tokyo, London and New York, and Parisians' high stress levels can partly be put down to the fact that they live literally on top of one another, squeezed into small apartments, packed into the city's 100 sq km (40 sq miles). There's intense competition for desirable living space. Paradoxically, this battle occurs in a city where 16 per cent of apartments lie vacant. Moreover, high

rents mean that many Parisians have neither the time nor the money to appreciate their city, being trapped in a routine they call *Métro-boulot-dodo* (commuting, working, sleeping). Nonetheless, for anyone fortunate enough to live in the city centre, the rewards far outweigh the demands. Human in scale, clean, safe, cosmopolitan and lively, Paris deserves its reputation as one of the best cities in which to enjoy the good life.

Parisians, as a whole, are such a diverse collection of races and cultures that it's virtually impossible to stereotype them. Still, there are ties that bind. Parisians are proud and often impatient, always complaining about their social services, yet often defending them, too. In general they are class-conscious and fashion-savvy, largely traditional when it comes to food and etiquette, refreshingly open-minded about art, politics and lifestyle. They're the most orderly people on the planet, and the most chaotic. They're forever in a hurry – and always late.

Appearances matter in a city where people-watching is a popular pastime. Almost everyone pays attention to *le look* (pronounced "louk"): an English word used to describe not only your wardrobe but also your "style". And if you change your style you are *relooké(e)*.

A French sociologist once claimed that in his country there were not three social classes but 63. One entrenched classification is BCBG *(bon chic, bon genre)*: the French equivalent of the British Sloane ranger or the American preppie. Their stamping grounds are Neuilly, Auteuil and Passy (known collectively as NAP), the rich suburbs of the 16th and 17th *arrondissements*. If you are BCBG, your clothes are well cut, but not daring or flashy. Another taxonomic is *bobo (bourgeois bohème)*. These are the sort of bohemians who can afford the high rents of St-Germain-des-Prés or the Marais. They're just as bourgeois as the BCBG crowd, only they play up their informality with more youthful clothes.

How Safe is Paris?

La sécurité has been a key political topic for several years, not least in the wake of the 2005 riots. According to statistics, the crime rate in France has shot up in recent years. In the Métro, a taped voice booms over the loudspeaker: "Take care of your wallets and personal belongings – pickpockets may be operating in the station." Still, despite the latest trends, Paris remains one of the safest – and most heavily policed – cities in Europe. The suburbs, however, are another story.

Breaking the rules

Paris is riddled with rules and regulations, but Parisians have a special talent for breaking them. Things like building codes, labour laws or pollution will probably not come to the visitor's immediate attention. What will hit home, however, are things like clouds of cigarette smoke wafting through public spaces marked "smoking forbidden". Parisian drivers park in the middle of the street and they stop paying parking tickets during presidential elections (traditionally, the victor declares an amnesty). In theory, you can be fined for allowing your dog to leave its mess, yet dog dirt is by no means rare on Paris pavements.

> *"One never sees Paris for the first time – one always sees it again..."*
> *–Edmondo De Amicis*

La politesse

This is not to suggest the city is one big free-for-all. Parisian anarchy does not extend to etiquette, and their reputation for rudeness is largely undeserved. Good manners are considered essential to everyday life. Indeed, *la politesse* can often become outright chivalry. Visitors would be well advised to follow the same rules of courtesy. Whether you're buying a baguette or a Hermès scarf, starting any transaction with a "*Bonjour Madame/Monsieur*," and finishing with "*Merci, au revoir*" will make the world of difference to the service you receive. If you forget, you may be reminded with an unspoken reprimand.

LEFT: car nostalgia – the ever-so-French 2CV. **ABOVE:** Parisian smile. **ABOVE RIGHT:** Paris is so romantic that it is often called the "city of love".

Taking to the streets

Somewhere in Paris, someone is on strike almost every day of the year. The expression for going on strike – *faire la grève* – refers to the still current practice of besieging Paris's Town Hall (located on what was once called Place de Grève) or marching from Nation and blocking streets all the way to Bastille. The strikes can involve many groups – transport workers, teachers, air traffic controllers, hospital staff, illegal immigrants, etc. These "social actions" might involve picketing school teachers, farmers dumping tomatoes on the Champs-Elysées or lorry drivers blockading roads. Perhaps going on strike is compensation for the decline of the trade unions and the weakening of political parties. But it can also seem rather more banal – a national sport in which Parisians are top of the league.

The protest march is part of the great Paris tradition of "the people" rising up. Parisians from all walks of life are willing to participate in street demonstrations for causes that matter to them. Several hundred thousand people packed the streets in 2003 to protest against the war in Iraq. In fact, there were so many marches and strikes that year, there was even a major protest march against strikes. ❑

THE MAKING OF PARIS

The Parisii tribe discovered it, the Romans usurped it, the Franks invaded it and Napoleon ruled it. The city's refined culture and revolutionary politics changed the world

Paris has been a site of human habitation since the Stone Age, and its history spans well over two millennia. A giddy whirl of invasions, uprisings, murders, building, demolishing, writing, painting, invention, song and dance; a past that's eternally present, reliably thrilling. Eventful, then, and lucky with it. Unlike many European cities, Paris almost entirely escaped wartime destruction in the 20th century: the buildings that were world-famous at the outbreak of war in 1939 are still standing.

The roots of the city

Paris has grown outwards, in fairly uniform rings from an island in the Seine, the Ile de la Cité. The foundations for the city as we know it today are deemed to have been laid down in around 300 BC by the Celtic tribe of the Parisii, who set up a trading settlement on the island. It was perfect for the transport of goods, from east to west by the river and from north to south along major overland routes that had converged there for centuries: the Seine was much wider then than today, and crossing it at the island was easier than elsewhere.

The author of a visitor's guide wrote, "One would be wrong if, seeing the vast number of books devoted to Paris, one imagined there was nothing more to be said." That was in 1765.

LEFT: *Napoleon on the Imperial Throne* by Ingres (1804).
RIGHT: Roman stonework at the Thermes de Cluny.

In 53 BC, some Gallic tribes failed to appear in Ambiani (Amiens) at the annual council convened by the Romans, who were in the process of colonising Gaul. Julius Caesar, Roman commander in Gaul, sensed rebellion and transferred the council to the Parisii settlement. The Romans realised the advantage of the position, and developed the site for themselves, naming it Lutetia. A town grew up with all the hallmarks of Roman civilisation, and it spread to the Left Bank. Buildings were also scattered on the Right Bank, including a hilltop temple to Mercury where, in around AD 250, Christian missionary St Denis, the first bishop of Paris, was beheaded; according to legend, he picked up his severed head and

walked 6,000 steps before being buried on the spot where the St-Denis Basilica now stands. The hill subsequently acquired the name Mons Martyrum (Martyr's Mound), now Montmartre.

Lutetia soon fell victim to sackings by barbarians. In 358, Emperor Constantine sent his son-in-law, Julian, to Gaul to deal with them. Julian promptly fell in love with Lutetia and some say that it was he who renamed it Paris. In 360 he became emperor of Rome, and rejected Christianity (officially tolerated since 313); this earned him the nickname "the Apostate".

Geneviève, patron saint of Paris

Just under a century later, in around 451, the armies of Attila the Hun circled for the kill. The Parisians prepared to flee, but were assured by the pious 19-year-old Geneviève that the Huns would not harm the city, provided they stayed with her and prayed. The marauders passed southwest of the town and ran straight into the swords of a hastily raised army of legionaries. Geneviève later became the patron saint of Paris.

She was still alive when Clovis I, king of the Salian Franks and founder of the Merovingian dynasty, invaded much of Gaul, seeing off the Romans and sweeping into Paris. He promptly made it his capital and reconverted it to Christianity. Later a basilica was built where he and St Geneviève were buried. The church was demolished; on its site now stands the Panthéon, the last resting place for France's great and good.

The Merovingian law of succession was simple: the empire was divided among the previous ruler's offspring. As a result, for the next 250 years, instead of serving as an administrative centre, Paris became a battleground for the murderous family bickering of Clovis's descendants.

CURRENT AFFAIRS

Attracted by the convenient transport route that was the large local river, the Parisii tribe set up camp on the Ile de la Cité in around 300 BC. But they were by no means the first people to put the Seine to good use: there's evidence of human habitation in these parts dating back to the Stone Age. One of the most dramatic finds occurred in 1991, when archaeologists working at Bercy in the 12th *arrondissement*, a mile or so upriver from the site of the Parisii settlement, unearthed several Neolithic dugout canoes, or *pirogues*, dating from 4500 BC – among the world's oldest known records of the use of canoes by hunter-gatherers. A nearby street was named Rue des Pirogues de Bercy, in honour of the find, and three of the craft are now exhibited in the Musée Carnavalet.

Into the Middle Ages

The Carolingians, who ruled from 751, moved the political centre away from Paris, which was left in the charge of a count and his municipal guard. Charlemagne died in 814, leaving his son Louis – the first Louis of many – in charge.

The Norman (or Viking) invasions of the mid-9th century brought Paris back into the limelight. After several sackings of the city, in 885 Eudes, count of Paris, had fortifications built around the Ile de la Cité. The first siege of Paris lasted a year and almost bore fruit: the Carolingian army came to the rescue. But King Charles ("the Fat"), instead of attacking the siege-weary aggressors, let them sail up the Seine to pillage Burgundy. In defiance of the king, Eudes took the crown and Carolingian unity dissolved. A period of instability followed, as the French crown was passed from one dynasty to the next. The Saracens appeared in the south, Hungarians in the east, and the Vikings ran amok. All in all, it was not a happy time. Finally, the power struggle saw Hugh Capet, son of Hugh the Great, a descendant of Eudes, become king of all France in 987. This marked the beginning of a new, long-lasting dynasty – the Capetians.

Paris prospered under the Capetians: new fountains were built to provide fresh drinking water, and armed *sergents de ville* walked a beat. With new churches and a cosmopolitan population, Paris soon became an intellectual hotspot. At the start of the 12th century, monks, scholars, philosophers, poets and musicians came to the city to learn, exchange ideas and teach.

Economic power rested in the hands of merchants and craftsmen, organised into guilds. The most powerful was the water merchants' guild, which included all river workers and gave its coat of arms to Paris. Philippe-Auguste (1180–1223) built Les Halles for the guilds and improved the docks. The guilds took care of levying taxes, town-crying and other municipal duties. In 1190, six guild members, so-called Grands Bourgeois (city dwellers), were chosen to act as the king's officers. Their number increased to 24. Later, Louis IX (1226–70) created three governing chambers; he was subsequently canonised. The Bourgeois became an independent political force, corrupt but striving for reforms. In 1200, the first student riot prompted Philippe-Auguste to found the University of Paris.

Most historians view the coronation of Hugh Capet (c.940–96) as the beginning of modern France.

LEFT: detail from a tapestry depicting the baptism of Clovis (*c.*1525). **TOP LEFT:** St Geneviève as a shepherdess with the Butte Montmartre in the background. **ABOVE:** Sainte-Chapelle stained glass. **ABOVE RIGHT:** Charlemagne, founder of the Carolingian dynasty.

The first revolution

By the mid-14th century the Capetians had been replaced by the Valois dynasty, and the devastating Hundred Years War with England began. In 1356, the English captured King Jean ("the Good") at Poitiers. Parisians, tired of incompetent leadership, rebelled; their leader was Etienne Marcel, a wealthy cloth maker and guild chairman. He also provided troop reinforcements to impoverished townspeople and peasants under Jacques Bonhomme, who chose the moment to start a revolt known as the *Jacquerie*.

In 1516, François I enticed Leonardo da Vinci to France. He lived near the king's residence in Amboise.

For support, Marcel unwisely chose the king of Navarre, Charles ("the Bad"), an ally of the English. When the Parisians learned of the alliance, they turned on Marcel, who was killed in July 1358. Three days later, Jean's son entered the capital. The new regent, the future Charles V (1364–80), hammered out a truce with the English. Paris was relatively well treated: the Parliament still met but its powers were curtailed.

But Parisians were seething. In 1382, during the reign of Charles VI (1380–1422), a group called the Maillotins rebelled against high taxes and were brutally repressed. Then, in 1407, they were enmeshed in the struggle for power between the Burgundian Jean ("the Fearless") and his cousin Louis d'Orléans. Jean had Louis murdered and, in 1409, took control of Paris.

The advance of the English

While Louis's Armagnac son, Charles, raised a new army, Paris celebrated. Into the fray stepped butcher Caboche, demanding reforms. All hell broke loose as Jean's authority slipped into Caboche's hands. Profiting from the reign of terror, Charles's army re-entered the city. With France torn apart by civil war, the English resumed hostilities and, siding with the Burgundians, beat the Armagnacs at the Battle of Agincourt in 1415.

Four years later, Jean "the Fearless" was murdered, whereupon Henry V of England married Catherine, daughter of the mad King Charles, and occupied Paris in December 1420. The dauphin, the legitimate French heir, had some support in the capital, but could not keep out the English. Joan of Arc, a 17-year-old girl from Lorraine, came to his rescue in 1429 by defeating the English at Orléans; a year later, Charles VII was crowned at Reims. However, Paris remained English until 1436, when Charles recaptured his capital and drove the English back to Calais.

By the early 16th century, Louis XII (1498–1515) was embroiled in the Italian Wars. His successor, François I (1515–47), began the struggle against the Habsburgs but was captured at Pavia in 1525. The Parisians paid his ransom and he moved into the Louvre. In his wake came Italian architects, painters, sculptors and masons, whose task was to reshape the city's lugubrious Gothic face. With the rebirth of the capital gathering pace, French culture also returned to life.

The advent of the printing press underpinned the Renaissance; however, it also helped spread the new gospel of Protestantism through Catholic France. Paris, dominated by the conservative Sorbonne theologists, pushed for measures against the Protestants, known as Huguenots, often burning religious agitators. Henri II's sons and heirs, François II (1559–60), Charles IX (1560–74) and Henri III (1574–89), proved unable to control France's religious factions; nor were they helped by the intrigues of the Queen Mother, Catherine de Médicis. The country was plunged into a religious war.

LEFT: battle of Neville's Cross during the Hundred Years War. **TOP LEFT:** Henri III, son of Catherine de Médicis. **ABOVE:** boatmen in front of Pont Notre-Dame.

War between the Henris

King Henri III's concessions to the Protestants infuriated the Catholics, led by Henri de Guise and his Holy League. In 1584, the Protestant Henri de Navarre, a Bourbon, became heir to the throne, but had to fight de Guise for the right to accede to power. To this end, in 1589, Henri III had de Guise killed. Paris threw up its barricades, and the Holy League's Council of Sixteen took power and deposed Henri III, who joined forces with Navarre. His army, however, sided with the Catholics. That summer, Henri III was murdered and Henri de Navarre became Henri IV.

Civil war dragged on for another five years. Paris was the stage for the Council of Sixteen's gruesome repression of real and perceived plots. In 1593, Philip II of Spain, who had entered the war on the Catholic side, pressed to usurp the French throne. Henri IV, in a brilliant piece of opportunism, chose that moment to convert to Catholicism, whereupon Paris welcomed him, and overnight the war-weary nation fell in line.

Henri IV patched up France spiritually and economically; in 1598, his Edict of Nantes set up guidelines for cohabitation between the religious groups. In 1610, Henri IV was murdered, and the young Louis XIII took to the throne.

THE EDICT OF NANTES

The Edict of Nantes, signed by Henri IV on 30 April 1598, enshrined religious tolerance in French law, and was a significant step on the road to the secularism of the French state that holds today. The Edict's immediate purpose was to put a stop to the long-running French Wars of Religion; in effect, they gave rights hitherto denied to French Protestants, also known as Huguenots, in what was a predominantly Catholic state. Once the Edict became law, all subjects of the French crown, with the exception of Muslims (who were later expelled, in 1610) and Jews, were granted freedom of worship, the right to work in any sphere, including for the state, as well as the right to bring grievances directly to the king.

The Bourbons

In spite of the massive debts incurred by their foreign wars, the Bourbons lavished huge sums on Paris, while keeping it on a short political leash. Two marshy islets east of the Ile de la Cité were amalgamated to become the residential Ile St-Louis. New bridges crossed the Seine. Avenues cut through the dingy labyrinth. Architects built new houses, parks, palaces and schools and restored the old ones. Cardinal Richelieu, who largely governed on behalf of the young Louis XIII (1610–43), founded the Académie Française. Under the Sun King, Louis XIV (1643–1715), the spending spree reached its zenith. His minister, Colbert, sanitised entire sections of the city and set up manufacturing plants. Louis XIV also had hospices constructed for the poor, and Les Invalides was built to house war veterans.

The influx of money and the proximity of the court attracted crowds to the capital. Theatres rang with the dramas of Racine and Corneille, and audiences roared at the comedies of Molière.

But trouble loomed. In 1648, Paris revolted, demanding greater political representation. The 12 provincial parliaments joined a body lobbying for change, as did a conspiracy of nobles under Prince Condé. This alliance, known as the Fronde, eventually collapsed, but Louis XIV later had his lavish palace built outside the city in Versailles, away from the Parisian mob.

ABOVE LEFT: the bloody St Bartholomew's Day Massacre. **TOP:** *The Death of Marat* (1793), by Jacques-Louis David. **BOTTOM:** Cardinal Richelieu. **RIGHT:** the taking of the Bastille.

The early 18th century was a time of great inequality in Paris. French high society enjoyed greater comforts and luxuries than ever before, and the court of the Sun King was a fertile breeding ground for debauchery and political intrigue. But the poor still had a raw deal. They were to make their displeasure felt with shattering consequences as the century drew to a close.

The revolutionary years

By the latter part of the 18th century, France's international renown rested increasingly on the writings of its intellectuals such as Voltaire, Rousseau and Diderot. But the poverty worsened; a bad harvest in 1788 caused the price of bread to soar and the people to become restless.

By 1789, France's debts had reached a critical level. King Louis XVI had to summon the Estates General, a legislative body of three estates: the Clergy, the Nobility and the rest of the populace, the Third Estate, to vote for reforms. Craftily, the king allowed only one vote per estate, so the huge Third Estate could be outvoted two to one by the smaller Clergy and Nobility. Eventually forced out, the Third Estate created a National Assembly to oppose the king. On 14 July, Parisians stormed the Bastille prison for weapons, proclaimed a Commune and formed a National Guard under liberal aristocrat and soldier Lafayette. The explosion of 1789 swept the past away. The First Republic was proclaimed and, in January 1793, Louis was guillotined in public, followed in October by Queen Marie-Antoinette. Paris was the epicentre of the French Revolution and its radical leaders Mirabeau, Danton and the fanatical Robespierre, egged on by Marat, whose murder in July 1793 threw the Reign of Terror into top gear. Anyone suspected of stepping out of line got the chop; in July 1794, it was Robespierre's turn. The young brigadier-general Napoleon Bonaparte finally ended the Revolution, after quashing a royalist uprising in 1795. Four years later he was First Consul. In 1804 he crowned himself emperor of a totalitarian and military state.

> *"Terror is nothing other than justice, prompt, severe, inflexible"*
> *–Maximilien Robespierre*

The Napoleonic Empire

A masterful administrator, Napoleon drew up plans for a Bank of France, reformed the judiciary and local government, improved secondary education, instituted the Légion d'Honneur and restored the Church. He greatly strengthened France's power in Europe, and its trade links with the rest of the world.

In Paris, Napoleon's architects and engineers improved the sewers and initiated a building boom. Paris wouldn't be the city it is today had it not been for Napoleon.

Though he ruled supreme at home, he could not have things all his way on the battlefield for ever. His glorious empire ended with Paris occupied after the Battle of Waterloo in 1815. Bourbon Louis XVIII headed a constitutional monarchy, focusing on law and order and laissez-faire economics. In cultural circles, Romanticism was in the air; one of the movement's bearers was Victor Hugo (1802–85). Inspired by the anti-establishment spirit of 1789, the Romantics railed against creaky academia and bourgeois respectability. The revolutionary spirit also remained in the Republican forces, who reached for the Parisian mob whenever despotism reared its head. In July 1830, Charles X revoked some electoral laws, sparking three days of rioting; he had to abdicate. His cousin, Louis-Philippe, Duke of Orléans, held power until 1848, when another revolution brought about his abdication in turn; the monarchy was finished.

The Second Empire

The first president of the Second Republic was Napoleon's nephew, Charles-Louis-Napoleon Bonaparte. The family traits didn't take long to show: he crowned himself Emperor Napoleon III in 1852, and arrested over 20,000 opponents to make his life easier.

The Commune

In 1870, Napoleon III went to war with Prussia. Two months later, he had been humiliatingly beaten, the Second Empire had become the Third

ABOVE: Boulevard Haussmann at the turn of the 20th century. **TOP RIGHT:** caricature of "J'accuse", article written by Emile Zola in defence of Alfred Dreyfus. **RIGHT:** French soldiers in the trenches, World War I.

Republic, and the Prussians were besieging Paris. In Bordeaux, the government of Adolphe Thiers waited for an uprising, which never materialised.

In January 1871, Thiers agreed to a ceasefire; the National Assembly ratified a peace treaty a month later. The Prussians marched through Paris, avoiding the eastern districts full of the starving and vengeful National Guard, which felt betrayed by the French government. Sensing trouble, Thiers moved his government to Versailles. He barely escaped the ensuing explosion.

In March, a Commune was proclaimed at the Hôtel de Ville after the bourgeoisie boycotted a municipal election. Civil war erupted and the Hôtel de Ville was burned. While the Communards hoisted red flags and argued over strategies, Thiers was busy raising a new army. The government forces succeeded where the Prussians had failed, and some 25,000 Communards were killed in the last weeks of May.

With the working class brutally tamed, Paris became host for the squabbles and plots of the Third Republic. The Republicans split into pro- and anti-clerical factions. In the 1890s, the left gathered around socialist Jean Jaurès. On the right were diehard monarchists and nationalists with a strong vein of anti-Semitism, as revealed by the Dreyfus Affair in the 1890s. This bitterly divisive scandal revolved around a Jewish army captain, Alfred Dreyfus, imprisoned on trumped-up spying charges. But amid the political acrimony, Paris hailed impressive new facilities: the first Métro lines were dug, the Eiffel Tower was built for the 1889 World Fair, and the first films were shown. Between 1880 and 1940, Paris was home to more artists than any other city.

World War I put a dampener on the high spirits, and in September 1914 the German artillery came within earshot. The city's military governor, Galliéni, rushed reinforcements (including the Paris taxi service) to the counter-offensive on the Marne; his rapid response ensured that the city was spared.

Normal life began to return after the armistice in 1918, though the daily sight of mutilated veterans was a reminder of the damage France had sustained. From the east came Russian émigrés, and from the west American writers and composers. In the 1930s, Paris became a temporary haven to the refugees of fascism in Europe.

AN ERA OF GRANDEUR

The Second Empire was a grandiose era. New railway lines were built, and Paris hosted the World Fair in 1855 and 1867. Basking in financial ease, the city abandoned itself to masked balls, Offenbach operettas and salon conversation. Its prefect, Baron Georges Haussmann, gave Paris a new face, gutting and rebuilding vast areas. Water mains and sewers were installed. Elegant boulevards and squares appeared; these served an aesthetic purpose, but also facilitated swift troop deployment and were hard to barricade.

Between the wars

With 1 million dead, millions of others crippled and the agricultural north destroyed by shelling, France's part in the victory over Germany in 1914 was bittersweet. Conservative Republicans and left-wing coalitions, including the Communist Party (founded in 1920), tried to come to grips with the economic and social after-effects of the Great War. The extreme right, meanwhile, made some important gains.

Fascist-type groups had appeared in France in the late 19th century. In the 1920s and 30s they proliferated, fuelled by general discontent and fear of Bolshevism, and inspired by Mussolini and Hitler. They focused their efforts on Paris, parading and campaigning against the internationalists, the socialists and, above all, the Jews. On 6 February 1934, a coalition of fascist factions attempted a *coup d'état* in Paris. It failed, but the left was finally goaded into concerted action. In 1936, a front of radicals, socialists and communists, headed by the socialist Léon Blum, won the election. The so-called Front Populaire promised to fight fascism and improve the workers' lot, but the initial euphoria was short-lived. The Front disappeared after a series of wildcat strikes.

De Gaulle was the first president of the Fifth Republic, still in place today.

World War II

When war broke out against Nazi Germany in September 1939, France hunkered down behind its fortifications along its eastern border, the Maginot Line, mobilised its ill-equipped army and waited. In Paris, Louvre curators prepared paintings for transport to safety.

On 14 June 1940, the Nazis marched into the City of Light after a lightning push through France from the Ardennes; the Germans had simply skirted the northern end of the Maginot Line. There was no siege, no National Guard, no *levée en masse*. Marshal Philippe Pétain, the 84-year-old hero of Verdun, became the head of a puppet regime in Vichy, in what was (at first) the unoccupied southern half of France.

While many Parisians were quiescent under the Nazi occupiers, and a number actively collaborated, there were those who bravely resisted, joining the Free French Movement led from London by General Charles de Gaulle. Their defiance often cost them their lives. On 6 June 1944, Allied forces landed in Normandy and advanced on Paris. Dietrich von Choltitz, the German commander, received orders to blow up the city, but chose to surrender instead; for this action he was dubbed "the saviour of Paris".

On 24 August 1944, Paris was liberated and, two days later, General de Gaulle paraded down the Champs-Elysées. De Gaulle immediately formed a provisional government, which lasted until 1946. Tourists returned in droves. Bebop and rock 'n' roll arrived from across the Atlantic.

Post-war thought was dominated by the dark ideas of writers such as Jean-Paul Sartre and Albert Camus. In addition, France lost two major colonial wars, the first in Indochina (1946–54) and the second in Algeria (1954–62).

May 1968: the barricades are back

A wave of bombings hit Paris in the early 1960s, when it became clear that President de Gaulle, who had come out of retirement to head the Fifth Republic in 1958, wanted to pull out of the Algerian quagmire. His manner in dealing with internal matters was patriarchal and authoritarian.

The 1968 agitation began uneventfully enough in March, with a sit-in by students to revise the antiquated university system. But instead of initiating a dialogue with the students, the *ancien régime* called in the CRS (the riot police) to restore order.

FAR LEFT: D-Day, 6 June 1944. **LEFT:** Adolf Hitler visits occupied Paris in 1940. **ABOVE:** the liberation of Paris, August 1944. **RIGHT:** former president Jacques Chirac.

On the night of 10 May 1968, the police stormed 60 barricades in the Quartier Latin. Unrest spread to the factories and other cities. France was soon paralysed and Paris was left in a state of siege. The state-run media broadcast heavily monitored programming, while Parisians received the news from France's periphery. At the end of the month, de Gaulle announced new elections and warned against impending totalitarianism. The Parisian bourgeoisie awoke, and an hour later, over 500,000 supporters of de Gaulle were flowing down the Champs-Elysées.

The Gaullists won the election, but were not in power for long. Discontent continued, and the President resigned in 1969, leaving his Republic to his ardent disciple Georges Pompidou.

Mitterrand and Chirac

The 1970s were a time of relative stagnation, so when the Independent Republican president Valéry Giscard d'Estaing lost to socialist leader François Mitterrand in 1981, it felt like the dawn of a new era. However, the contrary Parisian character revealed itself again in 1986, during the legislative elections. Voters on the left were dismayed by what they viewed as Mitterrand's capitulation to business interests, and

conservative forces, led by Paris mayor Jacques Chirac, swept in with a right-wing coalition; an unprecedented "cohabitation" was begun.

Chirac was a mass of contradictions. In his student days, he had been a member of the Communist youth movement, then a lieutenant fighting with French anti-independence forces in Algeria, and in the early 1970s, prime minister for two years under Giscard d'Estaing. As Paris mayor, he had a lot on his plate. May 1968 had reaffirmed the city's rebellious spirit, and Parisians now demonstrated at the drop of a hat.

But the 1993 elections maintained the swing to the right and two years later Chirac succeeded François Mitterrand as president. Mitterrand died in January 1996. Despite the disquiet about his personal integrity, the French mourned him. His *grands projets* made an indelible contribution to the Paris landscape. Besides, by 1997, Chirac's popularity had plummeted, and when he made the disastrous decision to dissolve the National Assembly and call new legislative elections in June, the socialist Lionel Jospin was swept in on a flood of votes as prime minister.

ABOVE: Nicolas Sarkozy, elected in 2007.
RIGHT: First Lady and singer-songwriter Carla Bruni.

Chirac's second term

By the end of 1999 Paris was benefiting from a strong economy. But in the mayoral elections two years later, Parisians, disenchanted with the sleaze-ridden administration of right-wing Jean Tibéri, voted for the more flamboyant Bertrand Delanoë, the first socialist mayor of Paris for 130 years. Delanoë quickly initiated a swathe of feel-good public events and attractions, notably the annual Paris Plage *(see page 111)*.

The French presidential elections of 2002 produced a dramatic run-off between Chirac and the xenophobic far-right agitator Jean-Marie Le Pen. Parisians took to the streets in vast numbers to express their opposition to Le Pen. Chirac finally won 82 per cent of the vote, the largest in the country's history. His opposition to the war in Iraq saw his approval ratings soar. But the bubble soon burst, with public protests against reforms to the state pension and benefit system.

Sarkozy comes to power

It seems Chirac will go down in the annals as a president of persuasive charm and energy, who promised much and achieved little. Perhaps his longest-lasting contribution will be the law he pushed through in 2000 to shorten the presidential term from seven to five years. His party's candidate to succeed him, Nicolas Sarkozy, won the presidency in 2007 with a clear six point lead over socialist Ségolène Royal, giving him a strong mandate for the sweeping economic and social reform he promised.

Sarkozy's taste for luxury and his marriage to former supermodel Carla Bruni have alienated some voters. In 2008 he unveiled plans for a series of "Grand Paris" projects, intended to improve transport connections between the city centre and the suburbs; it remains to be seen whether this will be his legacy. ❑

The Outsiders

Dictionaries translate *banlieue* as "suburbs", but whereas its English counterpart is relatively unproblematic, the French word is loaded

Banlieue means "outskirts". Historically, it was the loop of land within a distance of one league ("lieue") from a city's perimeter; nowadays the word applies to any residential area on the edge of a large city or town. Some *banlieues*, like St-Germain-en-Laye, west of Paris, are affluent and picturesque; but out of context, "la banlieue" puts most French people in mind of high-rise estates like La Courneuve, Argenteuil and Aulnay-sous-Bois, sinkholes of burned-out cars, delinquency and boiling-point tempers.

Such estates have been a running sore for years, and not only on the Paris periphery: similar ghettos can be found outside Lille, Lyon, Toulouse and elsewhere. Most were built in the 1960s and 70s, cheap housing for a growing workforce – in particular first- and second-generation immigrants from Algeria, Morocco and former French colonies in Africa. The effects of cack-handed urban and social engineering were compounded when industry slumped; and so began a vicious circle, whereby poor social facilities fuel local resentment, and chronic vandalism gives the state the perfect excuse not to invest. Sky-high unemployment goes without saying.

ABOVE: Banlieue angst in *La Haine*.
RIGHT: David Belle, in a scene from *Banlieue 13*.

In October 2005, the subject that many politicians and middle-class voters preferred to ignore punched its way to the top of the news. The trouble started in the Paris *banlieue* of Clichy-sous-Bois, where two teenagers, running from the police, climbed into an electricity substation and died. The resulting riots spread across the country; there were 23 nights of violence, 9,000 cars were torched, and a state of emergency was declared.

Still, not all of France was in denial. It's a measure of how heavy the topic weighs on the national conscience that there's even an established cinematic sub-genre, the "*banlieue* film", of which the best-known is Matthieu Kassovitz's incendiary 1995 hit *La Haine*; reportages such as the Taverniers' *De l'autre côté du périph'* are frequent; and there's the occasional film made "from the inside", like *Wesh Wesh, qu'est-ce qui se passe?* (2001). Indeed, it's one of the ironies of the *banlieues* that their cultural scenes should be so vigorous and influential. In fashion, the "banlieue look" has entered the mainstream.

Little has improved since 2005, yet the *banlieues* are at the heart of France's struggle to define and understand itself. Many residents feel fierce pride in their suburban roots – but they also know that the "ban" in *banlieue* can mean "exile". ❑

DECISIVE DATES

The Gallo-Roman era

c.300 BC
A Celtic tribe, the Parisii, settle on the Ile de la Cité.

58–52 BC
Julius Caesar conquers Gaul; Lutetia is founded.

c.AD 250
Gaul converts to Christianity.

451
St Geneviève's troops fend off Attila the Hun.

The Dark Ages

486
Frankish king Clovis expels the last Romans. In 496, he is baptised at Reims; in 508, he makes Paris his capital.

543
The St-Germain-des-Prés monastery is founded.

751
The Carolingian dynasty: Emperor Charlemagne rules from 768 to 814.

845–80
Paris sacked by the Vikings.

885
Count Eudes is king of the Western Franks in 888.

The Middle Ages

Paris develops into a city of learning and political power. It spreads north of the river.

987
The Capetian dynasty starts.

1108–54
Paris becomes an important trading centre.

1163
Notre-Dame is started.

1190–1223
The Louvre fortress is built.

1226–70
Louis IX's judicial reforms.

1246–8
Sainte-Chapelle is built.

1253
Sorbonne University created.

1340
Beginning of the Hundred Years War.

1358
Jacquerie uprising.

1364
Charles V moves his court to the Louvre.

1380
The Bastille prison is built.

1420
English rule until 1436, despite Joan of Arc's military campaign of 1429.

The Renaissance

Wars with Italy expose the French to new ideas of art, wealth and luxury.

1469
First French printworks.

1516
François I brings Leonardo da Vinci to France; rebuilding of the Louvre starts in 1528.

1559
Henri II is killed jousting.

1572
St Bartholomew's Day Massacre of Protestants.

1589
Henri III is assassinated.

1593
Henri IV becomes a Catholic.

1598
The Edict of Nantes ends the Wars of Religion.

1609
The Place Royale (now Place des Vosges) and Pont Neuf are built.

1610
Henri IV is assassinated.

"Le Grand Siècle"

Louis XIV spurs an age of extravagance by moving to Versailles and launching an opulent building programme.

1629
The Palais Royal is built.

1631
Launch of the first Paris newspaper, *La Gazette*.

1635
Académie Française set up.

1648–53
The Fronde rebellion.

1672–1705
The Grands Boulevards are built.

1677
Hôtel des Invalides finished.

1680
Comédie Française founded.

1682
Court moves to Versailles.

1686
The first café, Le Procope, opens in Paris.

Age of Enlightenment

The arts flourish, science develops and philosophers spread new ideas.

1715
Louis XIV dies and Philippe d'Orléans becomes regent.

1751
First volume of Diderot's *Encyclopédie* published.

1755
Place Louis XIV (now Place de la Concorde) is started.

1758
Panthéon is started.

The First Empire

The French Revolution leads to a republic then an empire under Napoleon Bonaparte.

1789
Bastille stormed; Louis XVI leaves Versailles for Paris.

1791
Louis is caught fleeing Paris.

1792
The Republic is declared; the royal family is imprisoned.

1793
Louis and Marie-Antoinette are guillotined.

1794
The ensuing Terror claims more than 60,000 lives. The Directoire takes over.

1799
Napoleon seizes power and is crowned emperor in 1804.

1806
Arc de Triomphe started.

1814
Napoleon is defeated; the Russians occupy Paris.

1815
Napoleon briefly regains power before his downfall at the Battle of Waterloo; the Bourbon monarchy is restored with Louis XVIII.

The Restoration

Two more revolutions shake Paris, unseating the monarchy once and for all.

1830
Charles X is overthrown and Louis-Philippe d'Orléans becomes "the Citizen King".

1837
First French passenger railway service.

1848
Louis-Philippe is deposed. Louis-Napoleon Bonaparte is elected president of the Second Republic.

The Second Empire

Under Louis-Napoleon, Paris becomes the most efficient, modern city in Europe.

1852
Louis-Napoleon crowns himself Emperor Napoleon III; the Second Empire begins.

1852–70
Baron Georges Haussmann redesigns the city.

1852
Le Bon Marché, the first department store, opens.

1855
Paris's first World Fair.

1862
Hugo's *Les Misérables* published.

1863
Manet's *Le Déjeuner sur l'herbe* causes a scandal.

1867
Second World Fair.

1870
Franco-Prussian War.

The Belle Epoque

New inventions and a great artistic élan.

1871
Defeated France signs an armistice with Prussia. During the Paris Commune, 25,000 people are killed.

1875
The Third Republic begins.

1887
Louis Pasteur founds the Institut Pasteur.

1889
Gustave Eiffel completes his tower for the World Fair. The Moulin Rouge opens.

1894–1906
Dreyfus scandal.

1894
President Sadi Carnot assassinated.

1895
Lumière brothers screen the world's first public film.

The Age of Anxiety

Social tensions multiply, and France is shaken by two world wars.

1900
The first Métro line opens. Pont Alexandre III, the Grand and Petit Palais are finished.

1914–18
World War I. Paris is saved from German attack by the Battle of the Marne.

1919
Versailles Peace Conference.

1924
André Breton publishes his Surrealist Manifesto.

1934
The Depression gives rise to riots and a series of strikes.

1936
Popular Front leader Léon Blum elected prime minister.

1939
World War II begins; France sides with Britain against Nazi Germany.

1940
Germany invades France; the Occupation begins.

1941–2
Paris Jews are deported.

1944
Paris liberated by the Allies. General de Gaulle in power until 1946, when the Fourth Republic is proclaimed.

1949
Simone de Beauvoir publishes *The Second Sex*.

1958
The Algerian crisis topples the Fourth Republic.

The Fifth Republic

De Gaulle returns as president of the Fifth Republic.

1958
Work begins on La Défense.

1962
End of the Algerian War.

1968
Strikes and student riots force de Gaulle to call an election. He wins.

1969
De Gaulle resigns; Georges Pompidou is president.

1972
The Tour Montparnasse is completed.

1973
The Boulevard Périphérique (ringroad) is opened.

1977
Centre Georges-Pompidou opens. Jacques Chirac elected mayor of Paris.

1981
Socialist François Mitterrand elected president. First TGV (high-speed) railway service.

1986
Chirac becomes prime minister in an unprecedented "cohabitation". The Musée d'Orsay and Cité des Sciences at La Villette open.

1988
Louvre Pyramid completed.

1989
Bicentenary celebrations of the Revolution. Inauguration of the Grande Arche de la Défense and Opéra Bastille.

1995
Chirac elected president.

1997
Socialist Lionel Jospin becomes prime minister in a second "cohabitation".

1998
France wins the football World Cup. The Bibliothèque Nationale de France is relocated to Tolbiac.

2000
Presidential term shortened from seven to five years.

2001
Bertrand Delanoë elected mayor of Paris.

2002
The euro replaces the franc. Chirac is re-elected.

2003
Chirac opposes the war in Iraq and his popularity soars, then plummets with a reform of the French state pensions and benefit systems.

2005
French voters say *Non* to the European Constitution. Chirac's standing in the opinion polls is at an all-time low. Riots flare up in the *banlieues* (suburbs).

2006
New tram service in the south of the city.

2007
Right-wing Nicolas Sarkozy is elected president.

2009
65th D-Day anniversary in Normandy. "Grand Paris" proposals unveiled.

SOFITEL

ARCHITECTURE

Paris is probably the loveliest and widest-ranging display of building styles in the world – and, with few exceptions, ancient and modern complement each other flawlessly

Two thousand years of history and seven centuries of artistic brilliance have made Paris a city rich in architecture. Although invasions, sieges, insurrections and city planners destroyed a number of the capital's early masterpieces, fine examples remain, making modern-day Paris one of the most beautiful, fascinating – and intact – cities anywhere in the world.

More fortunate than many of its European counterparts, Paris escaped catastrophe (by a whisker) in 1944. As Allied troops approached the city, Hitler ordered General Dietrich von Choltitz, the occupying governor of Paris, to blast every single historical edifice to pieces, so that the Allies' victorious entry would be made in a field of smoking ruins. But, at the last minute, loath to perpetrate such sacrilege, von Choltitz thankfully disobeyed the order. He surrendered the city, intact, to General Philippe Leclerc, liberator of Paris.

Paris is a textbook of architectural history, boasting a full set of French architectural styles, especially from the 12th century and the beginnings of the Gothic era onwards.

Over time, the best architects have preserved this heritage, while looking forward and making room for the new. This explains the amazing juxtaposition of different architectural idioms.

PRECEDING PAGES: the business district of La Défense. **LEFT:** old and new – the Louvre and its glass pyramids. **RIGHT:** the Thermes de Cluny hold a Roman bath.

Roman remains

Unsurprisingly, almost nothing remains of the wooden huts occupied by the Parisii. However, thanks to the Romans' development of a most durable concrete, their ruins can still be found in the Quartier Latin. Streets such as Rue St-Jacques and Boulevard St-Michel are built on ancient Roman roads. The vestiges of a bath can be seen in the garden at the Musée National du Moyen Age–Thermes de Cluny, and the ruins of the arena (Arènes de Lutèce) have also survived.

Unfortunately, nothing is left of the Merovingian and Carolingian eras (6th–9th centuries); the Vikings burned and pillaged Paris on several occasions during this period.

Romanesque and Gothic

The Romanesque era (10th–11th centuries), with its ponderous, gloomy structures, left hardly a trace either. The steeple of St-Germain-des-Prés church is a rare remnant. In the 12th century, Paris turned to the newest rage in religious architecture – Gothic, discerned by pointed arches and the use of ribbed vaults with flying buttresses, which allowed windows to replace walls and stone to soar towards the heavens.

Lighter, more slender and luminous than previous styles, Gothic coincided with the strengthening of the French crown and a religious fervour inflamed by the Crusades.

The most famous sacred building in Paris, Notre-Dame cathedral, epitomises the perfection of Gothic style. Its construction began in 1163 on the site of a Romanesque church, which had been built on the foundations of a Carolingian basilica, which in turn had been built on the site of a Roman temple. It took 200 years to finish. The building began to decay in the 17th century, but restoration by 19th-century Gothic revivalist Eugène Viollet-le-Duc (1814–79) only started in 1841. The restoration took nearly 23 years.

Close by stands Sainte-Chapelle, a fragile-looking church in High Gothic style, which differs from Notre-Dame in that the vast stained-glass windows are supported by only a thin framework of stone. It was built by Louis IX in 33 months to shelter the Crown of Thorns.

The Renaissance

War in Italy, in 1495, brought the French into contact with Renaissance grandeur, and the style, characterised by contempt for all Gothic forms and a rediscovery of antiquity, was imported to France. In architecture, the ribbed vault disappeared in favour of flat ceilings with wooden beams. Medieval fortresses gave way to genteel palaces with Greek-style colonnades.

Among Paris's main exponents of the Renaissance were architect Pierre Lescot (1510–78), whose finest work is the west wing of the Louvre, and Jean Goujon (1510–68), who sculpted the reliefs on Lescot's Louvre facade and worked

Above: the Gothic splendour of Notre-Dame de Paris. **Top Right:** the Pont Neuf is in fact the oldest bridge in Paris. **Right:** Renaissance style at the Hôtel Carnavalet.

on the Hôtel Carnavalet (1544). Goujon's work can also be seen on Lescot's Fontaine des Innocents, an example of Renaissance sensuality.

The Classical influence

At the end of the 16th century, while the Renaissance had succumbed to the Baroque in the rest of Europe, a desire for strength and clarity, born of rationalism, dominated architecture. French architects were still looking towards sobriety and Classicism; the Classical style is based on symmetry, simplicity of line and great, wide-open perspectives. The Pont Neuf (1606), the first bridge to be built without houses on it, was one of the first examples. During this period, large squares were created, surrounded by uniform buildings and displaying a statue of the king in the middle of the large central garden. The Place des Vosges, commissioned by Henri IV in 1609, was the first and most elegant of the Classical-style royal squares. Edged with graceful arcades, the square started out as the Place Royale, until it was renamed during the Revolution.

THROUGH THE AGES

Architecture in Paris embodies a wide spectrum of styles. Here are a few examples:
Gothic: Notre-Dame (1163–1345), Sainte-Chapelle (1245), Tour St-Jacques (1523)
Renaissance: Cour Carrée facade of the Louvre (1556), St-Eustache church (1532–1637)
Classical: Versailles (1668), Les Invalides (1677), Place Vendôme (1698)
Neoclassical: Panthéon (1790)
Second Empire: Opéra Garnier (1875)
Modern: La Défense, the Louvre Pyramid, Opéra Bastille (all three 1989), Bibliothèque Nationale de France (1998).

The grand style

The Sun King, Louis XIV, left his mark on Paris and its surrounding region, but imposed his personality most forcefully on the palace of Versailles. Begun in 1668, the palace symbolised the absolute power of the monarch and employed the top talents of the time: architects Louis Le Vau and Hardouin-Mansart, painter Charles Le Brun and landscape gardener André Le Nôtre. Other fine examples of the Classical style are the Palais du Luxembourg (1631) and the Hôtel des Invalides (1677).

After Louis's death, building was kept to a minimum until the 1750s, when the Neoclassical movement turned to forms lifted directly from antiquity, taking the utmost care to reproduce what recent progress in archaeology had brought to light. Jacques-Ange Gabriel laid out Place de la Concorde and built the Ecole Militaire, and Jacques-Germain Soufflot designed the Panthéon on the site of an older church.

With the coronation of a triumphant Napoleon and the installation of a new empire at the beginning of the 19th century came the triumphal arches (Arc de Triomphe du Carrousel and Arc de Triomphe) and the triumphal Neoclassical Rue de Rivoli.

The Haussmann effect

Except for a few upper-class neighbourhoods, post-Revolution Paris was a squalid city. Poverty-stricken communities, in filthy, narrow alleyways and miserable, overpopulated shacks, were constantly on the brink of revolt. For obvious sanitary reasons, but also to defeat riots, Napoleon III and the prefect Baron Georges Haussmann began a sweeping programme to redraw the city map in the 1850s. Medieval Paris all but disappeared: whole quarters were razed, and wide, tree-lined avenues, harder to barricade than narrow alleys, cut through the maze of backstreets.

Paris still bears the indelible stamp of Haussmann's achievements. After clearing out slums and opening up the area around the Louvre, he concentrated on expanding the system of boulevards through the city centre begun by Louis XIV. A small hill then known as the Butte St-Roch, occupied by windmills, a gallows and a pig market, was intended to be their centre. It is hard to picture that today as you stand on the busy Place de l'Opéra, looking at Garnier's opera house, the Second Empire's most sumptuous construction.

Monsieur Eiffel's tower

The second half of the 19th century was rich in architectural creativity. Wrought iron made its debut with the Grand Palais, the Pont Alexandre III and, of course, the iconic Eiffel Tower. Panned by writers and critics during its construction for the World Fair in 1889, the tower is now the symbol of Paris. The tower embodied the uneasy relationship between science, industry and art in Paris. As Gustave Eiffel's controversial creation rose higher and higher, bets were placed on when it would topple. When the engineer himself climbed its 1,665 steps to plant the French flag atop his iron latticework fantasy, crowds of ordinary Parisians who admired his vision cheered; the aesthetes stayed away.

Amazingly, the Eiffel Tower was originally intended to be merely a temporary exhibit, to be dismantled after the 1889 World Fair.

It was an eclectic era. Having burned down during the Commune of 1871, the Hôtel de Ville (City Hall) on the Right Bank was rebuilt in Renaissance style, while Sacré-Cœur cathedral fused neo-Byzantine and Romanesque styles. Numerous churches toed the neo-Gothic line. Reacting against these academic approaches and inspired by Japanese art, the Belgian Hector Guimard established the Art Nouveau movement. The sinuous organic forms and curving lines, natural and Baroque at the same time, were decried by some as "noodle style". Guimard designed several buildings in the 16th *arrondissement*, including the Castel Béranger (14 rue de la Fontaine), and also the city's Métro entrances, many of which, including those at Porte Dauphine and Abbesses, still remain.

The modern age

Both the modern movements of the 1920s and 1930s and Art Deco were born in the 16th *arrondissement*. Mallet-Stevens and Le Corbusier were the main exponents of the Cubic style of architecture, all pure lines and concrete. At the same time, a grandiose, Neo-classical form of modernism appeared, as epitomised by the Palais de Chaillot.

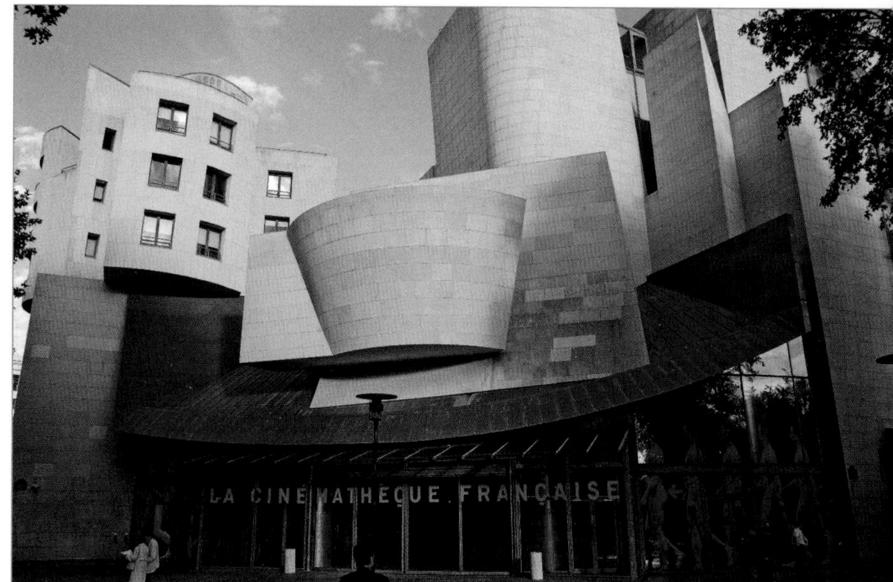

From the 1960s, Paris underwent a transformation. Facades were cleaned, the Métro was modernised and old parts of the city were demolished. New architectural projects were developed, keeping up with technical advances by building upwards (La Défense and the much-decried Tour Montparnasse), expanding indoor space (Centre Pompidou, Cité de la Villette, Palais Omnisports at Bercy) and experimenting with new materials that capture, reflect and admit light.

In the 1980s, Sino-American architect I.M. Peï designed a new entrance for the Louvre: a "landscape" of pyramids in stainless steel and specially made glass. Lauded for its beauty and efficiency, the central pyramid has undoubtedly earned its place on the city's architectural stage.

Like Peï's pyramid, the bankside Institut du Monde Arabe (designed in 1987 by Jean Nouvel) achieves a kind of harmony by reflecting the neighbouring buildings and the ever-changing Parisian sky. Gothic architecture, in its time, held a mirror to society in much the same way.

LEFT: the Grande Arche at La Défense (top) completes the *Axe historique* which runs through Paris and thus aligns with the Arc de Triomphe (bottom). **ABOVE:** the Cinémathèque Française, a Frank Gehry design.

Into the future

Innovation continues. The imposing 1997 Bibliothèque Nationale de France, also known as the TGB (Très Grande Bibliothèque), is at the heart of the "new" Left Bank, a vast renewal project in the 13th *arrondissement*. MK2 Bibliothèque, a cinema complex designed by Jean-Michel Wilmotte, opened nearby in 2003.

Two new footbridges have sprung across the river in the last decade: the Passerelle de Solférino between the Tuileries and the Musée d'Orsay, in 1999, and the Passerelle Simone de Beauvoir between the TGB and the Parc de Bercy in 2006. In the Parc de Bercy itself, the former American Center, a 1992 Frank Gehry building, became the new home for the iconic Cinémathèque Française in 2006. An even newer building, another Nouvel design, is the Musée du Quai Branly, a museum of art from Asia, Africa, the Americas and Oceania that opened in 2006 in the shadow of the Eiffel Tower.

To get a complete overview of the history of architecture in Paris, pay a visit to the permanent exhibition in Le Pavillon de l'Arsenal (21 boulevard Morland, 4th), itself a remarkable piece of 19th-century design, with natural light pouring through a superb glass roof. ❑

Paris on a Plate

This is a city that worships food – and recent years have brought plenty of notable new talents and intriguing new addresses to keep the dining scene alive

The news of the death of French food has been greatly exaggerated. Critics hail Spain, or London, or Sydney, or New York, as the "new France" – whereas Paris, they whine, is stuck in a rut. But that's not an entirely fair evaluation. It's important to remember when you eat in Paris, where the cooking of the whole country converges, that you're sampling a long-established cuisine: a vast, yet coherent repertoire of dishes, ingredients and techniques that have stood the test of time. A new ingredient or dish won't be welcomed into the cuisine until it proves itself worthy.

For the traveller, if not for locals, such conservatism is a boon. You want real French onion soup? You've got it, and there won't be any star anise or coriander in there. The menu says *steak au poivre*? That means it's *steak au poivre*: flat, rare, with creamy peppercorn sauce. No surprises. Everything is reassuringly real.

French cooking may be slow to evolve, but it's because France is a country that truly knows its food.The French are incredibly protective, disciplined and judicious in this regard.

This is not to say that contemporary and international experiences are not to be found. In recent years, a wave of young chefs has been opening snazzy yet relaxed restaurants serving French food with a fresh, contemporary face, and integrating (ever so cautiously) more exotic flavours like ginger, peanut, coriander, curry and lime. Even stellar chefs like Joël Robuchon and Alain Senderens have taken a more unbuttoned approach to their trade by opening their own bistros.

The international scene, although perhaps not as widespread as elsewhere, is also an integral part of the city's taste experience. Indeed, one thing that makes it exciting to eat in a country other than one's own is discovering the influences that immigrants from other places have brought to it. Paris has a lot of good North African, Vietnamese, Lebanese and Afro-island cooking; seek it out and you'll be rewarded.

LEFT: the palatial dining room at Le Meurice.
RIGHT: mouth-watering cakes at Pâtisserie Dalloyau.

Street food and cafés

Street vendors are a welcome sight, especially in winter, with chestnuts roasting over beds of coal, waffle irons and crêpe grills ever at the ready. Falafels are sold through the windows on the Rue des Rosiers. Middle Eastern kebabs and savoury turnovers are sold throughout the city. Ice-cream stands abound on the Ile St-Louis.

A VEGETARIAN DESERT

The vegetarian dishes of French cuisine are few and far between, which can be trying for herbivorous travellers. Even dishes that you're assured are meat-free often contain bacon or meat-based stocks. A solution is to order two meat-free starters instead of a main course, or to stick to simple egg and potato dishes. This, however, will soon seem repetitive. In an upmarket restaurant, you can telephone ahead and request a vegetarian meal; this gives the cook time to concoct something just for you. Another option is to explore the ethnic restaurants of the city which serve meat-free snacks as well as elaborate three-course meals.

To fill a picnic basket with traditional French fare, your best bet is a *charcuterie*, where you'll find ready-cooked dishes such as quiches, salads, pâtés, sausages, cheeses and prepared dishes like *poulet basquaise* (chicken with tomatoes and red peppers). Next, go to the bakery for a baguette or ready-made sandwiches.

If you're in a rush in the midst of shopping, traditional cafés will cater quickly while you give your feet a rest. Many will serve no more than simple baguette sandwiches. Others offer omelettes, or the quintessential café favourite, *croque-monsieur* (grilled ham and cheese on toast), or *croque-madame* (the same, but with a fried egg on top). Café salads are often hefty and filling, such as *Paysanne* (with potatoes, bacon and cheese) *Norvégienne* (with smoked salmon), *Landaise* (with duck breast), to name but three.

Bistros and brasseries

No restaurants are more popular – or more emblematic of Paris – than the neighbourhood bistros and brasseries. Brasseries (breweries) were introduced to the city in the 19th century, around the time when modern methods of brewing were being perfected. Many brasseries serve Alsatian specialities such as *choucroute* and

steins of beer; others specialise in shellfish. Outside the latter, you'll spot heaps of clams, mussels and langoustines on beds of ice, and burly men in overalls shucking oysters from dawn until dusk. All brasseries serve a wide range of dishes, including standard bistro fare. They're a jolly experience: spacious, clamorous and festive, usually decorated in Belle Epoque style.

For quieter, more intimate meals, opt for the bistros. These are smaller, more humble nooks, offering similar menus: *hareng pommes à l'huile* (smoked herring marinated in oil with warm potatoes), *œufs en meurette* (poached eggs with red wine sauce), *blanquette de veau* (veal in a white sauce), *coq au vin* (braised chicken in wine), *mousse au chocolat* (chocolate mousse) and *tarte Tatin* (caramelised upside-down apple tart). Some bistros have a regional bent, proudly boasting their provincial specialities. In Auvergnat bistros, think blue cheese, potatoes, walnuts and superb beef; with Southwestern ones, it's *foie gras* and duck; Basque flavours include hot pepper, salt cod and ham; and Provençal bistros guarantee ratatouille, lamb and *bouillabaisse*.

The name "bistro" supposedly derives from the days of the Allied occupation of Paris in 1814. Russian soldiers were forbidden to drink, so whenever they dived into a bar, they demanded their refreshments urgently – bistrot – to avoid being caught.

Far Left: the legendary Left Bank café Les Deux Magots. **Top Left:** bistros are a convivial affair. **Bottom Left:** quiches are a French staple. **Above:** a culinary work of art. **Right:** chef at work at plush Le Meurice.

The star experience

For those who want to dress up and spend a bomb on dinner, there are countless prestigious restaurants in the city. A Michelin guide will point you in the direction of establishments that meet these starry standards. Be ready to spend several hours at the table, to eat seven courses, and to have waiters buzzing around you like winged butlers. The food in starred restaurants (whether one star or three) should produce meals you'll remember for a lifetime, but some restaurants, unfortunately, rest on their laurels.

Contemporary French cooking

There is no single term for the recent sprouting of contemporary French restaurants: sleek, trendy, moderately priced, and with good, interesting food. Dinner usually consists simply of an *entrée*, *plat* and *dessert*. Dishes are lighter than in a bistro, less complicated than in starred establishments; the wine list will probably include international bottles; the service is pleasant; and the crowds are *branché* (fashionable).

All in all, they're a good way to get a taste of the future of French food. The only drawback is that (apart from what you find on the menus) they don't feel particularly French.

Food for thought

Not all visitors to Paris are as enthusiastic about certain French classics as the locals. Almost everyone knows that *escargots* are snails and *cuisses de grenouille* are frogs' legs, but many a tourist has unwittingly ordered calf's head *(tête de veau)*, expecting simply veal, or *andouillette* in hope of pork sausage only to discover tripe-filled concoctions. But dishes like these sound more frightening than they really are: after all, millions of French people relish their taste.

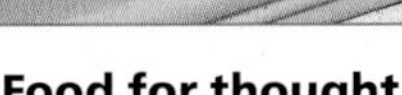

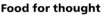

Part of the excitement of dining in France is having the option of – if not the appetite for – pig's ears, beef muzzle and blood sausage.

Fish, of the truly excellent kind, is not especially easy to find in Paris, and where one does find it, it comes at a price. Brasseries usually have a promising array, for example on their *plateaux de fruits de mer* (shellfish platters). Of course, it's generally in the more expensive restaurants that it will be cooked best. In France, meats tend to be served at one extreme or another: at the one end, raw (for example, *tartare de bœuf* or beef tartare) or *saignant* (rare); and at the other, *confit* (preserved) or cooked tender until falling from the bone. If you order steak, it will come rare unless you specify "*à point*" (medium) or "*bien cuit*" (well done). Don't hesitate to send a dish back if the meat is not cooked to your liking. Fish is trickier. At mid-range restaurants it tends to be overcooked, so if you like it just done, it's important to ask for your fish cooked "*rose à l'arête*" (rare at the bone).

Cheese

Nowhere in the world is there a wealth of cheese to match that of France, where cheese is considered so important that an entire dinner course is devoted to it alone. Between the main course and dessert, out comes the trolley or platter, laden with a delectably smelly array. The most pungent are generally cheeses such as Epoisses, Mont d'Or and Munster. If you prefer mild ones, steer instead towards goat's cheeses, young Comté or Mimolette. Blue cheeses vary greatly in creami-

LEFT: traditional decor for home-made desserts. **TOP, BOTTOM AND RIGHT:** cheese, bread, wine: a winning French combo. **FAR RIGHT:** mouth-watering beef dish.

ness and strength, but usually aren't too overpowering; Brie and Camembert are well known, mild and deliciously smooth. Try not to be overwhelmed by the number of options. It can take years to become familiar with French cheeses. Just remember two rules: in a cheese tasting, always start with the mildest cheese and work your way around to the strongest; and never steal the "nose" off a piece; always slice cheese in such a way as to preserve its shape, so the last person served won't be left with just the rind.

Drinks

It is usual to be offered an *apéritif* before a meal. A glass of champagne, white wine, or a *kir* (white wine with *cassis* – a blackcurrant liqueur) are most popular, but whisky and port are also common. Of course, you don't have to order an *apéritif*; you can jump straight to the wine list.

In the minds of the French, wine is the *de rigueur* accompaniment not only to French food, but to eating in general. In starred restaurants, a deal of care is generally taken over which wine will go with what, but in most casual places, the rule is drink what you like.

Simple restaurants, in addition to bottles, sell wine by the glass or by the jug: *un pichet de rouge* (a jug of red) will get you an inexpensive, potentially rough but entirely drinkable red wine. Beer is usually only ordered with sandwiches, Alsatian meals or Asian lunches; cider accompanies Breton and Norman specialities (crêpes or mussels). Several mineral waters are on offer; request *pétillante* for sparkling, *plate* for still, or *en carafe* for tap water.

The French meal

Entrée (Americans, take note) means starter, not main course. *Plat* is the main dish. *Dessert* is, not surprisingly, dessert or pudding. All three are often included in *prix fixe* (fixed-price) menus, although a choice of either *entrée* and *plat* or *plat* and *dessert* is increasingly common.

In unpretentious places, nobody minds if you order two *entrées* instead of a full meal. What is often frowned upon, especially in upmarket restaurants, is passing dishes around the table to share, as chefs take pride in balancing the flavours on each plate. For a widely roaming meal, opt for a *menu dégustation* (tasting menu).

Coffee is served after dessert. *Café* means espresso, strong and black. If you like milk, order a *café noisette*. *Café crème* (coffee with milk) is considered a breakfast drink. Finally, if you're avoiding caffeine, ask for a *café décaféiné* (*déca* for short) or *une tisane* (herbal tea).

Last but not least, the *digestifs* (after-dinner drinks), ranging from Cognac to Armagnac to Calvados to other liqueurs. Beware: too many and you'll pay for it in the morning. ❑

OTHER CUISINES

North African restaurants are probably the best-represented in the French capital, serving classic hearty dishes like *couscous* (steamed semolina with spicy meat or stewy vegetable toppings) and *tagine* (braised meat, often cooked with preserved lemons and dried fruits).

Japanese restaurants – from cheap and cheerful noodle joints to more swanky sushi specialists – are numerous in the 1st *arrondissement*, in and around Rue des Petits Champs; and for cheap Vietnamese, head for the Porte d'Italie neighbourhood, not far from student stomping grounds in the Latin Quarter.

For Indian fare (not just restaurants, but also eclectic grocers), explore the 10th *arrondissement* around the Gare du Nord.

African food can be had in Belleville, northeast of Place de la République, and good Lebanese food is dotted all over Paris.

Chic Shopping

Chic boutiques, mouth-watering food shops and strutting-edge fashions: welcome to the best collection of shops in Europe

Though shopping abroad is an increasingly predictable affair, Paris can still claim to offer something different. It hosts an incredible variety of shops and has, by and large, retained its tradition of small specialist addresses and personal attention.

Despite a tendency for fashion labels to aim for a citywide spread, there are fewer chain stores here than in most European capitals. With the exception of the Forum des Halles and a couple of small shopping centres, Paris remains largely free of the *centres commerciaux* (shopping malls) that disfigure its suburbs. Instead, boutiques ensure that Paris stays vibrant and alive.

The fashion industry is still a tangible presence in Paris; however, French designers no longer dominate the world fashion stage. But between the couture tags and the high-street chains, you can find boutiques with their own take on French style, retailers picking out exciting new talents, and the one-off boutiques of individual designers. And at some atelier-boutiques, in Bastille and Montmartre, you can buy direct.

Other aspects of French design are also worth exploring. Paris has a strong art and craft tradition, from the classic hallmarks of quality such as Lalique glass and Pierre Frey fabrics to contemporary design gurus such as Philippe Starck, and the rising talents Tsé & Tsé Associées and the Bouroullec brothers.

Then there's food, of course. Every *quartier* has its *chocolatiers*, *pâtisseries* and *boulangeries*, ripe-smelling cheese shops and bustling street markets.

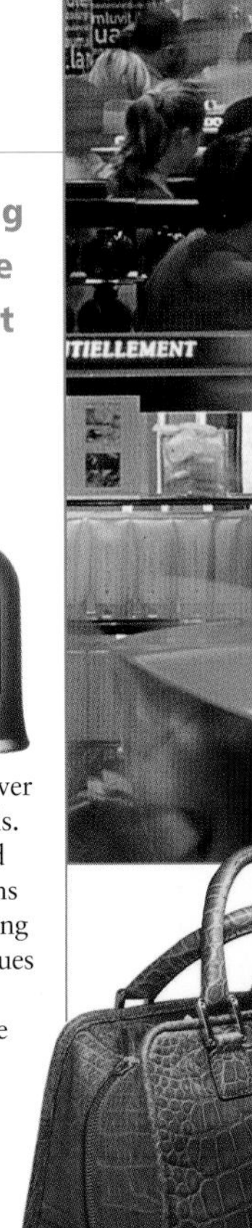

Left: all international luxury labels have stores in Paris, most to be found along the *chicissime* Avenue Montaigne, like Loewe, a Spanish leather-goods company.

Left: Paris has a long- and well-established reputation for beautifully made lingerie.

Right: for those who like dressing up a little, designer Jérôme L'Huillier (138–9 Galerie de Valois, 1st) produces sexy dresses in colourful geometric patterns.

ABOVE: for those with a passion for independent beauty brands, a visit to Sephora's cavernous flagship store at 70 avenue des Champs-Elysées is essential.

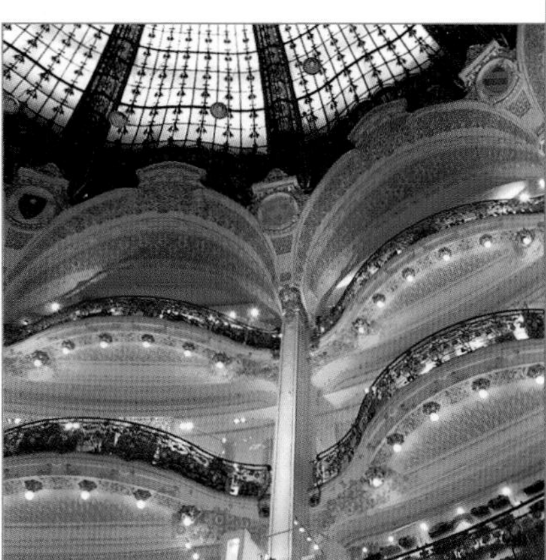

ABOVE: under its stunning Art Nouveau glass dome, Galeries Lafayette offers a colossal fashion choice, from hip designer labels and classical womenswear to popular labels. Also check out Le Labo and Trends which feature innovative young designers. There is an adjoining Lafayette Homme for men.

Palais Royal: the glorious arcades, once tranquil, are now buzzing – new boutiques include Marc Jacobs.

Rue de Rennes: the place to come to for shoes – and the city's oldest department store, Le Bon Marché, is just a short walk away.

Rue St-Honoré: home to purveyors of luxury goods and smart fashions, and the trend-setting (and still cool) concept store Colette.

Grands Boulevards: two behemoth department stores, Galeries Lafayette and Au Printemps, make this area a must, but there are also smaller boutiques nearby.

The Marais: youthful fashions, quirky gift boutiques and gay bookshops, all in beautiful, historic buildings.

St-Germain-des-Prés: the former literary hub is now fashion central – joining the big names are hot newcomers like Catherine Malandrino.

The Market Scene

The city's lively street markets are a vital part of life for many residents – and no two are the same

Visitors wanting a change from the cool chic of haute couture Paris should seek out a street market: there are more than 50. Foodies will be beguiled by the tantalising smells of the roving street food markets; photographers intrigued by the predominantly North African Marché d'Aligre; and browsers may prefer the *bouquinistes*, open-air booksellers whose stalls line the banks of the Seine. There are markets specialising in flowers, postcards and stamps, funky Left Bank markets selling second-hand designer clothes, rural markets overflowing with fresh farm produce and bargains or genuine antiques to be had at the city's regular flea markets. Best of all, markets are one of the best opportunities for visitors to experience the real buzz of the various *quartiers*.

Above: at the Puces de St-Ouen, although a few of the markets remain shabby, much of what is on sale is classy and often quite pricey. Many of the stalls have the allure of shops, and stallholders are knowledgeable enthusiasts. The whole complex has recently been listed as a historic monument in an attempt to preserve its character.

Left: the flea markets of Paris developed in the 19th century, as scrap-metal merchants and rag-and-bone men camped in the unbuilt zone outside the Thiers fortifications, thus avoiding the duties within the city walls.

Left, Above and Right: food markets say a lot about the way Parisians live. The key to most is that they sell fresh, quality ingredients. Prices are not cheap, but the emphasis is on the best that is in season. There are two main types of food market: the roving street markets that appear a couple of mornings a week, and the historic covered markets.

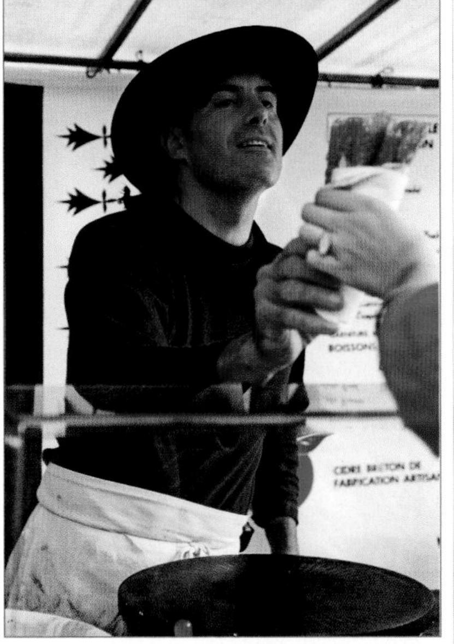

THE BEST MARKETS

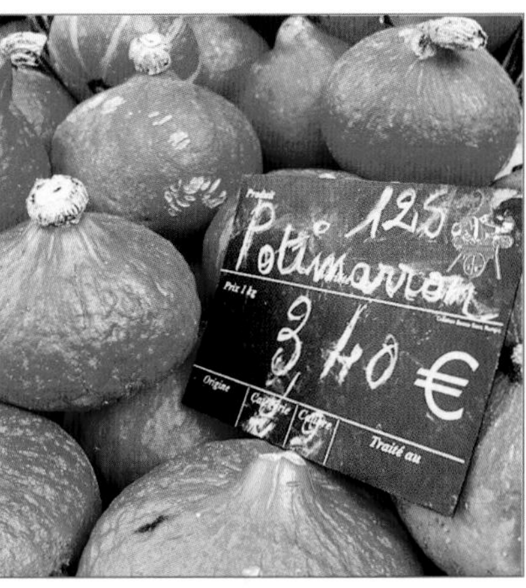

Paris is known for it many flea *(puces)* and food markets. Here are some of the best:

Marché de St-Ouen: in the north of Paris (Métro Porte de Clignancourt). Reputedly the largest flea market in Europe, with over 2,500 dealers spread over a dozen markets and arcades. A huge range of specialists, with prices to match. Be ready to bargain. Sat–Mon 8am–6.30pm.

Marché de Montreuil: tattier and more anarchic than St-Ouen, Montreuil (Métro Porte de Montreuil) sells car parts, tools and unwashed clothes. Sat–Mon.

Marché de Vanves: smaller than St-Ouen and Montreuil, Vanves (Métro Porte de Vanves) is a relaxed flea market within the *Périphérique*. Weekends.

Marché d'Aligre: the oldest flea market in Paris, on the square next to the Rue d'Aligre (Métro Ledru-Rollin) food market. Handful of stalls selling overpriced antiques and junk. Tue–Sun am.

Marché Bastille on boulevard Richard-Lenoir (Thur and Sun am; Métro Bastille) and **Avenue Daumesnil** (Tue and Fri am; Métro Daumesnil)**:** street markets with a great range of seasonal produce.

Rue Mouffetard: characterful food market street in the Latin Quarter (Métro Censier-Daubenton). Tue–Sat (closed for lunch) and Sun am

Marché St-Quentin: 85 boulevard Magenta, 10th (Métro Gare de l'Est), was built in the 1880s and remains the best-preserved cast-iron covered market. Stalls sell fresh produce and exotic snacks. Sat and Sun am.

PARIS AFTER DARK

The city's nightlife offers many options for eating late, drinking late, or dancing until dawn

Paris still isn't really a clubbing city, and stringent anti-noise laws mean most music venues can't stage late-night gigs. But there's no shortage of after-dark revelry if you know where to look. There has been a recent increase in the range and number of venues: upmarket clubs like Le Baron and Le Milliardaire attract the jet set; in 2005, an old warehouse on the bank of the Canal St-Martin was turned into giant arts and nightlife complex Point Ephémère; and in 2007, "hangars" underneath the Pont Alexandre III opened as glam club Le Showcase. And other stalwarts, like Les Bains Douches, La Flèche d'Or and Le Bus Palladium have been given new leases of life. There's also a lot of jazz, blues, *chanson* and world gigs, and lively backroom gig spaces to complement the larger, more traditional music venues. Keep your ears to the ground and look out for flyers and free listings booklets in bars.

ABOVE: La Flèche d'Or (102bis rue de Bagnolet, 20th) is an enjoyable anarchic music and clubbing venue housed in an old train station.

LEFT: enjoy an exotic gastronomic journey under the serene supervision of a gigantic Buddha, accompanied by smooth tunes from renowned DJs at Le Buddha-Bar (8/12, rue Boissy d'Anglas),

LEFT: Le Batofar (11 quai François Mauriac) is one of the city's most unusual club venues: a converted barge moored on the Seine. DJs play electro, rock, groove, soul, funk and hip-hop, and there are live gigs, too.

RIGHT: located in an upbeat street in a trendy neighbourhood in the heart of Saint Michel quarter, the Bistro de la Huchette will have you dancing to salsa beats all night long.

THE COCKTAIL HOTSPOTS

Parisian trendsetters still love the **Hôtel Costes** (239 rue St-Honoré, 1st), which has a sleek bar and plays classic "lounge music". Chez Justine (96 rue Oberkampf) attracts a large crowd with its comfy bar and classy decor. A sizzling atmosphere awaits you at the **Mezzanine de l'Alcazar** (62 rue Mazarine, 6th). For a more casual and exotic night, try **Andy Walhoo** (69 rue des Gravilliers, 3rd) to savour Moroccan tapas, funky decor and mint-and-vodka concoctions.

ABOVE: Mix Club (24 rue de l'Arrivée, 15th) is a massive venue. The music is house, and house only, and there is a popular gay tea dance on Sundays.

RIGHT: Nouveau Casino (109 rue Oberkampf, 11th), in the heart of the cool Oberkampf area, hosts good live music and hip club nights (Wed–Sat) – house, techno and electro.

LEFT: recently renovated, celeb haunt club Les Bains Douches (7 rue du Bourg-l'Abbé, 3rd) attracts a fashionable crowd and tourists. All music genres.

RIGHT: an iconic disco of the 1960s, Le Bus Palladium (6 rue Fontaine, 9th) has just reopened and it's cool all over again.

BELOW: Le Caveau de la Huchette (5 rue de la Huchette, 5th) is a Latin Quarter jazz basement that will take you right back to the jazz heyday of the 1950s.

Paris at the Movies

In 1895, the first public film screening was held in Paris – and the city and cinema have been inseparable ever since

If Paris feels eternally familiar, thank the movies. Indeed, you're in film-set Paris the second you get off the train at the Gare du Nord, filmed by Orson Welles *(F for Fake)*, Jean-Pierre Jeunet *(Amélie)* and many others. Next, naturally, you make your way to the Métro – an even more popular film location, used by everyone from Henri-Georges Clouzot to the Coen brothers. Perhaps you come out at the Champs-Elysées – another classic setting; as you walk up, imagine the Wehrmacht's daily parade coming the other way, as recreated to sobering effect in Jean-Pierre Melville's *L'Armée des Ombres*. And it's hard to miss the Eiffel Tower: not only filmed more times than it has rivets (the pioneering Lumière brothers were first – their 1900 portrait of the 11-year-old tower is still extant), it even starred in its own cartoon, *Bonjour Paris*.

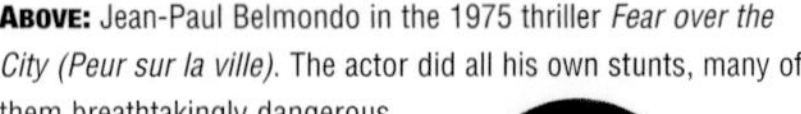

Above: Jean-Paul Belmondo in the 1975 thriller *Fear over the City (Peur sur la ville)*. The actor did all his own stunts, many of them breathtakingly dangerous.

Below: Christophe Lambert grabs a little down time in Luc Besson's light-hearted thriller *Subway*, set largely in the tunnels of the Métro and RER. The film helped define *le cinéma du look*: high on swagger and visual panache, low on substance.

Right: Vincent Cassel as a bad boy from the *banlieues* in Matthieu Kassovitz's ferocious 1995 agitprop drama *La Haine*, which won its director a major prize at the Cannes Festival that year. In its portrayal of the urban underclass, the film is still all too relevant.

GOOD OLD NEW WAVE

When people think of Paris movies, they often have in mind a small clutch of films – usually including *Breathless* and *The 400 Blows* – made by a small group of people in a short space of time. These Nouvelle Vague ("new wave") films were made between the late 1950s and mid-1960s, by a loosely affiliated group of directors opposed to what they saw as the stuffiness of cinema of the day; its leading figures were Jean-Luc Godard (pictured), François Truffaut, Claude Chabrol, Eric Rohmer and Jacques Rivette, all – except Truffaut, who died in 1982 – still working today. One of its few women directors was Agnès Varda, whose 1962 film *Cléo de 5 à 7* is one of the best of the bunch.

BELOW: Jean Seberg and Belmondo in probably the most famous Paris film, Jean-Luc Godard's *Breathless (A Bout de Souffle).*

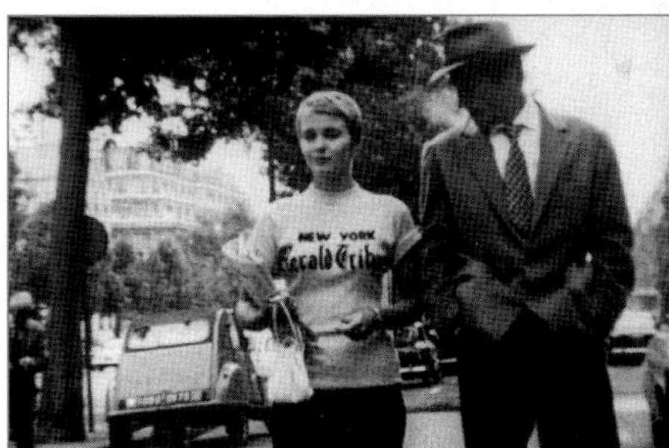

BELOW: Juliette Binoche stars in *Les Amants du Pont Neuf*, the film that nearly ended the career of its director, Leos Carax. The Pont Neuf itself was recreated, life-size, near Montpellier – at colossal expense.

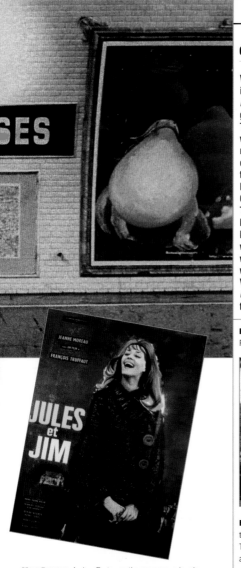

MAIN PICTURE: Audrey Tautou as the eponymous heroine of Jean-Pierre Jeunet's 2001 smash hit *Amélie (Le Fabuleux Destin d'Amélie Poulain).* The Métro stop shown is not, in fact, Abbesses – but a disused station used exclusively for filming.

ABOVE: François Truffaut's 1962 film *Jules et Jim* is probably the best-known screen tale of a love triangle; Jeanne Moreau plays its pivotal character. At various points in her career, Moreau has been an actress, writer, producer, director and a successful singer.

PLANETE SUR SEINE

PLANETE
SEINE
TOURING CLUB

ORIENTATION

The Places section details all the attractions worth seeing, arranged by area. The areas are shown on a colour-coordinated map on pages 70–1. Main sights are cross-referenced by number to individual maps

Paris is set in a natural basin, cut through the middle by the meandering River Seine and edged with gentle hills. Situated on longitude 2° 20'W and latitude 48° 50'N, roughly the same latitude as Vancouver in Canada, the city itself covers an area close to 100 sq km (40 sq miles), spanning 13 km (8 miles) from east to west, and 9 km (6 miles) north to south. On the map, 20 *arrondissements* (administrative districts) spiral out like a snail's shell, a pattern reflecting the city's historical development and successive enlargements. The Seine enters Paris close to the Bois de Vincennes in the southeast, and weaves gently past three small islands – Ile St-Louis, Ile de la Cité and, on its way out, Ile des Cygnes. Several hills rise up to the north of the river, including Montmartre, the city's highest point at 130 metres (425 ft), Ménilmontant, Belleville and Buttes Chaumont; and to the south, Montsouris, Mont Ste-Geneviève, Buttes aux Cailles and Maison Blanche. Mont Valérien is the highest point on the outskirts at 160 metres (525 ft), providing an immense panoramic view of Paris from the west. The lowest, at 25 metres (85 ft) above sea level, is at Grenelle.

The city is contained by the *Boulevard Périphérique*, a ringroad stretching 35 km (22 miles). Built in 1973 to try to reduce traffic jams, the Périph' is invariably congested itself, particularly during the rush hours, when an estimated 150,000 cars storm its 35 exits. Forming two concentric rings around Paris, the suburbs *(la banlieue)* are divided up into *départements* or boroughs. The inner ring incorporates Hauts-de-Seine, Val-de-Marne and Seine-St-Denis, and the outer ring consists of Seine-et-Marne, Essonne, Yvelines and Val-d'Oise. These counties, together with Paris and the Greater Paris conurbation around it, constitute the Ile-de-France region and are linked by eight major roads, five RER lines and an extensive rail network branching out in all directions from five stations in the capital. The city's calmest transport route is its river, barely ruffled by the daily flow of tourist and commercial boat traffic. Barges and pleasure boats on their way to Burgundy use the St-Martin and St-Denis canals to shorten their trip, cutting across the northeast of Paris. ❑

PRECEDING PAGES: ornate streetlamps on the Place de la Concord; the view from Pont Alexandre III. **LEFT:** Place de la Concorde, the obelisk and the Eiffel Tower at sunset.

PARIS TOP SIGHTS

Montmartre
pages 159–175

La Défense
pages 252–3

Arc de Triomphe
pages 156–7

Eiffel Tower
pages 234–5

Musée d'Orsay
pages 236–9

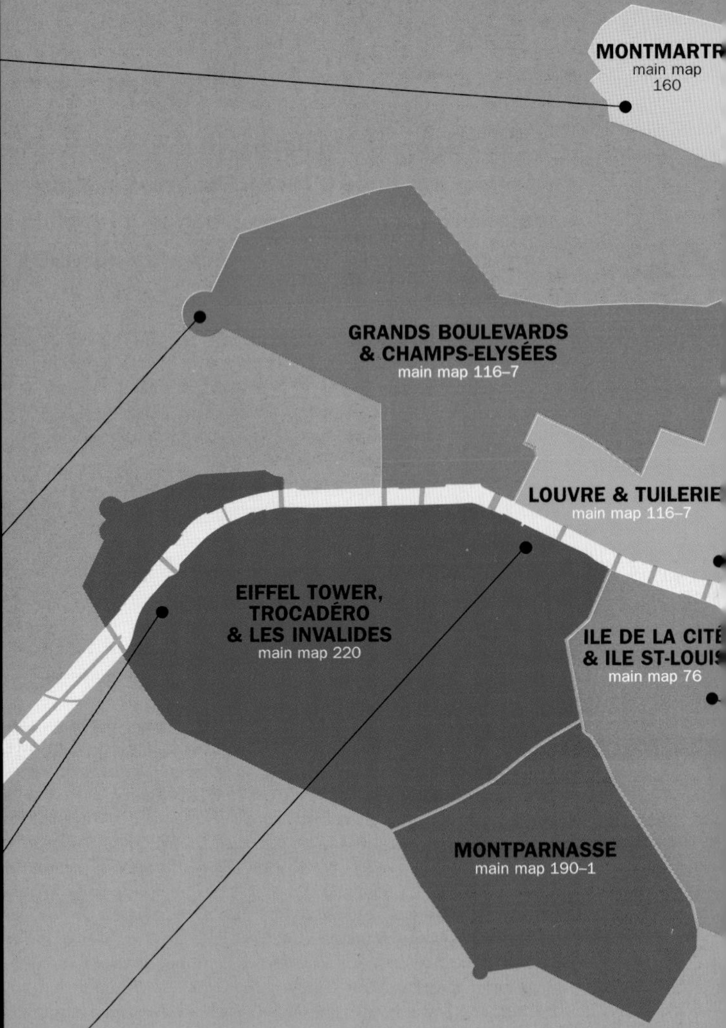

MONTMARTRE
main map
160

GRANDS BOULEVARDS
& CHAMPS-ELYSÉES
main map 116–7

LOUVRE & TUILERIES
main map 116–7

EIFFEL TOWER,
TROCADÉRO
& LES INVALIDES
main map 220

ILE DE LA CITÉ
& ILE ST-LOUIS
main map 76

MONTPARNASSE
main map 190–1

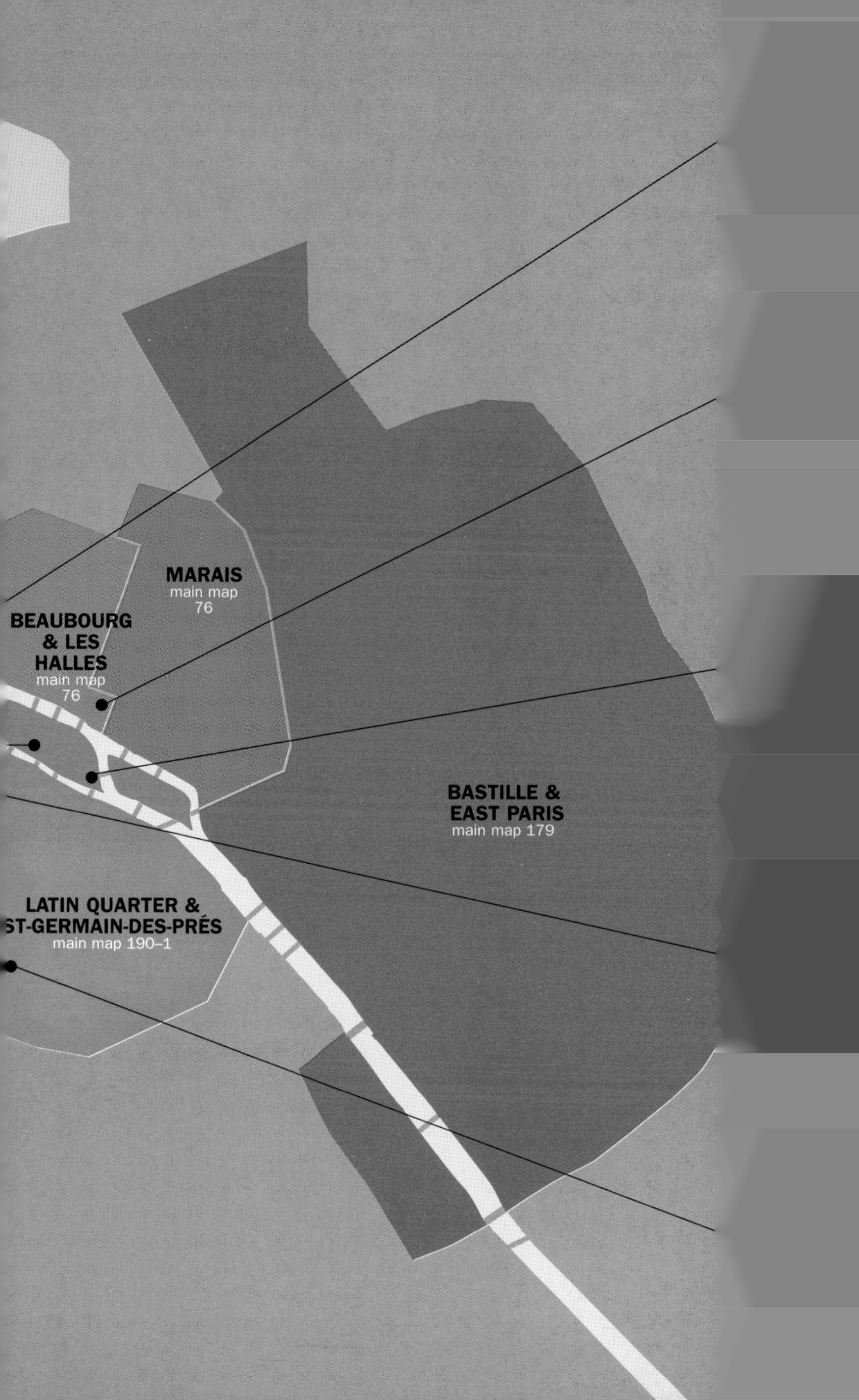
MARAIS
main map
76
BEAUBOURG
& LES
HALLES
main map
76
BASTILLE &
EAST PARIS
main map 179
LATIN QUARTER &
ST-GERMAIN-DES-PRÉS
main map 190–1

Paris

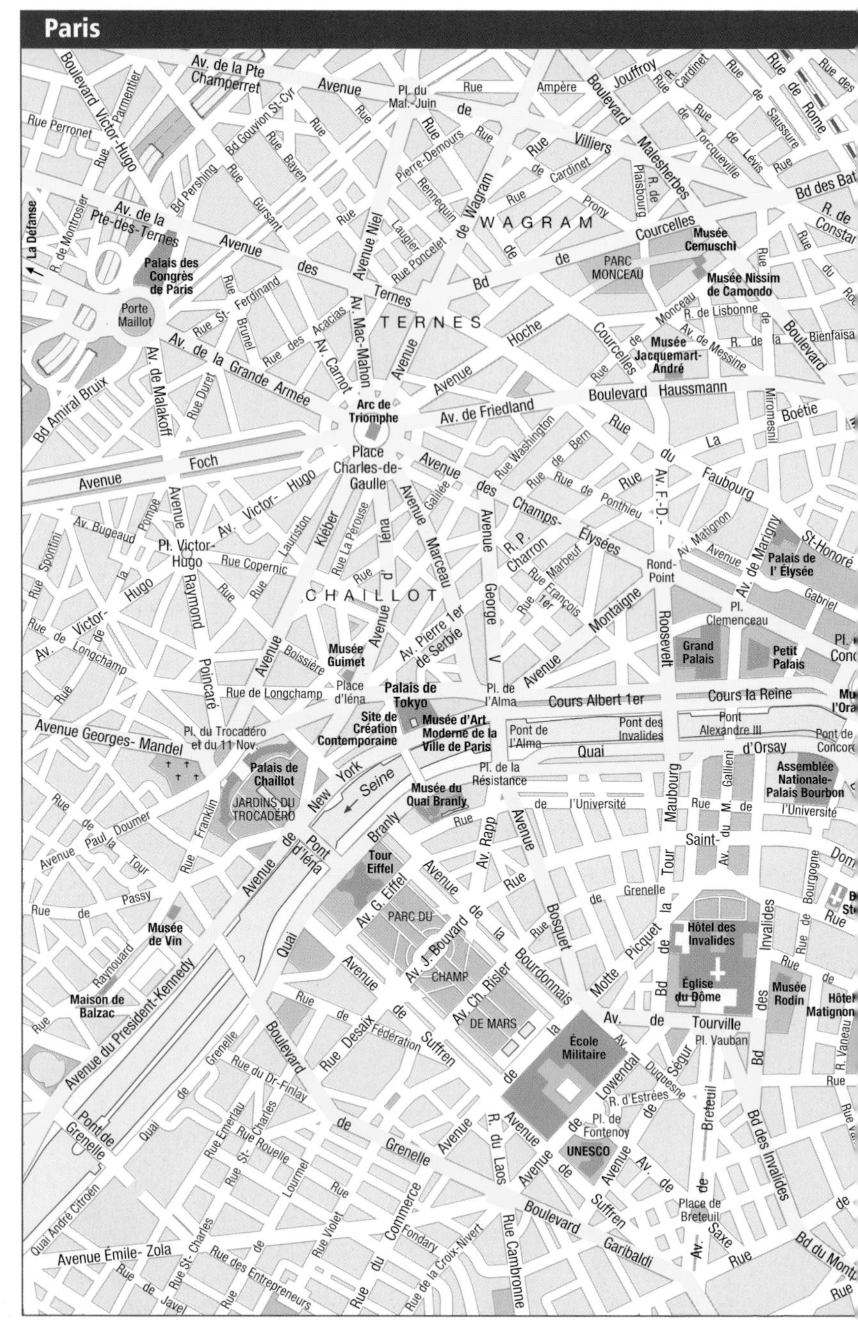

Arc de Triomphe
Place Charles-de-Gaulle
Palais des Congrès de Paris
Porte Maillot
Musée Cernuschi
Musée Nissim de Camondo
Parc Monceau
Musée Jacquemart-André
Palais de l'Élysée
Grand Palais
Petit Palais
Musée Guimet
Palais de Tokyo
Site de Création Contemporaine
Musée d'Art Moderne de la Ville de Paris
Palais de Chaillot
Jardins du Trocadéro
Musée du Quai Branly
Assemblée Nationale-Palais Bourbon
Tour Eiffel
Parc du Champ de Mars
Hôtel des Invalides
Église du Dôme
Musée Rodin
Hôtel Matignon
École Militaire
UNESCO
Musée de Vin
Maison de Balzac
Wagram
Ternes
Chaillot
Seine
La Défense
Avenue des Champs-Élysées
Boulevard Haussmann
Avenue Foch
Avenue de la Grande Armée
Avenue Kléber
Avenue d'Iéna
Avenue Marceau
Avenue George V
Avenue Montaigne
Cours Albert 1er
Cours la Reine
Quai d'Orsay
Avenue du Président-Kennedy
Avenue de Suffren
Avenue de la Bourdonnais
Boulevard Garibaldi
Boulevard de Grenelle
Avenue Émile-Zola
Pont d'Iéna
Pont de l'Alma
Pont des Invalides
Pont Alexandre III
Pont de Grenelle
Pl. du Trocadéro et du 11 Nov.
Pl. Victor-Hugo
Pl. de l'Alma
Pl. de la Résistance
Pl. Clemenceau
Pl. Vauban
Pl. de Fontenoy
Place de Breteuil

0
500 m
0
500 yds
CIMETIÈRE MONTMARTRE
Moulin Rouge
Basilique du Sacré-Cœur
St-Jean
Rue des Abbesses
R. Caulaincourt
Place de Clichy
Boulevard de Clichy
MONTMARTRE
Boulevard de Rochechouart
Pl. Pigalle
Bd Barbès
Rue d'Amsterdam
Rue Notre-Dame-de-Lorette
Rue La Bruyère
Rue Blanche
Rue de Clichy
Avenue Trudaine
Rue de Dunkerque
Rue Condorcet
Rue des Martyrs
Rue Rodier
Rue de Rochechouart
Rue de Maubeuge
R. de Maubeuge
Boulevard de Magenta
Gare du Nord
Rue du Faubourg St-Denis
Rue la Fayette
Rue de l'Aqueduc
Rue Louis Blanc
Rue St-Martin
Rue de Londres
Rue St-Lazare
Rue de Châteaudin
Rue la Fayette
Rue de Chabrol
Gare de l'Est
Rue du Faubourg
Quai de Valmy
Quai de Jemmapes
Canal St-Martin
Rue de la Grange
Rue St- Lazare
R. de la Chaussée
Rue de Provence
Folies Bergère
Rue Richer
Rue de Paradis
R. des Petites Écuries
Rue d'Hauteville
Rue du Fg Poissonnière
Boulevard Haussmann
R. Drouot
Rue Tronchet
Palais Garnier
Bd Montmartre
Bd Poissonnière
Bd des Italiens
Bd de Bonne Nouvelle
Boulevard de Strasbourg
Rue du Faubourg St-Martin
Rue du Château d'Eau
Bd de Magenta
Bd des Capucines
Th. des Capucines
Rue du Quatre-Septembre
La Bourse
Rue de Richelieu
R. de la Paix
Rue Cambon
Place Vendôme
Rue de Cléry
Rue Réaumur
Rue N.D. des Victoires
Bibliothèque Nationale-Richelieu
Bd St- Martin
Pl. de la République
Rue du Faubourg-du-Temple
Av. de l'Opéra
R. des Petits Champs
Rue Montmartre
Rue Montorgueil
Rue St-Denis
Boulevard Sébastopol
Rue St-Martin
Musée des Arts et Métiers
Rue de Turbigo
Rue St- Honoré
St-Roch
JARDIN DU PALAIS ROYAL
Rue du Louvre
Rue Etienne-Marcel
St-Eustache
MARAIS
Rue du Temple
R. de Bretagne
Rue Charlot
Boulevard du Temple
Boulevard Voltaire
JARDIN DES TUILERIES
Comédie Française
Palais Royal
Bourse de Commerce
Rue de Rivoli
Forum des Halles
Rue Berger
Rue Rambuteau
Rue Beaubourg
Rue des Archives
Rue de Turenne
JARDIN DU CARROUSEL
Quai des Tuileries
Seine
Quai Anatole-France
Quai Fr. Mitterrand
Musée du Louvre
Centre Georges Pompidou
Musée de l'Histoire de France
Musée National Picasso
Bd des F. du Calvaire
Musée d'Orsay
Pont Royal
Rue du Bac
Pont du Carrousel
Rue de Lille
Rue de l'Université
St-Merri
Rue du Temple
Rue Vieille du Temple
Rue des Francs-Bourgeois
Musée Carnavalet
Boulevard Beaumarchais
Pont Neuf
Quai de Conti
École Nationale Supérieure des Beaux-Arts
Institut de France
Palais de Justice
Hôtel de Ville
Quai de l'Hotel de Ville
Pl. des Vosges
Rue Bonaparte
Rue des Saints-Pères
R. Mazarine
Rue Dauphine
Quai d. Grands Augustins
Ste-Chapelle
Bd du Palais
Rue de la Cité
Île de la Cité
Hôtel d'Aumont
Rue St- Antoine
Maison de Victor Hugo
Boulevard St-Germain
St-Germain-des-Prés
Rue de Seine
R. St-André-des-Arts
Hôtel de Sens
Place de la Bastille
Rue de Grenelle
Rue du Four
St-Sulpice
R. St-Sulpice
Boulevard St-Michel
Notre-Dame
R. des Deux Ponts
Île St-Louis
Bd Henri IV
Boulevard Raspail
St-Julien-le-Pauvre
Quai de la Tournelle
Bd Morland
Quai Henri IV
Bd Bourdon
Bd de la Bastille
Théâtre National de l'Odéon
Rue Madame
Rue de Rennes
Rue de Vaugirard
Rue St-Jacques
Rue des Écoles
Rue Monge
Quai St-Bernard
Seine
Palais du Luxembourg
La Sorbonne
R. Cujas
R. Soufflot
Rue Clovis
Rue Jussieu
JARDIN TINO ROSSI
Quai de la Rapée
Rue Guynemer
JARDIN DU LUXEMBOURG
Panthéon
Rue Cuvier
Pont d'Austerlitz
Rue d'Assas
Rue A.-Comte
Boulevard St-Michel
JARDIN DES PLANTES

Recommended Restaurants, Bars & Cafés on page 85

ILE DE LA CITÉ AND ILE ST-LOUIS

Paris's Gothic heart, where the soaring towers and buttresses of Notre-Dame and the Sainte-Chapelle rise up next to the glowering fortress-prison of the Conciergerie, only a short walk from the 17th-century refinement of the Ile St-Louis

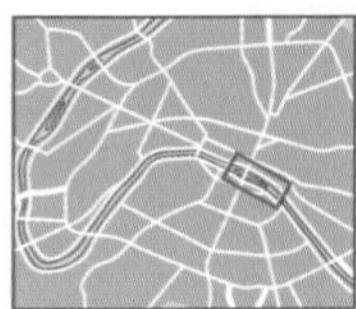

Main attractions
- NOTRE-DAME
- PALAIS DE JUSTICE
- SAINTE-CHAPELLE
- CONCIERGERIE
- MÉMORIAL DE LA DÉPORTATION
- MUSÉE ADAM MICKIEWICZ

The Ile de la Cité in the middle of the Seine is the birthplace and topographical centre of Paris, and has been its spiritual and legislative heart for more than 2,000 years. Invading the already established Parisii settlement in 53 BC, the Romans built a prefect's palace, law court and temple to Jupiter on the island. Across the river on the Right Bank, the Hôtel de Ville has been a cauldron of political debate since the Middle Ages (though the current building dates from the 1870s), while just to the north, the area of Les Halles fed the city's stomachs from 1110 until 1969. This is the core of the capital, an area which in many ways embodies the essence of Paris.

NOTRE-DAME ❶

www.cathedraledeparis.com
01 42 34 56 10 Mon–Fri 8am–6.45pm, Sat–Sun 8am–7.15pm
free Cité

The Ile de la Cité is dominated by the soaring cathedral, Notre-Dame de Paris, that fills the eastern end of the island. Gazing up at its finely sculpted facade, it's hard to imagine the building's condition when Victor Hugo *(see page 92)* wrote his novel *Notre-Dame de Paris* in 1830–1. He and fellow Romantics were appalled by the state of the building, and in 1841 succeeded in triggering a massive restoration programme, headed by Viollet-le-Duc *(see page 46)*. For 23 years, the meticulous architect repaired Notre-Dame from the foundations to the roof tiles, recreated stained-glass windows by copying extant ones and replaced sculptures destroyed in the Revolution, such as the Gallery of Kings, by studying those of other Gothic cathedrals.

LEFT: the Gothic towers of Notre-Dame.
RIGHT: design shop in chic Ile St-Louis.

Cité, Marais, Beaubourg and Les Halles

Recommended Restaurants, Bars & Cafés on page 85

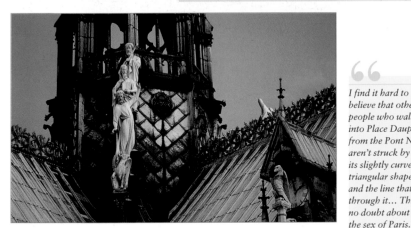

He also added a sacristy on the south side, now the **Trésor de Notre-Dame** (Mon–Fri 9.30am–6pm, Sat until 6.30pm, Sun 1.30–6.30pm; charge), housing the alleged Crown of Thorns, among other relics. *For more on Notre-Dame, see pages 86–7.*

Royal shrine

The church of "Our Lady" was built on the site of earlier pagan fertility worship by Celts and Romans. In the 6th century, Clovis, the conquering Frankish king, erected a Christian basilica, which was replaced by a Romanesque church. In 1159, the young bishop Maurice de Sully decided that Paris deserved bigger and better. Work on the cathedral began in 1163 and took just under 200 years to complete, following plans by Pierre de Montreuil, also the architect of Sainte-Chapelle.

Even before it was finished, Notre-Dame had become the venue for state ceremonies, funerals and thanksgivings; in 1239 Louis IX deposited the Crown of Thorns and other relics acquired on Crusade here, while Sainte-Chapelle was being built. Since then Notre-Dame has been witness to a string of historical events: in 1572, the cathedral's strangest wedding took place. The bride, Marguerite de Valois (a Catholic), stood at the altar, while bridegroom Henri de Navarre (a Protestant), called in his vows from the doorstep. Later, in 1589, Henri was crowned in the cathedral, having decided to convert to Catholicism. The famous comment attributed to him, "Paris is well worth a Mass" is almost certainly apocryphal.

Come the Revolution, Notre-Dame was ravaged by looters, who melted down and destroyed anything

> *I find it hard to believe that other people who walk into Place Dauphine from the Pont Neuf aren't struck by its slightly curved triangular shape, and the line that runs through it... This is, no doubt about it, the sex of Paris.*
>
> André Breton

ABOVE: Notre-Dame bell tower.
BELOW: the Portal of the Last Judgement.

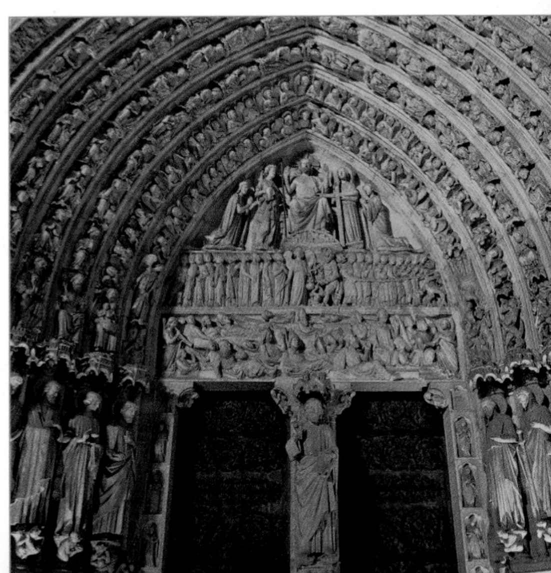

When the north–south Métro line 4 was being built in the first decade of the 20th century, its builders solved the problem of getting past the two channels of the Seine by building colossal iron frameworks, in the shape of flattened tubes, and driving them into the river bed. These tubes are the tunnels the trains have passed through ever since.

that hinted of royalty, lopping off the heads of the kings of Judah along the top of the main portals. The cathedral was then turned into a "Temple of Reason", and by the end of the Revolution was being used to store wine.

By the time Napoleon decided to be crowned emperor in 1804, the cathedral was in such a shabby state bright tapestries were hung up to cover the crumbling decor. Pope Pius VII attended reluctantly, and when he hesitated at the altar, Napoleon took the crown and to cheers of *"Vive l'empereur!"* placed it on his head himself. Another dramatic event came in August 1944, at the thanksgiving ceremony for the Liberation of Paris, when the leader of the new government, General Charles de Gaulle, was shot at during the Te Deum.

Gothic architecture

Notre-Dame is magnificent from any angle, but its facade is particularly impressive. Viewed from Place du Parvis, the twin towers soar to the heavens with dramatic grace. The three porticoes each have a distinct design: an asymmetry typical of medieval architecture. Originally, the stone figures were finely painted against a gilt background, to illustrate Bible stories for an illiterate populace.

On the left, the Portal of the Virgin depicts the Ark of the Covenant and the coronation of the Virgin. The Portal of the Last Judgement, in the middle, shows the Resurrection, the weighing of souls and their procession to heaven or hell. The Portal of St Anne portrays the Virgin and Maurice de Sully. Above the doorways, the rose window, depicting the Virgin and Child in deep blues and rich reds, is a miracle of engineering. Picture the rickety scaffolding and the armies of stonemasons, who with

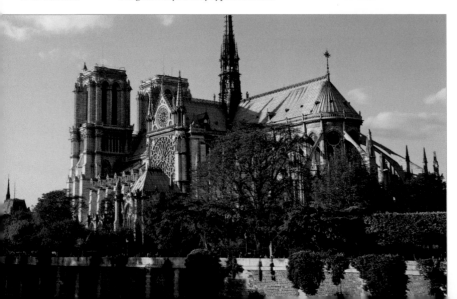

RIGHT: Notre-Dame choir during Mass. **BELOW:** riverside view of the cathedral.

simple measuring techniques constructed an intricate masterpiece that has lasted for 750 years. The glass, however, has been restored.

Tours de Notre-Dame

01 53 10 07 00 daily Apr–Sept 10am–6.30pm (June–Aug Sat–Sun until 11 pm), Oct–Mar 10am–5.30pm, last admission 45 minutes before closing time charge Cité

The ascent of the towers (be prepared to queue) is a religious experience for those who love heights and a taste of hell for claustrophobes and vertigo sufferers. The ascent is long (387 steps) and narrow, but the reward is a breathtaking view over Paris. "Emmanuel", the 13-tonne bell, is rung only on state occasions. Legend has it that the purity of its tone is due to the gold-and-silver jewellery thrown into its heated bronze by the most beautiful women of Paris.

Cathedral interior

Inside, the cathedral is bounded by 37 side chapels. Supported by flying buttresses, the vault of the chancel seems almost weightless, with stained-glass windows distributing rays of coloured light into the solemn shadows. The exquisite 13th-century north and south rose windows are the two star attractions. The spectacular north window still retains most of its 13th-century glass, but the south rose had to be reconstructed completely by Viollet-le-Duc.

The 18th-century carved choir stalls, depicting the life of the Virgin Mary, were commissioned by Louis XIV, fulfilling a vow his father made 60 years earlier that he would devote the east chancel to the Virgin if he were to have an heir. Louis XIII's statue stands behind the high altar, with Guillaume Coustou's *Pietà*.

Hôtel-Dieu ❷

1 place du Parvis Notre-Dame 4th courtyard daily free Cité

Just north of Notre-Dame is the Hôtel-Dieu, the oldest hospital in the city. Founded in 651 by Saint Landry, it was the recipient of generous donations from Louis IX during the 13th century. It has remained in the same

Delicate statues punctuate Notre-Dame's intricate western facade.

BELOW LEFT: memorial service for President François Mitterrand (1996). **BELOW:** the superb rose window.

Vedettes du Pont Neuf (tel: 01 46 33 98 38; www.vedettesdupontneuf.com) run cruises along the Seine lasting about an hour. Boats leave from the Square du Vert-Galant (Métro: Pont Neuf) every half-hour in the high season (see page 317).

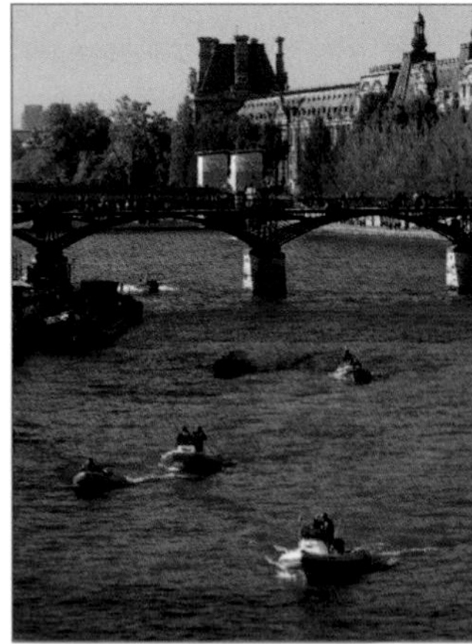

ABOVE: boat action on the Seine near Ile de la Cité.

location despite several fires throughout the ages. The current building was constructed by Baron Georges Haussmann in the 1860s and was the scene of intense battles between police and the Germans in 1944.

Crypte archéologique ❸

01 55 42 50 10 Tue–Sun 10am–6pm charge Cité

Underneath the parvis in front of the cathedral, inside the crypt, are excavations of buildings dating back to the Roman city of Lutetia in the 3rd century AD, including parts of a house inhabited by the Gallic Parisii, amid the remains of medieval cellars.

A short walk west of Notre-Dame are the imposing walls of the Palais de Justice and the Conciergerie.

Palais de Justice ❹

01 44 32 50 50 Mon–Fri 9am–6pm charge Cité

At one time, the Palais de Justice was a royal palace, and Louis IX had his bedroom in what is now the First Civil Court. In the 14th century, the monarchy, in the person of Charles V, moved out, and parliament, with full judiciary rights, moved in. A wander around the hushed corridors, past fleeting black-robed figures, might recall the tense days of the Revolution when the public prosecutor, Fouquier-Tinville, sent thousands of people to the guillotine. The present legal system is still based closely on the one founded by Napoleon Bonaparte.

SAINTE-CHAPELLE ❺

www.monum.fr 01 53 40 60 80 daily summer 9.30am–6pm, winter 9am–5pm charge Cité

Within the walls of the Palais de Justice, Sainte-Chapelle stands like a skeletal finger pointing heavenwards – an ethereal counterpoint to the stones of the establishment.

This miracle of High Gothic ingenuity is one of the most gorgeous buildings in Paris. Completed in just 33 months by Pierre de Montreuil and consecrated in 1248, the chapel was built to house the Crown of Thorns, bartered from the Venetians by Louis IX. Seemingly constructed without walls, the chapel's vaulted roof is supported by a thin web of

Notable Inmates

A prison for five centuries, the medieval Conciergerie housed, among others, Captain Montgomery, a Scot, who fatally wounded Henri II during a tournament in 1559, and Ravaillac, assassin of Henri IV in 1610. During the Revolution, its big-name inmates ran from figures of the *ancien régime* such as Marie-Antoinette – whose cell has been carefully reconstructed – and Louis XV's favourite mistress, Madame du Barry, to Charlotte Corday, murderer of the Revolutionary leader Marat, and her defender the poet André Chenier, and finally the revolutionaries themselves, such as Danton, Camille Desmoulins, St-Just and even the architect of the Terror, Robespierre. In the massacres of September 1792 that marked the beginning of the Revolutionary Terror, over 300 prisoners were killed here.

Recommended Restaurants, Bars & Cafés on page 85

stone, from which descend veils of richly coloured stained glass. A replica Crown of Thorns decorates the top of one of the pinnacles.

Built in two tiers, the lower chapel was designed for the palace staff, and is consequently smaller and gloomier. From the shadows, climb the spiral staircase into the crystalline cavern of the upper chapel. The soaring windows catch the faintest of lights, creating kaleidoscopes of colour that are still vivid, despite being nearly 800 years old. Depicted are 1,134 scenes from the Bible, which begin by the staircase with Genesis and proceed round the church to the 15th-century rose window. Regular concerts of chamber music are held in the chapel.

THE CONCIERGERIE ❻

www.monum.fr 01 53 40 60 80 daily Mar–Oct 9.30am–6pm, Nov–Feb 9am–5pm charge Cité

In the northeast wing of the Palais de Justice, the Conciergerie looks like an intimidating castle, its four towers rising menacingly above impenetrable walls. It isn't hard to imagine this fortress as a merciless medieval prison – which it was (although much of the facade is 19th-century). It was originally built as a palace, administered by the Comte des Cierges or royal concierge – hence the name, Conciergerie – but after Charles Martel's revolt in 1358 King Charles V moved his main residence to his new palace of the Louvre.

The Comte was in charge of the king's seals, lodgings and taxes, until

ABOVE: bars in the Salle des Gens d'Armes. **BELOW:** the Conciergerie is really stunning at night.

the Conciergerie was made a prison in 1391, when his job changed to that of chief gaoler. The Capetian palace came into its own during the Revolution, when it housed nearly 2,600 prisoners awaiting the guillotine, including Marie-Antoinette. Ironically, her prosecutor, Danton, resided in the next cell before his trip to the guillotine, as, in turn, did his nemesis Robespierre. In the merry-go-round of retribution, 1,306 heads rolled in one month at Place de la Nation. To the west is the Cour des Femmes, a rough courtyard where the women were allowed during the day.

The tower at the back is called Bonbec (the Squealer), for it was here, from the 11th century, that torture victims told all. At the front is the 14th-century clock tower containing the first public clock in Paris, still ticking today.

Inside, the original kitchens are still intact. They were built to feed up to 3,000 people using four huge fireplaces and have a Gothic canopied ceiling supported by buttresses. The adjacent Salle des Gens d'Armes is a magnificent four-aisled Gothic hall where the royal guards, or men-at-arms, used to live.

Exploring the Island

Escape the shadows of the Revolution on Quai des Orfèvres, on the south bank of the island, where goldsmiths *(orfèvres)* once fashioned Marie-Antoinette's jewellery, but which is now home to the Police Judiciaire (the equivalent of the English CID). Beyond the Square du

KIDS

The Ile St-Louis's most popular attraction (except on cold days) is edible: the famous ice creams of Berthillon, at 31 rue St-Louis-en-l'Ile, in over 100 delicious flavours. The shop stubbornly shuts in school holidays, but you can find its wares at many cafés nearby.

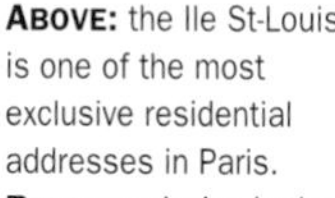

ABOVE: the Ile St-Louis is one of the most exclusive residential addresses in Paris.
BELOW: relaxing in the autumn sunshine on the Square du Vert-Galant.

Recommended Restaurants, Bars & Cafés on page 85

Vert-Galant and the statue of Henri IV, the river slides past the tip of the island. Pont Neuf, bisected by the island, is the oldest surviving bridge in Paris. It was made of stone, rather than wood, and was the first bridge to be built without houses on it. In 1985, the artist Christo wrapped the whole length of the Pont Neuf in golden fabric. Between 1994 and 2007, the bridge underwent a major restoration project completed in time for its 400th anniversary, as a result of which it is looks particularly resplendent today. No small part of the Pont Neuf's charm are the 385 grotesque faces below its cornices.

You can return to the east end of the island via the colourful Marché aux Fleurs in Place Louis-Lépine, opposite the Préfecture de Police and the Hôtel-Dieu *(see page 79)*.

In contrast to these forbidding structures, the market is an array of small glasshouses selling flowers and plants underneath classical black street lamps. On Sunday, the stalls become a market for caged birds, and the jabbering of parakeets fills the air.

On the north side of Notre-Dame is the Quartier des Anciens Cloîtres (Ancient Cloister Quarter), home and study area for 12th-century monks and scholars who belonged to the cathedral chapter, including the theologian Pierre Abélard, famous for his love letters to the beautiful Héloïse. The area was once a warren of medieval churches and houses until Haussmann razed them to the ground, moving 25,000 inhabitants to the suburbs, to create the present vista. As you pass along Rue de la Colombe, note the remains of the Gallo-Roman wall in the pavement.

Mémorial de la Déportation ❼

01 49 74 34 00 daily 9am–noon, 2–4.30pm free Cité

On the eastern tip of the island lies this bleak but moving monument commemorating the 200,000 French deportees (Jewish, homesexual or resistant) sent to their deaths in Nazi concentration camps. The chambers of this prison-like structure are engraved with quotations and the names of concentration camps.

On Rue St-Louis-en-l'Ile is the church of St-Louis-en-l'Ile, built in 1664 and originally designed by Le Vau. The side tower was added later, in 1765.

LEFT: florist on Ile St-Louis.

The Urban Nomad

One of the 19th-century's most towering literary figures, the poet Charles Baudelaire, lived on the Ile St-Louis, on the ground floor of the Hôtel de Lauzun – his window is to the left of the door – from October 1843 to September 1845. While here, the young writer took hashish with Théophile Gautier and friends, fell obsessively in love with his mixed-race mistress Jeanne Duval, and wrote several poems that were later to form part of *Les Fleurs du Mal*. Baudelaire had rarely lived at one address for such a long period of time: between his birth in 1821 and death in 1867 he lived at 45 different Paris addresses, and even this would not include the bolt-holes he spent a few nights in when fleeing from creditors – which was often. Perversely enough, the street named after him, Rue Charles-Baudelaire, is in the 12th *arrondissement* – a part of the city he never called home.

ILE ST-LOUIS

Away from the tourists and camcorders, across the pedestrian Pont St-Louis, Ile St-Louis is a privileged haven of peace and wealth. The island's elegance recalls the 17th century, the era of Louis XIII and Cardinal Richelieu, and its mansions are home to Paris's elite.

ABOVE: Ile St-Louis is dotted with tasteful art galleries.
BELOW: most brasseries and cafés on the island sell Berthillon ice creams.
RIGHT: the local *boulangerie.*

Musée Adam Mickiewicz 8

6 quai d'Orléans 01 55 42 83 88
by reservation, Thur 2.15–5.15pm
charge Pont Marie

Turning right along the south bank, you will come to this small museum. Adam Mickiewicz (1798–1855) was a Polish poet, living in Paris from 1832–40, who devoted his work to helping oppressed Poles. The 17th-century building includes a Polish library and memorabilia of the Polish composer Frédéric Chopin, who often visited and played here.

Continuing eastwards round the island to the north bank, you will pass the private mansion Hôtel Lambert. Built in 1640 by Louis Le Vau, architect to Louis XIV, who built many of the houses on the Ile St-Louis and also worked on Vaux-le-Vicomte and Versailles, it is now owned by the Rothschilds. Further on is another mansion, the Hôtel de Lauzun, where the poets Théophile Gautier and Charles Baudelaire lived in 1843–5 and where Baudelaire wrote part of *Les Fleurs du Mal*.

The building now belongs to the City of Paris, and is reserved for official guests. Behind, the Rue St-Louis-en-l'Ile is full of chic gift shops, bars, restaurants and quaint tearooms. Also on this street is the church of the same name. Built between 1664 and 1765, the **Eglise St-Louis-en-l'Ile** has a classic Baroque interior and hosts popular classical concerts. ❑

BEST RESTAURANTS, BARS AND CAFÉS

Restaurants

Price includes dinner and a half-bottle of house wine:
€ = under €25
€€ = €25–40
€€€ = €40–60
€€€€ = more than €60

Brasserie de l'Ile St-Louis

55 quai de Bourbon, 4th 01 43 54 02 59 L & D Thur–Tue, D only Wed. **€€** (set menu), **€€€** (à la carte) [p339, C3]

If you eat on the island, you pay for it. Here, at least, the terrace is marvellously placed for people-watching and admiring Notre-Dame's soaring buttresses. The menu is hearty Alsatian fare: terrine with Riesling, pork with apple marmalade and *choucroute*. Wines are reasonable; skip the overpriced coffee and ice cream and head for Berthillon instead.

L'Escale

1 rue des Deux Ponts, 4th 01 43 54 94 23 non-stop Mon–Sat. **€€** [p339, C3]

This old-fashioned, pleasantly bustling brasserie-cum-wine bar serves good, heartening dishes like leek quiches, *chou farci* and *clafoutis*. The wines are well sourced and affordable, and the chips are far better than the average brasserie frites.

Isami

4 quai d'Orléans, 4th 01 40 46 06 97 L & D Tue–Sat. **€€€** [p339, C3]

There is something marvellous about eating the freshest seafood imaginable and then stepping out onto a full view of the Seine on the Ile St-Louis. The sushi and sashimi are a work of art and the Seine-side dining room is cosy. This small Japanese restaurant has a minimalist menu to match the stripped-back decor. Prices reflect the quality. Book ahead.

Mon Vieil Ami

69 rue St-Louis-en-l'Ile, 4th 01 40 46 01 35 L & D Wed–Sun. **€€€** [p339, C3]

The Paris offshoot of lauded Strasbourg chef Antoine Westermann has at last brought some serious culinary distinction to the Ile St-Louis. In a light, modern approach to bistro cooking, some dishes draw on Alsatian tradition, others roam the French regions. A good-value lunchtime *formule* features a daily rotating *plat du jour*.

Le Pré Verre

8 rue Thénard, 5th 01 43 54 59 47 L & D Tue–Sat. **€€€** [p338, C3]

A delightful wine bar with a "néo-bistrot" design and welcoming atmosphere. The service is pleasant and the staff helpful. Serves French gastronomic food with a modern touch and exceptional wines.

Taverne Henri IV

13 place du Pont Neuf, 1st 01 43 54 27 90 non-stop Mon–Fri, L Sat. **€€** [p338, B2]

This diminutive spot on the Ile de la Cité is a good bet for some straightforward French cuisine and wines. Try the excellent eggs baked with blue cheese and ham, washed down with a glass of white Beaujolais. Prices are reasonable, especially given the location.

Bars and Cafés

Le Flore en l'Isle
42 quai d'Orléans, 4th. Tel: 01 43 29 88 27. Non-stop daily. [p339, C3]

The views from this café of the river and Notre-Dame are the main draw – that and, in summer, the Berthillon ice cream it serves. If you want something warmer and more substantial, it also does a range of brunch dishes based on eggs and seafood. The *gratin aux poires* is truly delicious.

RIGHT: there are numerous places to stop for refreshments on the Ile de la Cité.

NOTRE-DAME DE PARIS

On the eastern tip of the Ile de la Cité stands the Gothic cathedral of cathedrals, "parish church of the history of France"

Notre-Dame cathedral's fortunate position – at one end of an island, with river to its north and river to its south – has meant it never got hemmed in by urban clutter: visitors are all the better able to appreciate its beauty for the vast open space around it. It has had an eventful history. It stands on the site of a former Gallo-Roman temple to Jupiter, and was damaged by rioting Huguenots in 1548. It was sacked during the Revolution, then turned to new use as a "Temple to Reason" and a warehouse; it remained in poor repair – some city planners even propounded its demolition – until an extensive renovation programme was begun in the mid-19th century, after a campaign led by Victor Hugo. In 1991 another programme of restorations got under way, with a timetable that was expected to run for a decade. Work is still going on, but the results are simply stunning. Amazingly, the architect of this awe-inspiring monument is unknown.

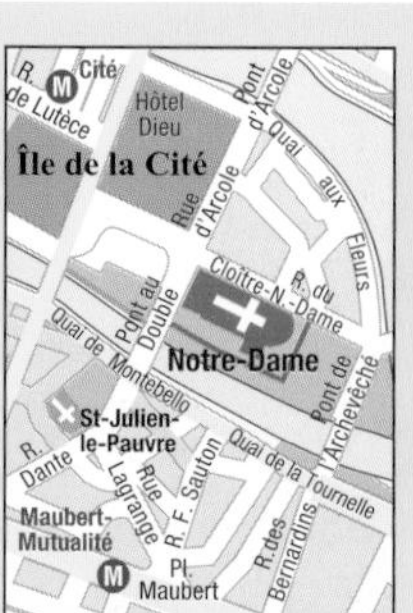

Essential info

www.cathedraledeparis.com

01 42 34 56 10

Mon–Fri 8am–6.45pm, Sat–Sun 8am–7.15pm

free

Cité

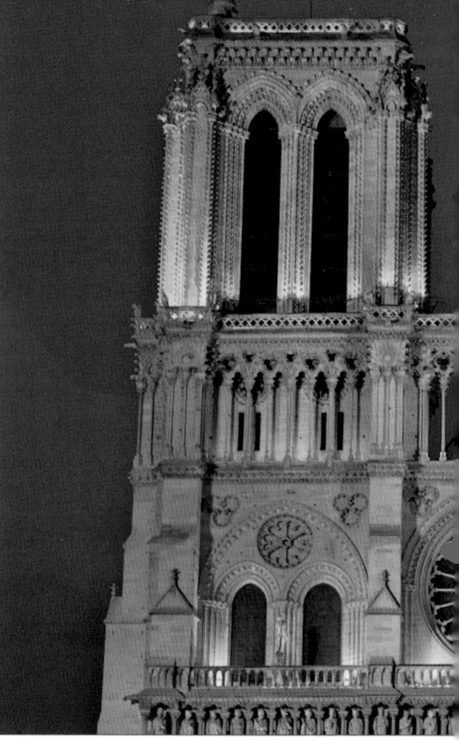

TOP LEFT: apostles flanking the left side of the Portal of the Last Judgement.

ABOVE: the cathedral is a superb venue for sacred music. As well as free organ concerts held daily at 4.30pm, prestigious vocalists (such as Barbara Hendricks, pictured) and ensembles perform here at various times in the year.

ABOVE: the cathedral, looking splendid in the evening light after the recent cleaning operation on its facade. Restoration work continues in other parts of the massive, complex structure.

BELOW: the chimera of Notre-Dame, the work of the 19th-century Gothic Revivalist Viollet-le-Duc, are among its most famous features.

HUGO, THE HUNCHBACK AND HISTORY

Notre-Dame's largest bell weighs 13 tonnes and was cast in the 14th century; it was recast in 1631, and is famous for the purity of its F-sharp tone. "The bells", of course, are a distinguishing element in one of the great love stories of literature: the love of the cathedral's hunchbacked bell-ringer, Quasimodo, for the beautiful Esmeralda, in Victor Hugo's 1831 novel *Notre-Dame de Paris*. Hugo had a special regard for the cathedral, then a tatty place seen by most as a leftover from a barbaric age; he said he was inspired to write the book by a graffito – "FATE" – he found in one of the towers.

RIGHT: Notre-Dame boasts three splendid rose windows, all masterpieces of stained glass.

BELOW: although right in the heart of the city, the streets and bridges around the cathedral are quiet and pleasant places – ideal for a breather during a long day's sightseeing.

3e Arrt
PLACE
DES VOSGES

Recommended Restaurants, Bars & Cafés on pages 100–1

THE MARAIS

Left behind by history for three centuries but now restored to vibrant life, this charming quarter offers elegant *ancien régime* mansions, trendy bars and boutiques, a whole array of intriguing museums and the city's oldest and most beautiful square

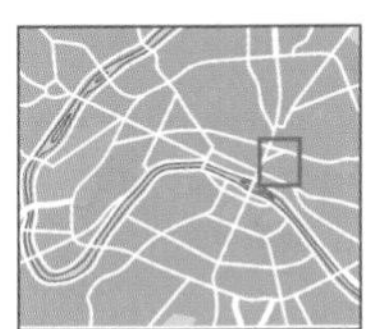

There's nowhere quite like the Marais, an elegant district that oozes charm and character. There's so much to recommend it: mansions and museums, chic boutiques and kosher grocers, gay bars and cosy cafés, all bundled together in a labyrinth of narrow streets and alleyways. Stretching west to east from Beaubourg to Bastille, straddling the 3rd and 4th *arrondissements*, with the Rue des Francs-Bourgeois pulsing across it like a central artery, the Marais offers a wonderfully compact package of history, local colour and plain fun. Few parts of the Right Bank have so much in so little space.

It's hard to believe that for many centuries the area was a mosquito-infested swamp ("marais" means marsh), cut right through the middle by Rue St-Antoine, the old Roman road. The marshes were drained in Philippe-Auguste's reign, and when Charles V moved his royal court from the Ile de la Cité to the area around the Tuileries in 1358, a royal influx to the Right Bank began.

In 1609, Henri IV had sumptuous accommodation built for his court all around the Place des Vosges, thereby shifting the political and financial focus from the Louvre. As a result, the finest architects and stonemasons in Europe descended on the Marais, building countless grand residences, or *hôtels particuliers*, for the nobility, each more spectacular than the last.

The Place des Vosges itself, initially known as the Place Royale, was the first planned square in Paris, and, with its red brick-and-stone facades tapering into arched walkways, remains as beautiful as ever.

LEFT: one of the elegant archways leading off the 17th-century Place des Vosges. **RIGHT:** artist at work in her atelier in the Village St-Paul.

Main attractions

- HÔTEL DE SENS
- PLACE DES VOSGES
- MAISON DE VICTOR HUGO
- JEWISH QUARTER
- MUSÉE CARNAVALET
- MUSÉE NATIONAL PICASSO
- MUSÉE COGNACQ-JAY
- MUSÉE DE L'HISTOIRE DE FRANCE

The Marais is one of the few Paris quarters where a large number of shops open for business on a Sunday, its busiest and most crowded day of the week.

ABOVE RIGHT: cool boutiques with up-to-the-minute fashions dominate the Marais. **BELOW:** Les Mots à la Bouche, the largest gay bookstore in Paris. **BELOW RIGHT:** retro kitchenware on Rue St-Paul.

THE MARAIS'S FALL AND RISE

The pendulum of fashion swung away from the Marais after Louis XIV moved his court to Versailles in the 1680s, and the nobility moved to the Ile St-Louis, then westwards to the Faubourg St-Honoré and the Boulevard St-Germain. During the Revolution, the area was abandoned to the people, and the Marais's graceful *hôtels* fell into disrepair.

In the 19th and 20th centuries, the quarter became a centre for small industries and craftwork, and successive developers dug up and widened its picturesque streets. In 1962, André Malraux, President de Gaulle's arts minister, set wide-scale renovation work in motion to preserve what had by then become a very run-down area. By the 1990s, the Marais had regained its status as one of the most fashionable – and costly – places to live in Paris.

The Jewish and working-class communities that once occupied the area have been marginalised by the relentless gentrification process. The character of the Marais is now defined by its designer boutiques, trendy bars and cafés, and a thriving gay community.

A TOUR OF THE OLD *HÔTELS*

Most of the *hôtels particuliers* have been converted into luxury apartments or offices, but several have been left intact and now house museums. A good place to begin a Marais tour is at the Hôtel de Ville (City Hall), on Rue de Rivoli *(see page 103)*, which marks its western boundary. Behind it is the 17th-century church of **St-Gervais-St-Protais** ❾ (Tue–Sun; free)

Recommended Restaurants, Bars & Cafés on pages 100–1

with a triple-tiered facade, Italianate steps and monstrous-looking gargoyles. The church is renowned for its 18th-century organ, and concerts are held here frequently.

Rue François-Miron leads from Place St-Gervais into the heart of the Marais. By the 1950s the houses here were practically derelict, but they have been carefully restored. At the corner of Rue Cloche-Perce is a half-timbered medieval house, and at No. 68 stands the **Hôtel de Beauvais** ❿, built by Catherine Beauvais in 1654 with money from Louis XIV, who had greatly enjoyed her favours. She is also said to have entertained archbishops here. A more innocent young Mozart stayed here on his first visit to Paris, at the tender age of seven.

Neighbouring Rue de Jouy contains **Hôtel d'Aumont** ⓫, designed by the Versailles architect Louis Le Vau *(see page 84)*, renovated and enlarged by François Mansart (1598–1666) and decorated by Charles Le Brun (1619–90). With a formal garden by Le Nôtre *(see page 124)*, the mansion now functions as the city's administrative court.

Hôtel de Sens ⓬

1 rue du Figuier 01 42 78 14 60 Tue–Sat 1.30–7pm free Pont Marie

Built in the late 15th century for the Archbishop of Sens, this turreted mansion is one of Paris's few surviving medieval residences, with immaculate gardens. Henri IV lodged his first wife Marguerite de Valois (Reine Margot) here when he could no longer stand her promiscuity. She continued to leave a trail of broken hearts, and when a jealous ex-lover killed her current beau, she had him beheaded. It now houses the Bibliothèque Forney, devoted to graphic and applied arts.

For a true Parisian lunch, Le Temps des Cerises in Rue de la Cerisaie (tel: 01 42 72 08 63), where 1,000 cherry trees used to grow, is a bistro that hasn't changed with the times, providing fresh market produce served by a team of jocular waiters.

BELOW: Rue des Francs-Bourgeois is a busy shopping street.

ABOVE: the Hôtel de Sully, a fine 17th-century mansion.

THE VILLAGE ST-PAUL

Opposite the Hôtel de Sens, the Rue de l'Avé-Maria intersects with the Rue des Jardins St-Paul, a block away. This leads into the Village St-Paul past two towers and ramparts, the remnants of the city wall built for King Philippe-Auguste around the year 1200, and which now shadow the antics of local schoolchildren. The restored "village" consists of a series of small courtyards and fountains, sheltering bustling antique shops and second-hand stalls. At night, it is tranquil beneath the halo of old street lamps.

Victor Hugo – Man of Many Words

Poet, dramatist, novelist, politician and figurehead of Romanticism, Victor Hugo (1802–85) lived at 6 place des Vosges from 1832 to 1848. His salon – now a museum *(see page 93)* – drew great luminaries of the day, including Balzac and Dumas. "The king of modern poetry reigned for 15 years, surrounded by his devoted courtiers, who were full of admiration for the master," wrote Eugène de Mirecourt, a regular. The museum traces Hugo's life, which he divided into three stages: before exile, during exile and after exile. In 1841 he was elected to the Académie Française, and accepted political posts under King Louis-Philippe. The 1848 Revolution threw him into the thick of political struggle, as a leader of democratic opposition to Louis-Napoleon. In 1851 he went into exile in the Channel Islands, where he wrote much of *Les Misérables* (1862). At the fall of the Second Empire in 1870 Hugo returned to Paris, and continued writing there until his death.

On Rue Charlemagne, wooden walkways running between the buildings have been restored to the way they were in the Middle Ages. Left along Rue St-Paul is an ancient passageway leading to the church of **St-Paul-St-Louis** ⓭, an amalgamation of two parishes, constructed by Jesuits in 1627 copying the Gesù church in Rome. Here, the hearts of Louis XIII and Louis XIV were kept as embalmed relics until the Revolution, when they were removed and sold to an artist, who crushed them to mix with oil for a varnish for one of his pictures. Later he gave what was left of Louis XIII's heart to the newly installed King Louis XVIII, in return for a golden snuffbox.

PLACE DES VOSGES

Rue St-Antoine is the ancient Roman road that led east out of the city. Built wide and straight in typical Roman fashion, it became a site for jousting tournaments until, in 1559, Henri II was fatally injured by a sliver from the shattered lance of Gabriel Montgomery, his Scottish Captain of the Guard. In a drastic bid to save his life, Henri's physician, Ambroise Paré, ordered the immediate decapitation of every prisoner awaiting execution and had their heads rushed to the surgery so that he could experiment on them in a bid to rescue his king. Needless to say he didn't succeed, and Henri died 10 days later. The unfortunate Montgomery lost his head, too.

At 62 rue St-Antoine, roughly halfway between Métro St-Paul and Place de la Bastille, stands the **Hôtel de Sully** ⓮ (courtyards open daily 10am–6.30pm), one of the finest mansions in the Marais. Under the courtyard's grumpy statues, Voltaire was beaten with clubs by followers of the Count of Rohan, following a slanging match between the two at the Comédie Française. Off the courtyard, the **Site Sully** annexe of the Jeu de Paume gallery (www.jeudepaume.org; tel: 01 42 74 47 75; Tue–Fri noon–7pm, Sat–Sun 10am–7pm; charge), which hosts exhibitions of photography and related topics.

The cosy garden with clipped privet hedges *à l'anglaise* is an unexpected surprise. A door in the back right corner leads to the **Place des Vosges** ⓯. Initially called the Place Royale, this enchanting 17th-century square, with a garden surrounded by 36 arcaded residences, was built by Henri IV as a showcase for his court.

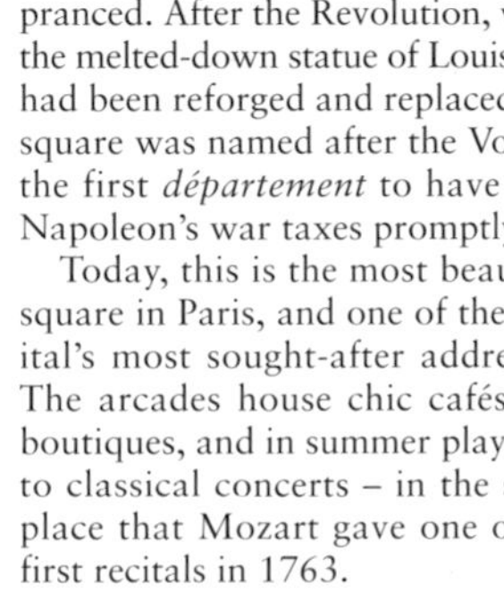

Here courtiers paraded, preened and pranced. After the Revolution, when the melted-down statue of Louis XIII had been reforged and replaced, the square was named after the Vosges, the first *département* to have paid Napoleon's war taxes promptly.

Today, this is the most beautiful square in Paris, and one of the capital's most sought-after addresses. The arcades house chic cafés and boutiques, and in summer play host to classical concerts – in the same place that Mozart gave one of his first recitals in 1763.

Maison de Victor Hugo ⓰

6 place des Vosges
01 42 72 10 16 Tue–Sun 10am–6pm free Saint-Paul

In the southeast corner of the square stands the house that was the Romantic writer's Paris home for 15 years. It's now a museum to the great man, containing portraits of his family, manuscripts, accomplished pen-and-ink drawings and pieces of furniture knocked together by Hugo in his spare time.

An aspiring Victor Hugo writing at a Marais café.

LEFT: hat shop in the Village St-Paul. **BELOW LEFT:** make your own jewellery at Matière Première in Rue de Sévigné. **BELOW:** the delightful Place des Vosges.

Rue des Rosiers, the main thoroughfare of the Jewish Quarter, tells the tale of its changing community. Central European bakeries and delis mix with Middle Eastern-style falafel outlets such as the ever-popular L'As du Fallafel.

THE JEWISH QUARTER

Between the northwestern corner of Place des Vosges and Rue Vieille-du-Temple runs the Rue des Francs-Bourgeois, a shopper's paradise crammed with boutiques and curiosity shops, many of which have retained the shop signs from their previous incarnations as butchers or bakers. A left-hand turning just past the Musée Carnavalet leads to Rue Pavée and the **Hôtel de Lamoignon** 17, built in 1584 for the Duchesse d'Angoulême. Sixty people were murdered here during the massacres of 2 September 1792. The *hôtel* now houses the city's historical library.

Rue des Rosiers, a little further on, is the hub of what remains of the Jewish Quarter. As the area has become increasingly popular with bar and boutique owners, the Jewish community has retreated to a small pocket centred on this narrow street lined with kosher delis, falafel stands and tiny shops packed with religious artefacts. Originally an Ashkenazi community, with its origins in Eastern Europe, the local Jewish population was depleted by the Holocaust. Numbers swelled again with an influx of Sephardic Jews from North Africa following the independence of Algeria in the 1960s, giving the area a Middle Eastern feel. Among the restaurants and bookshops around the synagogue, look out for Chez Marianne, the perpetually busy restaurant for Jewish specialities such as rollmops and falafels. Jewish history and decorative arts are treated in the Jewish Museum *(see page 97)*.

A few minutes south, behind St-Gervais-St-Protais, is the recently enlarged Mémorial de la Shoah.

Mémorial de la Shoah 18

17 rue Geoffrey l'Asnier, www.memorialdelashoah.org
01 42 77 44 72 Mon–Wed, Fri, Sun 10am–6pm, Thur 10am–10pm, closed Jewish holidays free
Pont Marie

The memorial has a permanent exhibition on the concentration camps, in which documents, photographs and personal artefacts are used to present an overview of Nazi deportation and extermination, and mov-

BELOW: try Sacha Finkelsztajn for its cheesecake, strudel and poppy-seed cakes.

ing personal stories. As the most important centre in Europe devoted to the Holocaust, it also contains a research centre, archive and auditorium. In the crypt, within a black marble star of David, an eternal flame burns for the Mémorial du Martyr Juif Inconnu (Memorial to the Unknown Jewish Martyr).

Rue des Rosiers leads on to the **Rue Vieille-du-Temple**, with one of the best and liveliest stretches of cafés and bars in Paris.

CARNAVALET AND PICASSO

Musée Carnavalet ⓳

✉ 23 rue de Sévigné, www.paris.fr/musees ☎ 01 44 59 58 58
🕒 Tue–Sun 10am–6pm € free
🚇 St-Paul

This is one of the most fascinating of the many Marais museums. Occupying two mansions, the main 16th-century Hôtel Carnavalet and the neighbouring 17th-century Hôtel Le Peletier, it covers the history of Paris chronologically from its beginnings as a Gallo-Roman settlement to its transformation into a modern-day metropolis. The evolution of the capital is traced through paintings, objets d'art, sculpture and costume. Madame de Sévigné, whose celebrated letters provide an insight into 17th-century Paris high society, lived in the Hôtel Carnavalet between 1677 and 1696, and there is a gallery here devoted to her life.

Research for the creation of the Wall of Names at the Mémorial de la Shoah took six archivists two years to complete. The names of 76,000 Holocaust victims are given by year of deportation and in alphabetical order.

ABOVE: Madame de Sévigné.
BELOW LEFT: the Musée Carnavalet boasts ornate gardens.

The Curious Cannonball

The three-day Citizens v State match of July 1830 was practically a friendly: a mere 600 rioters and 150 soldiers dead, the material damage largely cosmetic, the ousted king, Charles X, allowed to keep his head and take a boat to exile in England. So it's odd that such an unostentatious revolution should have left what must be, outside the museums, the niftiest emblem of the city's violent past. Stand at the junction of Rue du Figuier and Rue de l'Hôtel-de-Ville, look up at the Hôtel de Sens and you'll see it buried in the gable stonework, next to the left-hand turret: a cannonball the size of a fist. The iron sphere was fired on day two of the revolt – note the date, "28 juillet 1830", engraved underneath – from a beseiged army barracks on nearby Rue Charlemagne. Was it a warning shot? Was the cannoneer aiming at the second-storey window just below? And when the fighting was over, did no one ever think to dig it out?

At 47 rue Vieille-du-Temple stands the 17th-century mansion Hôtel Amelot de Bisseuil. The playwright Beaumarchais lived here in the 18th century, and he used it as the base for a gun-running operation to help the American fight for independence. These days it's a popular (if small) Paris photo opportunity, famed for the carved Medusa heads that scream from its heavy wooden doors.

Rue de Thorigny leads to one of the Marais's finest mansions, now home to the Musée National Picasso.

Musée National Picasso 20

5 rue de Thorigny, www.musee-picasso.fr 01 42 71 25 21 Wed–Mon summer 9.30am–6pm, winter 9.30am–5.30pm charge St-Paul

The Hôtel Salé was constructed with the booty of a 17th-century tax collector. Three centuries later, the French tax authorities scored another coup. Following his death in 1973, Pablo Picasso's family was faced with an enormous inheritance tax bill, and so, in lieu of payment, they donated to the French nation a vast collection of his works: 200 paintings, over 3,000 drawings and 88 ceramics, along with sculptures, collages and manuscripts, as well as Picasso's own collection of works by other artists like Cézanne, Matisse and Modigliani.

The museum shows all Picasso's periods, in chronological order, including the Blue, Pink, Cubist, Classical and Post-Cubist phases. The famous beach pictures of the 1920s and 1930s are here, as well as remarkable portraits of his model-mistresses, Marie-Thérèse and Dora Maar. There is also a lot of sculpture made of driftwood, scrap iron and bicycle parts, a reminder of Picasso's motto: "I do not seek, I find."

RIGHT: artist's palette.

A Spanish Genius

Born in Málaga in Spain, Pablo Picasso (1881–1973) settled in Paris at the age of 23, having studied art in Barcelona and Madrid. However, he never lost his Spanish touch: his works ooze life, humour and sex, in a career that could never be separated from his personal life. The central figure in 20th-century art, he passed through many phases, including his early Blue Period, as in the 1901 *Self-Portrait*, and Cubism. In the 1920s and 1930s he produced his most abstract work, but in 1937 he painted *Guernica*, on the Spanish Civil War. He stayed in Paris, in Rue des Grands-Augustins, during World War II, moving to the south of France afterwards. His last paintings were long considered a splashy, crude decline, but they have been rehabilitated as proof of his continuing inventiveness up to his death in 1973, in Mougins. He left behind a massive collection of paintings, sculpture, drawings and ceramics.

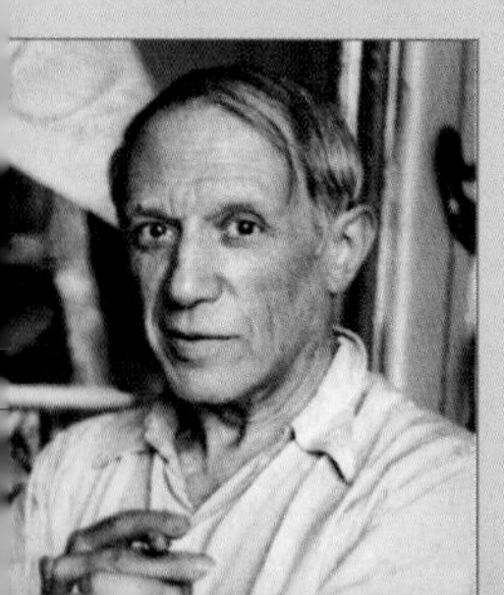

A Cluster of Museums

Musée Cognacq-Jay 21

8 rue Elzévir, www.paris.fr/musees 01 40 27 07 21 Tue–Sun 10am–6pm free St-Paul

The exquisite Hôtel Donon houses the art and antiques collection of Ernest Cognacq and his wife Louise Jay, founders of La Samaritaine department store. The collection, which includes works by Rembrandt and Canaletto, is displayed in a succession of salons and small rooms, which are furnished to give the feel of a private house.

Hôtel de Rohan 22

87 rue Vieille-du-Temple during exhibitions, times and details as for Musée de l'Histoire de France

Further west, this stunningly restored mansion is also part of the national archives and the Musée de l'Histoire de France *(see page 97)*. Even if you don't go inside, take a look in the courtyard at the superb sculpture of the horses of Apollo over the stables.

Musée de l'Histoire de France ㉓

60 rue des Francs-Bourgeois, www.archivesnationales.culture.gouv.fr 01 40 27 60 96 Mon, Wed–Fri 10am–12.30pm, 2–5.30pm, Sat–Sun 2–5.30pm charge Rambuteau

The Hôtel de Soubise is an exquisite 18th-century mansion, with a superb arcaded courtyard and exuberant Rococo decor. It is now the main home of France's history museum, with changing exhibits. Here, too, are the National Archives, in which over 6 million documents, on 290 km (180 miles) of shelving, demonstrate the nation's love affair with the rubber stamp. Across the street is the Crédit Municipal, the state pawnbroker. Nicknamed "*Ma Tante*" (My Aunt), it opened in 1777, and still functions.

Musée de la Chasse et de la Nature ㉔

62 rue des Archives, www.chassenature.org 01 53 01 92 40 Tue–Sun 11am–6pm charge Rambuteau

The Hôtel Guénégaud houses a display of stuffed animals and hunting-related objects with enjoyably quirky touches, such as "hunted species" that include unicorns.

Musée d'Art et d'Histoire du Judaïsme ㉕

71 rue du Temple, www.mahj.org 01 53 01 86 60 Mon–Fri 11am–6pm, Sun 10am– 6pm charge Rambuteau

The grand Hôtel St-Aignan is now a fascinating museum of Jewish art, culture, history and heritage.

ABOVE: art gallery in Place des Vosges. **BELOW:** ostentatious Rococo ceiling in the Hôtel de Soubise.

Rue Vieille-du-Temple is the epicentre of the Marais's cosmopolitan café culture. Trendy young types frequent the arty L'Etoile Manquante and La Perle *(see page 101)*, the picturesque Petit Fer à Cheval *(see page 101)*, wine bar-cum-bookshop La Belle Hortense and artfully distressed cocktail bar Les Etages. During early-evening happy hour, the gay community throngs the Amnésia Café or heads to Le Cox and the Open Bar on nearby Rue des Archives.

BELOW: the Marais streets are a showcase for urban style.
BELOW RIGHT: trendy design store.

QUARTIER DU TEMPLE

To the north of the Marais, the Quartier du Temple was once the headquarters of the Knights Templar. A medieval order of soldiers, originally formed to protect pilgrims in the Holy Land, the Templars owned large properties in France and were in charge of the royal treasury until 1307, when Philippe the Fair burned their leaders at the stake, and the order was disbanded. During the Revolution, the Temple Tower was a prison for the royal family; it was from here that Louis XVI went to the guillotine. It was razed by a superstitious Napoleon, and Haussmann replaced it with a wrought-iron covered market, the Carreau du Temple, which still sells second-hand and bargain clothes and cloth by the metre.

Along Rue Perrée lies all that remains of the Temple fortress, the **Square du Temple** ㉖, a tree-lined garden which echoes with the gentle sound of table tennis balls on its two outdoor tables. Not far from the Temple district, another 10 minutes along Rue Réaumur, is France's most prestigious technical college, the **Conservatoire National des Arts et Métiers**, and its recently renovated museum, the oldest dedicated to science and technology in Europe.

Musée des Arts et Métiers ㉗

60 rue Réaumur, www.arts-et-metiers.net 01 53 01 82 00 Tue–Sun 10am–6pm, Thur until 9.30pm charge Arts et Métiers

The best part of this fascinating museum of technology is the converted 11th-century chapel that houses, among other innovations, Foucault's pendulum (a copy of which hangs in the Pantheon, *see page 197*). There are also ancient cars and flying machines set on glass floors, and hands-on exhibits for children.

To end a visit to the Marais, head down Rue du Temple past the glitzy wholesale jewellery outfits to No. 41 and its courtyard. Once the headquarters of the Aigle d'Or, the last stagecoach company in Paris, it is a bustling corner, where the Café de la Gare theatre puts on alternative comedy and musical performances. ❑

Café Life

If you've never nipped into a café to make a phone call, met your lover on a *terrasse* or negotiated the crouch of the *toilettes*, you cannot truly claim to know Paris

The neighbourhood café is the Parisian's decompression chamber, easing the transition between *Métro-boulot-dodo* – commuting, working and sleeping. It offers a welcome pause in which to savour a *p'tit noir* (espresso) or an *apéritif*, empty the mind of troublesome thoughts and watch people go by. The café is also the place to meet friends, have a romantic tryst or even do business in a relaxed atmosphere.

The first café in France was Le Procope *(see page 207)* in 1686, and the literati soon began to congregate there, keen to exchange ideas. More sprang up all over the country, and it wasn't long before there was at least one in every village. In the 19th century, the neighbourhood *zinc*, named after its metal counter, became part of the fabric of French life. In Paris, each café developed its own character, and with the widening of the boulevards, their tables spilled out onto the pavements. By 1910 there were 510,000 *zincs* in France, but today café life is waning.

While the invasion of fast-food restaurants is partly to blame (a nearby McDonald's can slash a café's profits by 30 percent), changes in the French way of life are also culpable. When customers move out to homes in the suburbs, they tend to "cocoon", staying in to watch TV, and the local café eventually has to close. Then there are the ageing proprietors to consider: a café is traditionally a family business, but today fewer sons and daughters are prepared to take on gruelling 16-hour days.

Sadly, even the atmosphere of remaining cafés is not what it was. There is formica where once there was marble. Piped muzak and the beep of video games have replaced accordionists and the furious volleys of players on *baby-foot* machines. Only the Gauloise-fed haze (attitudes to the 1992 smoking ban are casual) and the hazards of the lavatories (some still holes in the ground) are the same.

Yet all is not lost. Authentic *zincs* can still be found in Paris, and many are thriving. Try stylish Café de l'Industrie on Rue St- Sabin, La Palette on Rue de Seine or the tiny but lovingly restored Le Cochon à l'Oreille on Rue Montmartre. For literary atmosphere there's Les Deux Magots, home to almost every Paris intellectual from Rimbaud to André Breton. At nearby Café de Flore, Sartre and Simone de Beauvoir wrote by the stove. "My worst customer, Sartre," recalled the *patron*. "He spent the entire day scribbling away over one drink."

But go soon, before things change too much, for this is one Parisian experience that demands to be savoured. ❑

ABOVE: pastries at Les Deux Magots. **RIGHT:** the archetypal Parisian café, Au Petit Fer à Cheval.

BEST RESTAURANTS, BARS AND CAFÉS

Restaurants

Price includes dinner and a half-bottle of house wine:
€ = under €25
€€ = €25–40
€€€ = €40–60
€€€€ = more than €60

L'Ambassade d'Auvergne

22 rue du Grenier-St-Lazare, 3rd 01 42 72 31 22 L & D daily. **€€** (set menu) **€€€** (à la carte) [p339, C1]
Auvergne fare is famously hearty, so make sure you come here hungry. One of this cheerful, almost rustic restaurant's signature dishes is the lentil salad, made with Puy lentils, bacon and shallots. End with a regional eau-de-vie, available to buy to take home if you like it.

L'Ambroisie

9 Place des Vosges, 4th 01 42 78 51 45 L & D Tue–Sat. **€€€€** [p339, D2]
A superb haute cuisine restaurant worthy of its royal location on Place des Vosges. Sumptuous seasonal ingredients are turned into stunningly sophisticated food by chef Bernard Pacaud – with prices to match. Still, the chance to sample his much-in-demand langoustines with a light curry sauce shouldn't be passed up if you can afford it.

Au Bascou

38 rue Réaumur, 3rd 01 42 72 69 25 L & D Mon–Fri. **€€** [p339, D1]
Generous meals from the Pays Basque: squid, roast lamb, stuffed peppers, *pipérade* and smoked tuna are on the menu in this small, friendly place. Exceptional wine list.

Chez Omar

47 rue de Bretagne, 3rd 01 42 72 36 26 L Mon–Sat & D daily. **€€** [p339, D1]
Couscous is king here, in an old brasserie setting. Popular with artists and the chattering classes. No reservations and no credit cards.

Le Dôme du Marais

53 bis rue des Francs-Bourgeois, 4th 01 42 74 54 17 L & D Tue–Sat. **€€** (set menu) **€€** (à la carte) [p339, D2]
This quiet, airy 18th-century dining room, topped with a glass dome, is unique. It is hard to believe that such a romantic place was once a pawnbroker's shop.

Guillaume

32 rue de Picardie, 3rd 01 44 54 20 60 non-stop Mon–Fri, D Sat. **€€** [p339, D1]
If there's no space on the terrace at this trendy new bar-restaurant, fear not – it has a large back room (with a huge peacock-feather chandelier). Cocktails cost a reasonable €8 each, and the champagne is discounted during the evening happy hour. The food is of the light variety: crostini with red tuna or guacamole, say.

Le Pamphlet

38 rue Debelleyne, 3rd ☎ 01 42 72 39 24 © L Tue–Fri, D Mon–Sat. €€ [p339, D1]
You'll find very fine cooking and a remarkably good-value menu at this discreet and comfortable restaurant in the northern Marais. Chef Alain Carrère's light market-inspired cooking includes superb fish from Brittany and seasonal game.

Le Petit Marché

9 rue de Béarn, 3rd ☎ 01 42 72 06 67 © L & D daily. €€€ [p339, D2]
The "little market" is one of the Marais's many hip bistros, and it pulls a matching fashion-conscious clientele without losing its friendly feel. The short, modern menu has a pronounced Asian slant: raw tuna flash-fried in sesame seeds and served with Thai sauce, or pan-fried scallops with lime. From the similarly laconic wine list, the house red is a good bet.

Aux Vins des Pyrénées

25 rue Beautrellis, 4th ☎ 01 42 72 64 94 © L Sun–Fri, D Mon–Sun. €€ [p339, D3]
A youthful bistro adorned with cheerful bric-a-brac. Food, such as squid risotto, fish tartare, lamb curry or satisfying steak, is a mix of mode and tradition, drawing a noisy young Parisian clientele.

LEFT: a vintage film poster in Au Petit Fer à Cheval, just one of the bar's interesting features. **ABOVE:** one of the many popular bistros in the Marais district.

Bars and Cafés

Andy Wahloo

69 rue des Gravilliers, 3rd. Tel: 01 42 71 20 38. Tue–Sat 6pm–2am. [p339, C1]
The name is Arabic for "I have nothing", and the Moroccan bar that bears it (founded by the people behind its neighbour 404 and London's Momo and Sketch) is a tiny little spot that's popular with a fashionable crowd. Expect mint-and-vodka concoctions and apple-flavoured hookahs. It gets really packed in the evening.

L'Apparemment Café

18 rue des Coutures-St-Gervais, 3rd. Tel: 01 48 87 12 22. Non-stop daily. [p339, D2]
This relaxed spot – distressed armchairs, jazz soundtrack, parlour games, lots to read and a low hubbub of conversation – feels a bit like someone's artfully bohemian flat. That's the intention. There are salads, meat and cheese dishes to eat, and some nice wines at the bar. Come on your own and read a book – plenty of people do.

La Perle

78 rue Vieille-du-Temple, 3rd. Tel: 01 42 72 69 93. Non-stop daily. [p339, D2]
This bar, another new addition to the Marais line-up, is almost always open: it doesn't close until 2am, and on weekdays opens at 6am. It's straight-forward, non-exclusive and has a pleasant neighbourhood feel. DJs spin in the evenings; food consists of salads and generous omelettes.

Au Petit Fer à Cheval

30 rue Vieille-du-Temple, 4th. Tel: 01 42 72 47 47. L & D daily (until 2am). [p339, D2]
Fin de siècle café/wine bar where an eclectic mix of locals and foreigners gathers around the original marble-topped horseshoe bar. Particularly atmospheric and a great favourite with the bourgeois-bohemian crowd. Solid food, rushed but genial service. An excellent place to people-watch.

Stolly's

16 rue Cloche Perce, 4th. Tel: 01 42 76 06 76. L & D daily. [p339, D2]
This Anglo bar, part of the city's Hip Bars stable, has been going strong for years: a drinking den that's a firm favourite on the expat circuit. There are long happy hours and a terrace, good vodka tonics and, unsurprisingly, a steady party vibe.

Recommended Restaurants, Bars & Cafés on pages 112–3

BEAUBOURG AND LES HALLES

One of the world's most popular venues, the "inside-out" Pompidou Centre has given this area its modern identity. But nearby around Les Halles – though blighted by failed 1960s redevelopment – there remain many traces of Paris's historic market district, one of the most pungently atmospheric parts of the city

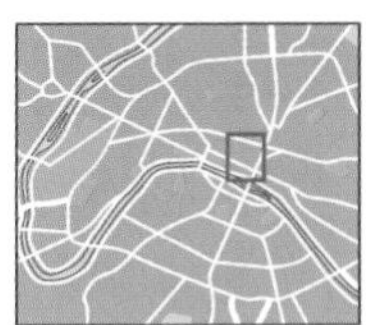

Main attractions
- **HÔTEL DE VILLE**
- **CENTRE GEORGES POMPIDOU**
- **FORUM DES HALLES**
- **RUE MONTORGUEIL**
- **EGLISE ST-EUSTACHE**
- **EGLISE ST-GERMAIN-L'AUXERROIS**

Sandwiched between the Louvre and Palais Royal to the west, and the Marais to the east, this central chunk of the Right Bank is one of the city's most hyperactive commercial and cultural areas. Its epicentre is the Forum des Halles, a vast and unlovely shopping and leisure complex. Next to the monumental grandeur of the Louvre, Les Halles is a scruffy poor relation, an unsightly multi-storey blot on the landscape. The other landmark building here is the Pompidou Centre, Paris's modern art museum. Unlike the 1970s monstrosity of Les Halles, this hulking mass of pipes, ducts and scaffolds painted in primary colours is strangely alluring, and one of the world's most visited sites.

Place du Châtelet, hard by the Seine, is a good starting point for exploring the area. Flanked by two theatres (Théâtre de la Ville and Théâtre du Châtelet, for opera and modern dance), it lies above one of Paris's biggest Métro and RER stations. To the northeast rises the Gothic **Tour St-Jacques**, a lone belfry once attached to a church that was destroyed during the Revolution. Look out for the statue of scientist and philosopher Blaise Pascal (1623–62), who carried out pioneering experiments on atmospheric pressure from the top.

HÔTEL DE VILLE 28

www.paris.fr 01 42 76 43 43
visits by arrangement free
Hôtel de Ville

Opening out at the eastern end of Avenue Victoria is the wide esplanade of the Hôtel de Ville (Mairie de

LEFT: Henri de Miller's giant sculpture in the Jardin des Halles, St-Eustache.
RIGHT: ice-skating fun in front of the Hôtel de Ville.

The famous cast-iron-and-glass buildings that housed the Les Halles food market, otherwise known as "pavillons Baltard", after the man who designed them, were torn down in 1969. All except one, which was transplanted to the suburb of Nogent-sur-Marne, where it's now an attractive and unusual concert venue (www.pavillon baltard.fr).

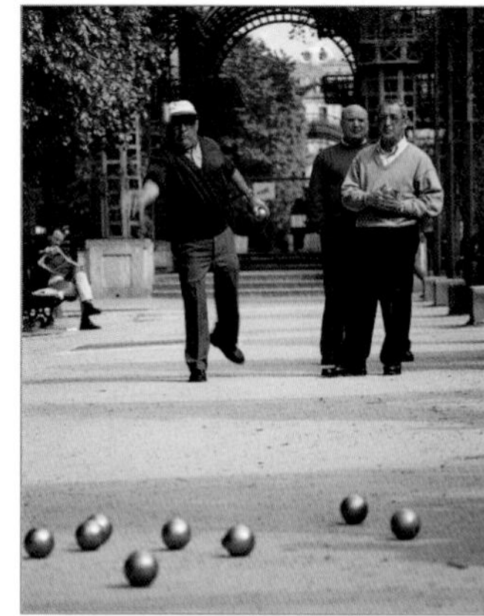

ABOVE: *jeu de boules.*
BELOW: homage to the great composer Igor Stravinsky: the Fontaine de Stravinsky by Niki de Saint-Phalle and Jean Tinguely.

Paris), ornate home of the city council. In medieval times, the square was the site of hangings and macabre executions. No traces of its horrific past remain; today, the pedestrianised Place de l'Hôtel de Ville, which overlooks the Seine, is a pleasant place to stroll through, especially in the evening, when the fountains and Town Hall are floodlit.

The elaborate neo-Renaissance building, with its splendid mansard roofs, carved facade and army of statues, was rebuilt after the original 17th-century Town Hall was burned down in the 1871 Commune. The most notable features inside are the majestic Salle des Fêtes (ballroom), a magnificent staircase and lots of chandeliers. Such grandeur and opulence are a fitting backdrop for the city's governing powers, and the grand halls are often used for banquets and ceremonial receptions.

At most times only an exhibition space is open to visitors, but the rest of the building can be seen on free guided tours, available by arrangement, tel: 01 42 76 50 49. In recent years the whole exterior has been cleaned, with the result that the building now looks thoroughly imposing outside and in. It's worth skirting around to Rue de Lobau at the rear of the Hôtel to see the two monumental bronze lions either side of the eastern entrance. These noble beasts are by the late 19th-century animal sculptor Alfred Jacquemart, who also made the colossal rhino in the square just west of the Musée d'Orsay *(see page 231)*.

Recommended Restaurants, Bars & Cafés on pages 112–3

QUARTIER BEAUBOURG

This area may, thanks to the Centre Pompidou, be synonymous with avant-garde architecture, but it's also one of the oldest parts of the city. Its parish church of St-Merri was at the centre of a local building boom in the 16th century, as the old medieval houses were steadily replaced by grand private mansions; the district remained a seat of nobility until the Revolution. Little of this architectural heritage remains today, however: many of the historic residences were pulled down in the 1930s, and the quarter was transformed further by the renovation of Les Halles in the 1960s and 1970s.

St-Merri 29

76 rue de la Verrerie, www.saintmerri.org 01 42 71 93 93 Mon–Sat 3–7pm free Châtelet

Off Rue St-Martin stands this richly adorned 16th-century church, built in Flamboyant Gothic style. Its bell, dating from 1331, is the oldest in Paris, and the organ used to be played by the composer Camille Saint-Saëns (1835–1921).

Between the church and the Centre Pompidou, the playful waterworks of the **Fontaine de Stravinsky** were inspired by the composer's ballet *The Firebird*. Created by artists Niki de Saint-Phalle and Jean Tinguely, the forms and figures in the fountain represent the story – a heart, a snake, a bare-breasted torso, pursed red lips and the firebird in the middle all spin and spit water in every direction. In fine weather, this square is a favourite picnic spot (though it's infested with pigeons). Alternatively, take a seat at one of the handful of cafés looking out at the colourful ensemble.

Rue des Lombards, between St-Merri and Les Halles, is a must-visit for jazz fans, with clubs such as Baiser Salé (No. 58), Au Duc des Lombards (No. 42) and Sunset/Sunside (No. 60) all hosting live performances by fine musicians, from world-famous names to exciting new talent.

LEFT: the imposing Fontaine des Innocents.

Fontaine des Innocents

The Fontaine des Innocents, a Renaissance fountain decorated with water nymphs by Pierre Lescot and Jean Goujon, stands in the Square des Innocents, between Place du Châtelet and Forum des Halles, formerly the site of the notorious Cimetière des Innocents. In use since the 12th century, the graveyard, encircled by a high wall, had become a putrid necropolis by the 18th century, as the dead – mostly paupers – were carried there among produce bound for the market at Les Halles. Gruesome tales are told about how people ground up bones for bread when Paris was under siege in 1590, and used the skeletons for firewood. By 1780, corpses were overflowing above street level and the area was teeming with rats, which started to gnaw their way into people's homes. It was recognised that something had to be done, so the cemetery was finally closed and its contents moved to the Catacombs, where the remains can still be seen *(see page 212)*.

Today, the square and fountain are a meeting place for the city's youth, and the pedestrianised Rue des Lombards is a centre for nightlife with bars, restaurants and the Duc des Lombards jazz club.

ABOVE: east facade of the Centre Pompidou.
BELOW: colourful sculpture in the Fontaine de Stravinsky.

CENTRE GEORGES POMPIDOU ㉚

www.centrepompidou.fr
01 44 78 12 33 Wed–Mon 11am–8pm charge Rambuteau

Known locally simply as Beaubourg, the Centre National d'Art et de Culture Georges Pompidou welcomes more than 8 million visitors a year. The basic idea was first mooted in 1969 by the cultivated president of the day, Georges Pompidou; the initial tender was put out in 1972. No fewer than 681 designs were put forward by architects around the world, but the winning partnership was Italian Renzo Piano and British Richard Rogers. The Centre opened to the public on 31 January 1977.

Rogers and Piano had placed all the infrastructure – escalators, lifts, ducts, etc – on the outside: this high-tech design caused uproar when it first opened, but its popular appeal soon silenced the critics.

As well as housing one of the world's most important modern art collections, the cavernous interior accommodates a large public library, an educational area, a performance space, auditorium and cinemas, and the neighbouring avant-garde music institute IRCAM. There's also an excellent art bookshop on the ground floor, and the swish restaurant **Georges** *(see page 112)* on the roof. The fifth-floor balcony and roof terrace enjoy magnificent views of the city, right across to Montmartre; the terrace also displays sculptures by Tinguely, Ernst and others.

Recommended Restaurants, Bars & Cafés on pages 112–3

Exhibits and activities

The **Musée National d'Art Moderne** is on the fourth and fifth floors. Incredibly, the works on display represent only a small proportion of the 50,000-strong collection, which is why the museum has regular rehangs, in order to rotate the works of art and give the public access to as many of them as possible.

The museum's permanent collection is arranged thematically, suggesting interesting confrontations and parallels between different periods and styles. Architecture and design are displayed alongside painting, sculpture and video art. Thus modern masterpieces by Matisse, Picasso, Kandinsky, Delaunay, Dalí and Grosz can be seen with post-war masters like Dubuffet, Johns, Warhol, Bacon and Merz, and works by contemporary artists like Boltanski, Sherman and Viola.

In recent years the Centre has boosted its cinematic presence, acting as another Cinémathèque, with comprehensive retrospectives of the likes of Martin Scorsese and Jacques Rivette. Hand in hand with such seasons is an active publishing programme, which produces attractive and scholarly books on the directors under examination.

Outside on the plaza are a reconstruction of Constantin Brancusi's studio, **l'Atelier Brancusi**, which he left to the state, and Jean-Pierre Raynaud's giant gold flowerpot. The plaza itself is a bustling space popular with street performers, buskers, barrel organists and portrait painters.

The Pompidou's primary-coloured pipes are not just for show: the blue convey air, the green transport water, the yellow contain electricity and the red conduct heating.

LEFT: statue outside the Hôtel de Ville.
BELOW: the tubed escalators add to the "inside-out" allure of the Centre Pompidou.

LES HALLES

When it comes to fashion, the eternally crowded Forum des Halles is something of a wash-out: mostly chain stores like H&M. Far richer pickings are to be had in the far nicer setting of Rue Etienne Marcel, a major *mode* thoroughfare of labels like Yohji Yamamoto, Barbara Bui and smaller, seriously hip labels.

The Les Halles quarter gets its name from the historic food market that stood from 1183 to 1969 on the spot now occupied by a vast shopping complex. Large-scale construction has been a feature of the area since 1851, when Napoleon III ordered architect Victor Baltard to design 10 colossal cast-iron hangars to go over the market. "Iron, nothing but iron" and "Make me some umbrellas" were the emperor's two instructions, and the resulting construction was an elegant masterpiece of 19th-century design, widely copied throughout France and abroad.

Stallholders, restaurant owners, pickpockets, artists, prostitutes and police inhabited this vast market, which novelist Emile Zola called "the belly of Paris". Unsurprisingly, the market had a strong presence in the literary output of the time. Zola set an entire novel here; Hugo described it in some detail in *Les Misérables*; and the area was a regular haunt of the Romantic poet and tormented bohemian Gérard de Nerval, who was born here and eventually ended his own life by hanging himself in a nearby cellar.

ABOVE RIGHT: statue in the courtyard of the massive Forum des Halles.
BELOW RIGHT: old-fashioned toy shop Le Nez de Pinocchio, in the Forum.

By the 1960s the site, already expanded in 1936, had become impractical – not least owing to traffic problems associated with bringing vast quantities of provisions to a site in the centre of the city. The market decamped to the suburbs of Rungis and the hangars were thoughtlessly pulled down, leaving a gaping hole that became a national joke. It was filled in the 1980s by the **Forum**

Rag Trade

Like any area not enshrined in administrative ink, Sentier has fuzzy boundaries: however, to most Parisians it is the top-right of the 2nd *arrondissement*, north of Rue Réaumur. This maze of narrow streets is the undisputed stronghold of the wholesale clothes industry. Most buildings are taken up by workshops and storerooms, and windows pour out a constant buzz of machinery. Sentier makes clothes and it makes fortunes: the secret of its success is not just its low-paid, often immigrant workforce but the ability of its workshops to take in the latest couture trends almost overnight. Sentier has its seamy side, but bits of it are worth a look, too: Rue Réaumur with its architectural collage, and the "Egyptian" Place du Caire *(see page 145)*. There are even signs of a mild shift upmarket, with dotcoms and media companies moving in among the workshops.

Recommended Restaurants, Bars & Cafés on pages 112–3

des Halles ㉛, an underground shopping mall with shops, a multiplex cinema, the Forum des Images film archive and cinema (which reopened in 2008 after an extensive refit, offering access to a wide variety of films, festivals, events, meetings and screenings) and an Olympic swimming pool. Combined with a massive RER/Métro interchange, the Forum has acquired a dodgy reputation as a hang-out for gangs of youths from the suburbs. In 2004, the Mairie de Paris launched a competition for redeveloping the Forum and re-landscaping the squares and gardens.

Paris's modern underbelly

Surrounding the market area are some remnants of a bygone age, with brasseries staying open around the clock (the early-hours clientele no longer formed by hard-working market porters, but exhausted party-goers) and sleazy Rue St-Denis, the age-old domain of prostitutes, albeit only in its northern reaches; the section adjacent to Les Halles is instead packed with small independent clothes shops, selling largely tacky streetwear and trainers.

The best place for a glimpse of the old Les Halles is **Rue Montorgueil**, a narrow, pedestrianised street packed with romantic cafés, wine and cheese merchants, garrulous butchers and colourful fruit and vegetable stalls. The street also contains the venerable *pâtissier* **Stohrer**, purveyor since 1730 of delectable cakes and tarts; its founder Nicolas Stohrer is said to have invented the rum baba. This short, attractive strip is one of a few places in Les Halles where it is easy to linger – even if you end up buying nothing more than a coffee.

Built in 1407, 51 rue de Montmorency was the house of alchemist Nicolas Flamelle who claimed to have created the philosopher's stone.

ABOVE: hip store Killiwatch sells vintage clothes and art and fashion books.
BELOW: books and record empire, FNAC.

ABOVE: cool, understated fashion at Barbara Bui.
BELOW: reflections, Les Halles.

St-Eustache 32

Rue du Jour, www.saint-eustache.org 01 42 36 31 05 Mon–Fri 9.30am–7pm, Sat 10am–7pm, Sun 9am–7pm free Les Halles

North of the Forum des Halles, this colossal, beautiful church is a rose among thorns. Modelled on Notre-Dame (note the flying buttresses), it took over a hundred years to build (1532–1637). The interior is a Renaissance feast of majestic columns, arches and stained-glass windows. Berlioz and Liszt played here in the 19th century, and concerts are held regularly – often for free – using the church's 8,000-pipe organ; a recent restoration included the addition of electronic equipment allowing the organ to be played from ground-level consoles. St-Eustache also has a prestigious choir, and is the burial place of French composer Jean-Philippe Rameau, and another personage with a musical connection – Mozart's mother.

Outside the church, a sculpture of a giant head and cupped hand by Henri de Miller attracts both children and pigeons to its benign seat *(see page 102)*. The stretch of gardens between Les Halles and St-Eustache is peopled by dog-walkers, loitering teenagers and down-and-outs. The green space features glass pyramids full of palms, papayas and banana trees. Metal walkways pass through them to the **Bourse du Commerce** (tel: 01 55 65 55 65; Mon–Fri 9am–6pm; free), a circular building erected in the 18th century as a corn exchange, and now a busy commodities market for coffee and sugar.

LES HALLES TO THE BEACH

Head back towards the Rue St-Honoré, south of Les Halles, an elegant street with a rich history and upmarket shops. A little further on, facing the eastern facade of the Louvre, is the church of **St-Germain-l'Auxerrois** ㉝ (tel: 01 42 60 13 96; daily noon–7pm). At midnight on 24 August 1572, the church's bells rang as the signal to start the St Bartholomew's Day Massacre *(see page 30)*, when thousands of Protestants were butchered on the orders of the Catholic Catherine de Médicis. Behind the church on the banks of the Seine is the historic La Samaritaine department store, which has been closed for major safety modifications since 2005 and is due to reopen in 2011.

Immediately in front of La Samaritaine is the Voie Georges Pompidou, the riverfront roadway that hosts much of the Right Bank portion of the annual **Paris-Plage** festivities *(see page 300)*. Every summer since 2002, the road has been shut to traffic, covered with tonnes of fine golden sand and kitted out with palm trees, deckchairs, refreshment kiosks, beach volleyball courts and a free lending library. The highly popular city-beach concept has been copied in other big cities, including Lyon, Toulouse, Berlin and Budapest. And in Paris, since 2006, the holiday fun has expanded across the river to the Left Bank. ❑

Every Sunday at 5.30pm, a free organ recital is held in the Eglise St-Eustache. The organ is the third-largest in France (those at Notre-Dame and St-Sulpice are first and second respectively), and the church's acoustics are excellent.

ABOVE: the Gothic gaze of St-Eustache.
BELOW: swimming by the Seine during Paris-Plage.

BEST RESTAURANTS, BARS AND CAFÉS

Restaurants

Price includes dinner and a half-bottle of house wine:
€ = under €25
€€ = €25–40
€€€ = €40–60
€€€€ = more than €60

Benoît

20 rue St-Martin, 4th ☎ 01 42 72 25 76 ⌚ L & D daily. **€€€** [p338, C2]
This celebrated vintage bistro (open since 1912), long renowned for its excellent cooking and very high prices, fell into the Alain Ducasse fold in spring 2004, but Ducasse has promised not to change its style. Forget fussy individual dishes – waiters will bring a whole terrine to the table and cut you a slab, or dish up beef and carrot casserole, or cassoulet, then tempt you with a slice of the heavenly prune-and-Armagnac ice-cream bomb that's the size of an igloo. Expect highly professional service, and an elegant crowd playing at bistros in what is actually a very chic establishment. Best to book ahead.

Au Chien Qui Fume

33 rue du Pont Neuf, 1st ☎ 01 42 36 07 42 ⌚ non-stop daily noon–2am. **€** [p338, B1]
The "smoking dog" has an extensive brasserie menu, including shrimp and langoustine salad, and duck à l'orange. All the classic desserts are on offer, including iced nougat and chocolate mousse. Not a bad place to lap up the late-night atmosphere in Les Halles.

Curieux Spaghetti Bar

14 rue St-Merri, 4th ☎ 01 42 72 75 97 ⌚ non-stop daily. **€** (set menu) **€€** (à la carte) [p339, C2]
As the name suggests, this three-year-old restaurant is a quirky place that serves spaghetti. What it doesn't say is that it's really rather trendy, with bold patterned walls and high leather-topped stools for seating. Portions are extremely generous, and the menu also includes other Italian fare such as carpaccio, osso bucco and bruschetta. Finish your meal with a glass of home-made limoncello.

L'Escargot Montorgueil

38 rue Montorgueil, 1st ☎ 01 42 36 83 51 ⌚ L & D daily. **€€€** [p338, C1]
Its heyday has passed, but the "snail of Montorgueil", its Second Empire decor intact, remains a glamorous, tourist-friendly restaurant nonetheless. Sadly, the cooking is no match for the surroundings, but if you stick to a dozen plump garlicky snails, you can still get a feel for its past splendour.

La Fresque

100 rue Rambuteau, 1st ☎ 01 42 33 17 56 ⌚ L & D Mon–Sat (until midnight). **€** [p338, C1]
Sitting elbow to elbow at one of the big wooden tables is part of the charm here, as is the decor (white faience tiles, frescoes). Bistro fare like beef stew and duck are excellent, and the staff are friendly if sometimes harrassed. There is always one vegetarian main course.

Georges

6th floor, Centre Georges Pompidou, place Beaubourg, 4th ☎ 01 44 78 16 80 ⌚ L & D Wed–Mon (until 1am). **€€€** [p339, C2]
The chic clientele don't go to Georges's restaurant for the food but to see and be seen in a unique setting at the top of the Centre Pompidou. With globular, brushed-aluminium pods, bright Pop Art colours, transparent tables, hip DJs and one of the finest restaurant views in the city, Georges is an art installation in its own right.

Le Hangar

12 impasse Berthaud, 4th ☎ 01 42 74 55 44 ⌚ L & D Tue–Sat. **€€** [p339, C1]
Minimalist yet cosy, this modern bistro is just steps from the Pompidou, hidden in an alley.

Pan-fried foie gras with puréed potatoes is always on the menu, as well as a towering chocolate soufflé. No credit cards.

Joe Allen

30 rue Pierre Lescot, 1st
01 42 36 70 13 non-stop daily. €€ (set menu) €€€ (à la carte) [p338, C1]
The Paris outpost of the Joe Allen chain has been going for over 30 years, and is still one of the better American eating establishments in Paris. In a decor of brick walls and dark wooden floors, contented Parisians dine on things like Caesar salad, quesadillas and very good cheeseburgers.

Au Pied de Cochon

6 rue Coquillière, 1st
01 40 13 77 00 non-stop daily. € (set menu) €€ (à la carte) [p338, B1]
In its heyday, the legendary all-night brasserie catered for the market workers; now it's rather more upmarket, if a little touristy. But the house speciality remains the same: grilled pig's trotter with béarnaise sauce. If that isn't your thing, there are oysters and seafood. And the onion soup is a good cure for hangovers.

La Tour de Montlhéry

5 rue des Prouvaires, 1st
01 42 36 21 82 L & D daily. €€€ [p338, B1]
This long-standing, late-opening (until 5.30am) purveyor of solid French food, also known as Chez Denise, is great fun. Portions are copious, the red-checked dining room cosy and the atmosphere friendly. The traditional menu runs to steaks, great home-made chips, some game, some offal and a few fish dishes.

LEFT: L'Escargot Montorgueil is a good place to have, you guessed it, snails. **ABOVE:** mouthwatering *pâtisserie*.

Bars and Cafés

Bistrot Beaubourg
25 rue Quincampoix, 4th. Tel: 01 42 77 48 02. L & D daily (until 1am). [p338, C2]
This designer café opposite the Centre Pompidou is a study in style over substance. Food is mediocre, considering what you pay, but it's fine for a light bite to eat and a spot of people-watching. Either gaze out from the terrace onto the Pompidou forecourt or turn your gaze inwards, to the café's habitués.

Le Café des Initiés
3 place des Deux-Ecus, 1st. Tel: 01 42 33 78 29. Non-stop daily. [p338, B1]
From crumbling old corner café comes trendy hang-out: this fashionable drinks purveyor has ergonomic red bench seating, a long zinc bar, swish black lamps and elegant flower arrangements in glass vases. It's friendly, too.

Le Père Fouettard
9 rue Pierre-Lescot. Tel: 01 42 33 74 17. L & D daily (noon–midnight). [p338, C1]
A warm and cosy bistro, with cheerful service, a young clientele and its fair share of regulars. Totally relaxing, the café terrace is leafy in summer, heated in winter. Cheap prices, and good food if you stick to the standards such as brochettes of beef from the Aubrac region, roast suckling pig, chocolate tart or spice roasted apples. Vegetarian options as well. Good wines by the glass.

Le Petit Marcel
65 rue Rambuteau, 4th. Tel: 01 48 87 10 20. L & D daily (until midnight). [p338, C1]
In a great location, a stone's throw from the Centre Pompidou, this quaint café/bar is a real find. Art Nouveau tiles decorate the interior. Salads, omelettes, steak frites, crumbles and brownies. Good drinks selection and very friendly service. No credit cards.

Le Tambour
41 rue Montmartre, 2nd. Tel: 01 42 33 06 90. Non-stop daily. [p338, B1]
There's nowhere else in Paris quite like this 24-hour bar. Inside it looks like a junk shop, its decor a mash-up of all manner of old Métro signs, stray statues, old books and even older customers (there are lots of students, too). The moustachioed owner is usually on hand, swapping animated bar-room philosophies with the regulars. Priceless.

Centre Pompidou

The inside-out museum of modern art is a world icon of contemporary architecture

President Georges Pompidou was a moderniser – and had a lasting fondness for the arts. He compiled an anthology of French poetry and it was he who proposed the building of a major cultural centre in Beaubourg. The chosen design, by the then-unknown duo Richard Rogers and Renzo Piano, put the air-conditioning ducts and escalators on the outside, which made for an adaptable space within. The Centre Pompidou opened in 1977; its multi-disciplinary set-up – the largest museum of modern art in Europe, plus a public library and cinemas – was an instant hit. It had a revamp at the end of the 20th century. Entrance to the forum and library is free, but you have to pay to go up the escalators.

Below: colourful statue in the Fontaine de Stravinsky by Niki de Saint-Phalle and Jean Tinguely, on Place Igor-Stravinsky.

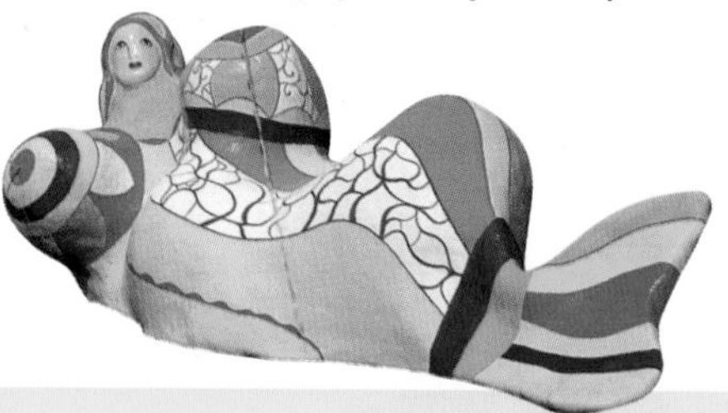

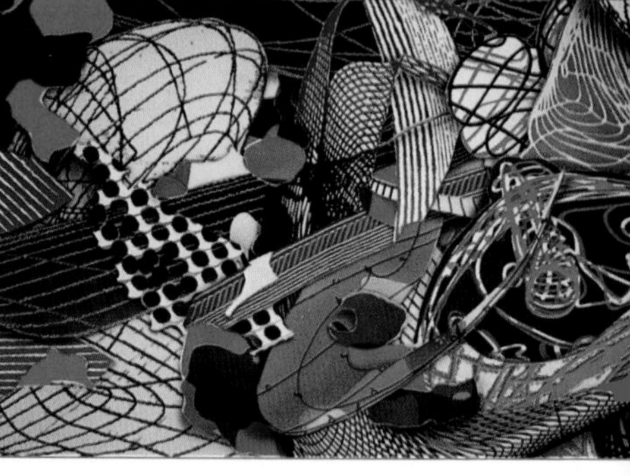

Above: *Polombe* by Frank Stella, 1994.

Below: in 2000, the Centre opened a swish restaurant on the rooftop, Georges *(see review page 112)*.

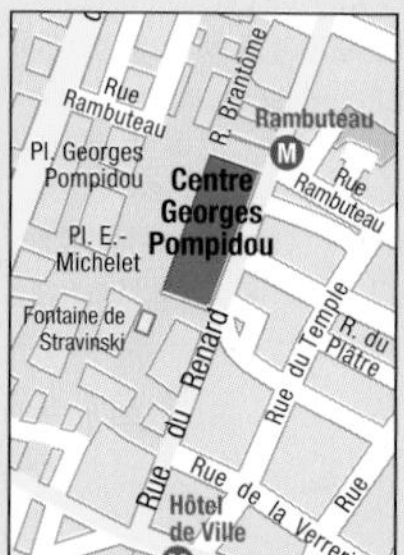

Essential info

- *www.centrepompidou.fr*
- *01 44 78 12 33*
- *Wed–Mon 11am–8pm*
- *charge*
- *Rambuteau*

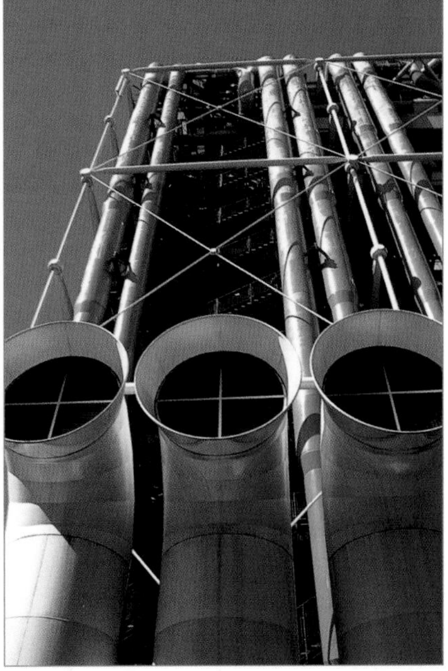

INSIDE AND OUT

The collection at the Pompidou is far too large to be displayed, even in such a cavernous setting: there are 50,000 works of art in all, and only 600 or so can be exhibited at once. Level four contains post-1960s art: here you'll find architecture, design and sections on movements like Arte Povera and Anti-Form. On level five is work produced between 1905 and 1960 by Matisse, Picasso and Braque, as well as Klee, Kandinsky, Magritte, Miró, Ernst and more. Art isn't confined indoors; on the plaza is Jean-Pierre Raynaud's *Pot Doré*, a giant gold flowerpot on a white pedestal, and to the south of the Centre is the Fontaine Stravinksy by Niki de Saint-Phalle and Jean Tinguely.

ABOVE: the escalators are contained in glass tubes, and their views of the plaza and, once at the top, a huge swathe of the city, including Montmartre, are superb.

ABOVE: Constantin Brancusi's beautiful bronze *Muse Endormie*, just one among dozens of the sculptor's works on display in the reconstruction of his studio, the Atelier Brancusi.

MAIN PICTURE: the revolutionary high-tech design of the Centre Pompidou in all its glory.

ABOVE: the colour-coded pipes outside the Centre.

Louvre and Grands Boulevards

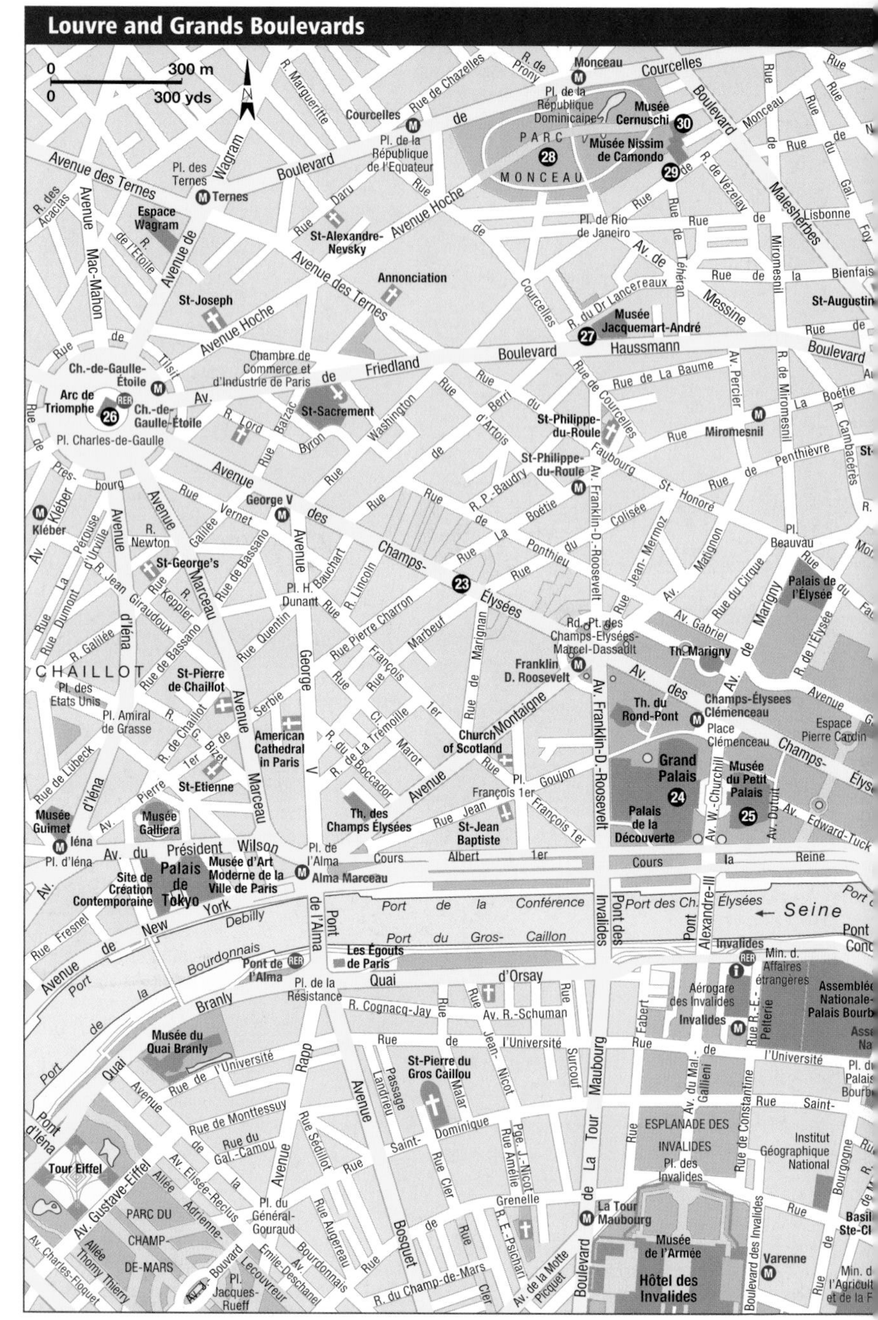

Louvre and Grands Boulevards

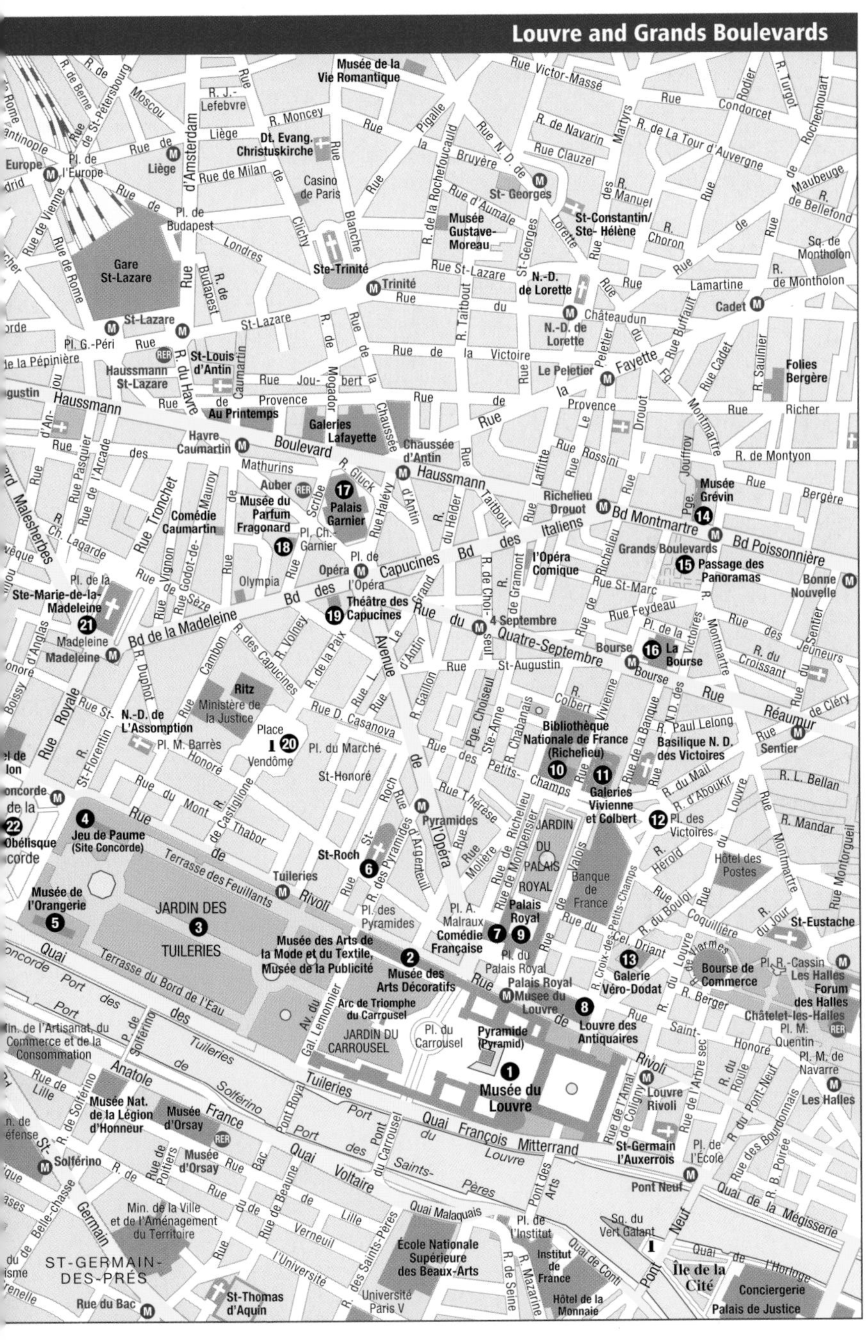

A. MAÌLLOL

Recommended Restaurants, Bars & Cafés on pages 134–5

THE LOUVRE AND QUARTIER DES TUILERIES

Royal Paris: the queen of all art museums, the gracious Tuileries gardens, a fascinating mix of smaller museums, the urban oasis of the Palais Royal and, tucked away, the world's most charming shopping arcades

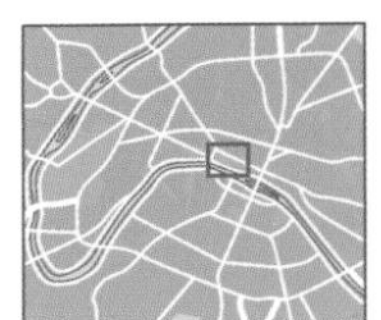

On the Seine's Right Bank beautifully laid-out gardens stretch into ostentatious squares, and wide tree-lined boulevards overflow with upmarket restaurants and designer boutiques. There are royal palaces, an opulent opera house and the world's most famous museum. Meticulously planned by Haussmann, the elegant buildings, boulevards and open spaces engulf the visitor in 19th-century grandeur.

This chapter covers the royal heart of Paris, from the Louvre and Palais Royal westwards to the Jeu de Paume gallery and the Musée de l'Orangerie at the far end of the Tuileries gardens. The grand squares – Place de la Concorde, Place Vendôme and Place de la Madeleine – with the Champs-Elysées, the Grands Boulevards and the Opéra are covered in the next chapter.

MUSÉE DU LOUVRE ❶

www.louvre.fr 01 40 20 50 50 Wed–Mon 9am–6pm, Wed, Fri until 9.45pm charge Palais Royal-Musée du Louvre

Once the seat of royalty, the Musée du Louvre has been the home of fine art since a colony of painters and sculptors moved into the empty halls after King Louis XIV left for Versailles in 1682. The Louvre's art collection goes back even further, to 1516, when François I invited Leonardo da Vinci to be his royal court painter, and he brought with him his masterpieces the *Mona Lisa* and *Virgin of the Rocks*.

Originally built as a fortress in 1190 by Philippe-Auguste to protect a weak link in his city wall, the Louvre was transformed into a royal château in the 1360s by Charles V,

Main attractions

- MUSÉE DU LOUVRE
- LOUVRE PYRAMID
- JARDIN DES TUILERIES
- MUSÉE DE L'ORANGERIE
- RUE DE RIVOLI
- COMÉDIE FRANÇAISE
- PALAIS ROYAL
- GALERIE VIVIENNE
- PLACE DES VICTOIRES

LEFT: sculpture by Aristide Maillol in the Jardin des Tuileries.
RIGHT: style, culture and cuisine at the Louvre's Café Marly.

> *I don't know how you visit museums, but for a long time I used to fall into the common trap of wanting to see everything.*
>
> François Mitterrand, at the inauguration of the Louvre Pyramid

who established his extensive library in one of the towers. Successive monarchs demolished, rebuilt and extended various sections until Louis XIV moved out. The squatters who consequently took up residence in the palace included Guillaume Coustou, sculptor of the Marly Horses, now one of the Louvre's most prized exhibits. A fine artistic reputation grew out of the decaying passageways and galleries and, in the 18th century, the fine arts academy, which had joined the Académie Française and other academic bodies in the royal apartments, set up salons for artists to exhibit their work, a tradition which lasted for more than 120 years.

From palace to museum

After the Revolution, in a moment of creative fervour, the new regime decided to open the palace as a museum, thereby fulfilling the plans of Louis XVI, the king they had just beheaded. Opened in August 1793, the museum benefited from the collection of royal treasures, augmented by Napoleon's subsequent efforts to relocate much of Europe's artistic wealth, following his victorious military campaigns in Italy, Austria and Germany. After Napoleon was defeated at Waterloo in 1815, a large number of the stolen masterpieces were reclaimed by their rightful owners. But many more remained.

In 1981, the newly elected President Mitterrand commissioned a massive renovation of the Louvre, one of his *grands projets*, transferring in the process the Finance Ministry from the Richelieu Wing to Bercy, in eastern Paris, in order to free up more space for the vast collection. When it was finally finished, the *Grand Louvre*, already a vast museum, had doubled in size, making it the world's biggest.

RIGHT: mix art and cuisine at the Louvre's Café Marly. **BELOW:** the old palace seen under the new Pyramid.

Recommended Restaurants, Bars & Cafés on pages 134–5

The Pyramid

In 1989 the emphatically modern Louvre Pyramid, designed by Chinese-American architect I.M. Pei, opened above the Louvre's new main entrance. A celebration of angles, the pyramid's 666 panes of glass are held together by stainless-steel nodes and cables. The glass reflects and to many minds complements the lines of the surrounding building; however, to traditionalists, such modernism amid such historic beauty is a heresy – the same criticism that was levelled against the now-beloved Eiffel Tower when it was first erected. The Pyramid stands on the Royal Axis, or Triumphal Way, an alignment of monuments, regal and triumphal, leading from the Louvre's Cour Carrée all the way to the Grande Arche at La Défense.

Of course, it was not just designed to dazzle. The Pyramid also serves an important practical purpose, as it allows light to flood into the sunken court where you buy your ticket, along with three smaller pyramids that illuminate the area where a cluster of shops, restaurants, cafés and an exhibition area are situated. This exhibition area, called the Medieval Louvre, shows the palace at different stages of its development. It is also a location for the twice-yearly Paris fashion shows.

However, the Pyramid entrance gets very congested, so try to avoid peak times such as Sundays. There's an alternative entrance at 99 rue de Rivoli, which takes you in via the swanky Carrousel du Louvre shopping centre (a treasure trove of chic and cheerful gifts and souvenirs), or

ABOVE: the Pavillons Turgot and Richelieu. **BELOW:** the Pyramid is the main entrance to the museum.

Paris Museum Pass

If you plan to visit several museums during your stay, it may be worth investing in a Paris Museum Pass. Valid for two, four or six days, this gives free and no-waiting access to over 60 museums and monuments in and around Paris. Advantages include skipping queues to get into permanent collections (though it does not cover temporary exhibits); the cost is €30 for two days, €45 for three, or €60 for five. It is sold at participating museums and tourist offices; for full details and a complete list of the museums, see www.parismuseumpass.com. Note that most museums are closed on Monday or Tuesday, and some public holidays. *See also page 295.*

you can enter directly from Palais Royal-Musée du Louvre Métro. There are special queues for museum pass-holders *(see page 121)*, who can also use the Porte des Lions entrance.

A tour of the treasures

From the central Hall Napoléon, escalators whisk visitors off to various parts of the complex, divided into three separate sections: Sully (east wing), Denon (south wing) and Richelieu (north wing), with the exhibits on three levels. Although star attractions are well signposted, the free map provided is essential.

ABOVE: the Sculpture Hall at the Louvre. **BELOW:** Guillaume Coustou figures in the Sculpture Hall.

A good exhibition to start your visit with is the Medieval Louvre, en route to the Crypte Sully under the Cour Carrée, where the remains of Philippe-Auguste's fort and keep, and some of the artefacts discovered in the excavations to build the underground complex, can be seen. Pieces of Charles VI's parade helmet were found at the bottom of the well in the keep in 1984, and a replica of the helmet is on display in the Salle St-Louis.

Up on the ground floor of the Sully and Richelieu wings are Oriental Antiquities, including the Mesopotamian prayer statuette of Ebih-il (dating from approximately 2400 BC), with its striking lapis lazuli eyes, as well as the black basalt Babylonian *Code of Hammurabi* (1792–1750 BC), which is one of the world's first legal documents.

Greece to the Renaissance

On the south side of the Sully Wing you will find the graceful Hellenic statue *Venus de Milo* (2nd century BC), bought by the French government for a thousand francs in 1820 from the Greek island of Milos. From here, head on into the Denon Wing to see the Etruscan sarcophagus of a *Reclining Couple*. Continuing along the ground floor, you will reach the Italian Sculpture section and its famous masterpieces, such as Michelangelo's *Slaves* (1513–20), sculpted in marble for Pope Julius II's tomb but never finished, and Canova's neoclassical *Psyche Revived by the Kiss of Cupid* (1793).

In the Denon Wing, on the first floor, is the work of art that everyone wants to see for themselves, the *Mona Lisa* (1503) – *La Joconde* in French. The first incumbent in the Louvre, Leonardo da Vinci's small painting of a Florentine noblewoman rests securely behind bulletproof

Recommended Restaurants, Bars & Cafés on pages 134–5

glass since her knife assault in the 1980s. It now hangs in pride of place in the restored Salle des Etats, along with Veronese's superb *The Wedding Feast at Cana* and other Venetian paintings by Titian and Tintoretto. The €4.7 million cost of the refurbishment was met, believe it or not, by Japan's Nippon Television Network, which also forked out €1.7 million to upgrade the gallery housing the *Venus de Milo*. Other Italian masterpieces include works by Fra Angelico, Raphael and Caravaggio.

Delacroix to Rembrandt

On the same floor is the Grande Galerie, starting at the top of the Escalier Daru opposite the *Winged Victory of Samothrace* (2nd century BC), a Hellenistic stone figure commemorating a sea victory. Here hang 19th-century French paintings, with Delacroix's *Liberty Leading the People*, Géricault's *Raft of the Medusa* and David's *Sabine Women*. Spanish Paintings, with masterpieces by El Greco and Goya, is close by.

The second floor of Richelieu and Sully Wings are entirely given over to paintings, including Rembrandt's masterly portrait of his second wife, *Bathsheba Bathing* (1654), and his Dutch compatriot Vermeer's telling portrayal of domestic life in the 1660s, *The Lacemaker*. The beautifully renovated Richelieu Wing houses a vast collection of French sculpture on the ground floor and is focused around two splendid sculpture courts, starring Guillaume Coustou's two giant Marly Horses.

> *The Louvre is like the morgue – one goes there to identify one's friends.*
>
> Jean Cocteau

LEFT: the headless *Winged Victory of Samothrace*. **BELOW:** Géricault's expressive *Raft of the Medusa*.

André Le Nôtre (1613–1700) is France's most celebrated gardener. Creator of the French formal garden, he designed those at Versailles, the Champs-Elysées and the Tuileries, where his family had gardened for three generations.

Musée des Arts Décoratifs 2

✉ 107 rue de Rivoli, www.ucad.fr ☎ 01 44 55 57 50 ◷ Tue–Fri 11am–6pm, Sat–Sun 10am–6pm € charge Ⓜ Palais Royal-Musée du Louvre

In a separate wing of the Louvre are three other museums which complement the main collection. This one surveys interior design and applied art from medieval tapestries to extravagant Empire furniture and 20th-century design, including Art Nouveau and Art Deco. A recent renovation programme removed old false floors and opened up the central nave. There are medieval and Renaissance galleries, a jewellery collection and period rooms such as the lavish bedroom of Baron William Hope.

Musée des Arts de la Mode et du Textile

Details and opening times as for Musée des Arts Décoratifs

In the same wing on Rue de Rivoli, this museum covers Paris fashions and textiles from the 16th century until today. Each year it mounts a big display focusing on a different aspect of its collection (which comprises 16,000 costumes, 35,000 fashion accessories and 30,000 textile pieces) from the earliest existing dresses to the ground-breaking designs of big-name couturiers of the 20th century, such as Schiaparelli and Christian Dior.

Musée de la Publicité

✉ www.museedelapub.org; other details as for Musée des Arts Décoratifs

Upstairs in this wing, the "Advertising Museum" was designed for the millennium celebrations by French architect Jean Nouvel, who turned to the city for inspiration. It is home to a comprehensive collection of posters – around 100,000 in all, starting from as early as the Middle Ages – press, TV and radio adverts and promotional memorabilia, complemented by interactive displays, slide shows and videos. Only a fraction of the vast collection can ever be exhibited at one time.

BELOW: the Arc de Triomphe du Carrousel. **BELOW RIGHT:** sunbathing in the Tuileries.

Map on pages 116–7
Recommended Restaurants, Bars & Cafés on pages 134–5

A WALK IN THE TUILERIES

The **Jardin des Tuileries** ❸ offers shade, statues, fountains and a place in which to relax and pretend to read *Le Monde*. Once a rubbish tip and a clay quarry for tiles (*tuiles*, hence the name), the garden was initially created in 1564 for Catherine de Médicis in front of her palace, to remind her of her native Tuscany. Louis XIV's celebrated gardener André Le Nôtre redesigned it in 1664, giving free rein to his predilection for straight lines and neatly clipped trees.

Louis XIV, however, was far more interested in Versailles, and the Tuileries gardens were, surprisingly, opened to the public. They quickly became the first fashionable outdoor area in which to see and be seen, triggering the appearance of Paris's first deckchairs and public toilets. One of the earliest hot-air balloon flights was launched from here, in 1783.

The Tuileries Palace for which the gardens had been created – which "closed off" the two wings of the Louvre – burned down in 1871, during the Paris Commune, leaving the gardens as a permanent park.

Sculpture, paths and ponds

The Tuileries were renovated in the 1990s, restoring Le Nôtre's original design and incorporating a sloping terrace and enclosed garden. The Passerelle de Solférino footbridge across the Seine, opened in 1999, provides a quick route from the gardens to the Left Bank and Musée d'Orsay.

Approaching the gardens from the Louvre, you pass through the Arc de

Refreshments in the Tuileries gardens can be had at Café Very (tel: 01 47 03 94 84), on the north side of the central path towards the Place de la Concorde. In fine weather, its terrace is almost always packed, though it also seats 100 indoors.

ABOVE: *Spring* by Art Nouveau poster artist Eugène Grasset (Musée des Arts Décoratifs). **BELOW:** the Tuileries' pool is the focal point of the geometrically designed park.

ABOVE: relaxing in the Jardin des Tuileries. **BELOW LEFT:** the annual funfair held in the Jardin des Tuileries.

Triomphe du Carrousel, the smallest of the three arches (the others being the Arc de Triomphe and the Grande Arche at La Défense) on the Triumphal Way. Erected in 1809 by Napoleon to commemorate his Austrian victories, this arch is a garish imitation of the great triumphal arches built by the Romans, and the four horses galloping across its top are copies of four bronze horses that were stolen by Napoleon from St Mark's Square in Venice to decorate his memorial. After his downfall in 1815, the originals were returned.

In front and a little to the right of the arch, where the Tuileries Palace once stood, is a collection of sculptures of sensuous nudes, produced between 1900 and 1938 by Aristide Maillol, adorning ornamental pools and hedge-lined pathways. More works by sculptors such as Rodin and Le Pautre, along with copies of ancient works and a selection of modern sculpture by, among others, Dubuffet, Etienne-Martin, Ellsworth Kelly, Laurens and David Smith, can be found scattered around the park.

Continue westwards along the Terrasse du Bord de l'Eau, where Napoleon's children played under the watchful gaze of their father, to the hexagonal pool – still a favourite spot for children with boats, and seagulls with attitude. Here, facing each other, are the twin museums of the Jeu de Paume and the Orangerie. These buildings are all that remain of the Palais des Tuileries, after the fire that engulfed the royal residence during the 1871 Commune.

Recommended Restaurants, Bars & Cafés on pages 134–5

Jeu de Paume (Site Concorde) ❹

www.jeudepaume.org 01 47 03 12 50 Tue noon–9pm, Wed–Fri noon–7pm, Sat–Sun 10am–7pm charge Concorde

Once the real tennis court of the Tuileries Palace, the Jeu de Paume is now a light, airy exhibition space that is the main base of France's national photography centre. Its approach is multi-disciplinary, featuring video, installation and film, documentary and art photography. The centre's other Paris building is the Hôtel de Sully in the Marais *(see page 92)*.

Musée de l'Orangerie ❺

www.musee-orangerie.fr 01 44 77 80 07 Wed–Mon 9am–6pm charge Concorde

The list of canvases here is impressive: 22 Soutines, 14 Cézannes – including one of *The Bathers* that was cut in three, then stuck back together again (look for the joins) – 24 Renoirs, 28 Derains and a pile of Picassos, Matisses and Utrillos. The highlight, though, is the unforgettable, extraordinarily fresh series of water lilies by Claude Monet, conceived especially for two oval rooms upstairs. Donated by the artist in 1918, the eight vast curved panels hover between abstraction and decoration.

During extensive renovations at the Orangerie, workers uncovered a wall dating back to Charles IX's reign (*c.*1566). The museum reopened in 2006, with part of its Walter-Guillaume collection in new rooms beneath the Tuileries.

Aristide Maillol (1861–1944) started sculpting at the age of 40, concentrating his efforts on large, bronze, nude women – 20 of which adorn the Tuileries.

LEFT: *Portrait de Madame Cézanne* by Paul Cézanne (Walter-Guillaume collection, Musée de l'Orangerie). **BELOW AND BELOW LEFT:** Claude Monet's *Water Lilies*.

At 226 rue de Rivoli, chocolate-lovers should not miss Angélina, a late 19th-century Viennese salon de thé *famous for its rich and intense hot chocolate l'Africain.*

RIGHT: antique Napoleon pipe at the Louvre des Antiquaires. **BELOW:** gilded Joan of Arc in Place des Pyramides. **BELOW RIGHT:** Rivoli bookshop Galignani.

RUE DE RIVOLI

The long Rue de Rivoli starts in the Marais, then runs past the Louvre and along the Tuileries – where its north side becomes a pedestrian arcade topped with Haussmannian apartments – to Place de la Concorde. It was built to commemorate Napoleon's victory over the Austrians at Rivoli, north of Verona, in 1797, but was completed well after the emperor's demise. Amid the souvenir shops, the presence of two English-language bookshops (Galignani and an outpost of WH Smith) and shirt-maker Hilditch & Key are a legacy of the English, who often stayed here in the 19th and early 20th centuries, notably at the Hôtel Meurice. Nearby is Angélina *(see margin)*.

Parallel to Rue de Rivoli is the ancient Rue St-Honoré. Once full of noble residences, it still has some elegant facades and ornate shopfronts, but the area, long considered staid and straight-laced, has been transformed by the arrival of influential designer boutiques and so-called concept stores, of which the first and still the best-known is Colette.

St-Roch 6

✉ 296 rue St-Honoré
☎ 01 42 44 13 20 ⏲ daily 8am–7.30pm € free Ⓜ Pyramides

This Baroque church contains the tombs of royal landscape gardener Le Nôtre, the playwright Corneille and philosopher Diderot. In 1795, Royalist insurgents were shot dead on the church steps on the orders of a young general named Napoleon Bonaparte (the bullet holes are still visible). The church is slowly being renovated; its spotlessly clean, honeyed stone facade is particularly fine.

On nearby Place des Pyramides is a shiny equestrian statue of Joan of Arc (one of four statues of the Maid

Recommended Restaurants, Bars & Cafés on pages 134–5

of Orléans in the city), wounded here in battle when fighting against the English in 1429.

Comédie Française ❼

1 place Colette, www.comedie-francaise.fr 08 25 10 16 80 Palais Royal-Musée du Louvre

The French national theatre overlooks two squares named after the writers Colette and Malraux. The company that started life with Molière and his acting troupe *(see page 130)* was given the official stamp in 1680 by Louis XIV. It has been in the present building since 1799, and the plays of Racine, Molière, Corneille and Shakespeare continue to form the backbone of its classical repertoire.

Louvre des Antiquaires ❽

2 place du Palais-Royal, www.louvre-antiquaires.com 01 42 97 27 27 Tue–Sun 11am–7pm free Palais Royal-Musée du Louvre

On Place du Palais-Royal, now a popular spot for stunt-mad rollerbladers, is this massive building, built as a department store, and now home to some 250 upmarket antique dealers. Specialists take in everything from fine art, porcelain and furniture to Chinese and Japanese ivories, antique jewellery and scientific instruments. The area was cleared by a paranoid Napoleon following an attempt on his life in 1800, when two Royalists planted explosives in a cart, but the bomb missed his carriage.

TIP

If you want to try a performance of classic French theatre, take note that at the Comédie Française's main Salle Richelieu there are "reduced visibility" tickets available for €5, and that those aged under 28 can buy all tickets – even, sometimes, in the best seats – for €12. Also, any of the cheapest seats still unsold go on sale an hour before each performance, for €5.50.

ABOVE: top-notch food and presentation at Le Meurice.
BELOW LEFT: celebrated restaurant Le Grand Véfour.

Hotel with History

The sumptuous Hôtel Meurice (228 rue de Rivoli, *see page 287)* is one of Paris's grandest hotels, with a spa, Michelin-starred restaurant, supremely elegant cocktail bar and sumptuous decor. During the Nazi Occupation, however, it was the German headquarters. It was here in August 1944 that General Dietrich von Choltitz, military governor of Paris (he was only promoted to the job on the 7th), received direct orders from Hitler to blow up most of the city in advance of the Allied liberation. Von Choltitz famously refused – an act of disobedience that earned him the sobriquet "saviour of Paris" and the presence of French generals at his funeral 22 years later.

With Allied troops swarming into Paris, a young French officer ran into the suite occupied by von Choltitz, who was at his desk. "Do you speak German?" shouted the Frenchman; "Probably better than you," was the general's laconic reply. He allowed himself to be taken prisoner.

ABOVE: flying the flag on the Palais Royal.
BELOW RIGHT: one of many local antiques dealers.

PALAIS ROYAL ❾

The Palais Royal is a timeless and tranquil spot. The palace was built on the site of a Roman bathhouse for Cardinal Richelieu, Louis XIII's chief minister from 1624. On Richelieu's death in 1642, it was passed to the Crown, and became the childhood home of Louis XIV. At the beginning of the 18th century, the dukes of Orléans, descendants of Louis XIV's younger brother, took up residence, and the palace turned into a den of debauchery, with the infamous "libertines' suppers" thrown regularly by the Regent, Philippe d'Orléans.

In 1780, to compensate for his family's profligate spending, Louis-Philippe of Orléans, known as *Philippe-Egalité* due to his liberal ideas, enclosed the gardens at the back of the palace with an elegant three-storey arcade, spaces in which were let as shops, theatres, restaurants, cafés, sideshows and brothels. The Jardins du Palais Royal became a focal point of Parisian life, as a place where all classes could mingle freely; the duke forbade the police entrance to the palace precincts, and gambling and prostitution were rife.

Birthplace of revolution

It was also a hotbed of radical ideas, and it was famously from a café table in the Palais Royal that Camille Desmoulins made an impassioned speech on 12 July 1789 calling on the people of Paris to take arms against the royal government, which led directly to the storming of the

Master of Comedy

Born Jean-Baptiste Poquelin in Paris in 1622, Molière, playwright, actor, director and stage manager, wrote 12 enduring comedies, including *Tartuffe* (1669) and *Le Bourgeois Gentilhomme* (1671). After studying law, he formed an acting troupe with the Béjart family (including his lover, Madeleine Béjart). He also changed his name to Molière, perhaps to spare his father the embarrassment of an actor in the family. The troupe had an unsuccessful start, but after Molière polished up his act in the provinces, they became Louis XIV's court entertainers.

In 1673, at 51, Molière collapsed on stage with a haemorrhage while playing *Le Malade Imaginaire*, in which an old man feigns death; he died hours later. In 1680 the king merged his company with a rival's, creating the Comédie Française. The great thespian lived at 40 rue de Richelieu, and is commemorated by the Molière Fountain close by. The giant chair in which he was sitting when he died is in a case in the theatre's foyer.

Recommended Restaurants, Bars & Cafés on pages 134–5

Bastille two days later. After the Revolution the complex continued to be one of the social hubs of Paris, until the Palais was reclaimed by the Orléans family after the demise of Napoleon. The Palais Royal was seriously damaged during the Commune (1871), but was faithfully reconstructed in the following years.

Today, the Palais Royal houses the Ministry of Culture. In the main courtyard stand 250 black-and-white-striped columns of varying heights, erected by artist Daniel Buren in 1986. At weekends it echoes with the squeals of delighted children, who love to play around them. The garden, once a meeting place for revolutionaries, is now a tranquil oasis – with some fine restaurants – while the eccentric mix of shops ranges from old-fashioned specialists in medals and lead soldiers to make-up, vintage couture and upmarket interior design. In recent years some seriously glam fashion labels have boosted the arcades' pulling power considerably: newcomers include Marc Jacobs, Rick Owens and Didier Ludot.

Bibliothèque Nationale de France (Richelieu) ⑩

58 rue de Richelieu, www.bnf.fr 01 53 79 59 59 exhibitions Tue–Sat 10am–7pm, Sun noon–7pm charge Bourse

North of the Palais Royal is the former mansion of Cardinal Mazarin, which became the royal library and so the foundation of France's national library. Most of the collection has been transferred to the massive building at Tolbiac *(see page 214)* – last (and least successful) of Mitterrand's *grands projets*. The book collection is one of the biggest in the world, and includes Charlemagne's illuminated Bible, as well as manuscripts by Rabelais, Hugo and Proust. The Richelieu building now houses the collections of prints, drawings, maps, music and manuscripts. The main reading room, designed by Henri Labrouste in 1863, is an architectural masterpiece. Downstairs, the **Cabinet des Médailles** (open afternoons; charge) contains coins and objets d'art from the royal collections that were seized during the Revolution.

Jean-Paul Sartre, sculpted outside the Bibliothèque Nationale de France (Richelieu).

BELOW LEFT AND RIGHT: the tranquil enclosed gardens and elegant colonnades of the Palais Royal.

ABOVE: neoclassical clock, Galerie Vivienne. **BELOW:** chic restaurant on Rue St-Honoré.

Opposite the library, across Rue de Richelieu, the charming **Square Louvois** contains one of the most beautiful fountains in Paris, which represents the four "female" rivers of France – La Loire, La Seine, La Garonne and La Saône.

GLORIOUS *GALERIES*

The area between the Palais Royal and Rue du Faubourg-Montmartre is laced with picturesque covered shopping arcades. The 20 or so *galeries* represent a fraction of the number that existed in the early 19th century. By the 1840s there were over 100 such *passages*, built by speculators who snapped up the land of the dispossessed aristocracy that came onto the market after the Revolution, and making imaginative use of the new technologies of the era with their combination of iron and glass to create a light, airy, and yet enclosed space. They became the ideal places in which to discover novelties, inventions and the latest fashions, while keeping out of the city's mud-splashed, carriage-laden thoroughfares.

Galeries Vivienne and Colbert

The best-preserved and most elegant of these shopping arcades is **Galerie Vivienne ⓫**, first opened in 1826, which has a fine mosaic floor, intricate brass lamps, graceful glass canopies and restored wooden shopfronts. It has been colonised by art galleries, upmarket clothes designers, restaurants and a very pretty tea room, A Priori Thé *(see margin tip*

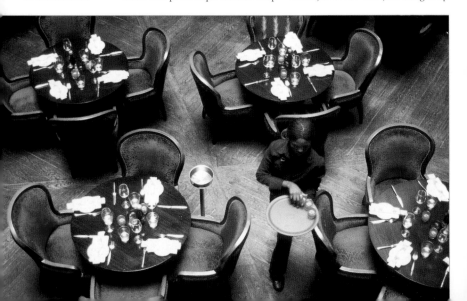

right). The adjoining **Galerie Colbert** has a spectacular glass dome. Formerly an annexe of the Bibliothèque Nationale, it has been renovated to house a variety of art institutions.

Victory Square

Adjacent to these arcades is the **Place des Victoires** ⓬, an archetypal royal square designed in 1685 by Louis XIV's architect Jules Hardouin Mansart as a backdrop for the equestrian statue of his patron the Sun King (a bronze copy from 1822 – revolutionaries destroyed the original). The square became a model for squares across France. It was designed to give the impression of an entirely enclosed space, but this effect was destroyed by the opening up of Rue Etienne Marcel in 1883. Nowadays a large number of its surrounding mansions are occupied by designer boutiques (Apostrophe, Mercadel, Kenzo and more).

Heading south down Rue Croix-des-Petits-Champs for about five minutes, you reach the most beautiful and atmospheric passageway in Paris, **Galerie Véro-Dodat** ⓭ (opposite Rue Montesquieu), with polished mahogany facades, brass lamps and skylights all beautifully preserved. It is named after the duo of wealthy pork butchers who financed the arcade's construction in 1826, fitting it with the new technology of the day: gas lighting. One of its main attractions is the picture-perfect brasserie the Café de l'Epoque, a good spot for lunch. ❑

FOOD

A Priori Thé, in the Galerie Vivienne, is an elegant *salon de thé* that spills out into the gallery's main passageway. As well as teas and coffees, it serves light snacks and a very good cheesecake.

LEFT: funky shop display in Rue St-Honoré. **BELOW LEFT:** Galerie Vivienne, the most fashionable of all the Parisian galleries. **BELOW:** French dressing, Rue de Rivoli.

BEST RESTAURANTS, BARS AND CAFÉS

Restaurants

Price includes dinner and a half-bottle of house wine:
€ = under €25
€€ = €25–40
€€€ = €40–60
€€€€ = more than €60

L'Absinthe

24 place du Marché, 1st
01 49 26 90 04
L Mon–Fri, D Mon–Sat.
€€€ [p338, A1]
Although they don't serve absinthe here and it is more chic than bohemian, it is still a lot of fun. The well-prepared bistro-style food includes chestnut velouté, crayfish ravioli and pear tatin with walnut sauce and caramel. The terrace is one of the best in Paris, and there are exhibits of contemporary artists (works for sale).

L'Ardoise

28 rue du Mont-Thabor, 1st
01 42 96 28 18 L & D Tue–Sun. **€€** [p338, A1]
A successful, modern bistro, which offers a good-value menu written on a blackboard – the *ardoise* in question. The typical bistro cooking is careful, even if the surroundings are rather utilitarian.

La Ferme Opéra

55–7 rue Saint-Roch, 1st
01 40 20 12 12 daily until 8pm (Sat & Sun until 7pm). **€** [p336, A4]
Most of the ingredients are organic. On the menu you'll find salads, sandwiches, soups, a hot *plat du jour* and savoury tarts.

Le Fumoir

6 rue de l'Amiral-de-Coligny, 1st 01 42 92 00 24
L & D daily, Br Sun. **€€** (set menu), **€€€** (à la carte) [p338, B2]
With an admirable location facing the eastern facade of the Louvre, spacious, sophisticated Le Fumoir is renowned for shaking some of the best cocktails in town, including a remarkable choice of martinis. Come lunch and dinner it morphs into a restaurant serving light pan-European cooking (monkfish with peas, sea bass with ginger, rack of lamb and polenta), with a popular Sunday brunch. Offers one of the best happy hours in town.

Le Grand Véfour

17 rue de Beaujolais, 1st
01 42 96 56 27 L Mon–Fri, D Mon–Thur.
€€€€€ [p338, B1]
Hiding under the arches of the Palais Royal is one of the most beautiful restaurants in Paris. Le Grand Véfour opened its doors in 1784 and has fed the likes of Napoleon and Victor Hugo. Today it serves grand classic haute cuisine – lobster salad, oxtail parmentier and clever desserts – in the hands of imaginative chef Guy Martin.

Kinugawa

9 rue du Mont-Thabor, 1st
01 42 60 65 07 L & D Mon–Sat. €€€ (set menu) €€€€ (à la carte) [p338, A1]
Paris has some seriously good Japanese restaurants, and this is one of the best and longest-established – firm favourite with film stars, too. Each of the set menus is a good introduction to its prowess: faultless quality and presentation in dishes like turbot sashimi and egg custard studded with gingko nuts and chunks of whitebait.

Restaurant du Palais Royal

110 galerie de Valois, 1st
01 40 20 00 27 L & D Mon–Fri, Sat in summer. €€€ [p336, B4]
The most attractive terrace on the Palais Royal and the finest of the restaurants circling the inner gardens. The food is not wildly imaginative but lives up to the view. The menu features langoustine cappuccino and red mullet with polenta.

La Rose de France

24 place Dauphine, 1st
01 43 54 10 12
L & D. €€€ [p338, B2]
Charming little restaurant in a quiet street serving fresh produce from the market. Traditional French cuisine for a good price. The staff speak English.

Scoop

154 rue Saint-Honoré, 1st
01 42 60 31 84
Tue–Fri noon–4pm, Sat–Sun 11am–5pm. € [p338, B1]
Although, as the name suggests, Scoop is in part an ice-cream parlour, it is also a fun and funky place to have lunch. Choose from an all-day menu of home-made soup, sandwiches, salads and a few hot dishes before trying the unctuous ice creams.

LEFT AND ABOVE LEFT: impeccable service and dainty treats at Le Grand Véfour. **ABOVE RIGHT:** exquisite food at grandiose hotel-restaurant Le Meurice.

Takara

14 rue Molière, 1st 01 42 96 08 38 L & D Tue–Fri, D Sat–Sun. €€€ (set menu) €€€€ (à la carte) [p338, B1]
Another superb Japanese, this one is the city's oldest: it's been in business since the 1960s. The specialities here, not readily available at other addresses in Paris, are the communal hot-pots shabu shabu and sukiyaki, in which diners cook the ingredients themselves at the table. Not cheap, but well worth the outlay.

Bars and Cafés

Café Marly
Palais du Louvre, Cour Napoléon, 93 rue Rivoli.
Tel: 01 49 26 06 60.
L & D daily (until 2am).
[p338, B1]
With views of the Louvre Pyramid, this designer museum café is abuzz with Parisian intelligentsia and tourists. The food, modern and light, is prepared to a high standard, but steeply priced. You may have to wait for a seat.

Juvéniles
47 rue de Richelieu, 1st.
Tel: 01 42 97 46 49.
Mon–Sat noon–11pm.
[p338, B1]
Popular wine bar run by British ex-pat Tim Johnston, who offers a truly special selection of wines as well as tapas, simple *plats du jour* and a cheeseboard that celebrates the great British Stilton.

Willi's Wine Bar
13 rue des Petits-Champs, 1st.
Tel: 01 42 61 05 09.
L & D Mon–Sat (until 11pm). [p338, B1]
More of a wine bistro than a wine bar, British-owned Willi's has a phenomenal wine list (Côtes du Rhône are the speciality), but also serves ambitious food, including rich, wine-sauced seasonal game. Very popular with the area's stockbroking and fashion sets.

The Louvre

The largest museum in the world – a matchless treasure trove of paintings, sculpture, decorative art and antiquities

The Musée National du Louvre has something for everyone. The palace that houses it is in itself a building of breathtaking beauty, and its galleries form a labyrinth of corridors. Getting lost may be a good way to find unexpected gems, but wander for too long without direction and you might miss even the major collections. Use the map on the right, or pick up one showing current exhibitions at the information desk on your way in. If it all gets too much, you can leave the museum and return on the same day, or you can rest and get a bite to eat at one of the Louvre's cafés and restaurants (one of the best is Café Marly, with a terrace overlooking the pyramid, *see page 135*). The museum also has some excellent shops selling souvenirs – but don't try to see everything in one day; go back again, and get lost in a different place.

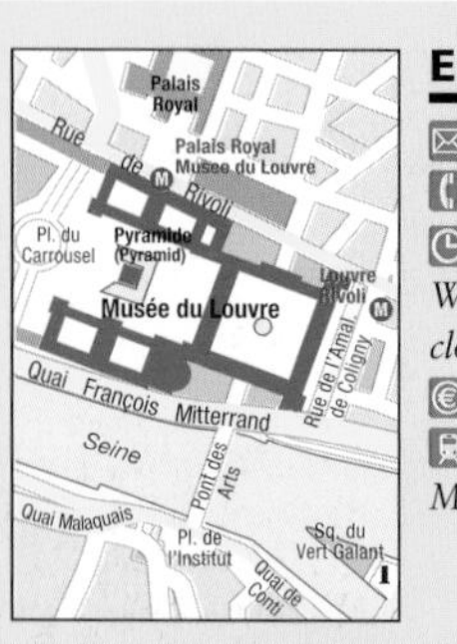

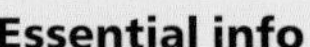

Essential info

www.louvre.fr

01 40 20 50 50

Wed–Mon 9am–6pm, Wed, Fri until 9.45pm; closed Tues

charge

Palais Royal-Musée du Louvre

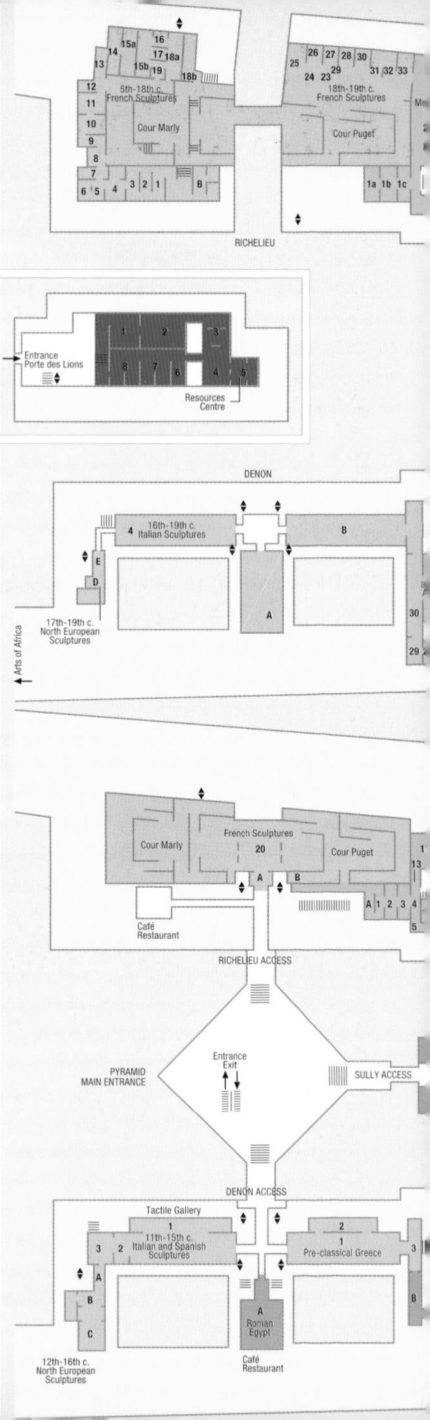

5th-18th c. French Sculptures
Cour Marly
18th-19th c. French Sculptures
Cour Puget
RICHELIEU
Entrance Porte des Lions
Resources Centre
DENON
16th-19th c. Italian Sculptures
17th-19th c. North European Sculptures
Arts of Africa
French Sculptures
Cour Marly
Cour Puget
Café Restaurant
RICHELIEU ACCESS
PYRAMID MAIN ENTRANCE
Entrance
Exit
SULLY ACCESS
DENON ACCESS
Tactile Gallery
11th-15th c. Italian and Spanish Sculptures
Pre-classical Greece
Roman Egypt
12th-16th c. North European Sculptures
Café Restaurant

Ground Floor

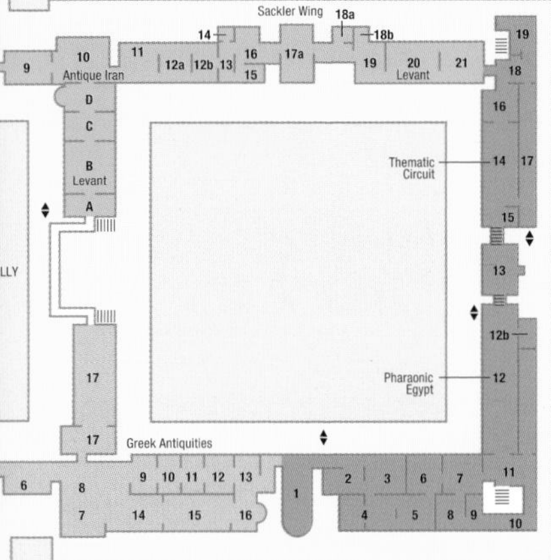

Oriental Antiquities and Islamic Art

Sculptures

Egyptian Antiquities

Greek, Etruscan and Roman Antiquities

History of the Louvre, The Medieval Louvre

Arts of Africa, Asia, Oceania and the Americas

Lower Ground Floor

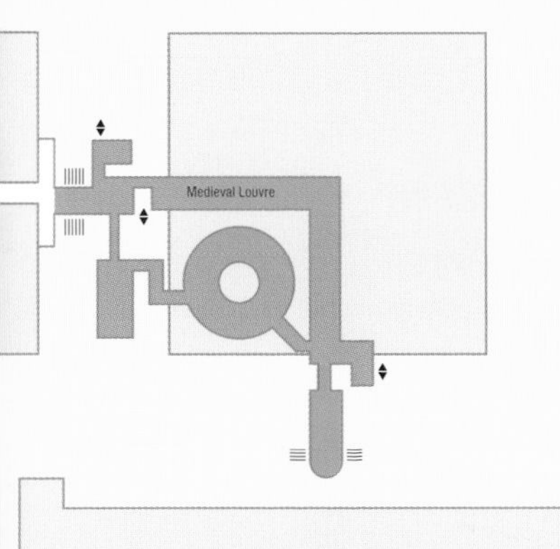

THE HIGHLIGHTS

***The Seated Scribe* (2500–2350 BC)**
This Ancient Egyptian figure is made from painted limestone and alabaster, with eyes of rock crystal (Sully, 1st floor).

Persian *Winged Bull* glazed tiles (*c.*500 BC)
A glazed, moulded relief from the palace of the Persian king Darius I at Susa (present-day Iran).

The *Venus de Milo* (*c.*2nd century BC)
The iconic Greek marble statue is on display in a gallery parallel to the Galerie des Antiquités.

***Virgin and Child in Majesty* (*c.*1270) by Cimabue**
This Early Renaissance masterpiece was acquired by Napoleon (Denon,1st floor).

***Venus and the Graces Presenting Gifts to a Young Woman* (*c.*1483) by Sandro Botticelli**
One of a pair of frescoes from the Villa Lemmi near Florence, thought to have been commissioned for a wedding (Denon, 1st floor).

***Mona Lisa* (1503–6) by Leonardo da Vinci**
The most famous Renaissance smile is better-displayed than ever, in a purpose-built new gallery.

***The Rebellious Slave* (1513–5) by Michelangelo**
One of a pair of unfinished sculptures intended for the tomb of Pope Julius II (Denon, ground floor).

***The Card Cheat* (*c.*1635) by Georges de la Tour**
A rich but unworldly young man falls in with a gang of card-sharps (French 17th-century painting).

***The Astronomer* (1668) and *The Geographer* (1668–9) by Vermeer**
Painted by Vermeer to celebrate the progress of science in Europe in the 17th century (Richelieu, 2nd floor).

***The Bather* (1808) by Ingres**
This celebrated figure was reused by Ingres 50 years later for his painting *The Turkish Bath* (French 19th-century painting).

***Raft of the Medusa* (1816) by Géricault**
A stirring vision of suffering based on a true story of shipwreck and cannibalism (Grande Galerie).

***Liberty Leading the People* (1830) by Delacroix**
Iconic painting of the July Revolution by the leader of Romanticism (Grande Galerie).

The Main Collections

Egyptian antiquities
The collection spans the period from the 4th millennium BC to the 4th–6th centuries AD.

Oriental antiquities and Islamic arts
The collection is mainly from the eastern Mediterranean, and holds the oldest item in the museum – a 7,000-year-old neolithic statue from Ain Ghezal.

Greek, Roman & Etruscan antiquities
A comprehensive collection which includes the mythical *Venus de Milo* and the *Three Graces*.

French painting 17th–19th century
Works are arranged in chronological order, from the Late Gothic period to the mid-19th century.

French sculpture
French sculpture dominates the collection in the courtyards of the Richelieu wing.

Italian and Spanish painting
The Italian galleries contain early masterpieces, but the Spanish collection is patchy.

Northern Schools
Six new rooms show Northern European paintings of the 18th and 19th centuries.

Decorative arts
One of the least-known aspects of the Louvre is the extensive decorative arts collection.

Graphic arts
The Louvre has a vast stock of drawings and engravings by Michelangelo, Raphael, Dürer and more, which are shown in changing exhibitions.

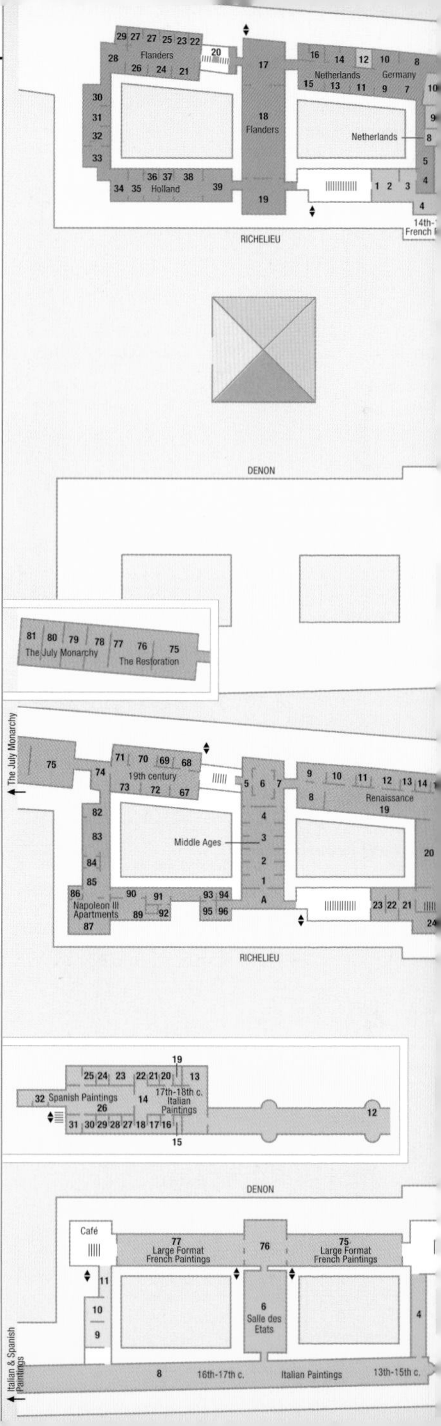

Second Floor

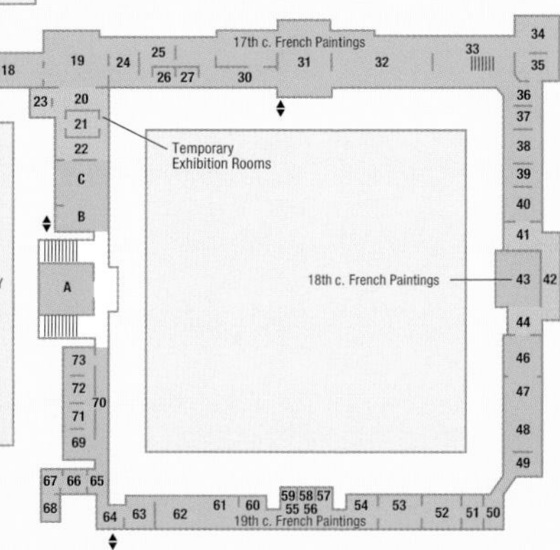

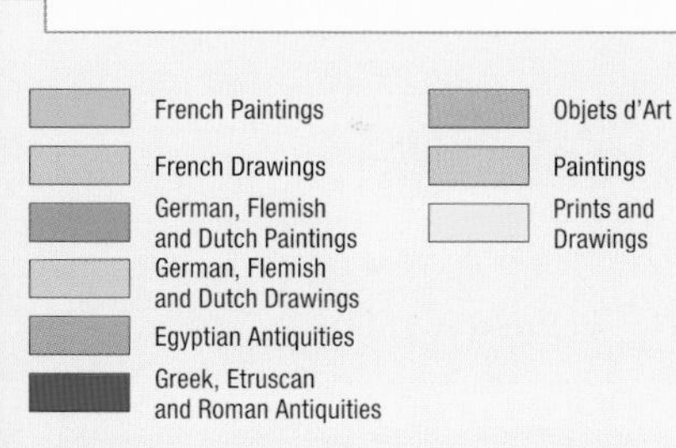

First Floor

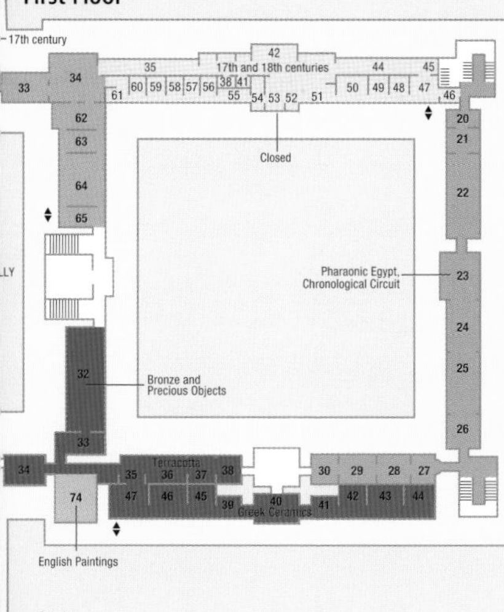

EGYPTIAN ANTIQUITIES AND ISLAMIC ARTS

The museum's spectacular Egyptian collection is very popular. Its core originates from the victory spoils of Napoleon's Egyptian campaign of 1798. The collection was subsequently expanded, largely through the efforts of the famous Egyptologist Jean-François Champollion (1790–1832), the first person to decipher hieroglyphics. Beyond the pink granite *Giant Sphinx*, insights into Egyptian life and the Nile culture are given through a thematic presentation on the ground floor, followed by a chronological presentation on the first floor. The later rooms follow religion and funerary rites.

The oriental antiquities collection (essentially from the eastern Mediterranean) may be overshadowed by the Egyptian collection, but it is no less important. The most spectacular items are the reconstructions of palaces at Susa and Khorsabad. The palace of Persian king Darius I at Susa (in present-day Iran) was constructed in around 510 BC. Other highlights include Cypriot terracotta figures and stag-shaped vessels, Mycenaean pots with geometric decoration, carved ivory, chalcolithic vessels from the Negev and the Neolithic statue from Ain Ghezal, discovered in 1985.

ABOVE: female figurine (*c.*4500 BC) in terracotta from Mesopotamia (northern Syria).

BELOW: an Egyptian relief.

Above: this portrait of the famous beauty and socialite Juliette Récamier was painted in 1802 by François Gérard, a pupil of the master of French Neoclassical painting, David.

Below: dating probably from the 2nd century BC, the marble Venus de Milo with its serene gaze, soft curves and naturalistic drapery rivals the *Mona Lisa* as an icon of female beauty. She was discovered, minus her arms, on the island of Melos in 1820 and promptly purchased by the French government for 6,000 francs. Various authorities have suggested that her left hand might have been holding the golden apple that was presented to Venus by Paris of Troy.

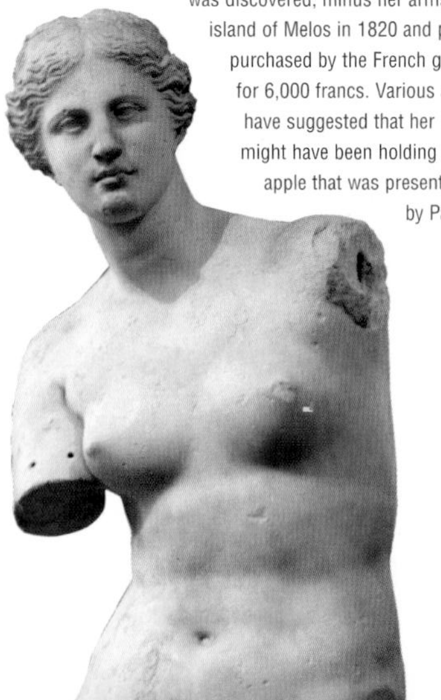

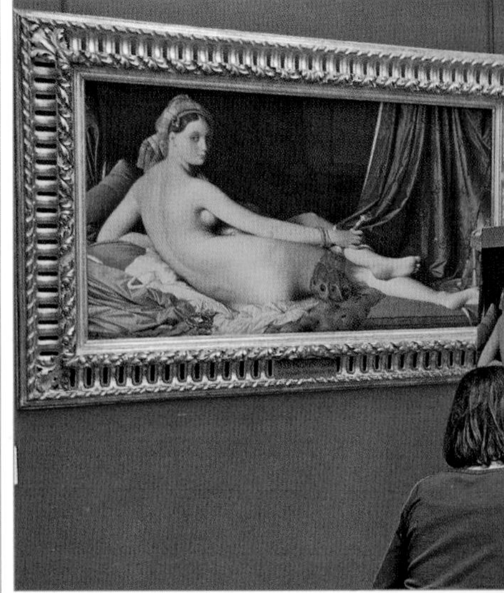

TRUTH? WHO CARES

Dig it or deplore it, Dan Brown's global bestseller *The Da Vinci Code* has been good news for the Louvre, as has the film of the novel: large parts of both were set here. Whereas St-Sulpice Church has been driven to put up signs reminding visitors that the events in the book are fiction, the Louvre has seen no harm in giving its public what it seems to want – so there's now a dedicated audio guide, the *Da Vinci Code Soundwalk*, available at the entrance to Denon wing. It's narrated by gravel-voiced Jean Réno, with bombastic music and sound clips from the movie, and it "unlocks the mystery" of 30 paintings in the Louvre collections.

LEFT: Delacroix's world-famous *Liberty Leading the People* is a painting whose dimensions are as epic as its theme, at over 3 metres (9 ft) wide. It dramatises the Revolution of July 1830, which ended the reign of Charles X.

LEFT: ever since the Louvre first opened, it has been popular with artists wishing to study the techniques of the masters.

BELOW: the dreamy *Psyche Revived by Cupid's Kiss*, sculpted around 1787 by the Venetian Antonio Canova.

ABOVE: a young man succumbs to the temptations of gaming, wine and luxury and is caught in the act of cheating in Georges de la Tour's masterly painting *The Card Cheat* (*c.*1635) – see the player on the left pulling an ace from his belt behind his back.

Recommended Restaurants, Bars & Cafés on pages 154–5

GRANDS BOULEVARDS AND CHAMPS-ELYSÉES

This area is a paradise for shoppers and strollers, with giant stores and grand fashion houses, glittering gourmet palaces and chic modern cafés, celebrated monuments and intimate mansion-museums, all amid some of Paris's most magnificent vistas

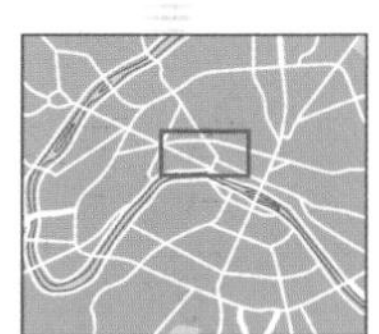

North of the Palais Royal lie the Grands Boulevards, a string of wide avenues running from east to west. Their oldest sections date from the 17th century, when Louis XIV tore down the medieval walls around Paris and created wide, open spaces bordered with trees for his subjects. In the 19th century, Baron Haussmann extended the string westwards along Boulevard Haussmann. The western boulevards became the preserve of the rich (as chronicled by Marcel Proust, who frequented the glittering local social events and salons), while the east was the playground of the city's industrial workers, lined with vaudeville theatres, restaurants, bars, brothels and, later, cinemas. Today the boulevards are dominated by mass-market clothing chains and discount outlets, but if you look up, the plate-glass traces of Second Empire extravagance can be seen in the ornate balconies and facades.

THE GRANDEST AVENUE

To the west, at a haughty distance from the populist strip, is the grandest of Parisian avenues, the Champs-Elysées, begun by Le Nôtre in 1667 as an extension of the Tuileries. Initially the promenade reached only as far as the Rond-Point des Champs-Elysées; over 100 years passed before the rest, stretching up to the Arc de Triomphe, was completed. Its reputation has ebbed and flowed with the centuries: today, chic restaurants, cafés and nightclubs are joining the fashion and luxury goods shops that appeared there through the 1990s, heralding the monumental avenue's comeback as one of the world's premier shopping destinations.

Main attractions

- PALAIS GARNIER
- GRANDS MAGASINS
- PLACE VENDÔME
- LA MADELEINE
- RUE DU FAUBOURG-ST-HONORÉ
- PLACE DE LA CONCORDE
- THE CHAMPS-ELYSÉES
- GRAND PALAIS
- PETIT PALAIS
- ARC DE TRIOMPHE

LEFT: the Place de la Concorde fountains are at their resplendent best at night.
RIGHT: restaurants in the Opéra district have retained their elegant Belle Epoque style.

ALONG THE BOULEVARDS TO THE OPÉRA

Traces of the Grands Boulevards' early pomp can be seen in one of the easternmost sections, Boulevard St-Denis (around Strasbourg St-Denis Métro), in the two triumphal arches erected by Colbert in the 1670s in honour of Louis XIV's military victories, the **Porte St-Denis** and **Porte St-Martin**. When they were built they stood on the very edge of the city, and greeted new arrivals from the north.

A short walk from the Palais Garnier is another, smaller opera house, the Opéra Comique (Place Boieldieu, tel: 01 42 44 45 40). This very pretty venue hosts a mixture of chamber orchestras and musicals.

Musée Grévin ⓮

✉ 10 boulevard Montmartre, www.grevin.com ☎ 01 47 70 85 05 ◷ Mon–Fri 10am–6.30pm, Sat–Sun 10am–7pm € charge Ⓜ Grands Boulevards

Heading westwards, the first place of interest, especially if you have kids in tow, is Paris's venerable wax museum. It's full of cheerfully incompatible figures – from Marie-Antoinette and Gandhi to virtual heroine Lara Croft, Elton John and of course national football hero Zinédine Zidane – and a hall of mirrors. The lavish decor of this century-old establishment is a confection of Venetian Rococo, rosewood and marble, and the staircase by Rives is an architectural gem.

To the left of the Grévin is the **Passage Jouffroy**, with a shop selling cinema books (many in English and/or out of print) and memorabilia, antique silver and the old-fashioned, affordable Hôtel Chopin. Next door is the soothing **Café Zephyr**, one of few cafés with style on the Grands Boulevards.

RIGHT: Art Deco atmosphere at Drouant restaurant. **BELOW:** the opulent Opéra Garnier.

Recommended Restaurants, Bars & Cafés on pages 154–5

Across the busy boulevard is the **Passage des Panoramas** ⓯, one of the earliest of the covered arcades. It was opened in 1800 on the site of a former aristocratic mansion, and Parisians flocked here to see the giant painted panoramas of different cities that were exhibited in two great rotundas. The shop **Stern Graveur** has been engraving fine notepaper and wedding invitations since 1840; other shops sell lingerie, floaty clothes, vintage vinyl and old postcards, but above all this *passage* is a haven for philatelists, with half a dozen specialist stamp dealers.

La Bourse ⓰

place de la Bourse, www.euronext.com 01 49 27 55 55 guided tours Mon–Fri, call to book charge Bourse

Emerging from the arcades, head south to Paris's imposing stock exchange, also known as **Palais Brongniart** after its architect Alexandre Brongniart. Built in 1808, the grand colonnaded building is one of the most distinctive neoclassical constructions of the Napoleonic era.

Rue du Quatre-Septembre leads from here to Place de l'Opéra. This broad square is lined by elegant shops, luxury hotels and cafés, notably **Café de la Paix**, where you can join the chic clientele enjoying coffee and croissants, or a glass of wine and oysters later in the day. Just remember, the prices match the luxurious setting.

Palais Garnier – Opéra National de Paris ⓱

place de l'Opéra, www.operadeparis.fr for visits 08 92 89 90 90 daily 10am–5.30pm, guided tours in English Wed, Sat, Sun 11.30am, 2.30pm charge for guided tours Opéra

Soaring above the square is Paris's celebrated, now fully restored opera house, the Palais Garnier. It is now only part of the Opéra National de Paris with the Opéra Bastille, which has taken charge of larger, more ambitious opera and ballet productions, but the newcomer can never challenge the original "Paris Opera" in the style stakes. In 1860 architect Charles Garnier was commissioned

When it was built, the Palais Garnier was the largest performance venue in the city. It has 1,991 seats, 334 boxes, 1,606 doors, 7,593 keys, 450 fireplaces and 6,319 steps.

BELOW LEFT: detail from Marc Chagall's ceiling at the Opéra.

Egypt-sur-Seine

Place du Caire, in the Sentier garment district – just north of Sentier Métro, up rue d'Aboukir – is one of Paris's curios, off the tourist trail. This was the site of the so-called *Cour des Miracles* in the 1600s, home to beggars who spent their days around the city, apparently disabled, blind or deaf. At night they returned here, and immediately shed their wooden legs and eye patches – hence the "miracles". Not until 1667 did Louis XIV's police chief La Reynie clean up this notorious den of iniquity of all kinds. Today the square is notable for the bustle of multiracial porters lugging rolls of cloth or racks of finished clothes between workshops, as well as its mementoes of Napoleon's campaign in Egypt: the north side is covered with sphinxes and hieroglyphics. In the middle of the panel just below the roofline is the face of a man with an enormous nose – not Gérard Depardieu, but a local 19th-century scoundrel called Bouginier; Hugo mentions him in *Les Misérables*.

Rue St-Honoré, and its even more elegant continuation west of Rue Royale, Rue du Faubourg St-Honoré, form the traditional heartland of Parisian high fashion. St-Honoré, beginning at the Palais Royal, has cutting-edge boutiques as well as big names like John Galliano; the really grand fashion houses (Dior, Laroche, Hermès) are clustered together on Rue du Faubourg. The concentration of chic is just dazzling.

BELOW: the Colonne de la Grande Armée, Place Vendôme.

by Napoleon III to build an opera house for the imperial capital, and his lavish designs were wholly in tune with the pomp and opulence that characterised the Second Empire, creating a style in themselves.

The facade and exterior are covered in sculptures of great composers and allegorical figures representing spirits of music and dance, including voluptuous nudes that caused a scandal when first unveiled. The profusion of marble and gilt inside is almost oppressive in its excess, but the glamour of the Opéra's foyers is undeniable. The grand staircase was conceived by Garnier as the ultimate celebrity catwalk: "Everything is designed so that the parade of spectators become themselves a performance." The five-tiered auditorium, dripping in red velvet and gilt, is dominated by a 6-tonne chandelier, which famously crashed down on the audience during a performance in 1896. The auditorium ceiling was painted by Marc Chagall in 1964, commissioned by André Malraux. The visit also takes in the **library** and **museum**, with scores, portraits, costumes and sets.

Behind the Opéra is the **Musée du Parfum Fragonard** ⓲ (9 rue Scribe, www.fragonard.com; tel: 01 47 42 04 56; Mon–Sat 9am–6pm, Sun until 5pm; charge), a compact museum tracing 5,000 years of perfumery. A heady fragrance permeates the air, in a beautifully restored 19th-century town house. Also nearby across Boulevard des Capucines is the **Théâtre des Capucines** ⓳ (Mon–Sat 9am–5.30pm), where legendary music-hall singer and actress Arletty began her career in the 1930s, and which also has a small museum.

Grands magasins

The area just behind the Opéra, along Boulevard Haussmann, is dominated by the *grands magasins* (department stores). **Galeries Lafayette** and **Au Printemps**, both established in the late 19th century, have remained rivals ever since. Galeries Lafayette is especially famed for its splendid Art Nouveau central hall, topped with a vast stained-glass dome *(see Shopping on pages 56–7)*.

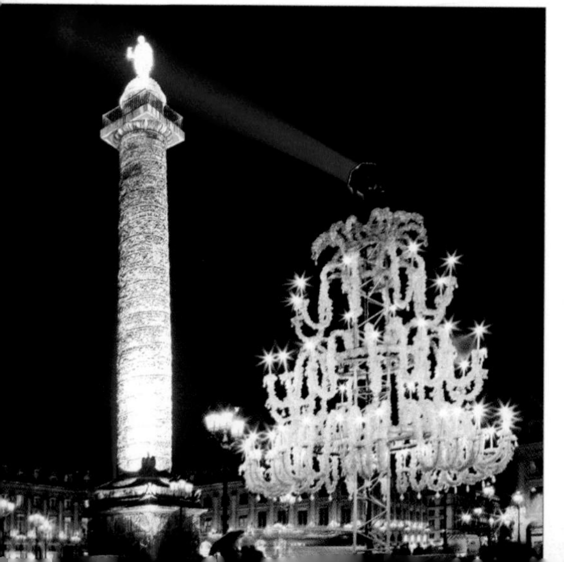

Where Gourmets Gather

The Place de La Madeleine boasts shops devoted to mustard (**Boutique Maille**, No. 6), caviar (**Caviar Kaspia**, No. 17) and truffles (**La Maison de la Truffe**, No. 19), and famous delicatessens, **Hédiard** (No.21) and **Fauchon** (Nos 24–26). Prices and service are usually better elsewhere, but it's still fun to look around. The cheese shop **La Ferme Saint-Hubert**, on one of the square's tributary streets (21 rue Vignon), is famous for its exquisite finely aged cheeses. Across the street is **La Maison du Miel** (No. 24), devoted to honey. **La Maison du Chocolat** (nearby at 8 boulevard de la Madeleine), is one of three outlets for Robert Linxe, the city's most renowned chocolatier.

THE LUXURY QUARTER

One essential side of Paris: the streets and squares southwest of the Opéra are the number-one home of the fine foods, high fashion and exquisite jewellery that have made the city world capital of luxury for two centuries.

Place Vendôme 20

Centre of a grand vista between Palais Garnier and Rue de Rivoli, octagonal Place Vendôme is perhaps the smartest square in Paris. Laid out in 1699 by Colbert to glorify Louis XIV – whose equestrian statue was subsequently replaced in the centre by an imitation of Trajan's Column, glorifying Napoleon's exploits – it is now home to luxury jewellers and designers such as Boucheron, Van Cleef & Arpels, Bulgari, Cartier, Chaumet and Dior. Here, too, are big financial institutions such as the J.P. Morgan merchant bank, and of course the Ritz, at No. 15. The luxury hotel is now most famous as the place where Princess Diana had her last meal before her fatal car crash in August 1997.

Eglise de la Madeleine 21

place de la Madeleine 01 44 51 69 00 daily 9.30am–7pm free Madeleine

From just south of Place Vendôme chic, boutique-laden Rue St-Honoré leads to the church of **Sainte-Marie-de-la-Madeleine**, rising up amidst roaring traffic and expensive shops. This giant neoclassical temple was

It's only natural that the jewellery shops on Place Vendôme should attract the interest of the criminal fraternity. A famous robbery took place in 1970, not in real life but on film: the heist in Jean-Pierre Melville's gangster classic Le Cercle Rouge, *carried out by Alain Delon, Yves Montand and Gian Maria Volontè, is one of the best ever filmed.*

LEFT: the superb Art Nouveau central hall of fashion emporium Galeries Lafayette.
BELOW: the neoclassical Eglise de la Madeleine.

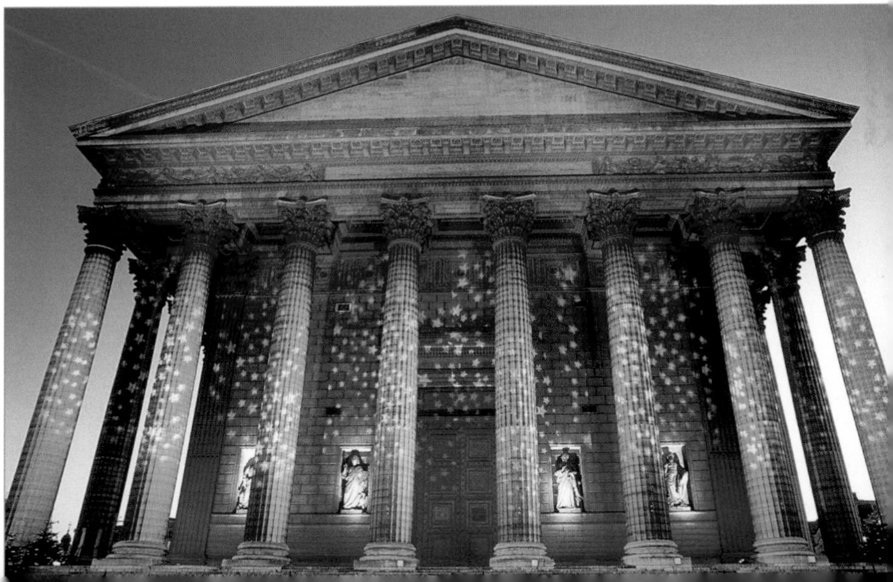

The two fountains designed by German architect Hittorf on the left and right of the obelisk are modelled after those of St Peter's Square in Rome.

commissioned as a self-aggrandising exercise by Napoleon, but more recently has become a favourite venue for celebrity weddings and funerals. In the square around it the mouth-watering displays at food-stores **Fauchon** and **Hédiard** are tourist attractions in their own right.

Place de la Concorde ㉒

Rue Royale runs from La Madeleine to Place de la Concorde, designed for Louis XV by Jacques-Ange Gabriel as a hub of spectacular vistas to north, south, east and west. The square has been the site of many historical events since its completion in 1763, notably the decapitation of Louis XVI by the Revolutionaries in 1793. Majestic in the middle of the traffic chaos, the central obelisk was a gift from the Viceroy of Egypt in 1829; the 3,300-year-old column, weighing 220 tonnes, took four years to reach Paris. On the north side of the square is a pair of grand neoclassical mansions, flanking the Rue Royale: the one on the right is the French Navy Ministry, the other is the opulent Hôtel de Crillon, where Benjamin Franklin signed the Treaty of Friendship between the newly formed United States of America and King Louis XVI in 1778.

The Champs-Elysées ㉓

Initiated by Louis XIV in 1667, the Champs-Elysées was originally laid out by landscape architect Le Nôtre to create a visual extension of the Tuileries gardens running west from the Louvre. The broad avenue, lined with elegant gardens and rows of trees, was continued after the completion of the Arc de Triomphe in 1836. By the 1900s the Champs, in contrast to the rather downmarket Grands Boulevards, had reached a

RIGHT: Ladurée is famed for its *macarons*. **BELOW:** the Champs-Elysées is often referred to as the most beautiful avenue in the world.

Map on pages 116–7

Recommended Restaurants, Bars & Cafés on pages 154–5

zenith of popularity and elegance, attracting stylish and moneyed types from all over the world to linger on its animated café terraces.

The sophisticated spectacle on the avenue evaporated in World War I, but made a brief and giddy comeback during the 1920s. This was followed by the Depression, World War II and, post-war, traffic problems, as the Champs shifted from a luxury address to a commercial one distinguished by cinemas and airline offices in the 1950s, '60s and '70s. By the 1980s it was quite dowdy, with an atmosphere comparable to a tatty shopping mall.

Determined to resurrect the area, Jacques Chirac, then Mayor of Paris, budgeted the equivalent of €75 million to renovate, modernise and beautify the Champs: street parking was replaced by underground car parks; new street furniture was added, including handsome teak benches and retro Art Nouveau newspaper kiosks; dove-grey granite paving stones were laid; and the number of trees doubled. Parisians gave the avenue a second look. A turning point came in 1999 when Ladurée, the venerable Parisian tearoom on Rue Royale, opened a Champs-Elysées branch, at No. 75. Today, the Champs is considered not only elegant again, but a cool place to hang out.

Browsing the Champs

The main shopping stretch of the Champs-Elysées runs from the Rond-Point to the Arc de Triomphe. Landmark stores are the **Virgin Megastore** at Nos 52–60, where you can sample CDs until midnight; **Guerlain** (No. 68), with its Rococo facade and sumptuous interior; the Aladdin's cave of beauty products, **Sephora** (No. 70); and **Louis Vuitton**, at No. 101.

In the last few years a number of swanky concept stores have opened up as well, including one from luxury leather goods purveyor **Lancel** at No. 127, and a couple, bizarrely enough, by carmakers Toyota and Renault. The latter, the **Atelier Renault** at No. 53, features a swish café that serves a good choice of cocktails and light meals and has a fine view of passers-by. There's also a temple to all things beer, **Culture Bière** at

The boutiques on Avenue Montaigne offer the epitomy of Parisian chic.

BELOW: shopping arcade on the Champs-Elysées.

Haussmann's Handiwork

Because they're so often described as "Haussmannian", it's frequently assumed that the buildings that went up in the French capital's mammoth restructuring between 1853 and 1870 were actually designed by Baron Georges-Eugène Haussmann (1809–91) himself. But Haussmann, then Prefect of Paris, was just the project's coordinator; he was not an architect by any means. In a curious twist of fate, his plans entailed the demolition of the building he was born in, to make way for the elegant boulevard that bears his name.

ABOVE: Petit Palais exhibit. **BELOW:** the Petit Palais's ornate Belle Epoque style.

No. 65. Owned by Heineken, this boutique-lounge-restaurant-gallery is innovative and reasonable value: they even do a beer sorbet.

Most of the grander designer outlets are concentrated around Avenue Montaigne and Avenue George V. This is fashion land, where prices for the majority are prohibitive, but window shopping is free. Most of the brands here are established megastars – the likes of Dior, Chanel and Prada – but in the last few years they've been joined by younger, hipper labels **Paul & Joe**, at 2 avenue Montaigne; **Jimmy Choo**, at No. 34; and **Bonpoint**, at No. 49. The Montaigne Market, at No. 57, is the avenue's sole multi-brand emporium, stocking an ever-changing selection in different price brackets.

On Rue François 1er (No. 18) is a de luxe branch of boutique **Zadig & Voltaire**, with limited-edition pieces not found in its other stores. Fashionable bars and restaurants have also mushroomed in the surrounding streets, such as Senso, Tanjia, Spoon and Market *(see pages 154–5)*.

Galeries Nationales du Grand Palais ㉔

✉ 3 avenue du Général Eisenhower, www.grandpalais.fr ☎ 01 44 13 17 17 ⏲ Wed–Mon 10am–10pm, Thur until 8pm € charge 🚇 Champs-Elysées-Clémenceau

Between the Champs and the Seine stands the huge, glass-domed **Grand Palais,** built for the 1900 World Fair, but which for decades has served as

Recommended Restaurants, Bars & Cafés on pages 154–5

central Paris's largest exhibition centre. The building's grand nave closed in 1993 after a metal rivet fell from its roof, but after more than a decade of work it reopened in 2006 as good as new: a glorious Belle Epoque masterpiece of glass and iron, covering a vast open space decorated with Art Nouveau motifs. Since reopening, it has been the venue for all manner of events and activities: DJs, a light installation, a Christmas funfair and fashion shows, as well as several major art exhibitions.

The Grand Palais is also home to the **Palais de la Découverte** (www.palais-decouverte.fr; tel: 01 56 43 20 20; Tue–Sat 9.30am–6pm, Sun 10am–7pm; charge), the city's original science museum. It covers astronomy, biology, chemistry, physics and earth sciences through interactive experiments. Sadly, there's very little labelling in English.

Musée du Petit Palais ㉕

avenue Winston Churchill, www.petitpalais.paris.fr 01 53 43 40 00 Tue–Sun 10am–6pm free Champs-Elysées-Clémenceau

Across Avenue Winston Churchill from the Grand Palais is its smaller neighbour, inspired by the Grand Trianon at Versailles with its polychrome marble, magnificent long gallery and arcaded garden. The Petit Palais houses the municipal collection of fine and decorative arts, and it too reopened in 2006 after being thoroughly refurbished. The renovation work has brought in a lot of extra natural light, which greatly benefits the eclectic collection that lives here. Its main strengths are paintings of the 19th and early 20th centuries, including works by Bonnard,

Since the early 1990s, the Champs-Elysées quarter has been gaining new lustre, now the location for many of the avant-garde, fashionable and spectacular restaurants in Paris.

LEFT: plate from the Petit Palais collection. **BELOW:** Claude Monet's *Soleil couchant sur la Seine à Lavacourt, effet d'hiver*, Petit Palais.

Guarding the Palais de l'Elysée.

BELOW: a giant buddha sculpture inside the Musée Cernuschi.

Cézanne, Courbet and Sisley; but there are also Greek and Roman antiquities, icons, tapestries, ceramics and sculpture, and some fabulous Art Nouveau furniture.

Arc de Triomphe 26

✉ place Charles-de-Gaulle, www.monum.fr ☎ 01 55 37 73 77 ⏲ Apr–Sept daily 10am–11pm, Oct–Mar until 10.30pm € charge 🚇 Charles de Gaulle-Etoile

Crowning the Champs-Elysées is this great memorial to megalomania. The Arc de Triomphe was commissioned by Napoleon in 1806, but the arch, ornately carved with heroic images of Revolutionary battles and the emperor's victories, was not completed until long after his death, in 1836. Napoleon's only chance to pass under it came when his body was triumphantly returned to Paris for reburial in Les Invalides in 1840. Beneath the arch is France's Tomb of the Unknown Soldier, laid to rest in 1920. Since 1923 an eternal flame has been here too, rekindled each evening at 6.30pm with a wreath-laying ceremony. The platform above the arch can be reached via a lift, and offers one of the finest Paris views.

BELLE EPOQUE MANSIONS

Much of the old Paris that was swept away by Haussmann around his Grands Boulevards was replaced by opulent mansions typical of France's Belle Epoque, several of which now house intriguing small museums.

Musée Jacquemart-André 27

✉ 158 boulevard Haussmann, www.musee-jacquemart-andre.com ☎ 01 45 62 11 59 ⏲ daily 10am–6pm € charge 🚇 Miromesnil

This collection of art and furniture once belonged to wealthy collector Edouard André and his wife, erstwhile society portrait painter, Nélie Jacquemart. It includes a small Uccello masterpiece, *St George and the Dragon*, and works by Bellini, Donatello, Rembrandt, Titian, Boucher and David. The house and its ornate decor are also a magnificent example of Belle Epoque taste.

Recommended Restaurants, Bars & Cafés on pages 154–5

Parc Monceau ㉘

daily 7am–8pm, Apr–Oct until 10pm
free Monceau

A 19th-century version of a theme park, with an English-style garden and lake, a fake Egyptian pyramid, Venetian bridge and Greek colonnade.

Musée Nissim de Camondo ㉙

63 rue de Monceau, www.ucad.fr
01 53 89 06 40 Wed–Sun 10am–5.30pm charge Monceau

Overlooking the park, this stately home modelled on the Petit Trianon at Versailles was built for a wealthy Jewish banking family. Its remarkable collection of 18th-century tapestries, porcelain, objets d'art, furniture and paintings was left to the state in 1935 by the passionate collector Count Moïse de Camondo in memory of his son Nissim, killed in action in 1917.

Musée Cernuschi ㉚

7 avenue Velasquez, www.cernuschi.paris.fr 01 53 96 21 50
Tue–Sun 10am–6pm free

One of the most important collections of oriental art in Europe, thanks to financier Henri Cernuschi, who amassed his holdings in China and Japan in 1871–3 and then built this residence beside Parc Monceau to house them. Extensive renovation, completed in 2005, has brought more space and natural light to the army of terracotta tomb figures, bronze vessels, Buddhist statues and fine ceramics. ❑

ABOVE: the spiralling staircase of the Musée Jacquemart-André. **BELOW:** Parc Monceau's Greek colonnade.

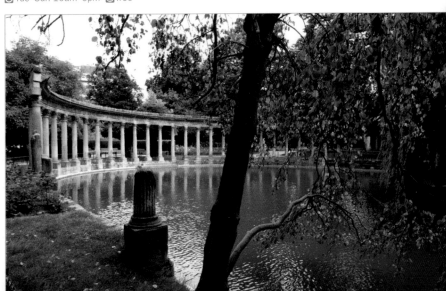

BEST RESTAURANTS, BARS AND CAFÉS

Restaurants

Price includes dinner and a half-bottle of house wine:
€ = under €25
€€ = €25–40
€€€ = €40–60
€€€€ = more than €60

Alain Ducasse au Plaza Athénée

25 avenue Montaigne, 8th 01 53 67 65 00 L Thur–Fri, D Mon–Fri. **€€€€** [p335, C3]
Cooking elevated to art from France's first recipient of six Michelin stars (three apiece for two restaurants), in the hands of his acolyte, Christophe Moret. Expect truffles in abundance, but also superb vegetables from Provence, where Ducasse first made his name. The listed neo-Rococo decor has been rejuvenated with a shower of glittery crystals to match the scintillating cuisine and graceful service. Reservations essential.

Drouant

16–18 place Gaillon, 2nd 01 42 65 15 16 non-stop daily. **€** (Sun brunch), **€€€€** (à la carte) [p336, A4]
This old stalwart has recently had a make-over, and it's now one of the most talked-about places in town. Star Alsace chef Antoine Westermann has revived the humble hors d'oeuvre tradition here, so you can eat the food in more or less any order you feel like, and friendly sharing is encouraged. Dishes include Thai beef salad and a modish deconstructed version of eggs in mayonnaise.

Guy Savoy

18 rue Troyon, 17th 01 43 80 40 61 L Tue–Fri, D Tue–Sat. **€€€€** [p334, B2]
Savoy's imaginative haute cuisine has (belatedly) earned the highest Michelin rating. The son of a gardener, Savoy has an obsession with vegetables that anticipated the recent trend by more than a decade. He doesn't hesitate to pair truffles with lentils or artichokes.

Ladurée – Salon de Thé

16 rue Royale, 8th 01 42 60 21 79. **€** [p334, C2]
This oh-so-civilised tearoom is a true Paris institution and a wonderful place to start the shopping day. World-famous for its melt-in-the-mouth macaroons.

Lavinia

3 boulevard de la Madeleine, 1st 01 42 97 20 27 L Mon–Sat. **€€** [p335, E3]
A restaurant/bar on the first floor of Paris's largest wine emporium. You can drink anything you buy with no corkage fee. The best approach is to order the simpler dishes and select a different glass of wine for each one with a little help from the expert sommeliers.

Aux Lyonnais

32 rue St-Marc, 2nd 01 42 96 65 04 L & D Tue–Fri, D only Sat. **€€€** [p336, B3]
This pretty vintage bistro (opened 1890), with its *banquettes* and Belle Epoque floral tiles, has been transformed by superchef-entrepreneur Alain Ducasse to bring a modernised take on Lyonnais cooking. The iron casserole of slow-cooked seasonal vegetables is a must. Other specialities include crayfish and frogs' legs from the Dombes.

Market

15 avenue Matignon, 8th 01 56 43 40 90 B & L Mon–Fri, D daily, Br Sat–Sun. **€€€** [p335, D3]
Popular contemporary restaurant, run by globe-trotting star chef, Jean-Georges Vongerichten, next to the glamorous new Parisian headquarters of Christie's auctioneers. East-meets-West style preparations and an international crowd against a slick backdrop.

LEFT: bright and breezy Café Le Nôtre, on the Champs-Elysées. **RIGHT:** exquisite display of cakes.

Savy

23 rue Bayard, 8th Tel: 01 47 23 46 98 L & D Mon–Fri. € (set menu), €€€ (à la carte) [p335, C3]
Amid all the fashionable designer haunts around the Champs-Elysées, Savy remains resolutely traditional. The food focuses on the meaty, rustic cuisine of the Auvergne and Aveyron in central France, although excellent fish is brought in daily from Brittany.

Sens: La Compagnie des Comptoirs

23 rue de Ponthieu, 8th Tel: 01 42 25 95 00 L & D daily. €€€ [p335, D3]
Twin brothers X and Y Pourcel, already proprietors of restaurants in Mauritius and Montpellier, have staked a claim in Paris. This is a swish, grey loft-style setting with a menu inspired by French trading posts: dishes include steamed lacquered duck with pumpkin purée or cep cappuccino with a poached egg.

Senso

16 rue de la Trémoille, 8th Tel: 01 56 52 14 14 L & D Mon–Fri, D only Sat. €€€ [p334, C3]
The Conran-designed dining room provides a calm and sophisticated respite from the frenzy of the Champs-Elysées. The summery modern cooking by young Marseille-born chef Frédéric Duca scans Provence and the rest of the Mediterranean in dishes like stuffed squid, chicken tagine and John Dory with courgette flowers. Simpler light meals are also served in the bar.

Spoon, Food & Wine

14 rue du Marignan, 8th Tel: 01 40 76 34 44 Fax: 01 40 76 34 37. L & D Mon–Fri. €€ (set menu) €€€ (à la carte) [p335, C3]
The prototype of Ducasse's mix-and-match global kitchens has spawned half a dozen siblings around the world. You choose a main course of fish or meat and then decide on sauces and side dishes. Desserts are often of American inspiration. The wine list is packed with New World vintages. Book ahead.

Taillevent

15 rue Lamenais, 8th Tel: 01 44 95 15 01 L & D Mon–Fri. €€€ (set menu) €€€€ (à la carte) [p334, C2]
One of the most illustrious haute cuisine restaurants in town (three Michelin stars), but surprisingly unstuffy. The food is magnificent: the earthy signature spelt cooked "like risotto" with bone marrow, black truffle, whipped cream and parmesan is heavenly. Hushed service and one of the world's greatest wine lists. Booking well ahead is, naturally, essential.

Bars and Cafés

Café Jacquemart-André
158 boulevard Haussmann, 8th. Tel: 01 45 62 04 44. Daily 11.45am–5.30pm. [p335, D2]
This sumptuous café pulls in local residents as well as museum-goers. While waiting for your lunch salad to arrive (served with smoked salmon, breast of duck, etc.), look up at the *trompe l'œil* ceiling by Tiepolo, and a gallery of 17th-century faces staring down at you.

Café Le Nôtre
Pavillon Elysée, Carré Marigny, 10 avenue des Champs-Elysées, 8th. Tel: 01 42 65 85 10. B, L and D daily. [p335, D3]
This pretty, wedding-cake-style pavilion in the gardens of the Champs-Elysées offers everything from breakfast to lunch, dinner, tea and snacks. Famous for its pastries.

Café de la Ville
34 boulevard Bonne-Nouvelle, 10th. Tel: 01 48 24 48 09. Non-stop daily. [p336, C3]
The gang behind fashionable Oberkampf Café Charbon have expanded and refurbished their western outpost. The place now has a trendy clubbing area, a lounge and exhibition space. The mood is relaxed and buzzy, drinks are affordable and varied.

Culture Bière
65 avenue des Champs-Elysées, 8th. Tel: 01 42 56 88 88. Non-stop daily. [p335, C3]
It was an unusual pitch: a "beer bar" on the glitzy-again Champs-Elysées. But this innovative boutique-gallery restaurant concept from Heineken is pretty sleek and good value with it. Try the beer sorbet or the crêpes topped with *confit de bière*. Or just have a beer.

The Arc de Triomphe

Built by Napoleon and visited by millions – the Triumphal Arch is the focal point of French national pride

It's the most recognisable Paris landmark after the Eiffel Tower and, in the words of its website, "the most illustrious symbol of French history"; victory parades flowed through it in 1919 and 1944; Victor Hugo lay in state beneath it in 1885. Access for visitors is via an underpass; such is the traffic chaos encircling it at all times that crossing the road would be tantamount to suicide. The roof of the Arc is reached by a narrow staircase or a small lift, and the view from the top, out over Paris in all directions, is simply glorious.

Below: on major national festivities, such as Bastille Day and Armistice Day, an enormous tricolour is flown underneath the main arch.

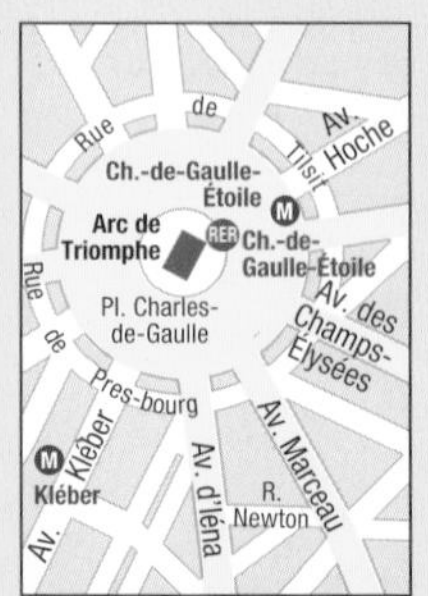

Essential info

Place Charles-de-Gaulle, *www.monum.fr*

01 55 37 73 77

daily 10am–10.30pm, Apr–Sept until 11pm

charge

Charles de Gaulle-Etoile

Above: one of the four main sculptural groups on the exterior base of the Arc, unusual in that its subject matter isn't martial – Peace, created by Antoine Etex in 1815.

ABOVE: carved on the inside of the monument are the names of the generals who fought in the Napoleonic wars.

BELOW: gigantic living doll during the parade staged by Jean-Paul Goude for the bicentenary celebrations of the French Revolution.

STANDING TALL

In conception, the Arc de Triomphe was a typical piece of Napoleonic self-advertisement, intended to honour the military triumphs of his armies. Work began on it in 1809, but it wasn't finished until 27 years later (laying the foundations alone took two years, and work was halted several times) – by which time Napoleon was dead. For all that, the names of his 128 major battles were carved on its sides, along with the names of the 660 generals who took part in them, and the entire structure is richly adorned with sculptures depicting battle scenes and allegories, of which the most famous is Rude's *Le Départ des Volontaires* (also known as *La Marseillaise*). It stands 50 metres (164 ft) tall, set on the axis that runs from the Louvre, through the Arc du Carrousel and out west to the Grande Arche de la Défense.

BELOW: viewed from the air, it's easy to appreciate why the square around the Arc de Triomphe is called L'Etoile ("Star") – no fewer than 12 avenues radiate out from it.

RIGHT: an eternal flame burns above the Tomb of the Unknown Soldier, buried here in 1920 and honoured every Armistice Day.

Recommended Restaurants, Bars & Cafés on pages 172–3

MONTMARTRE

One of the great birthplaces of bohemia, cabaret and modern art, Montmartre threatens to surrender to its own clichés, without ever quite doing so. The maze of steep, narrow streets around the hill still have a unique atmosphere, and even seedy Pigalle has reinvented itself with a new sense of cool

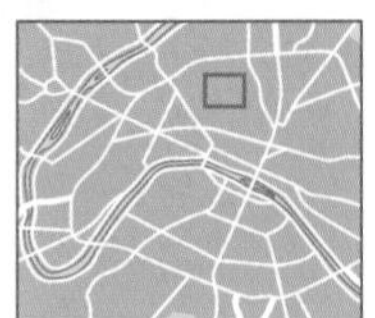

Main attractions
MOULIN ROUGE
PIGALLE
SACRÉ-CŒUR
PLACE DU TERTRE
ESPACE SALVADOR DALÍ
MUSÉE DE MONTMARTRE
AU LAPIN AGILE
CIMETIÈRE DE MONTMARTRE

The "village" of Montmartre occupies the highest point of Paris, nestling on a hillside in the 18th *arrondissement*, north of the city centre. Extending from sometimes seedy yet always vibrant Place Pigalle in the south to the sugar-white cupolas of Sacré-Cœur, this urban village is an alluring huddle of small steep streets and hidden steps.

In parts Montmartre resembles a country hamlet, with ivy-clad cottages and cobbled squares. Elsewhere, neon, fast food, sex shows and tourist buses set the tone. Follow the golf caps up to Place du Tertre, filled with tourist bistros, tatty gift shops and would-be artists, and Montmartre will seem brash and commercial. Enter a narrow side street, veer down a deserted flight of steps and you will be alone, wandering in one of the city's most charismatic quarters.

MONTMARTRE'S BEGINNINGS

Montmartre has always stood slightly apart from the rest of Paris. Legend has it that in AD 250 the Romans decapitated St Denis, first bishop of Paris, and two priests on the hill. St Denis picked up his head and walked off with it to where the Basilica of St-Denis now stands *(see page 265)*. The hill became known as *Mons Martyrium* (Martyrs' Mound). As local bar owners point out, people have been picking their heads out of the gutters of Montmartre ever since.

In the 12th century a Benedictine convent settled on the hill, and 400 years later Henri IV took shelter in it when laying siege to Paris in 1589. His only conquest of the campaign, it appears, was the 17-year-old abbess. The last Mother Superior

LEFT: the Sacré-Cœur offers one of the best views of the French capital.
RIGHT: funky café Un Zèbre à Montmartre, on Rue Lepic.

In the 1920s, Pigalle was taken over by sex-shop owners, pawn-brokers and sleazy hotels. Nowadays, it's still Paris's red-light district, dominated by by tacky strip joints and seedy sex shops.

here was guillotined during the Revolution at the age of 82, despite her deafness and blindness, and the convent buildings were destroyed.

Revolution has been the district's speciality ever since. In 1871, its inhabitants seized 170 cannons to defend themselves after the fall of Paris to the Prussians. The Thiers government sent troops to recapture them, but the generals were overwhelmed, lined up on the hill and shot – so beginning the Paris Commune *(see pages 32–3)*.

For much of the 19th century, Montmartre was mined for gypsum, and retained a country charm with its vineyards, cornfields, flocks of sheep and 40 windmills. This charm and the hill's lofty isolation attracted artists and writers. Painters and their models frequented Place Pigalle, and people flocked to the Moulin Rouge. Impressionism, Fauvism and Cubism were conceived in the lofts, bars and dance halls of Montmartre.

When the bohemians migrated to Montparnasse, Montmartre was left to sex-shop owners, pawnbrokers and cheap hotels, and for many years afterwards it was synonymous with sleaze. Yet today, the village is fashionable once more. Dingy strip bars have been transformed into chic rock clubs and the narrow streets are lined with buzzing cafés, quirky design shops, offbeat second-hand shops and hippy-chic boutiques. A new generation of bohemians is reclaiming Montmartre.

THE CHARMS OF PIGALLE

The traditional gateway to Montmartre, at the foot of the *Butte* or hill, Pigalle is also the place where modern nightlife was invented.

Moulin Rouge ❶

✉ 82 boulevard de Clichy, www.moulinrouge.fr ☎ 01 53 09 82 82 ⏲ shows daily 9pm, 11pm € charge Ⓜ Blanche

Montmartre

1. Rue Poulbot
2. Place du Calvaire
3. Impasse du Tertre
4. Rue Norvins
5. Place Dalida
6. Place Pacqueur

0 – 200 m
0 – 200 yds

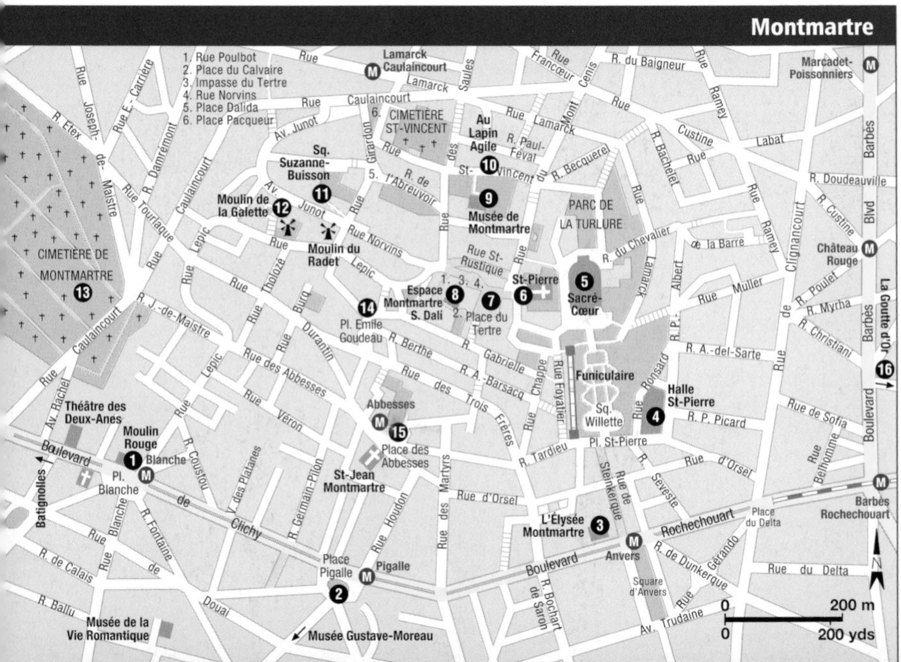

Recommended Restaurants, Bars & Cafés on pages 172–3

The kitschy Moulin Rouge with its signature neon windmill still does a roaring trade as tourists flock to see the high-kicking cabaret girls in feathers strut their stuff. Of all the glitzy Parisian floor shows it is probably the most tame and traditional, but the club's history is gloriously scandalous. Toulouse-Lautrec sat here sketching the working girls' energetic cancan; in 1896, the annual Paris Art School Ball at the Moulin Rouge was the scene of the first all-the-way stripteases, by one of the school's prettiest models. She was arrested and imprisoned, and students went to the barricades in the Quartier Latin, proclaiming "the battle for artistic nudity" – two died in subsequent scuffles with police.

Modern Pigalle

Next door to the Moulin Rouge, teenagers and suburbanites gather at **La Loco**, a huge, train-shaped disco, pumping with house, dance music and mainstream pop. A few doors away at 100 boulevard de Clichy, the **Théâtre des Deux Anes** offers a dose of typical Parisian cabaret.

A little further east along Boulevard de Clichy lies sprawling **Place Pigalle** ❷ itself. Less artistic attractions abound in Pigalle (or "Pig Alley", as it was once known to American soldiers), for this has been the core of the Paris sex trade for decades. In the surrounding streets, tassled curtains provide glimpses of smoky interiors, signs promote live sex shows and aggressive bouncers attempt to entice tourists into "naked extravaganzas". But, Pigalle's reputation has been changing

EAT

Some of the finest breads and most irresistible *pâtisseries* imaginable can be found just south of Pigalle at the shop of Arnaud Delmontel, 39 rue des Martyrs (closed Tue). Specialities include beautifully subtle cinnamon and raisin bread, and fabulous fruit tarts. He has another shop on the north side of the Butte Montmartre at 57 rue Damrémont (closed Mon).

LEFT AND BELOW LEFT: the Moulin Rouge still trades on the image of Toulouse-Lautrec.

Pigalle Nightspots

Popular venues include: **Elysée Montmartre** (72 boulevard Rochechouart), the district's oldest music hall, which has been revitalised as a concert venue and dance club, with one of the best sound systems in Paris; **Folies Pigalle** (11 place Pigalle), a strip club turned hip club, with a Sunday evening gay tea dance; **Le Moloko** (26 rue Fontaine), a hang-out for models, playboys and transvestites; **Le Divan du Monde** (75 rue des Martyrs), another old venue full of memories of the 1890s that's now a cool, relaxed nightclub and music venue with an eclectic programme; **La Cigale** (120 boulevard de Rochechouart), an old vaudeville house built in 1885 that now hosts big-name acts; and the **Bus Palladium** (6 rue Fontaine), an iconic disco hall in the 1960s (Serge Gainsbourg mentioned it in a song, and Dalí, Roman Polanski and the Beatles all hung out here), was refitted and reopened in 2006 with an all-new sound system, and a new programme of live music, club events and even stand-up comedy.

Montmartre's first funicular railway was built in 1900, driven by a water-filled counterweight; the current system, put in place in 1991, is electric. Bus and Métro tickets are valid for the short and dramatic ride up or down the steep slope.

from sleaze centre to trendy nightspot. The cabarets that occupied half the houses on Rue des Martyrs in the 18th century are being taken over by hip clubs – such as **Le Divan du Monde** at No. 75 – and bars.

Nothing symbolises the revival of Pigalle better than the state of the **Elysée Montmartre** ❸. Founded in 1807, rebuilt by Eiffel in 1889, frequented by Lautrec and used to host wrestling and boxing in the 1950s, this historic music and dance hall has been reborn yet again as one of the city's best live rock and club venues, hosting both big names and the up-and-coming. It's worth a visit for the Belle Epoque facade alone.

CLIMBING THE *BUTTE*

The wide esplanade at the foot of the Butte Montmartre, above Anvers Métro, is Square Willette.

Halle St-Pierre ❹

2 rue Ronsard, www.hallesaintpierre.org 01 42 58 72 89 daily 10am–6pm charge Anvers

Just off the square is this former market hall designed by Victor Baltard, the original architect of Les Halles *(see page 108)*, which is now a cultural centre housing a museum of "outsider" and Naïve art. The highly individual works are by artists from over 30 countries, many of them self-taught. Several shops in the area specialise in cheap textiles, which often attract professional designers.

Impossible to miss from Square Willette, overlooking the tide of human activity that ebbs and flows beneath it, is the vast white bulk of the Sacré-Cœur. To reach it, you can either walk up through the square, laid out in terraces in 1929, or take the *funiculaire* (funicular railway – Métro tickets are valid for travel).

Sacré-Cœur ❺

33 rue du Chevalier-de-la-Barre, www.sacre-coeur-montmartre.com 01 53 41 89 00 basilica daily 6am–10.30pm, crypt and dome daily summer 9.30am–7pm, winter 10am–5.30pm charge for crypt and dome Anvers

BELOW: the spectacular view from the tower of the Sacré-Cœur.

This domed basilica was conceived by a group of Catholics in 1871, who vowed to build a church to the Sacred Heart if Paris was delivered from the Prussian siege, and to expiate the sin represented by the atheist Commune, which had begun in Montmartre. The heart of one of the men, Alexandre Legentil, is preserved in a stone urn in the crypt. The Church took responsibility for the project in 1873, and work started two years later. Paul Abadie, the chief architect, based his design on the Romano-Byzantine cathedral of St-Front in Périgueux.

The bone-white colour of the building comes from its Château-Landon stone, which secretes calcite when it rains, bleaching the walls. Its mediocre architecture, added to its symbolic censure of a popular uprising, has made the Sacré-Cœur one of Parisians' least favourite monuments.

Completed in 1914 but not consecrated until after the war in 1919, the dome offers a stunning view over Paris, up 237 spiral steps (the second-highest vantage point over the city, after the Eiffel Tower). From the stained-glass gallery beneath there is a good view of the cavernous interior which, apart from a massive mock-Byzantine mosaic of Christ (1912–22) by Luc Olivier-Merson on the chancel ceiling, has little to offer.

Outside on the terrace, crowds gather in the early evening to drink wine, strum guitars and watch the glittering lights of Paris, overlooked by statues of Joan of Arc and St Louis on horseback.

ABOVE: Aristide Bruant mural in Montmartre.
BELOW LEFT AND RIGHT: the Sacré-Cœur was built in 1876, much later than its architectural style implies.

ABOVE: selling nudes and watercolours on Place du Tertre.
BELOW RIGHT: detail from Renoir's *Le Moulin de la Galette* (1876).

Around the Sacré-Cœur

Next to the Sacré-Cœur, the simple church of **St-Pierre de Montmartre** ❻ is the second-oldest in Paris (after St-Germain-des-Prés, *see page 204)*, dating from 1133, and the only remaining vestige of the Abbey of Montmartre, where the nuns used to live. After the Revolution the church was abandoned, until it was reconsecrated in 1908. If you are here on Toussaint (All Saints' Day – 1 November), visit the small, romantic graveyard behind the church, as this is the only day of the year when it opens.

To the west, **Place du Tertre** ❼ is the tourist trap of Montmartre, laden with kitschy overpriced bistros and craft shops selling junk. The square, once the site of the village hall, now throngs with coachloads of tourists. Artists began exhibiting here in the 19th century, and now there are legions of mediocre (and sometimes aggressively pushy) painters on the square. This oppressive commercialisation makes it a place best avoided by day. It's far more appealing at night, when the square is lit up by fairy lights and retains an animated charm.

Just off the square on place du Tertre, **La Mère Catherine** lays claim to being Paris's first bistro. Originally a revolutionary drinking den (where Danton pronounced the immortal words, "Eat, drink, for tomorrow we shall die"), the story goes that during the Allied occupation of 1814, the old inn greeted Russian soldiers. As they ordered their drinks (forbidden by the Rus-

Salvador Dalí

A true eccentric, Catalan painter Salvador Dalí (1904–89) was desperate to go to Paris in the 1920s, for it was the world's art capital, already conquered by fellow Spaniards Picasso and Joan Miró. After studying art in Madrid and befriending the future film director Luis Buñuel, he reached Paris in 1926. With the help of introductions from the two older Spanish artists, and motivated by his "Catalan sense of fantasy", Dalí held his first Surrealist exhibition the same year. Through Miró, Dalí met other Surrealists, many of whom he was to quarrel with later. Picasso said that Dalí's imagination reminded him of "an outboard motor continually running", and the painter himself wanted to "systematise confusion". As well as painting, Dalí produced films and books, including an autobiography. "Every morning when I wake up," he stated, "I experience an exquisite joy – the joy of being Salvador Dalí – and I ask myself in rapture, 'What wonderful things is this Salvador Dalí going to accomplish today?'"

sian military authorities) they shouted "*bistrot*", meaning "quickly", thereby founding a Paris institution.

Don't be put off by the masses on the square; escaping them is easy. From Place du Tertre, winding Rue Poulbot leads through Place du Calvaire – the smallest square in Paris, with a spectacular view, and a cosy magnet for lovers and drinkers – to another kitschy artistic attraction.

Espace Montmartre Salvador Dalí 8

11 rue Poulbot, www.daliparis.com 01 42 64 40 10 daily 10am–6pm charge Abbesses

Over 330 sculptures and drawings by the Catalan Surrealist painter are exhibited in unusual settings, including his famous clocks, intended to represent "the fluidity of time".

A few minutes' walk to the north, **Rue des Saules** crosses **Rue St-Rustique**, a quiet, rustic street leading away from the buzz of Place du Tertre, which contains the **Auberge de la Bonne Franquette** (tel: 01 42 52 02 42). It was originally called Le Billard en Bois; Vincent Van Gogh and Auguste Renoir both painted here, and the crossroads outside and other street scenes nearby were immortalised by the paintings of Maurice Utrillo. Other frequent visitors to the auberge were Cézanne, Toulouse-Lautrec, Monet, Pissarro and Sisley, and novelist Emile Zola.

OLD MONTMARTRE

The further you move from the Sacré-Cœur and Place du Tertre, the easier it is to get a scent of the days when Montmartre really was just a village.

Musée de Montmartre 9

12 rue Cortot, www.museedemontmartre.fr 01 49 25 89 37 Tue–Sun 11am–6pm charge Lamarck-Caulaincourt

This charming museum chronicles the life and times of Montmartre and the artists' quarter in a 17th-century manor, the oldest house on the *Butte*. It was originally the country home of Rosimund, an actor in Molière's theatre company who

Street artists conjure up quick portraits in the Place du Tertre.

BELOW LEFT: traditional *cartes postales*.
BELOW: street performers check out their competition.

Tranquil Square Suzanne-Buisson is a popular place to play the quintessentially French game of boules.

suffered the exact same fate as his master: in 1686 he died during a performance of *Le Malade Imaginaire*, just as Molière had done 13 years earlier *(see page 130)*. Many artists had studios here, including Renoir, Dufy and Utrillo; the composer Erik Satie (1866–1925) lived in the same street. The museum is an evocation of past simplicity, gaiety and bohemian living, with pictures by Kees van Dongen (1877–1968) and Dufy, Toulouse-Lautrec posters, reconstructions of Utrillo's favourite café, complete with zinc counter top and absinthe bottles, and an artist's studio, with yellowing photographs and a wonderful view over Paris.

Nearby on Rue St-Vincent is Montmartre's famous vineyard, **Le Clos Montmartre**, planted in 1933 in memory of the vines cultivated here since the Middle Ages. In early October, the grape harvest attracts hundreds of volunteers, and the streets host processions and parties. Around 300 litres of wine are sold at auction, with the proceeds going to Montmartre pensioners.

Au Lapin Agile ⑩

22 rue des Saules, www.au-lapin-agile.com 01 46 06 85 87
Tue–Sun 9pm–2am charge
Lamarck-Caulaincourt

Opposite the vineyard stands this legendary cabaret. It was the headquarters of the avant-garde around 1900, a restaurant-cabaret where Renoir and the Symbolist poet Paul Verlaine laid tables, and Guillaume Apollinaire sang with fellow poet Max Jacob. Picasso paid for a day's meals at the Lapin with one of his *Harlequin* paintings – now worth millions. Today a tourist attraction, the smoke-stained inn still has its old wooden tables, original paintings by Gill and Cubist Fernand Léger – and cabaret every evening.

TRANQUIL MONTMARTRE

Far from the helter-skelter animation of Pigalle and Place du Tertre, the west of Montmartre, on the other side of St Vincent cemetery, is a puzzle of little old streets and tumble-down houses. Take the steps from Place Constantin-Pecqueur, off Rue

BELOW: step back in time Chez Eugène.
BELOW RIGHT: Le Clos Montmartre vineyard.

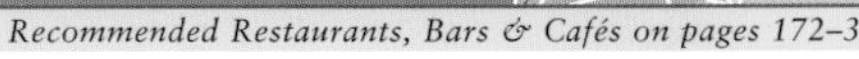
Recommended Restaurants, Bars & Cafés on pages 172–3

Caulaincourt, to **Square Suzanne-Buisson** ⓫, one of the most romantic corners of Montmartre, with a terrace and antiquated lamps. The square occupies the former garden of the Château des Brouillards, an 18th-century folly inhabited at different times by Renoir and the mad poet Gérard de Nerval (who hanged himself in Les Halles in 1855, leaving a note saying, "Don't wait for me, for the night will be black and white"), and which was later turned into a dance hall. During the 19th century, the "château" could only be seen when the *brouillards* (thick fogs) of Montmartre lifted, hence the name. In the middle of the square, a statue of St Denis washes the blood off his head while watching the old men playing *boules*.

Avenue Junot, beside the square, is one of the widest, most expensive streets in Montmartre. Constructed in 1910, the avenue cut through the ancient maquis scrubland that used to cover the hillside, where windmills turned their graceful sails and goats scampered among the trees.

The street's 1920s Art Deco elegance has attracted the cream of Montmartre society – singer Claude Nougaro lived in the big ochre house. **Le Hameau des Artistes** (No. 11) still provides artists' studios. **Maison Tristan Tzara** (No. 15) is named after the eccentric Romanian Dadaist who once lived here, and was designed especially for him by the Austrian architect Adolf Loos.

Below, between Avenue Junot and Rue Lepic, is the last of the great windmills of Montmartre, the **Moulin de la Galette** ⓬. Built in 1604, the mill became an illustrious dance hall

Surreal sculpture of the writer Marcel Aymé (1902–68) in a square named after him in Montmartre. His shorts stories convey a vivid sense of the fantastic.

LEFT: the Place Dalida honours the *chanteuse* who lived in Montmartre. **BELOW LEFT:** the Lapin Agile inn sign.

A Happy Bunny

The tiny Lapin Agile ("Nimble Rabbit") on Rue des Saules is the oldest surviving cabaret from Montmartre's high-kicking heyday. When it first opened in 1855 it was known as the Cabaret des Assassins, according to tradition because a gang of robbers had once broken in and killed the owner's son; but in 1875 it acquired the name it still bears today, when the painter André Gill painted a sign showing a rabbit escaping from a copper saucepan. The word "agile" described the bunny's nifty getaway, but was also a pun on the painter's name: A Gill. By the early 20th century, the cabaret was a popular spot in which painters and artists met and talked; Utrillo depicted it more than once, and Picasso's 1905 painting *Au Lapin Agile* cemented its renown. The fame still holds good: US comedian Steve Martin wrote a successful play, *Picasso at the Lapin Agile*, in the 1990s, and visitors still flock to the Lapin to hear old-fashioned French songs from as far back as the Middle Ages.

Rue des Abbesses is a hub of Montmartre's boho bar scene. Le Sancerre *(see page 173)* bursts at the seams every night; further along is the slightly calmer Le Chinon (No. 49); and the wine shop Caves des Abbesses (No. 43) has a tiny wine bar. Down the hill, La Fourmi *(see page 173)* draws a young arty set, while weekend sunseekers head to the *Butte's* east side for the terrace at L'Eté en Pente Douce (23 rue Muller).

RIGHT: Au Grain de Folie – a rare vegetarian restaurant. **BELOW:** archetypal Parisian café which inspired the film *Amélie*.

in the 19th century. Artists and writers living in Montmartre often hosted parties here, and it was on one such occasion that Auguste Renoir began sketches for his famous painting *Le Moulin de la Galette* (1866). Emile Zola held a party here to celebrate the success of his novel *L'Assommoir* (1877), set in La Goutte d'Or, just to the east. The novelist lived below the village, on Boulevard de Clichy.

Much earlier, in the 1814 siege of Paris, its owners the four Debray brothers had fought fiercely to save their windmill from the Russians – one of them was subsequently crucified on its sails. Today, the windmill is better-protected, as a notice proclaims, "Residence under electronic, radar and guard-dog surveillance".

Picturesque Rue Lepic, leading from the windmill and past the Moulin du Radet, descends to Place Blanche. This old quarry road housed Vincent Van Gogh and his brother Theo, an art dealer, at No. 54 for two years in the late 1880s. During that time Van Gogh is said to have exhibited his paintings at Le Tambourin, a seedy cabaret on Boulevard de Clichy, until the owner demanded that he remove them as they disturbed her customers.

Further down the hill, Rue Lepic turns into a quaint but slightly grubby market street, lined with mouth-watering shops selling pastries and exotic produce. Grab a drink at the picturesque **Le Lux Bar** (No. 12) or **Les Deux Moulins** (No. 15), where Amélie Poulain worked as a waitress in the eponymous movie.

Cimetière de Montmartre ⓭

✉ 20 avenue Rachel ☎ 01 53 42 36 30 🕒 mid-Mar–Oct Mon–Fri 8am–6pm, Sat 8.30am–6pm, Sun 9am–6pm; Nov–mid-Mar closes daily at 5.15pm € free Ⓜ Blanche

Just west of Rue Lepic, the area's artistic bias is reflected in Montmartre's cemetery. The tombs are elegantly sculpted, and their inmates famous: here lie the 19th-century novelists Stendhal and Alexandre Dumas, poet and critic Théophile Gautier, the painter Edgar Degas, the dancer Vaslav Nijinsky, composers Hector Berlioz and Jacques Offenbach, and a bust of Emile Zola (his body was moved to the Panthéon). Film director François Truffaut was also laid to rest here, in 1984.

Heading back into Montmartre, cut left off Rue des Abbesses into Rue Ravignan, for a detour to **Place Emile-Goudeau** ⓮, a particularly attractive square. At No. 13, modern art studios have replaced the wooden ramshackle building called **Le Bateau-Lavoir**, so named because it resembled a floating laundry. This artists' den housed Picasso and fellow Cubists Braque and Van Dongen in its narrow, ship-like corridors. Picasso painted *Les Demoiselles d'Avignon* (1907) in his chaotic studio, recalling the prostitutes of Barcelona, and Apollinaire and Max Jacob liberated verse form in the rooms alongside. Unfortunately, the building burned down in 1970, just as it was about to be renovated.

Turning left out of the square, take the Passage des Abbesses, a little further on, down to pretty **Place des Abbesses** ⓯ and its remarkable Art Nouveau Métro station, designed by Hector Guimard (*see page 171*). Rue des Abbesses is a focus of Montmartre life, with bustling cafés, grocery stores, wine merchants and trendy shops. The trio of streets east of the station – Rue de la Vieuville, Rue Yvonne-le-Tac, Rue des Trois Frères – are lined with designer boutiques, offbeat second-hand shops, little galleries supporting local artists and "boho" bars that are especially lively in the evenings.

AROUND MONTMARTRE

La Goutte d'Or ⓰

To the east of Montmartre is the old working-class district of La Goutte d'Or, centred around Barbès-Rochechouart Métro station. Vividly described by Zola in *L'Assommoir*, the district may still be one of the poorest and most run-down in the city, often marked by a heavy police presence, but it's also one of the liveliest. The conglomeration of Islamic butchers, African grocers, West Indian bakers, Jewish jewellers and Arab tailors is a never-ending spectacle of sight, sound and smell. Over 30 nationalities live in the streets around Rue de la Goutte d'Or and Rue des Poissonniers. Cut-price clothes are sold at the huge flagship store of the Tati chain on Boulevard Rochechouart.

Parisian-born Emile Zola (1840–1902) reveals in his novel L'Assommoir *the poverty and squalor below the glamour of Second Empire Paris.*

BELOW LEFT: Cimetière de Montmartre.
BELOW: Art Nouveau Abbesses station.

Tucked away among the atmospheric streets of La Nouvelle Athènes is a hidden gem. The Musée de la Vie Romantique is a lovely, evocative museum, dedicated to the novelist George Sand and her intellectual circle of friends – Flaubert, Delacroix, Liszt and, of course, her lover Chopin. The museum has a pretty garden, open to the public for tea among the roses and wisteria.

In an attempt to develop the area, the Fédération Française du Prêt à Porter (Ready-to-Wear Association) and the Mairie de Paris have tried to make Rue des Gardes a new centre of fashion. Ten couture boutiques of "emerging talent" have opened in the street (Métro Château-Rouge).

La Nouvelle Athènes

South of Pigalle, this area has been rediscovered in the last few years. In the early 19th century writers, artists and composers, among them Chopin and George Sand, as well as actresses and courtesans came to live here, leading it to be dubbed the "New Athens". Place St-Georges and the exclusive residential streets off Rue des Martyrs give an idea of its grander past, as do two museums: the **Musée Gustave Moreau** (14 rue de La Rochefoucauld, www.musee-moreau.fr; tel: 01 48 74 38 50; Wed–Mon 10am–12.45pm and 2–5.15pm; charge), which overflows with fantastical paintings and drawings that the Symbolist painter left to the state, and the **Musée de la Vie Romantique** (16 rue Chaptal; www.paris.fr/musees; tel: 01 55 31 95 67; Tue–Sun 10am–6pm; charge; *see margin left*).

RIGHT: purchases from bargain Montmartre institution, Tati.
BELOW: typical Montmartre stairway.

Rue Clauzel is an enclave of retro clothing outlets, bric-a-brac and boho clothes shops, while the lower half of Rue des Martyrs has several good bakeries and delis.

Batignolles

West of Place de Clichy, this area developed in the 19th century with a very different atmosphere from that of the grand mansions and apartment blocks in the western half of the 17th *arrondissement*, around Parc Monceau. Sliced through by huge railway depots, it still retains its authentic urban fabric, with old workers' cafés, budget hotels, craft workshops and picturesque alleys and courtyards, but is also being colonised by quirky boutiques and arty bistros. Two of the unusual boutiques in Batignolles are doll maker **L'Atelier de Maître** (8 rue Brochant) and **Buteux** (10 rue Brochant), a fine wig maker who specialises in work for the theatre, but rents out hairpieces for all occasions.

Square des Batignolles was once an empty space, where the Fêtes des Batignolles were held. Transformed in 1862 into Napoleon III's idea of a London park, it still has its 19th-century chalets, kiosks, glass-enclosed lookout and miniature river and waterfall. Black swans cruise its little lake. Towards the *Périphérique*, a great swathe of former railway land is being made into an all-new park, the **Parc Clichy-Batignolles**. ❑

Recommended Restaurants, Bars & Cafés on pages 172–3

The Métro

Wandering through white-tiled tunnels following *Correspondance* signs is as essential a part of the Parisian experience as strolling the squares and boulevards

Deep beneath the streets of Paris is another city, with its own shops, cafés, market stalls, hairdressers, banking facilities, musicians, artists, beggars and pickpockets, even its own police force and its own microclimate. Temperatures here occasionally exceed 30°C (86°F), while wind speeds through the tunnels can reach up to 40 km (25 miles) per hour.

In Luc Besson's 1985 thriller, *Subway*, audiences had a glimpse of this surreal world and the characters who make the Métro their home. In real life, every night around 1,000 people take refuge underground, most because they have nowhere else to go.

Construction of the Paris Métro began in 1898. The first line, 10.3 km (6.4 miles) long, between Porte de Vincennes and Porte Maillot, opened on 19 July 1900. Since then the Métro has extended in every direction, and is hailed as one of the world's cheapest and most efficient underground rail systems, carrying 3½ million passengers daily on over 200 km (124 miles) of track to 370 stations on 14 Métro, five RER and two railway lines.

The massive station at Châtelet-Les Halles is the hub of the network. Five Métro lines and three RER lines meet here, disgorging millions daily into its labyrinth of corridors. As you search this nightmarish warren for an exit, you may wonder if you'll ever come up for air. Trudging the Métro's 75 km (47 miles) of corridors, it seems unsurprising that the Parisian's average body weight is among the lowest in the industrialised world.

At no point in the city are you further than 500 metres (550 yds) from a Métro station. Some station entrances retain their elegant Art Nouveau features, designed by architect Hector Guimard, characterised by soft flowing lines and motifs evoking the growth of plants. Two that are still covered by his beautiful iron-and-glass pavilions are at Porte Dauphine and Abbesses.

Underground, walls are mostly covered in white tiles, apart from a few stations such as St-Michel, with a mosaic ceiling, and Bastille, with scenes from the Revolution.

In an attempt to make commuting slightly more bearable, the RATP (which runs the Métro and city buses) organises a variety of cultural events, from photography exhibitions to fashion shows, classical concerts to puppet theatre. Less organised but equally ubiquitous are the train-hopping buskers and beggars, hoping to profit from a captive audience – it's calculated that the average Parisian spends a year and four months of his or her life below ground. ❑

ABOVE AND RIGHT: the reliable Parisian Métro.

BEST RESTAURANTS, BARS AND CAFÉS

Restaurants

Price includes dinner and a half-bottle of house wine:
€ = under €25
€€ = €25–40
€€€ = €40–60
€€€€ = more than €60

L'Auberge du Clou

30 avenue Trudaine, 9th
☎ 01 48 78 22 48 ⊙ L & D daily. **€€** (set menu), **€€€** (à la carte) [p336, B2]

This cosy *auberge* is particularly lovely in winter when a log fire crackles upstairs. But there's nothing old-fashioned about the imaginative cooking. A la carte, spices and Asian influences complement French ingredients. Choose between the lamb tartare, shrimp beignets or spicy langoustines with pineapple. The set menus are more conventional. Tables outdoors in summer. No credit cards.

Le Bouclard

1 rue Cavallotti, 18th
☎ 01 45 22 60 01 ⊙ L Tue–Fri, D Mon–Sat. **€€** [p336, A1]

Everything here is still cooked *façon grand-mère*, from the macaroni with foie gras to the braised chicken with tarragon and vanilla. Among the delicious desserts: chocolate fondant cake and warm pie with pears.

Casa Olympe

48 rue St-Georges, 9th.
☎ 01 42 85 26 01 ⊙ L & D Mon–Fri. **€€** [p336, B2]

Olympe Versini is one of Paris's best-known female chefs. Her fixed-price menus are a culinary bargain, and the house speciality is oven-roasted lamb shoulder, served with potatoes, tomatoes and garlic. Unusually for a simple bistro, an original selection of (affordable) wines by the glass are offered for each course.

Chez Jean

8 rue St-Lazare, 9th ☎ 01 48 78 62 73 ⊙ L & D Mon–Fri. **€€** (set menu), **€€€** (à la carte) [p336, B2]

This popular brasserie boasts a lovely, high-ceilinged dining room, a high staff-to-diners ratio and a set menu that's excellent value. The slow-cooked farmhouse pork with apricot chutney is a stand-out dish, as are the cherries soaked in eau-de-vie and the melting chocolate *cannelé* come dessert time.

Chez Michel

10 rue de Belzunce, 10th.
☎ 01 44 53 06 20 ⊙ D Mon, L & D Tue–Fri. **€€** (set menu) **€€€** (à la carte) [p337, C2]

One of the flag bearers of the wave of small, excellent regional restaurants that's been spreading across Paris in the last decade. Chef-proprietor Thierry Breton (from Brittany, of course) does fine, hearty food like marinated salmon

with purple potatoes and rabbit braised with rosemary and Swiss chard. Blackboard specials, at extra cost, follow the seasons. The desserts are equally fabulous; choose from the St-Honoré or the typical – and perfect *far breton*. Booking recommended.

Chez Toinette

20 rue Germain-Pilon, 18th. 01 42 54 44 36 D Mon–Sat. **€€** (set menu), **€€€** (à la carte) [p336, B1]

Where many places in this part of town shamelessly fob off the unwitting tourist with overpriced fare, this amiable bistro has a good and good-value blackboard menu that might run to steaks, wild boar terrine, a lovely warm goat's cheese salad and prunes soaked in armagnac.

La Famille

41 rue des Trois-Frères, 18th. 01 42 52 11 12 D only Tue–Sat. **€€** [p336, B1]

A recent addition to the Montmartre restaurant scene, La Famille has immediately become one of the hippest. The interior is tastefully simple (powdery white walls and graceful, suspended lampshades) – a clean canvas on which to show off exciting creations such as raw shrimps served with passion fruit, pan-fried tuna with grilled polenta, and pink grapefruit sorbet.

Au Grain de Folie

24 rue La Vieuville, 18th. 01 42 58 15 57 L & D daily. **€** [p336, B1]

Self-named "a vegetarian place for non-vegetarians", this is a quaint spot for a healthy bite on your way to the *Butte*. It feels like the cluttered kitchen of an organic French farm. Sit at a gingham-covered table and enjoy a bowl of home-made soup, a crispy vegetable platter or a slice of savoury tart. Doesn't accept credit cards.

LEFT: ethnic food offers a vegetarian alternative.
ABOVE: regional salads are often served as mains.

Pétrelle

34 rue Pétrelle, 9th 01 42 82 11 02. D Tue–Sat. **€€** (set menu) [p336, C2]

The no-choice set menu served at this haute cuisine restaurant is a stunning bargain – perhaps marinated sardines and tomato relish, rosemary-scented rabbit and poached figs – but that doesn't mean you should ignore the carte, which brings on tournedos Rossini or, in winter, various game dishes. The place is very popular with designers and movie actors.

Le Relais Gascon

6 rue des Abbesses, 18th. 01 42 58 58 22. L & D daily. **€** [p336, B1]

This busy, good-value, bistro is a fine choice when you're on a Montmartre walkabout. Their speciality is a *salade géante* served in a big earthenware bowl. Note that the place fills up quickly at weekends.

Bars and Cafés

L'Etoile de Montmartre

26 rue Duhesme, 18th. Tel: 01 46 06 11 65. Daily 7.30am–2am. [p336 A1]

Café *à la française* and genuine Montmartre charm are to be found in this archetypal Parisian restaurant with friendly staff. A classic hang-out for Parisians living in the heart of the 18th arrondissement. The epitome of a local neighbourhood café.

La Fourmi

74 rue des Martyrs, 18th. Tel: 01 42 64 70 35. Non-stop daily. [p336, B1]

This retro-industrial bar was once a bistro, now given a modish modern make-over. The big windows pour light into the sand-coloured interior, and the attractive zinc bar counter is lit by industrial lamps. They play good music, and the piles of flyers for local gigs and club nights make it a good source of nightlife tips.

Le Sancerre

35 rue des Abbesses, 18th. Tel: 01 42 58 08 20. Non-stop daily. [p336, B1]

Le Sancerre is one of the cornerstones of the Montmartre bar scene. The terrace is always packed, the music (sometimes live) always loud, the crowd largely young, hip, arty and eclectic. There's a good choice of beers, wines and the standard cocktails; food-wise, there are decent salads and a variety of daily specials. Pavement chairs allow you to enjoy the scene.

CABARET LIFE

Cabaret used to be high kicks, frou-frou and unbridled revelry; today, it's high kicks, sequins, tasteful nudity and good behaviour

It wasn't until the Revolution that costumed masquerades and dancing became a democratic phenomenon; previously they'd been confined to the powdered world of the aristocracy. But by the 19th century, every stratum of Paris society had its *bals*, *café-concerts* and cabarets, though the different classes stuck to separate parts of the city: the chic crowd frequented establishments on the Grands Boulevards and Champs-Elysées, while the bohemians and lower classes whooped it up in Montparnasse. Another populist hotspot, especially in the 1890s, was the hill of Montmartre, with iconic cabarets Le Moulin Rouge, Le Chat Noir and Au Lapin Agile *(see page 167)*. Cabaret's heyday didn't last beyond the 1920s, and today's surviving examples are too expensive to qualify as populist entertainment, their tightly choreographed routines only occasionally catching the atmosphere of yesteryear. Still, they're good fun: the best are Le Lido *(see page 296)* and Le Moulin Rouge *(see pages 160–1)*.

ABOVE: modern cabaret costumes, like this one at the Folies Bergère, are much more scanty than their 19th-century counterparts. Could this be why the tickets are so much pricier?

TOP LEFT: the iconic Mistinguett performed her risqué routines at the Folies Bergère, the Moulin Rouge and Eldorado.

LEFT: the short-lived Montmartre cabaret Le Divan Japonais is still remembered today thanks to this poster by Toulouse-Lautrec.

RIGHT: the facade of Le Moulin Rouge, still Pigalle's most recognisable landmark and still going strong.

ABOVE: the Belle Epoque cabarets of Montmartre were especially popular with the writers and artists of the day – figures such as Pierre-Auguste Renoir, who painted this famous view of revellers at the Moulin de la Galette.

ABOVE: Aristide Bruant, shown on this advertisement by Toulouse-Lautrec, was an entertainer who flourished in the Montmartre cabarets: his act was largely song, with some comedy thrown in. He later became a cabaret owner.

HIGH KICK HIGHLIGHTS

Cabaret wouldn't be cabaret without its dancers – female dancers, that is. The first cancan performers were often part-time courtesans, but the leading lights of cabaret's Belle Epoque heyday – figures such as La Goulue and Jane Avril (shown in the centre of the poster, left; on stage is the singer Yvette Guilbert, recognisable by her black gloves) – were purely entertainers. Avril and La Goulue were huge stars and made a lot of money, though La Goulue lost hers in unlucky business ventures. Another hugely popular dancer in later years was Josephine Baker (right), a Missouri dancer who made her Paris premiere in 1925 and wowed the capital with her frenetic dancing and the briefest of costumes: a skirt made of bananas and little else. Soon she was a fixture at the Folies Bergère and one of the most popular entertainers in France; Hemingway described her as "the most sensational woman anyone ever saw". Baker recorded the iconic Paris song "J'ai deux amours" in 1931.

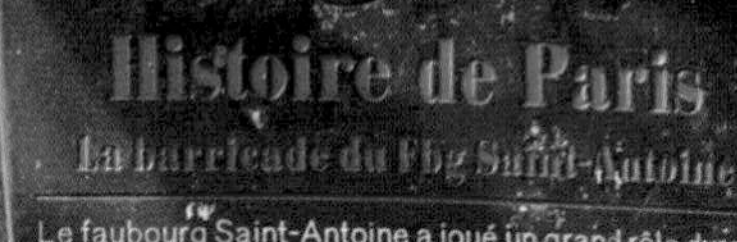
Histoire de Paris
La barricade du Fbg Saint-Antoine
Le faubourg Saint-Antoine a joué un grand rôle durant les révolutions de 1789, de juillet 1830 et de février 1848. Par trois fois, ses artisans et ouvriers ont contribué à la chute de la monarchie. L'insurrection de juin 1848 a été décrite par Victor Hugo dans "les Misérables", notamment l'énorme barricade élevée à l'entrée des rues de Charenton et du Faubourg-Saint-Antoine. Près d'elle furent abattus, le 25 juin 1848, le général Négrier et l'archevêque de Paris, Mgr Affre, venu
parlementer. Le 26 juin, à dix heures du matin, le général Lamoricière la fit tomber, mais, pour en finir avec la révolte ouvrière, ses troupes durent encore enlever une à une les 65 barricades échelonnées dans la rue du Faubourg-Saint-Antoine entre les places de la Bastille et de la Nation.

Recommended Restaurants, Bars & Cafés on pages 186–7

BASTILLE AND EAST PARIS

St-Germain and Montmartre may have the fame, but the tree-lined avenues, grungy alleyways, canalside walks and bohemian-chic streets east from the Bastille form one of the most vibrant parts of the modern, multicultural city

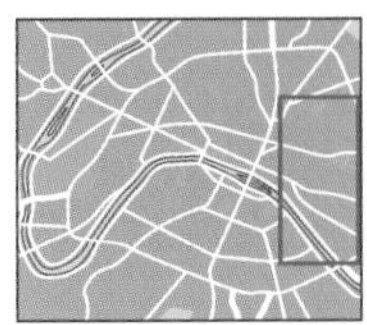

Main attractions

- PLACE DE LA BASTILLE
- OPÉRA BASTILLE
- OBERKAMPF
- CANAL ST-MARTIN
- CIMETIÈRE DU PÈRE-LACHAISE
- BERCY VILLAGE
- PARC DE BERCY
- CINÉMATHÈQUE FRANÇAISE

Traditionally, Paris has been divided into the Right and Left Banks (north and south), but these days the division between the east and west is more marked. The eastern side of Paris has long been associated with the workers and – unsurprisingly – social rebellion, beginning with that most famous revolutionary act of them all, the storming of the Bastille. This was the heartland of the Paris Commune, and today trade unions still begin their May Day marches and other big demonstrations at Place de la Bastille.

Architecturally, the east of the city suffered under the reforming drive of the 1960s and 1970s. However, it is the tantalising whiff of a less salubrious past, of a grittier, less conventional Paris, that makes the most appealing areas in the east – namely Bastille, Oberkampf and, to a lesser extent, République – intriguing alternatives to the bourgeois conservatism prevailing in the western *arrondissements*. The east is certainly very run-down in parts, but however much sophistication and glamour may be lacking, creativity and youthful energy abound.

LEFT: Faubourg St-Antoine played an important role in the French Revolution.
RIGHT: permanent fixture at the bar of Le Kitch, in the hip Oberkampf quarter.

QUARTIER DE LA BASTILLE

Once a fearsome symbol of royal strength, the Bastille and its surroundings fell into disrepair after the prison was destroyed during the Revolution. On 14 July 1789, when crowds stormed the prison, freeing the inmates – all seven of them – Louis XVI was unimpressed, recording in his diary, "Today – nothing." Following the dismantling of the Bastille, an enterprising workman made sculptures of the prison from the rubble and sold them to local councils, who

In Place de la Bastille, be sure to look down at the pavement: marked in the paving slabs – wherever possible, between the multiple lanes of cars – is the outline of the old fortress, demolished within five months of its storming in July 1789.

were denounced as anti-Republican if they refused the price demanded.

The medieval Bastille covered present-day **Place de la Bastille** ❶ and the Arsenal to the south, at the junction of the Seine and Canal St-Martin. The modern square is a wide, busy traffic hub, with the Colonne de Juillet in the middle. The tall column was erected to commemorate the victims of the 1830 and 1848 revolutions, who are buried underneath it.

Opéra National de Paris – Bastille ❷

box office 130 rue de Lyon, www.operadeparis.fr 08 92 89 90 90 guided tours, days and times vary, tel: 01 40 01 19 70 charge for tours Bastille

Dominating the square, this giant structure is now Paris's primary venue for opera and ballet, having taken over pride of place from its opulent predecessor the Palais Garnier *(see page 145)*. Ever since it was opened by Mitterrand in 1989, the "new" opera has been the subject of much polemic from politicians, critics,

musicians and public alike. Aside from its appearance (half a goldfish bowl attached to a black triumphal arch), the opera house is actually coming apart, and nets are in place to keep the concrete tiles on its outer walls from falling on people's heads.

The district to the east has changed enormously over the past 20 years. Old crumbling streets have been gentrified, and old crumbling inhabitants have moved out. Some of the rebellious charm remains in streets

RIGHT: art for sale on Boulevard Richard-Lenoir. **BELOW:** the modern Opéra Bastille. **BELOW RIGHT:** busy Place de la Bastille.

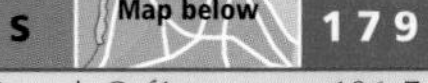

Recommended Restaurants, Bars & Cafés on pages 186–7

such as Rue de Lappe and Rue de Charonne, but the influx of the upwardly mobile has led to an epidemic of dimly lit bistro-bars. Designer boutiques and trendy cafés have sprouted up, particularly on Rues Keller, Charonne and de Lappe, and clothes shops have replaced many of the furniture stores on Faubourg-St-Antoine. Rue de la Roquette is a buzzing nightlife centre.

Le Balajo and **La Chapelle des Lombards** are two Latin clubs on Rue de Lappe that attract a mix of local Latinos and tourists. **Théâtre de la Bastille** on Rue de la Roquette (nothing to do with the Opéra, as the tatty decor proves) offers Paris's most challenging dance works.

At 17 rue de la Roquette, **La Rotonde** is a chic bar – a far cry from its past life as a brothel, whose owner was shot dead by a blind accordion player. Off Rue du Faubourg-St-Antoine, you can wander through passages of workshops producing furniture, rugs and jewellery, as they have for centuries. **Passage du Cheval Blanc** leads off from the Bastille, with courtyards named after the months of the year. **Passage de la Main d'Or**, further east, is equally intriguing.

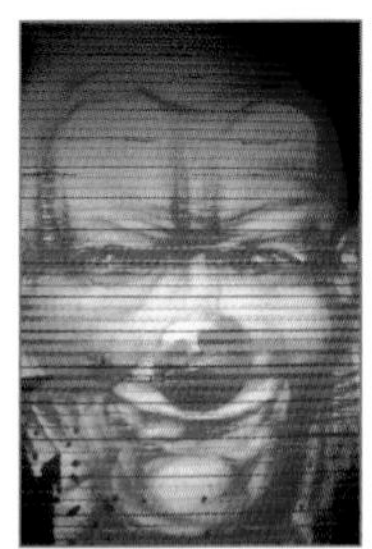

The east of Paris is where you'll find the most eccentric, hip bars and cafés, like the Clown Bar.

Bastille and the East

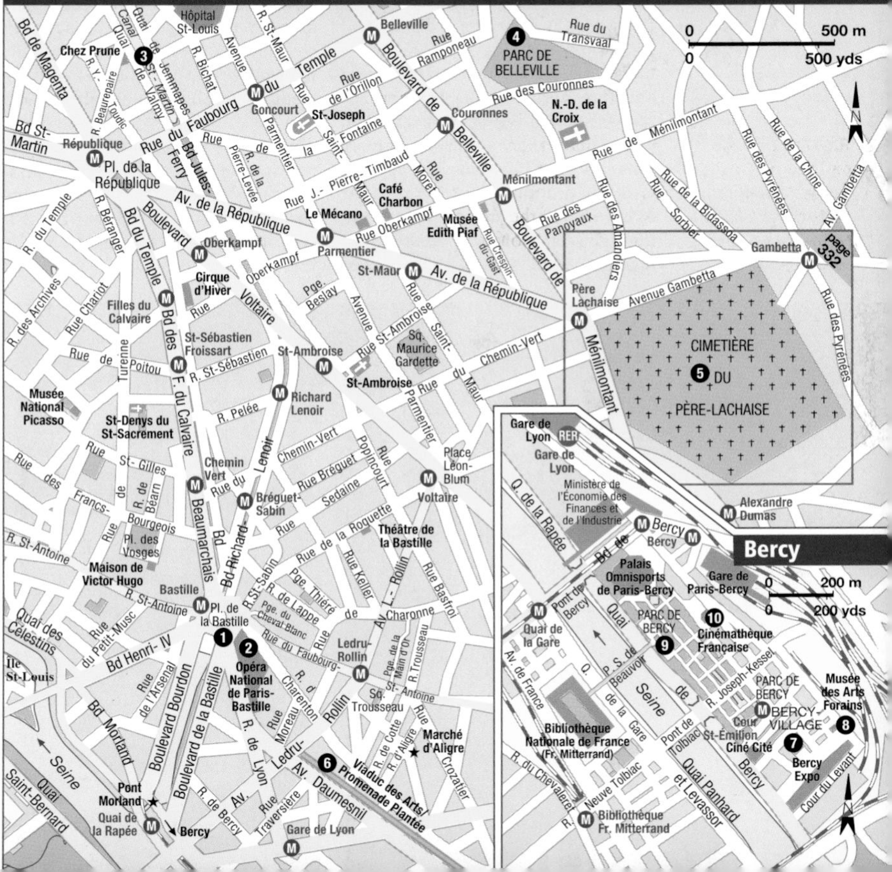

Hôpital St-Louis
Chez Prune
Belleville
Parc de Belleville
Rue du Transvaal
0 500 m
0 500 yds
République
Pl. de la République
Goncourt
St-Joseph
Couronnes
N.-D. de la Croix
Rue de Ménilmontant
Ménilmontant
Café Charbon
Le Mécano
Musée Edith Piaf
Oberkampf
Parmentier
St-Maur
Av. de la République
Gambetta
page 332
Cirque d'Hiver
Filles du Calvaire
Père Lachaise
Avenue Gambetta
St-Sébastien Froissart
St-Ambroise
Sq. Maurice Gardette
Cimetière du Père-Lachaise
Musée National Picasso
St-Denys du St-Sacrement
Richard Lenoir
Chemin Vert
Bréguet-Sabin
Place Léon-Blum
Voltaire
Gare de Lyon
Ministère de l'Économie des Finances et de l'Industrie
Alexandre Dumas
Bercy
Maison de Victor Hugo
Bastille
Pl. de la Bastille
Théâtre de la Bastille
Palais Omnisports de Paris-Bercy
Gare de Paris-Bercy
0 200 m
0 200 yds
Opéra National de Paris-Bastille
Ledru-Rollin
Sq. Trousseau
Marché d'Aligre
Quai de la Gare
Parc de Bercy
Cinémathèque Française
Parc de Bercy
Bercy-Village
Musée des Arts Forains
Cour St-Émilion
Ciné Cité
Bercy Expo
Viaduc des Arts/Promenade Plantée
Bibliothèque Nationale de France (Fr. Mitterrand)
Bibliothèque Fr. Mitterrand
Pont Morland
Quai de la Rapée
Île St-Louis
Seine

On Canal St-Martin is one of the city's foremost alternative cultural venues, Point Ephémère (200 quai de Valmy, tel: 01 40 34 02 48). A 1930s former warehouse, it has been converted into artists' studios, a gig and nightclub venue, music studios, a gallery and a café.

BELOW: friendly barmen at the delightful Bar du Peintre, on Avenue Ledru-Rollin.

OBERKAMPF AND RÉPUBLIQUE

As a rule, Paris is a city that doesn't change that quickly, but recent history has proved Oberkampf the exception. This area just north of Bastille has come a long way from the slums of Edith Piaf's childhood. Even ten years ago this was just another run-down district, but these days it is one of the hippest neighbourhoods in town. Remember, though, this is the east, so we're talking urban rather than glamour. The vanguard may have moved on, but the bars, restaurants and clubs that make it so vibrant still remain.

Rue Oberkampf is the hippest limb of the 11th *arrondissement*, especially at the upper end, east of Avenue de la République, where there's a high concentration of cafés and bars and unusual shops. Look out for trendy bars **Le Mécano** and **Café Charbon**, with its club venue alongside, the **Nouveau Casino**.

If you're looking for some of the old flavour of the area, wander down the side streets off Rue Oberkampf. Rue St-Maur, which crosses Rue Oberkampf, and Rue Jean-Pierre Timbaud are lined with tiny Middle Eastern food stores and cafés.

Canal St-Martin ❸

The Canal St-Martin begins at Pont Morland by the Seine, disappears undergound at Bastille (supposedly to allow troops faster access to subdue potential uprisings), then re-emerges in the 10th *arrondissement* near Place de la République and leads up to Place Stalingrad, before continuing eastwards as the Canal de l'Ourcq through the Parc de la Villette *(see page 246)*. The canal was dug in 1821 as a transport link for the area's factories and warehouses, many of which now house art galleries and small shops.

The canal is shielded by trees, dotted with small squares and crossed by iron bridges. It is a popular strolling and busking ground, particularly on balmy summer evenings. The bend in the canal is where you'll find the trendy **Chez Prune** café *(see page 186)*, and a row of pastel-coloured shopfronts belonging to **Antoine et Lili**. On the opposite bank is the

Recommended Restaurants, Bars & Cafés on pages 186–7

Hôtel du Nord, subject and title of a 1930s French movie classic. The old hotel now hosts anglophone stand-up comedy nights.

With its nine locks, the canal also makes for an attractive boat trip (Paris Canal; tel: 01 42 40 96 97; www.pariscanal.com).

BELLEVILLE AND MÉNILMONTANT

More than 60 nationalities make Belleville the melting pot of Paris. It is gradually becoming gentrified, which adds yet another layer of complexity. There are no major tourist attractions, five-star hotels or three-star restaurants, but it is a fascinating neighbourhood for an off-the-beaten-path excursion. In the 19th century, Belleville was a fertile country village whose springs were tapped to channel water into Paris. There are still a few old stone *regards* left – control stations for the aqueducts, particularly in the little lanes that wind around **Parc de Belleville** ❹.

The park is a terraced crescent of green atop a hill with a panoramic view of Paris. An "air" museum occupies one of the terraces. The **Maison de l'Air** (27 rue Piat; tel: 01 43 28 47 63; Tue–Fri Mar–Oct 1.30–5.30pm, Nov–Feb 1.30–5pm; charge) is an air-measuring station hooked up to a weather satellite, with amazing views over the city. A permanent exhibition demonstrates the alarming levels of air pollution in Paris.

Legend has it that Edith Piaf was born under a lamp-post in the Rue de Belleville, outside No. 72. There is now a plaque over the doorway that claims: "On the steps of this house, on 19 December 1915, was born, in the greatest poverty, Edith Piaf, whose voice would later take the world by storm."

The tiny **Musée Edith Piaf** (5 rue Crespin-du-Gast; tel: 01 43 55 52 72, by appointment only; donations requested), run by some of her true fans, is a touching tribute to the diminutive queen of French *chanson*.

Incorporating part of Rue Oberkampf, the eastern district of **Ménilmontant** is another hotbed of alternative culture. The area is home to a large number of the city's immigrants, forming an ethnic pastiche of cultures. It's not unusual to find a kosher butcher shop, Chinese DVD store and a Turkish snack kiosk on the same corner.

Marcel Carné's classic film Hôtel du Nord *was not filmed on the bank of the Canal St-Martin at all, but in a superb reconstruction of the hotel and the lock in front of it, built by the great set designer Alexandre Trauner in the suburban film studios at Boulogne in southwest Paris.*

LEFT: Belleville-born *chanteuse* Edith Piaf. **BELOW:** Amélie Poulain on a bridge over the Canal St-Martin, from the eponymous international hit movie.

Cimetière du Père-Lachaise 5

boulevard Ménilmontant, www.pere-lachaise.com 01 55 25 82 10 mid-Mar–Oct Mon–Fri 8am–6pm, Sat 8.30am–6pm, Sun 9am–6pm; Nov–mid-Mar closes daily at 5.15pm free Père Lachaise

ABOVE: Père Lachaise is one of the most illustrious resting places in Paris.
BELOW RIGHT: historic-listed restaurant Le Train Bleu.

The great tourist draw in the east is this giant cemetery, an oasis of peace in Paris. The list of famous people buried here reads like a who's who of the city's history – Abélard and Héloïse, Apollinaire, Balzac, Edith Piaf, Oscar Wilde, Molière, Proust, Gertrude Stein, Sarah Bernhardt, Chopin and, of course, Jim Morrison, the cemetery's most visited grave, manned by a stony-faced attendant. You can get a free map at the entrance, or purchase a better one from shops that border the cemetery or sellers by its gates.

The cemetery was the site of the last battle of the Paris Commune *(see pages 32–3)* against the troops of the right-wing Versailles government on 27 May 1871. At dawn the next day, the remaining 147 Communards were lined up against a wall and shot. They were buried in a ditch where they fell, and the **Mur des Fédérés** (Federates' Wall) has become a socialist shrine. Nearby are monuments to both world wars.

SOUTH OF THE BASTILLE

The area south of Place de la Bastille has become a potent symbol of urban regeneration in the 21st century. A disused railway viaduct and dilapidated wine-warehouse district have been brought back to life, and are now thriving commercial and recreational centres.

Relics of Revolution

Père Lachaise is atmospheric, tranquil, and packed with the mortal remains of the great and good. But a little to the south is another graveyard that's much less known, yet just (in its way) as interesting: the **Cimetière de Picpus** (35 rue de Picpus, 12th; tel: 01 43 44 18 54; Métro Picpus). It's part of a still functioning convent, and houses the bones of thousands guillotined in the Revolutionary years: 1,298 of 1,306 people executed in nearby Place du Trône (now Place de l'Ile-de-la-Réunion) in July 1794 are here. Off a lovely walled garden is "the cemetery of nobility", with family plots belonging to the Chateaubriands, La Fayettes, Montalamberts, Crillons, La Rochefoucaulds and more. There are also two mass graves, discovered in 1929, in one of which are the bones of the poet André Chénier. As you walk around, you may pass nuns in white lace bonnets – and feel as if Paris is very far away.

Recommended Restaurants, Bars & Cafés on pages 186–7

Viaduc des Arts ❻

15–121 avenue Daumesnil, www.viaducdesarts.fr 01 44 75 80 66 Gare de Lyon

Built in 1859, during the golden age of the railways, the Viaduc de Paris supported a railway that ran from Bastille to the Bois de Vincennes, at a time when the area between Gare de Lyon and Bastille was a thriving den of artisan workshops. But, as the railways declined in the 20th century, the viaduct fell into disrepair. Thankfully, it was saved from demolition, and reopened in 1998 as the Viaduc des Arts. The arches beneath the viaduct have been converted into glass-fronted *ateliers* (workshops) and craft boutiques. The diversity of creativity here is impressive, and from the street you can watch furniture makers, upholsterers, dress- and jewellery designers and painters all at work.

After exploring the shops under the viaduct you can take one of the city's most unusual walks along the former tracks on top, all the way across the south of the Bastille quarter. The railway tracks have been replaced by the **Promenade Plantée**, a leafy walkway planted with herbs and roses that provides a welcome green breathing space amongst the urban regeneration. Stretching for some 4 km (2½ miles) along the viaduct, and continuing at ground level through the Jardin de Reuilly and eastwards to the Bois de Vincennes, the promenade is accessible via staircases from the street.

FOOD

The Marché d'Aligre (Rue d'Aligre, Tue–Sun until 1pm) is one of Paris's best and cheapest open-air food markets. Sharing the same square at the end of the street, the covered market hall the Marché Beauveau (Place d'Aligre, Tue–Sun 8am–1pm and 4–7pm) sells a wealth of oysters, foie gras, cheeses and, in season, wild boar and venison.

LEFT: designers at work under the arches of the Viaduc des Arts.
BELOW: France's revered screen couple, Yves Montand and Simone Signoret, are buried in Père Lachaise.

Cruises along the Canal de l'Ourcq to La Villette leave from the Quai de la Loire, parallel to the Bassin de La Villette, and are organised by Canauxrama (13 quai de la Loire; tel: 01 42 39 15 00; www.canauxrama.com) and Paris Canal *(see page 181).*

RIGHT: shops on the cobbled streets of Bercy Village. **BELOW:** students in Parc de Bercy.

Wandering among the rose bushes today, it's hard to imagine the thunder of steam trains chugging their way to the Bois de Vincennes. It makes a very pleasant walk and an excellent way to see the city from a completely different angle.

BERCY

For centuries, wine was brought to Paris by boat from Burgundy to the river port of Bercy. Today, it's Paris's newest neighbourhood. The city is busy reclaiming the old river port, while creating a "new" Left Bank across the river, around the glass towers of the National Library *(see page 214)*. A fully automated, driverless "Meteor" Métro line was opened in 1998 (line 14, the first new Métro line since 1935), linking both areas to central Paris (stops at Bercy and Cour St-Emilion for the park and village, and Bibliothèque François Mitterrand for the New Left Bank; line 6 also goes to Bercy and Quai de la Gare on the Left Bank). The two areas were linked in 2006 by a new footbridge, the elegant **Passerelle Simone de Beauvoir**.

Old stone-walled warehouses and cobbled streets have been given a new lease of life in the shape of **Bercy Village** ❼ (www.bercyvillage.com). The car-free village, centred on the cobbled Cour St-Emilion, is full of boutiques, restaurants and cafés. Parisians visit its Club Med complex to enjoy a themed meal or drink designed to inspire them to book a holiday. The futuristic UGC Ciné Cité is Paris's biggest multiplex cinema, with 18 screens showing both mainstream and arthouse films, usually in their original language with French subtitles.

Musée des Arts Forains ❽

53 avenue des Terroirs de France, www.pavillons-de-bercy.com 01 43 40 16 22 by appointment charge Cour St-Emilion

Another less obvious attraction is this delightful collection of antique fairground attractions. The beautifully crafted carousels, amusement stalls, organs and mechanical figures are displayed in the Pavillons de Bercy, a former wine depot. It's officially only open to groups, but individuals can call ahead to join a group tour.

Recommended Restaurants, Bars & Cafés on pages 186–7

Parc de Bercy ❾

The busy road running down Quai de Bercy is backed by this vast park, graced by centuries-old chestnuts and plane trees. This charming belt of green has nine themed sections, among them Le Jardin Romantique and Le Jardin du Philosophe. The Maison du Jardinage (House of Gardening) is an 18th-century building where green-fingered people share their secrets. The park has a lake filled with water from the Seine, neoclassical ruins and a trio of ornate bridges.

On the north side of the park, the former American Center juts out among the houses and offices around the park. According to architect Frank Gehry, it expresses the spirit of a "younger country with fewer laws and fewer constraints" than Europe. It's now the magnificent and long-awaited new home for the **Cinémathèque Française** ❿ (51 rue de Bercy; www.cinematheque.fr; tel: 01 71 19 33 33; *see below*).

The reclaimed area is also the site of the vast new Ministry of Finance, whose edifice extends out over the Seine as if it were intended to be a bridge. Its architects, Paul Chemetov and Borja Huidobro, claim it is "the monumental entrance which the east of Paris had always lacked".

The neighbouring structure, the **Palais Omnisports de Paris-Bercy**, is a state-of-the-art sports hall seating 17,000 spectators, which offers a varied menu of concerts and sporting events from Thai boxing to opera recitals and reggae festivals. For the current programme, see www.bercy.fr or tel: 01 40 02 60 60. ❑

ABOVE: the pyramid-shaped POPB (Palais Omnisports de Paris-Bercy).

BELOW LEFT: Frank Gehry's cubist building now houses the iconic Cinémathèque Française.

Screens on the Green

Paris loves its cinema, and so loves its cinemas: here you'll find some of the best in the world, with some of the best programming. The big story of recent years has been the reopening in 2006 of its most prestigious picture house, the **Cinémathèque Française**: bigger, more streamlined and more ambitious than ever. Frank Gehry's Cubist building in Bercy went up in 1992 for another customer, but was cleverly re-purposed (a monthly guided tour shows how) to give the CF its fifth home in 70 years. Four screens under one roof replace the previous two under two; there are projectors digital and traditional; a museum, guarded by the robot from *Metropolis*; an exhibition space for temporary shows; and a bookshop and restaurant. The feel is light, airy and inviting, and the parkside location is lovely.

Though the setting is spacious, the programme barely fits into the quarterly 112-page booklet. There are retrospectives of filmmakers contemporary, vintage, underprized and forgotten, themed seasons, B-movie strands, kids' screenings, a new emphasis on art and avant-garde cinema, shorts, even dance films… and a lively programme of conferences, talks and classes. A truly inspiring place.

BEST RESTAURANTS, BARS AND CAFÉS

Restaurants

Price includes dinner and a half-bottle of house wine:
€ = under €25
€€ = €25–40
€€€ = €40–60
€€€€ = more than €60

Astier

44 rue Jean-Pierre Timbaud ☎ 01 43 57 16 35 ⓒ L & D daily. **€€** [p337, E4]
A traditional, well-known bistro in the north of Paris. Home cooking with an inventive touch and a few classics, all for a modest price. Try the escargots, beef with morels or chocolate praline pots. Alternatively, test out the famous cheese and wine lists. Booking is advised.

Auberge Pyrénées-Cévennes

106 rue de la Folie-Méricourt, 11th ☎ 01 43 57 33 78 ⓒ L Mon–Fri D Mon–Sat. **€€** [p337, E4]
Bring an appetite for French soul food like *caviar du Puy* (green lentils in vinaigrette) or Lyonnais-style endive salads topped with chunky bacon. The humble *cassoulet* and earthy Sabodet sausage are richly satisfying. Good-value wines from Morgon. For dessert, the tarte tatin takes pride of place.

Bofinger

5 rue Bastille, 4th ☎ 01 42 72 87 82 ⓒ L & D daily. **€€** (set menu) **€€€** (à la carte) [p339, E3]
A classic brasserie that claims to be the oldest in the city, with a stunning Art Nouveau interior. It serves excellent *fruits de mer* and some of the best Alsatian *choucroute* (sauerkraut) in Paris. The more creative dishes can sometimes disappoint.

Chez Prune

71 quai Valmy, 10th ☎ 01 42 41 30 47. ⓒ L & D daily. **€** [p337, D3]
A cornerstone of the Canal St-Martin area. This is one of the best places in Paris to watch the world go by. Good food at lunchtime and tapas-style snacks at night.

Comme Cochons

135 rue de Charenton, 12th ☎ 01 43 42 43 36 ⓒ L & D Mon–Sun. **€** (lunch menu) **€€** (à la carte) [p339, E4]
The big terrace is a great place for people-watching and browsing an honestly priced range of wines. Eat here before or after walking the nearby Promenade Plantée, elevated railway tracks now planted with roses and shrubs.

Crêperie Bretonne Fleurie

67 rue de Charonne, 11th ☎ 01 43 55 62 29 ⓒ L & D Mon–Fri, D Sat. **€** [p339, E3]
For economy and speed, it's hard to beat a crêpe. This authentically Breton spot near Bastille is one of the best places in town for that particular regional staple – served with a choice of fillings that includes ham, cheese, egg, onions and mushrooms. The approved accompaniment is cider; you can have a crêpe for dessert, too, filled with chocolate sauce and ice cream.

L'Encrier

55 rue Traversière, 12th ☎ 01 44 68 08 16 ⓒ L & D Mon–Fri, D Sat. **€** (set menu), **€€** (à la carte) [p339, E3]
One of those cosy restaurants that you dream of stumbling across: amazing value, traditional decor, an open kitchen, bubbly local crowd, cheerful staff and decent food: fried rabbit kidneys on salad dressed with raspberry vinegar, home-made terrine or goose magret with honey. Finish up with the delicious profiteroles. No reservations.

L'Oulette

15 place Lachambeaudie, 12th ☎ 01 40 02 02 12 ⓒ L & D Mon–Fri. **€€€** [p339, E4]
Chef Marcel Baudis is equally at home with creative dishes and traditional fare. The

LEFT: the beautiful interior of the Bofinger brasserie.

fixed-price menu (lunch and dinner) is particularly good value, and during the winter months the exciting *menu des gastronomes* provides the best glimpse of Gascon cooking in the city. Good wine list.

Paris Main d'Or

133 rue du Faubourg-St-Antoine, 11th ☎ 01 44 68 04 68 ⓒ L & D Mon–Sat. **€€€** [p339, E3]

This is an authentic slice of Corsica in Paris. The food displays a characteristic mix of sea and mountain ingredients and centuries of Genoan influence: superb Corsican charcuterie, aubergine baked with ricotta-like brocciu cheese, herby stews, fish soups and superb roast kid. It's also a good place to discover the island's wines and unusual eaux-de-vie. Liveliest at night. The lunch menu provides more standard bistro fare, with a few Corsican elements thrown in.

Le Train Bleu

Gare de Lyon, 12th ☎ 01 43 43 09 06 ⓒ L & D daily. **€€** [p339, E4]

Climb the main station staircase, busy with commuters and pigeons, and suddenly you're in the glittering rooms of a fabulous Belle Epoque restaurant. The menu offers traditional dishes (including foie gras, sole meunière and profiteroles) that are a bit pricey, but for atmosphere this place is hard to beat.

Bars and Cafés

L'Abreuvoir

103 rue Oberkampf, 11th. Tel: 01 43 38 87 01. Non-stop Mon–Sat. [p337, E4]

The "watering trough" is one of the relatively quiet gems on the Oberkampf scene. Candlelit tables, a bar decorated with rock and roll posters and knick-knacks, and a range of unusual beer-based cocktails (like Casse-Tête, which is beer, rum and peach liqueur) make it a good place to spend a few hours in.

Bar à Nénette

26 rue de Lappe, 11th. Tel: 01 48 07 08 18. Daily 5pm–2am. [p339, E3] Rue de Lappe is another street full of bars, and although its heyday is over, there are always people lurching along it. Nénette's happy hour lasts until 10pm, with plates of sausages or cheese, and friendly customers.

Bistrot à Vins Mélac

42 rue Léon-Frot, 11th. Tel: 01 43 70 59 27. L & D Tue–Sat (until midnight). [p339, E3]

Wine bar/shop/ "vineyard" (there are a few vines on the exterior wall) crowded with workers at lunchtime. Cheese and specialities from the Auvergne region are paired with a wide choice of wines.

Café Charbon

109 rue Oberkampf, 11th. Tel: 01 43 57 55 13. L & D daily (9am–2am, until 4am Thur–Sat). [p337, E4]

The former coal *(charbon)* shop with its *fin de siècle* atmosphere – lofty ceilings, ornate mirrors and red-leather sofas – is a fixture of east Paris's café culture.

Chez Justine

96 rue Oberkampf, 11th. Tel: 08 26 10 11 22. Daily 8am–2am. [p337, E4]

Laid-back and easy-going bar-restaurant. Resident DJ and music throughout the venue. This venue witnessed Charlie Winston's first Parisian concert.

Le Jemmapes

82 quai des Jemmapes, 10th. Tel: 01 40 40 02 35. Non-stop daily. [p337, D3]

Unusual flavoured vodkas are the speciality at this ever-popular canalside café-bar; it's packed at weekends, especially the terrace. Good beers and a relaxed vibe are two more reasons to pay a visit.

Plein Soleil

90 avenue Parmentier. Tel: 01 48 05 41 06. D 7.30am–2am. [p337, E4]

Trendy bar-café with a cosy sun-filled terrace and DJ nights on Thur, Fri and Sat.

Au P'tit Garage

63 rue Jean-Pierre-Timbaud, 11th. Tel: 01 48 07 08 12. Sun–Mon 6pm–2am. [p337, E4]

Rue Jean-Pierre-Timbaud is bar-hopping heaven – the street is one string of largely good drinking dens. This one's possibly the best: a jumble of assorted junk-shop furniture, cool crowd, nice cheap drinks and good choices of music.

Rosso

4bis rue Neuve-Popincourt, 11th. Tel: 01 49 29 06 36. Tue–Sun 6pm–2am. [p337, E4]

Arty Rosso is a sister operation to Le Zéro Zéro (89 rue Amelot). The eponymous cocktail is vodka, Triple Sec and framboise; there are also Daiquiris and a handful of beers.

L'épouvantail
autoportrait
SAIGYO
Moundarren
carrément
Zen
Moundarren
l'extase du
papillon

Recommended Restaurants, Bars & Cafés on pages 206–7

THE LATIN QUARTER AND ST-GERMAIN-DES-PRÉS

Writers, artists and thinkers have made these districts their home since Roman times. Nowadays, fashion rules as much as philosophy on the Left Bank, but the literary legacy lives on in its historic colleges, cafés, theatres, book stalls and street markets

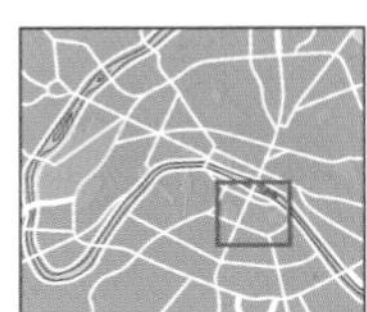

The Latin Quarter and St-Germain-des-Prés, side by side, make up the heart of the Left Bank. Once the home of artists and intellectuals, they have changed over the past few decades, with high fashion replacing high art. Nevertheless, the *Rive Gauche* maintains its charm in its beautiful tree-lined boulevards, narrow streets, manicured parks and imposing monuments. This is the place to stroll, imbibe and look cool. Sit in the shaded parks and on café terraces by day, and scan the menus in the fairylit streets by night.

THE DIVIDING BOULEVARD

What is generally referred to as the Latin Quarter lies east of Boulevard St-Michel, which runs from Place St-Michel on the banks of the Seine, to cross Boulevard St-Germain in front of the ancient Roman baths of Cluny – a reminder that this was once part of the Roman city of Lutetia. This maze of ancient streets and squares has been the stamping ground of students for nearly eight centuries, and Latin was virtually its mother tongue until Napoleon put a stop to it after the Revolution.

To the west of the Boulevard St-Michel is St-Germain-des-Prés, the historical centre of literary Paris and Existentialism, with the oldest church in Paris at its heart, but now chock-a-block with designer boutiques. If St-Germain's literary credentials remain intact it is thanks to Flammarion, Gallimard, Grasset and smaller publishers, who have refused to be tempted by luxury groups' lucrative offers for their premises. As for the three monuments to the district's literary heyday – the Café des

Main attractions

- MUSÉE NATIONAL DU MOYEN AGE
- LA SORBONNE
- EGLISE ST-ETIENNE-DU-MONT
- LE PANTHÉON
- MOSQUÉE DE PARIS
- ARÈNES DE LUTÈCE
- JARDIN DES PLANTES
- MUSÉUM NATIONAL D'HISTOIRE NATURELLE
- INSTITUT DU MONDE ARABE
- JARDIN ET PALAIS DU LUXEMBOURG
- ST-SULPICE
- EGLISE ST-GERMAIN-DES-PRÉS

LEFT: La Hune, the city's best-known bookshop, keeps St-Germain's literary credentials alive and well.

RIGHT: warm welcome at bistro Le Mauzac.

Latin Quarter, St-Germain-des-Prés and Montparnasse

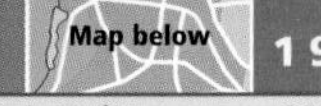

Recommended Restaurants, Bars & Cafés on pages 206–7

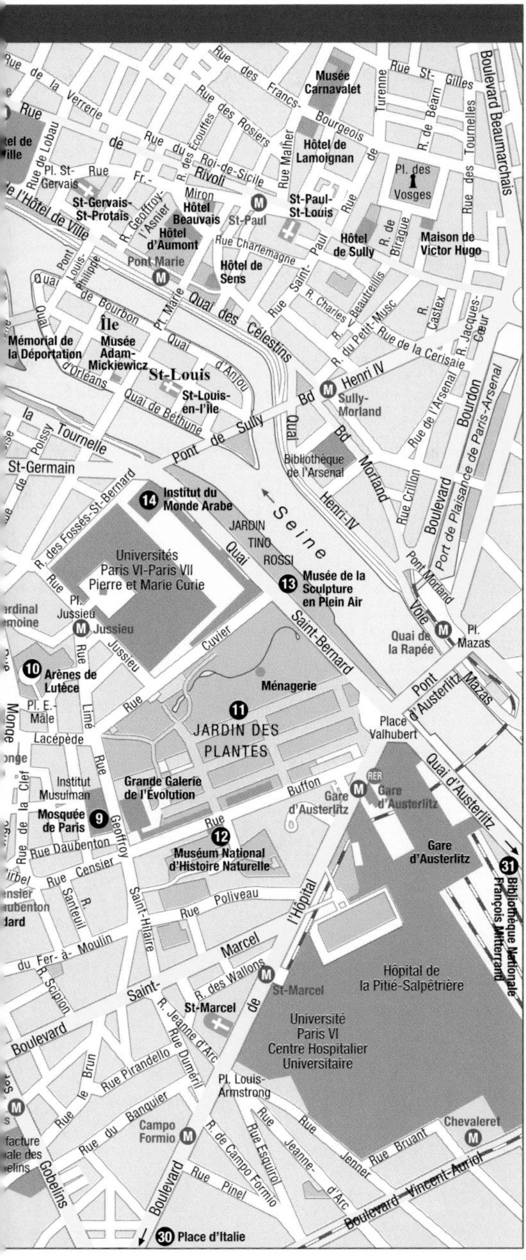

Deux Magots, Café de Flore and Brasserie Lipp – they are certainly thriving, even if their current clients are more likely to have Cartier than Camus on their minds.

THE LATIN QUARTER

Settled by the Romans in 53 BC and a cradle of philosophy and art since the Middle Ages, the Quartier Latin conjures up contradictions and delights in paradox, epitomised by the words of student and poet François Villon in 1456, as he declared "I laugh in tears." Villon debated with professors at the Sorbonne by day, and drank with thieves in the brothels of St-Michel by night.

Villon's legacy of rebellion survived him. In 1871, Place St-Michel was the headquarters of the Commune. Then in May 1968 – a turning point in the history of post-war France – demonstrations at conditions in the Nanterre faculty led to students tearing up the old cobblestones of Boulevard St-Michel to hurl at riot police. Hundreds of students were arrested, but a year later General de Gaulle relinquished power.

The Latin Quarter had been the centre of academic life in France since the 13th century, and the university had enjoyed immense privileges (included that of obliging all who entered it to speak Latin). After 1968, however, the University of Paris was decentralised to the suburbs, and the ancient cobblestones were buried under concrete. Protests, albeit far more subdued, still take place these days, and roads are sometimes blocked by squatting students, but the academic-hothouse atmosphere of the old Quartier has gone.

Nevertheless, the Latin Quarter remains a place of happy incongruity, where countless Greek souvlaki vendors stand amid traditional cafés spilling over the pavements, and arthouse cinemas occupy buildings with ancient academic facades.

Along the Boul' Mich

Across the river from the palaces of justice and salvation (the Préfecture de Police and Notre-Dame), **Place St-Michel ❶** revels in recklessness. Its fountain depicting St Michael and a surprised dragon often seems buried under scooters, lovers and *clochards* (tramps), sitting philosophically amid the youthful chaos. Extending south from the square, the grand Boulevard St-Michel (Boul' Mich to the locals) will nourish the senses, the mind as well as the stomach, with an eclectic assortment of stalls, bookshops, alternative cinemas and fast-food joints.

ABOVE: classical music posters on the gates of St-Julien-le-Pauvre.
BELOW: flower stall in St-Germain-des-Prés.

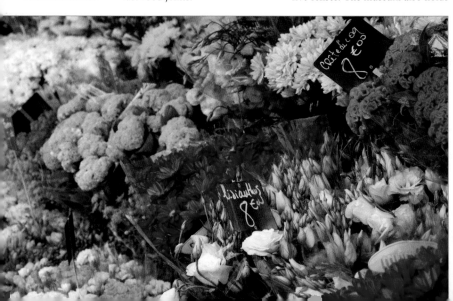

Musée National du Moyen Age – Thermes de Cluny ❷

6 place Paul-Painlevé, www.musee-moyenage.fr 01 53 73 78 16
Wed–Mon 9.15am–5.45pm
charge Cluny-La Sorbonne

At the crossroads of Boul' Mich and Boulevard St-Germain stands the fine Hôtel de Cluny, built in 1485–98 and a rare example of a late-medieval urban mansion. Once the residence of the Abbots of Cluny, these Flamboyant Gothic walls house one of the world's finest collections of medieval artefacts. Many of its treasures reflect life in religious communities, such as illuminated manuscripts, embroideries, stained glass, liturgical vestments and various church furnishings.

Among the numerous tapestries is the exquisite 15th-century *La Dame à la Licorne* (The Lady and the Unicorn) on the first floor of the rotunda. The six panels are beautifully worked in the millefleurs style of design, using rich, harmonious colours to create a delicate allegory on the worth of the five senses. The museum also holds

Recommended Restaurants, Bars & Cafés on pages 206–7

21 of the original heads of the kings of Judah, sculpted in 1220 for the facade of Notre-Dame but vandalised during the Revolution.

The Hôtel de Cluny was constructed on the remains of a huge Gallo-Roman bathhouse complex, believed to have been built in AD 200 by the guild of *nautae* (boatmen) – ships' prows are carved on the arch supports of the *frigidarium* (cold bathhouse). As elsewhere in their empire, the Romans living in Lutetia regarded bathing as the essence of civilisation.

Cluny's medieval garden is not a reproduction of a medieval garden but an imaginative modern evocation of the Middle Ages, taking its inspiration from objects in the collection and evoking the two spheres of the spiritual and the profane that governed the medieval world.

Latin lanes

Heading east along Boulevard St-Germain you'll reach Place Maubert, a bustling market square at the centre of a network of small, medieval streets lined with a jumble of boutiques revealing their shadowy interiors to the curious. The **Musée de la Préfecture de Police** ❸ (4 Rue de la Montagne-Ste-Geneviève; tel: 01 44 41 52 50; Mon–Fri 9am–5pm, Sat 10am–5pm; free), on the second floor of a pretty bleak police station, houses an intriguing collection of macabre objects, weapons and documents, including many relics of Napoleon's much-feared police chief Joseph Fouché.

St-Julien-le-Pauvre ❹

1 rue St-Julien-le-Pauvre
01 43 54 52 16 daily
9.30am–1pm, 3–6.30pm free
Cluny-La Sorbonne

Back on the banks of the Seine, quiet repose is to be found in this tiny 12th-century church, in the shadow of Notre-Dame. The Italian poet Dante is said to have prayed here in 1304. In the garden you can sit under a 300-year-old false acacia. Behind it is Rue du Fouarre, named after the bales of hay on which students used to perch during open-air lectures in the Middle Ages.

A section of the six-panel, 15th-century tapestry La Dame à la Licorne, *in the Hôtel de Cluny.*

BELOW: café life on the Boul' Mich, a favourite student hang-out.

Most of the striking stained-glass windows in the side chapels of church St-Séverin are by 19th-century Chartres master Emile Hersch.

La Huchette

The streets around St-Julien and across Rue St-Jacques make up the Quartier de la Huchette, remarkably missed by Haussmann's 19th-century boulevard-building and today one of the most engaging and liveliest parts of the Left Bank.

Shakespeare and Company at 37 rue de la Bûcherie follows in the footsteps of Paris's most famous English bookshop, founded in 1921 by Sylvia Beach in Rue de l'Odéon, which published the first edition of Joyce's *Ulysses*. It closed down during World War II, and the present shop was founded in 1956 by American George Whitman – who's still a regular presence, though he's passed on day-to-day running of the shop to his daughter Sylvia. It stocks a wide range of literature, from the Bard to the Beatniks, and famous expatriate writers such as William Burroughs and James Baldwin were frequent visitors. Today, it still stays open until midnight.

Le Petit Pont close by is a perfect spot from which to see the lights of the Seine shimmer at night. Here, the Quais St-Michel and Montebello offer picture-book views of the Ile de la Cité. By day, ancient bookstalls line the river banks, offering expensive antique volumes.

Trial by Revolutionary council has been replaced with jazz at the **Caveau de la Huchette** (5 rue de la Huchette, *see page 298*). Danton and Robespierre selected guillotine victims in the cellars where musicians now jam. At No. 10, a young Napoleon dreamed of power.

RIGHT: Left Bank statue.
BELOW: bookshops are a regular sighting in the Latin Quarter.

St-Séverin ❺

3 rue des Prêtres-St-Séverin 01 42 34 93 50 daily 11am–7.30pm free Cluny-La Sorbonne

This beautiful Flamboyant Gothic church is famous for its palm-tree vaulting and twisting spiral columns, fine stained glass, mighty organ loft and the oldest bell in Paris in its bell tower, dating from 1412.

La Sorbonne ❻

17 rue de la Sorbonne, www.sorbonne.fr 01 40 46 22 11 tours by appointment free Cluny-La Sorbonne

Continue south along Rue St-Jacques and you'll come to the vast complex of the Sorbonne. Established in 1253 by King Louis IX (St Louis) and his confessor Robert de Sorbon, France's oldest university has been rebuilt many times since its inception as a dormitory for 16 theology students, when it began to attract thinkers from all over Europe.

In 1469, France's first printing press was set up here by three Germans summoned by Louis XI, which encouraged the growth of intellectual life. Sorbonne alumnus Cardinal Richelieu rebuilt the university in the 1630s, but it was closed down during the Revolution, and allowed to become dilapidated. Napoleon then reopened, revitalised and expanded it to become once more the most important university in France. Since decentralisation in 1970, though, there are 13 universities in Paris, and the Sorbonne has lost its force, if not its reputation.

The 17th-century chapel, commissioned by Richelieu and containing his marble tomb, overlooks the university's main courtyard. Above the tomb, beautifully carved by François Girardon, hangs a hat believed to be the cardinal's. Legend has it that the hat will fall when Richelieu's soul is released from hell.

Across Rue St-Jacques is the **Collège de France** (www.college-de-france.fr; tel: 01 44 27 12 11; Oct–June Mon–Fri and Sat am; free), set up by François I in 1530 on the inspiration of the great humanist Guillaume Budé, to offer a more liberal education unfettered by the intolerance and dogmatism of the Sorbonne.

Bookworms can find an abundance of material in the famously learned 5th and 6th *arrondissements*. The Boulevard St-Michel is full of bookshops catering to students; Gibert Joseph (at No. 26) also has good second-hand titles, some in English. Two anglophone bookshops worth finding are tiny Abbey Bookshop (29 rue de la Parcheminerie, 5th); and Village Voice (6 rue Princesse, 6th), notable for its frequent readings and events.

LEFT: scooters are a good way to get around the capital. **BELOW:** the Chapelle de la Sorbonne, where Cardinal Richelieu is buried.

Today the college still has its academic independence, even though financially dependent on the state; lectures are open to the public without charge. Next door, the Lycée Louis-le-Grand is the school from which the 19th-century poet Charles Baudelaire was expelled, and in which Jean-Paul Sartre taught.

The bowling on Rue Mouffetard offers a pleasant alternative to the line of cheap bistros and souvenir shops.

Montagne Ste-Geneviève

Further along Rue St-Jacques the ground rises to the top of Montagne Ste-Geneviève, site of the hermitage of the devout woman credited with saving the city from destruction by Attila the Hun in AD 451 *(see page 26)*. She became the city's patron saint, and the hilltop her shrine.

St-Etienne-du-Mont ❼

✉ place Ste-Geneviève ☎ 01 43 54 11 79 ⏲ Tue–Fri 8.45am–7.30pm, Sat 8.45am–noon, 2–7.45pm, Sun 8.45am–12.15pm, 2.30pm–7.45pm € free 🚇 Cardinal Lemoine

Built in a mixture of Late Gothic and Renaissance styles in the 16th century, this beautiful church was part of the abbey of Ste-Geneviève, closed by the Revolution. Inside, the remains of the saint are buried in an ornate shrine. Playwright Jean Racine (1639–99) and the scientist and philosopher Blaise Pascal (1623–62) are also buried here, and a marble slab near the entrance marks the spot where the Archbishop of Paris was stabbed to death by a priest in 1857.

RIGHT: the intellectual tradition persists. **BELOW:** hip, arty café on popular Rue de Buci.

Le Panthéon ❽

✉ place du Panthéon, www.monum.fr ☎ 01 44 32 18 00 ⏲ daily Apr–Sept 10am–6.30pm, Oct–Mar 10am–6pm € charge 🚇 Cardinal Lemoine

St-Etienne shares its commanding hilltop site with this monumental edifice. It was intended to be a new church to Ste-Geneviève, rashly promised by Louis XV when he recovered from a serious illness in 1744. Money was short, however, so public lotteries were organised to raise funds. Designed by neoclassical architect Jacques-Germain Soufflot (1713–80), who drew inspiration from Rome's Pantheon, the building was only finished just in time for the Revolution. The Revolutionaries had no use for a vast new church, however, so in 1791 it was designated a pantheon or resting-place for the "Founders of Liberty", a monument to rival the royal mausoleum at St-

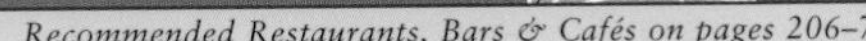
Recommended Restaurants, Bars & Cafés on pages 206–7

Denis *(see pages 265–6)*. Thus Voltaire, who was transferred from the country, and Jean-Jacques Rousseau came to lie in the crypt, to be joined later by Victor Hugo, Emile Zola and Louis Braille. Nobel Prize-winning scientists Pierre and Marie Curie joined them in 1995, and the remains of World War II Resistance hero Jean Moulin were reburied here in 1964; the man who read his eulogy at the ceremony, André Malraux, did not join him until 1996.

After the Revolution, the use of the Panthéon yo-yoed from church to necropolis to church to headquarters of the Commune, until it finally became a lay temple and tomb in 1885. The interior is in the shape of a Greek cross, with the iron-framed dome towering above the centre. Frescoes by Puvis de Chavannes on the life of St Geneviève line the south wall; her glorification is portrayed on the upper section of the dome. Foucault's 67-metre (220-ft) pendulum hangs from the centre of the dome, returned here from the Musée des Arts et Métiers in 1995; the one hanging there today is a replica.

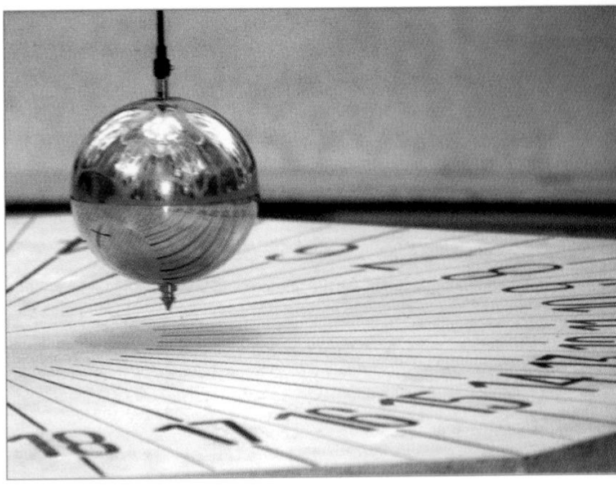

Rue Mouffetard

Rue Mouffetard, originally the road to Rome, is one of the oldest streets in Paris; narrow, crowded, and full of cheap and cheerful places to eat. In its lower half is a street market (Tue–Sat, Sun am) around the Gothic church of **St-Médard**. Walk there via the picturesque **Place de la Contrescarpe** (a few minutes from Place du Panthéon eastwards), a lively place to sit and people-watch

ABOVE: Léon Foucault's pendulum inside the Panthéon.
BELOW LEFT: cheap eateries near popular Rue Mouffetard.

The Illustrious Dead

The Panthéon is one of the world's most exclusive clubs. To take up residence, you need to be a high achiever, French – and dead. It also helps if you're a man, as all but two of the 73 people interred within are men; the two women are Marie Curie and Sophie Berthelot, who only got in with her husband, chemist Marcellin Berthelot.

Here are some of France's greatest writers, Rousseau, Voltaire, Hugo and Zola; scientists, like the Curies; and politicians, including a president, Sadi Carnot, who was assassinated in 1894.

Others took longer to get to the Panthéon, as if their membership took a while to be ratified: André Malraux was reinterred here in 1996, 30 years after his death; and Alexandre Dumas *père* only joined the illustrious throng in 2002 – in a coffin draped in blue velvet with the motto of the Three Musketeers, "One for all, all for one". A lapse between death and national consecration was also the lot of the man who designed the Panthéon, J.G. Soufflot: he had to wait 59 years.

with students skipping class, amid a maze of surrounding streets.

In the corner house (No. 1) Rabelais (1494–1553) composed his risqué rhymes, as had François Villon a century earlier. At No. 122, towards the bottom of the hill, the well carved onto the facade dates from Henri IV's reign.

ABOVE: skeletons galore inside the Grande Galerie de l'Evolution, Muséum National d'Histoire Naturelle.
BELOW RIGHT: children will love the pink flamingoes at the Ménagerie of the Jardin des Plantes.

THE JARDIN DES PLANTES

East of Rue Mouffetard is a quieter section of the Left Bank, the site of one of Paris's oldest parks, a distinguished mosque and intriguing museums and other attractions.

Mosquée de Paris 9

2 place du Puits-de-l'Hermite, www.mosquee-de-paris.org
01 45 35 97 33 tours Sat–Thur 9am–noon, 2–6pm charge
Monge

This green-and-white mosque was built in Hispano-Moorish style in 1922 by French architects to commemorate North African participation in World War I. Incorporating the Institut Musulman, the complex of buildings includes a museum of Muslim art, a patio inspired by the Alhambra in Granada, and an impressive selection of carvings and tiles. There is also a library, a restaurant, a delightful Moroccan tearoom and a Turkish bath.

Arènes de Lutèce 10

rue Monge daily summer 8am–10pm, winter 8am–5.30pm
free Cardinal Lemoine

Behind a nondescript wooden doorway is the ancient gladiatorial arena of Roman Lutetia. The 15,000-seat arena – destroyed by barbarians in

Exotic Imports

When the Jardin des Plantes was expanding in the early 18th century, the royal doctor, Fagon, and botanists such as Tournefort and the three Jussieu brothers travelled far and wide bringing back seeds from around the world. The wild and wonderful collection of flora that resulted includes a 2,000-year-old American sequoia, a Ginkgo biloba and a Persian iron tree. A laricio pine was grown from a seed brought back from Corsica in 1774, and the pistachio tree is almost 300 years old. The oldest Lebanese cedar in France, planted in 1734, was brought from Kew Gardens in England by the Jussieu brothers' nephew, Bernard de Jussieu. The story goes that after dropping and breaking the pot containing the young plants, he nurtured the seedlings in his hat. The oldest tree in Paris, a false acacia or Robinia brought from America in 1635, is also here. The most attractive features for children are the zoo, the 18th-century maze and the Grande Galerie de l'Evolution, part of the Muséum National d'Histoire Naturelle *(see page 199)*.

AD 280 – was unearthed during the construction of Rue Monge in 1869; Victor Hugo led the campaign to preserve it. Today, the arena where gladiators fought serves as a children's playground, and on fine days echoes with the clink of *pétanque* balls.

Jardin des Plantes ⓫

✉ rue Geoffroy-St-Hilaire ☎ 01 40 79 56 01 ⏲ daily 7.30am–7.30pm € free 🚉 Gare d'Austerlitz

Paris's botanical garden was inaugurated in 1640 as a medicinal herb farm for Louis XIII. The oldest tree in Paris, a false acacia planted in 1635, is here. The garden expanded in the 1700s, with the addition of a maze, amphitheatre and exhibition galleries. In 1889, the Galerie de Zoologie opened in the grounds, to display and study the millions of specimens brought back by globe-trotting naturalists and explorers.

Opened in 1794, the **Ménagerie** or zoo (daily 9am–6pm; charge) is popular with children, with its panthers, monkeys, orang-utan, flamingoes, reptile house and petting zoo.

Muséum National d'Histoire Naturelle ⓬

✉ 36 rue Geoffroy-St-Hilaire, www.mnhn.fr ☎ 01 40 79 54 79 ⏲ Wed–Mon 10am–6pm € charge 🚉 Gare d'Austerlitz

France's official natural history museum – one of many institutions created just after the Revolution, in 1793 – has galleries on palaeontology, mineralogy, geology and even a

TIP

Film buffs will enjoy the three cinemas in the Action mini-chain: Grand Action, Action Ecoles (5 and 23 rue des Ecoles, 5th) and Action Christine (4 rue Christine, 6th): all screen a rich variety of international arthouse fare, classic and modern.

LEFT: the mosque's green-and-white square minaret and main courtyard.
BELOW: the beautiful flower displays in the Jardin des Plantes; in the background the stunning Grande Galerie de l'Evolution.

The famous Poilâne bread, dark, dense and with a deliciously sour-sweet flavour, can be bought at the Poilâne HQ at 8 rue du Cherche-Midi in the 6th *arrondissement* (there's another branch in the 15th). The daily queues are testimony to its impeccable quality.

microzoo, but its great attraction is the lavishly restored **Grande Galerie de l'Evolution**. Its objective is to illustrate principles of evolution and dramatise the impact of human behaviour on the natural environment. The hall has retained elements of a 19th-century museum – parquet floors, iron columns, display cases – but has been completely modernised and equipped with the latest audio-visual techniques and interactive displays (mostly in French). The museum's *pièce de résistance* is the great herd of stuffed African animals that sweeps through the atrium.

RIGHT: Russian restaurant Dominique (19 rue Bréa) mixes folklore and Left Bank sophistication.
BELOW: the shuttered windows inspired by the screens of Moorish palaces at the Institut du Monde Arabe.

Musée de la Sculpture en Plein Air (Jardin Tino Rossi) ⓭

✉ quai St-Bernard ◷ Mon–Fri 8am–dusk, Sat–Sun 9am–dusk
€ free 🚇 Gare d'Austerlitz

For a riverside stroll, leave the Jardin des Plantes at Place Valhubert and head west to this park-cum-modern sculpture exhibit. It's not the prettiest space, and noisy by day, but it takes on a whole new character on summer evenings, when it's a venue for free salsa and tango sessions.

Institut du Monde Arabe ⓮

✉ 1 rue des Fossés-St-Bernard, www.imarabe.org ☎ 01 40 51 38 38
◷ Tue–Sun 10am–6pm € charge
🚇 Jussieu

One of the most striking buildings on the Seine is this high-tech blend of modern and traditional Arab styles, symbolic of the Institute's *raison d'être* – to deepen cultural understanding between the Western and Islamic worlds. A cultural centre and museum of Arab-Islamic art and civilisation, the nine-storey palace of glass, aluminium and concrete was designed by Jean Nouvel: its southern facade is a flat patterned wall of gleaming symmetry that recalls traditional Arab latticework. Its light-sensitive camera-like irises are supposed to open and close according to the movement of the sun, but have been plagued with problems, and most stay fixed at one setting. Views from the roof terrace-restaurant are breathtaking.

ODÉON AND LUXEMBOURG

The Odéon district acts as a buffer between the boisterous Latin Quarter (5th *arrondissement*) and the more refined St-Germain-des-Prés (6th *arrondissement*). From St-Michel Métro, walk along Rue St-André-des-Arts to the **Cour de Rohan**. It's worth popping in to admire the picturesque courtyards with Renaissance facades. Turn left into **Rue de l'Ancienne-Comédie**, the next street along, where **Le Procope**, the first-ever café in Paris and credited with introducing coffee to the city in 1686, is still doing good business *(see page 207)*.

At Carrefour de l'Odéon, a statue of the Revolutionary leader Georges Danton marks the spot where his old house once stood. Fellow Revolutionary Camille Desmoulins lived at No. 2 before storming the Bastille in 1789. Others plotted in neighbouring streets, which now shelter some of the most bourgeois boutiques and apartments in Paris.

From here, Rue de l'Odéon – first street in Paris to have gutters and pavements – leads to Place de l'Odéon and the neoclassical **Odéon-Théâtre de l'Europe** ⓯ (www.theatre-odeon.fr; tel: 01 44 85 40 40), founded by the Comédiens Ordinaires du Roi in 1782. Recently restored, this is one of France's leading public theatres, and as the "Theatre of Europe" hosts many international productions – albeit mostly performed in French.

Jardin du Luxembourg ⓰

rue de Vaugirard · daily summer 8am–dusk, winter 9am–dusk · free · Odéon/RER Luxembourg

Beautifully landscaped, this is the quintessential Paris park, a haven of manicured greenery where young couples rendezvous under plane trees by the romantic Baroque Fontaine de Médicis, while children sail boats across the carp-filled lake in the

ABOVE: *pâtissier* supremo and chocolate wizard Pierre Hermé (72 rue Bonaparte). **BELOW:** Jardin du Luxembourg, the Paris park par excellence.

ABOVE: St-Germain-des-Prés is now a hub of chic boutiques. **BELOW:** literary St-Germain.

middle. Statues of queens of France gaze down from the terrace, while the thwack of tennis balls disturbs the quiet reverie of sunbathers and smartly clad nannies push babies in expensive prams.

On Wednesdays and weekends, the famous Guignol puppet show is performed in the **Théâtre des Marionnettes**. More serious entertainment is found by the corner with Rue de Vaugirard, where people play chess under the fragrant orange trees. There are 200 varieties of apple and pear trees in the garden, and an apiary that produces hundreds of kilos of honey a year. The **Musée du Luxembourg** (19 rue de Vaugirard, www.museedu luxembourg.fr; tel: 01 42 34 25 95; Tue–Thur, Sat 10.30am–7pm, Mon, Fri 10.30am–10pm, Sun 9.30am–7pm; charge) puts on crowd-pulling major exhibitions.

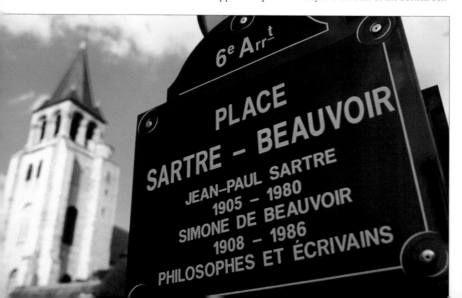

Palais du Luxembourg ⓱

www.senat.fr 01 44 54 19 49
guided tours by appointment
free Odéon/RER Luxembourg

The palace that presides over the gardens was built for Marie de Médicis after the murder of her husband Henri IV, on the site of a mansion that had belonged to Duke François of Luxembourg. Its Italianate style, modelled on the Pitti Palace in Florence, was intended to remind her of home. The widowed queen moved into the palace in 1625, but was forced into exile by Richelieu before its completion. During the Revolution it was used as a prison, and in World War II it was the German headquarters. Today it is the seat of the French Senate, and the adjacent Petit Luxembourg is the residence of its president.

St-Sulpice 18

place St-Sulpice, www.paroisse-saint-sulpice-paris.org 01 46 33 21 78 daily 7.30am–7.30pm free St-Sulpice

From the Petit Luxembourg, Rue Garancière leads to this imposing church. Apart from one of the finest organs in Europe (used for many recitals) and Delacroix's *Jacob Wrestling with the Angel*, inspired by the painter's own struggle with art, the great cavern of a church has little to offer, but now draws throngs of fanatical readers of *The Da Vinci Code*.

In front of the huge colonnaded facade, with mismatching towers, is a square with an amusing fountain made by Joachim Visconti in 1844. The square is the site of the **Foire St-Germain** in June and July, with antiques, poetry and ceramics fairs, children's events and street theatre.

ST-GERMAIN-DES-PRÉS

Historic heart of literary Paris, St-Germain-des-Prés covers an area roughly from St-Sulpice to the Seine. Its elegant streets now house chic boutiques, yet it retains a sense of animation, with cafés spilling out onto the pavements. In the 1940s the area became a breeding ground for literature and ideas. Existentialists, inspired by Jean-Paul Sartre, Simone de Beauvoir and Albert Camus, gathered in local cafés such as Les Deux Magots and Café de Flore.

The days of black sweaters and beret-clad Existentialists locked in

FOOD

The best-known organic market in Paris is the Marché Biologique Raspail, between Rue du Cherche-Midi and Rue de Rennes. It draws a savvy crowd from all over Paris every Sunday morning.

LEFT: stained glass window, St-Sulpice.
BELOW LEFT: a Parisian literary institution, the Café de Flore.
BELOW: picking up a good read at a *bouquiniste* along the Quai des Grands-Augustins.

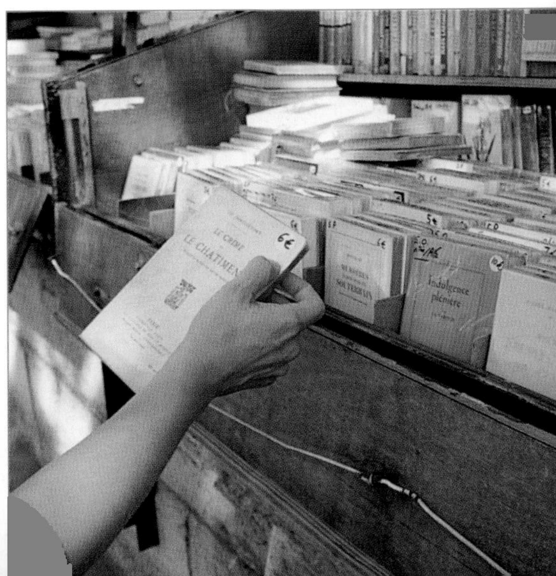

One of the most popular bridges in Paris is the cast-iron Pont des Arts – an appropriate name for a footbridge that spans the river between the Institut de France and the Louvre. It was built in 1804, but by the 1970s had been severely damaged by three boat collisions and was closed to the public. It was rebuilt from the original plans and reopened in 1984; today it's a popular spot for picture-taking and picnics.

debate are well and truly over; the area has been colonised by designers and antique dealers. The **Marché St-Germain** shows how things have changed. Tastefully restored, the old stone market hall now contains fashion shops, a swimming pool and an auditorium, as well as a local market.

The hub of St-Germain is the junction of Boulevard St-Germain and Rue Bonaparte, with, opposite each other, **Café de Flore** and **Les Deux Magots**, which serve some of the best hot chocolate in Paris – and some of the most expensive. Once favourite haunts of the literati, these cafés are now packed with tourists. Also here is the sleek **La Hune** bookshop, crammed with literature and books on art, architecture and performing arts, in French and English. It stays open until midnight, and feels most "St-Germain" after dark.

Eglise St-Germain-des-Prés ⓳

✉ www.eglise-sgp.org ☎ 01 55 42 81 33 ⏲ Mon–Sat 8am–7.45pm, Sun 9am–8pm € free 🚇 St-Germain-des-Prés

Overlooking the crossroads is the oldest church in Paris, begun in AD 542, when it was built as a basilica for holy relics. It is named after St Germain, cardinal of Paris, who is buried here. Ransacked and rebuilt over centuries, the heavily restored 11th-century building is a blend of simple Romanesque, Early Gothic, Baroque tombs and 19th-century wall paintings. In the small square alongside stands Picasso's tribute to his friend, the poet Apollinaire.

Musée National Eugène Delacroix ⓴

✉ 6 place Furstenberg, www.museedelacroix.fr ☎ 01 44 41 86 50 ⏲ Wed–Mon 9.30am–5pm € free 🚇 St-Germain-des-Prés

Heading east down Rue Jacob, filled with fascinating antiques and design shops, you pass Place Furstenburg, with the studio where Romantic painter Eugène Delacroix (1798–1863) lived from 1857 to his death, while he painted the murals in St-Sulpice. Now a museum, it has engaging sketches and memorabilia.

BELOW: the picturesque Pont des Arts at night.

Ecole Nationale Supérieure des Beaux-Arts ㉑

14 rue Bonaparte, www.ensba.fr
01 47 03 50 00 exhibitions Tue–Sun 1–7pm charge
St-Germain-des-Prés

Paris's finest art school fills two *hôtels* fronting the Quai Malaquais. Begun in 1608, the main building was a monastery until the Revolution; the School of Fine Arts moved here in 1816, and today holds exhibitions of students' work and works from its extensive collection, notably of French and Italian Old Master drawings.

Close by is the imposing **Institut de France** ㉒, seat of the Académie Française, established in 1635. The select members of the illustrious institution are guardians of the French language, protecting it from the insidious onslaught of English.

Musée de la Monnaie ㉓

11 quai de Conti, www.monnaiedeparis.fr 01 40 46 56 66
Tue–Fri 11am–5.30pm, Sat–Sun noon–5.30pm charge Pont Neuf

Next door is the neoclassical **Hôtel des Monnaies**, designed by Jacques Antoine for Louis XV to replace an earlier royal mint, and completed in 1775. The *hôtel* now houses a comprehensive museum of France's money and medals.

Quai des Grands-Augustins is the oldest quay on the Seine, and is lined with antiquarian bookshops and antique dealers. Picasso lived for 20 years on Rue des Grands-Augustins, which branches off the quay. ❑

ABOVE: browsing for a bargain at the San Francisco Book Co. (17 rue Monsieur-le-Prince).
BELOW LEFT: writer Jean-Paul Sartre, a St-Germain legend.

Left Bank Rendezvous

Cafés have played a huge part in Paris's intellectual, political and artistic development. In the 18th century, Café Voltaire (1 place de l'Odéon), named after its most famous regular, was the place where he met fellow philosopher Diderot to discuss their Enlightenment theories. The tormented 19th-century poets – Verlaine and Mallarmé – threw Symbolist ideas at each other here and, much later, in the 1920s, American writers Ernest Hemingway and F. Scott Fitzgerald extolled the café's "sudden provincial quality". Other writers in Paris between the world wars spent hours in Le Procope *(see page 207)*, and Jean-Paul Sartre and Simone de Beauvoir consolidated the highbrow reputation of Les Deux Magots (6 place St-Germain-des-Prés) in the 1940s. Art Deco Café de Flore (172 boulevard St-Germain), just opposite, was another Sartre favourite. And for decades French politicians have congregated at Brasserie Lipp, just across the road.

BEST RESTAURANTS, BARS AND CAFÉS

Restaurants

Price includes dinner and a half-bottle of house wine:
€ = under €25
€€ = €25–40
€€€ = €40–60
€€€€ = more than €60

L'Alcazar

62 rue Mazarine, 6th 01 53 10 19 99 L & D daily, Br Sun. **€€–€€€** [p338, B2]
Sir Terence Conran's contribution to the Paris restaurant scene was to transform this old music hall into a designer brasserie. A *réussite* with Parisians and tourists alike. The atmosphere is easygoing and the menu competitively priced.

Allard

41 rue St-André-des-Arts, 6th 01 43 26 48 23 L & D Mon–Sun. **€€** (set menu) **€€€** (à la carte) [p338, B3]
The dark Art Nouveau decoration makes this one of the loveliest bistros in Paris, with two intimate, atmospheric rooms evocative of Left Bank life. The traditional food – think duck with olives, roast lamb, etc. – is very good.

Les Bouquinistes

53 quai des Grands-Augustins, 6th 01 43 25 45 94 L Mon–Fri, D Mon–Sat. **€€€** (set menu) **€€€** (à la carte) [p338, B2]
Guy Savoy's stylish Seine-side bistro continues to draw a fashionable crowd. Chef William Caussimon's modernised take on bistro cooking is seen in dishes such as tuna prepared three ways, sea bass *a la plancha* (on a metal plaque), and foie gras with peaches.

Brasserie Lipp

151 boulevard St-Germain, 6th 01 45 48 53 91 daily 11.45am–00.45am. **€€€** [p338, A3]
Brasserie Lipp remains the fashion barometer of Paris. To be offered a table on the first floor is social suicide, but swagger in on the ground floor nodding to passing celebs and the unthinkable ascent can be avoided. The rather dull brasserie food is variable, but nobody cares.

Chez René

14 boulevard Saint-Germain, 5th 01 43 54 30 23 L & D Tue–Sat. **€€** (set menu) **€€€** (à la carte) [p339, C3]
Classic French bistro, one block from the Seine with a small outdoor terrace. It serves groaning plates of daily specials such as an excellent coq au vin, a perfectly aged entrecôte Bercy for two, and a fine selection of cheeses and charcuterie.

Le Comptoir

9 carrefour de l'Odéon, 6th 01 44 27 07 97 non-stop daily. **€€** (set menu), **€€€** (à la carte) [p338, B3]
One of the biggest stories in the restaurant world in recent years, Yves Camdeborde's bistro serves a no-choice €40 meal in the evening that's so good you have to book months ahead. The brasserie dishes served at lunch are no mean fare, either: iced cream of chicken soup, or rolled saddle of lamb.

Lapérouse

51 quai des Grands-Augustins, 6th 01 43 26 68 04 L & D Mon–Fri, D Sat. **€€** (set menu), **€€€€** (à la carte) [p338, B2]
Diners at this 17th-century institution have included Hugo and Proust. Its run of self-contained individual dining rooms used to lock on the inside, hence Lapérouse's rumoured popularity with ministers and their mistresses; the main dining room is hardly less romantic. The refined classical cooking is as elaborate as the decor. Prices reflect the riverside setting. Lunchtimes are relatively quiet, and the lunch set menus are less pricey.

LEFT: the chef at the lovely bistro Allard.
RIGHT: eating alfresco on bustling Rue de Buci.

Moissonnier
28 rue des Fossés St-Bernard, 5th ☎ 01 43 29 87 65 ⏲ L & D Tue–Sun. €€ [p339, C3]
A Parisian institution serving specialities from the Jura and the Rhône. Dishes include a *saladier lyonnais* (salad served with crisp bacon, hard-boiled eggs and chicken livers) and *quenelles de brochet* (pike dumplings).

L'Ourcine
92 rue Broca, 13th ☎ 01 47 07 13 65 ⏲ L & D Tue–Sat. €€ [p338, B4]
Talented young chef Stéphane Danière produces updated versions of French regional dishes, combining seasonal produce with more cosmopolitan flavours. Tables are tightly packed into a minimalist but attractive room in a 17th-century building.

Pierre Gagnaire à Gaya Rive Gauche
44 rue du Bac, 7th ☎ 01 45 44 73 73 ⏲ L & D Mon–Sat. €€€ [p338, A2]
Food at this recent arrival, a clever reworking of a famous fish restaurant, costs far less than at Gagnaire's HQ in the 20th. The piscine stars run from illustrious langoustine and sole to more humble cod; there are some nicely inventive dishes, too, such as red snapper daubed with peppered caramel.

Le Voltaire
27 quai Voltaire, 7th ☎ 01 42 61 17 49 ⏲ L & D Tue–Sat. €€€ [p338, A2]
Not the least of this vintage bistro's attractions is its riverside setting; others include the polished service and the food, which runs the gamut from elegant salads and rustic grub like sautéed rabbit to luxury dishes like lobster omelette. Cosy, but chic at the same time.

Ze Kitchen Galerie
4 rue des Grands-Augustins, 6th ☎ 01 44 32 00 32 ⏲ L & D Mon–Fri, D only Sat. €€€ [p338, B2]
Former Guy Savoy protégé William Ledeuil, who used to run Les Bouquinistes around the corner, branched out on his own in this arty modern bistro. The successful fusion fare is bursting with ideas, but centred around sushi-style raw fish preparations, spicy condiments and main course meat and fish speed-cooked *a la plancha* and served with Asian-style condiments.

Bars and Cafés

Le Bar Dix
10 rue de l'Odéon, 6th. Tel: 01 43 26 66 83. Daily 6pm–2am. [p338, B3]
A favourite with students and the economy-minded for decades, this bar has a cramped upper bar done out with old Jacques Brel record sleeves, and a basement romantically lit by candles. The drinks of choice are cheap reds by the glass or the home-made sangría.

Café de Flore
172 boulevard St-Germain, 6th. Tel: 01 45 48 55 26. Non-stop daily. [p338, A3]
Of the two celebrated "intellectual cafés" on Boulevard St-Germain, this (the other being Les Deux Magots) is the better. Prices are just as steep, but the prevailing language among customers here is French, not English; and you do see the occasional student writing an essay on a table.

Café de la Mairie
8 place St-Sulpice, 6th. Tel: 01 43 26 67 82. Non-stop daily. [p338, A3]
This place is always packed. Strangely, given its ringside view of St-Sulpice church, there never seem to be many tourists – stranger, when you remember it was frequented by Camus and Miller. Perhaps it's the low-marks food or rather gruff service.

Le Pousse au Crime
15 rue Guisarde, 6th. Tel: 01 46 33 41 91. Tue–Wed 11pm–2am and Thur–Sat 11pm–dawn. [p338, A3]
With no fewer than three bars, you can request your favourite music to dance to. A must in Saint-Germain-des-Prés. Two floors with just one motto: party! €15 entry on Fri and Sat.

Le Procope
13 rue de l'Ancienne Comédie, 6th. Tel: 01 40 46 79 00. Daily 10.30am–1am. [p338, B3]
Founded in 1686 by Francesco dei Coltelli, this is the city's oldest café. Enjoy lunch or dinner in the very place where Voltaire, Danton, Robespierre, Marat and Benjamin Franklin once sat.

La Rhumerie
166 boulevard St-Germain, 6th. Tel: 01 43 54 28 94. Daily noon–2am. [p338, A3]
This 77-year old café serves delicious cocktails and rums with *accras* (fritters), crab toasts and other exotic specialties.

Jardin du Luxembourg

The quintessential Paris park has leafy pathways, statues, *boules*, a bandstand, a boating pond and a lovely, civilised atmosphere

The Jardin du Luxembourg is one of the largest parks in Paris: 25 hectares (63 acres). It's also one of the loveliest, with its atmosphere of quiet panache and relaxed bonhomie. Its regulars, a mongrel crowd of smart locals, students, artists, joggers, and nuns from the nearby convents, refer to it by the affectionate nickname "Luco", a shortening of the Roman name for the area, Lucotitius. As well as an art museum (the Musée du Luxembourg, *see page 202*), the park contains an apiary, an orangery, a bandstand, both tennis and basketball courts, *boules* pitches, tables for chess, as well as a small café. The grand Palais du Luxembourg, located on its northern edge, was constructed in 1615 for Queen Marie de Médicis, who ordered a building in Florentine style to remind her of the Pitti Palace of her childhood. Since 1958, it has been home to the French parliament's upper house, the Senate.

Above: a view of the Palais du Luxembourg, centrepiece of the park.

Left: Arthur Jacques Le Duc's 1886 work *Harde de Cerfs* is a suitably noble group for the elegant setting.

Below: many people come to the tranquil gardens simply to read.

Essential info

rue de Vaugirard, www.senat.fr/visite/jardin/index.html

daily summer 8am–dusk, winter 9am–dusk

free

Odéon/ RER Luxembourg

ART IN THE PARK

The park is studded with nearly 100 sculptures, of varying styles, eras and subject matters. Famous artists are a dominant group: Baudelaire, Flaubert, Verlaine and George Sand; the face held up by the young boy to the right is Victor Hugo's, part of the sculpture *Le Marchand de masques* that also features the faces of Balzac and Berlioz. Historical figures are also present: Blanche de Castille, St Geneviève and Marie de Médicis, among others; and allegorical subjects include a scaled-down version of the Statue of Liberty. All together, they make the park something of an open-air museum.

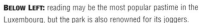

BELOW LEFT: reading may be the most popular pastime in the Luxembourg, but the park is also renowned for its joggers.

BOTTOM LEFT: horses in the Fontaine de l'Observatoire.

BELOW: colourful toy sailing boats are available for hire on the ornamental pond directly in front of the Palais du Luxembourg.

MONTPARNASSE AND BEYOND

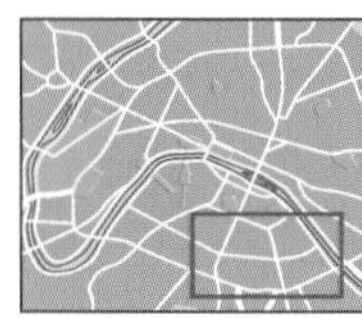

Once a backwater, Montparnasse has a unique place in modern culture – at some point between 1910 and 1939, Picasso and Matisse, Lenin and Stravinsky, Hemingway and Joyce could all be found here. Their legacy lives on amid tower blocks and redevelopment schemes, in a thriving café and nightlife scene

Main attractions

- MUSÉE DU MONTPARNASSE
- MUSÉE BOURDELLE
- MUSÉE ZADKINE
- TOUR MONTPARNASSE
- CIMETIÈRE DU MONTPARNASSE
- LES CATACOMBES
- BIBLIOTHÈQUE FRANÇOIS-MITTERRAND

The once-rural area southwest of the Jardin du Luxembourg was christened Mount Parnassus – after the classical home of Apollo and his Muses – by a local poetry society in the 17th century, when they gathered on quarry mounds to recite verses. In the early years of the 20th century, the area became a magnet for artists, composers and revolutionaries, including Chagall, Léger, Soutine, Picasso, Modigliani, Lenin and Stravinsky. Some decamped from Montmartre because of the inflated rents; others were émigrés in search of refuge or a new beginning, drawn to a place that embraced freethinkers and the avant-garde. They rented studios in the newly built-up area, and gathered in cafés and brasseries such as Le Select, Le Dôme, La Rotonde and La Coupole. Their bohemian lifestyle is as much a part of the Paris myth as the era's legacy of artworks *(see page 215)*.

After World War II, writers and philosophers such as Jean-Paul Sartre, Simone de Beauvoir, Henry Miller and Louis Aragon moved in, patronising the same cafés clustered around the lively **Carrefour Vavin**, where the district's inescapable artery, the **Boulevard Montparnasse**, crosses Boulevard Raspail. Now relabelled Place Pablo Picasso, the Carrefour still throbs with life well into the early hours. Further east, the Closerie des Lilas was another favourite artistic haunt *(see page 216)*.

AROUND MONTPARNASSE

Above the Carrefour on Boulevard Raspail stands Rodin's dramatic **Statue de Balzac**. This sculpture so shocked the Société des Beaux-Arts when unveiled at the 1898 Salon – by showing the great writer in a dressing gown – that it was turned down, and only finally cast and installed here in 1939.

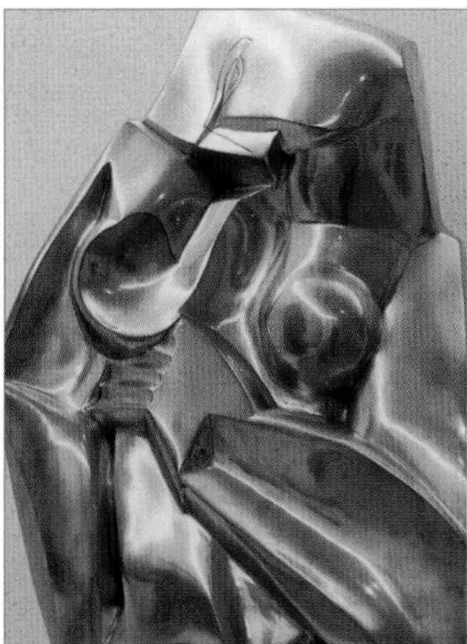

Musée du Montparnasse ㉔

21 avenue du Maine, www.museedumontparnasse.net 01 42 22 91 96 Tue–Sun 12.30–7pm charge Montparnasse-Bienvenüe

Tucked away down one of the small alleys of artists' studios that formerly littered Montparnasse, this museum was once a studio and art school run by Russian avant-garde artist Marie Vassilieff. Exhibitions focus on different aspects of the area's artistic heritage, with photos and art works.

Musée Bourdelle ㉕

16–18 rue Bourdelle, www.paris.fr/musees 01 49 54 73 73 Tue–Sun 10am–6pm free Montparnasse-Bienvenüe

A showcase for the work of Modernist sculptor Antoine Bourdelle, spread over his former apartment and studio. A pupil of Rodin, Bourdelle is best known for his friezes on the Théâtre des Champs-Elysées.

Musée Zadkine ㉖

100bis rue d'Assas, www.paris.fr/musees 01 55 42 77 20 Tue–Sun 10am–6pm free Vavin

Among the influx of émigrés from Russia was Cubist sculptor Ossip Zadkine, who moved into this tiny house and studio in 1928. His sculptures are displayed around the house and garden, along with his drawings and engravings, and paintings by his wife Valentine Prax.

Tour Montparnasse ㉗

33 avenue du Maine, www.tourmontparnasse56.com 01 45 38 52 56 daily 9.30am–11pm, winter until 10.30pm charge Montparnasse-Bienvenüe

The district, however – and the whole southern skyline – is dominated by this lumbering 59-storey tower, built in 1974 and the only skyscraper in central Paris (as no more have been allowed since then). If you've a head for heights and the stomach for a lightning-fast lift, the roof terrace offers superb views of Paris. At the foot of the tower, by an ugly shopping centre, is **Place du 18 Juin 1940**, commemorating the day when General de Gaulle sent his famous BBC radio message urging the French to carry on

The Fondation Henri-Cartier-Bresson opened in 2003. Its mission is "to preserve the independence and keep alive the spirit" of the photographer. The Fondation is located at 2 impasse Lebouis, 14th arrondissement. *Métro: Gaîté. Tel: 01 56 80 27 00; www.henricartier bresson.org.*

FAR LEFT: Cimetière du Montparnasse. **LEFT:** Zadkine sculpture. **BELOW:** the famous Montparnasse brasserie Le Dôme.

Baudelaire, one of the star residents of Montparnasse cemetery, has two memorial stones: the first is his grave, in the sixth division; the second is the cenotaph on Avenue Transversale, an errily lifelike recumbent sculpture of the poet watched over by a brooding figure representing Ennui.

RIGHT: sculpture in Musée Bourdelle. **BELOW:** new floating Piscine Joséphine-Baker.

resisting German occupation: "We have lost a battle, but not the war."

Behind the tower is the **Gare Montparnasse**, which serves north-western France. In the mid-19th century, thousands of Bretons emerged from this station, fleeing rural poverty and famine in Brittany, hence the many crêperies in the area.

Cimetière du Montparnasse 28

boulevard Edgar-Quinet 01 44 10 86 50 mid-Mar–Oct Mon–Fri 8am–6pm, Sat 8.30am–6pm, Sun 9am–6pm, Nov–mid-Mar closes daily at 5.15pm free Raspail

Boulevard Edgar-Quinet, as well as some nice cafés and a lively morning market on Wednesdays and Saturdays, contains the third of Paris's giant cemeteries, with Père Lachaise and Montmartre. Among those buried here are artists Antoine Bourdelle and Man Ray, composer Saint-Saëns and writers Charles Baudelaire, Guy de Maupassant, Jean-Paul Sartre and Irish writer and long-term local resident Samuel Beckett.

Les Catacombes 29

1 avenue Colonel Henri Rol-Tanguy, www.paris.fr/musees 01 43 22 47 63 Tue–Sun 10am–4pm charge Denfert-Rochereau

If you're still in macabre mood after the Cimetière, visit this labyrinth beneath Place Denfert-Rochereau, where the neatly stacked skulls, femurs and tibias of some 6 million departed souls line long passage-

Recommended Restaurants, Bars and Cafés on pages 216–7

ways. The former Roman quarries were converted into ossuaries in 1785, when cartloads of skeletons were removed from the overflowing cemeteries at Place des Innocents and other areas. Take a torch, and someone to hold your hand, as the inscription on the door reads: "Stop. You are entering the empire of the dead."

AROUND PLACE D'ITALIE

Place d'Italie ㉚ is the traffic hub of the 13th *arrondissement*, where old districts alternate with soulless 1960s tower blocks. The square is dominated by the modern Centre Commercial Italie, but more down to earth is the food market on Boulevard Auguste-Blanqui (Tue, Fri, Sun am).

Les Gobelins is the oldest part of the neighbourhood. Traces of a Gallo-Roman necropolis were discovered here, and the tomb of the first Archbishop of Paris, St-Marcel. The district's name stems from the **Manufacture Nationale des Gobelins** (42 avenue des Gobelins; tel: 01 44 08 52 00; tours Tue, Thur 2pm; charge), the tapestry factory founded in 1662. Visitors can watch weavers at work.

Hidden just south of Place d'Italie is the tranquil, villagey *quartier* of **La Butte-aux-Cailles**. In the 1900s the hill was still covered with working windmills and water mills. Its narrow, cobbled streets offer some of Paris's friendliest, cheapest bars. The hub of activity is around the Rue de la Butte-aux-Cailles and Rue des Cinq-Diamants. A few trendy restaurants have opened here, but it's still an unassuming, delightful area to visit.

Chinatown is a close neighbour, roughly bordered by Avenue d'Italie and Avenue d'Ivry – a mini-city of skyscrapers where streets are lined with kitsch gift shops, Thai groceries, Vietnamese pho noodle bars and Chinese *pâtisseries* and tearooms.

THE "NEW" LEFT BANK

The "new" *Rive Gauche* is Paris's biggest urban renewal project since the 1860s, when Baron Haussmann sliced up the city's medieval heart to carve out his tree-lined boulevards. New streets and buildings are going up in a zone of rusty factories and disused railway tracks extending south from Gare d'Austerlitz. With

SHOP

Chinatown's shops are a treasure trove of gaudy decorations, trinkets and figurines, alongside elegant rice bowls, fine teas and tea sets, and good-quality Chinese dresses. Tang Frères (48 avenue d'Ivry, 13th) is a sprawling Chinese grocery store with aisle upon aisle of exotic goods, including fruit, herbs and teas, all at reasonable prices.

BELOW LEFT: lovely tearoom L'Oisive-Thé, Butte-aux-Cailles.

Off the Waterfront

The new Left Bank has provided a new focus for the expanded Paris-Plage jamboree, which brings sand, palm trees and seaside fun to the city in July and August *(see also page 111)*. An annual smash hit ever since it started in 2002, Paris-Plage grew to include the south side of the river in 2006. The fun on the Left Bank revolves around a new floating swimming pool, Piscine Joséphine-Baker, that's moored up by the Bibliothèque Nationale.

It's a purpose-built barge that features a huge sun deck, cafeteria and children's play area, as well as – of course – a generous 25-metre (79-ft) swimming pool. The water for the pool is pumped from the river itself, before being treated to crystalline cleanliness for swimmers to splash in. As a final masterstroke, a huge, sliding glass roof covers the pool, and when the sunshine's hot enough, it's pulled back to let in the open air. There's even a packed programme of exercise classes.

ABOVE: the facade of the Bibliothèque Nationale François-Mitterrand.
BELOW: evening drinks at Cabaret Pirate.

the new national library as its centrepiece, the area is gradually taking shape as new offices, apartments and schools go up, and the **MK2-Bibliothèque** multiplex cinema draws in the public at weekends. Art galleries, upmarket cafés, restaurants and boutiques have cropped up, and the **Rue Louise-Weiss** is the focus of a small gallery scene. In an unusual display of solidarity, the galleries have synchronised openings.

Bibliothèque Nationale François-Mitterrand ㉛

quai François-Mauriac, www.bnf.fr
01 53 79 59 59 Tue–Sat 10am–7pm, Sun 1–7pm charge
Bibliothèque François Mitterrand

Designed by Dominique Perrault and opened in 1997, the library cost over €1 billion to build. Its 90-metre (300-ft) -high glass towers are meant to evoke open books on end, set on top of a plank-covered plinth 305 metres (1,000 ft) long. Like it or not, the library is undeniably impressive.

Nightlife on the Seine

The new Left Bank is to have its own "Latin Quarter", with 30,000 students on a new campus around a giant rehabilitated grain store. Streets have been extended to the Seine and the river banks landscaped, and this is Paris's hottest new nightlife area, with boats and barges where you can eat, drink and dance: the **Batofar**, **Cabaret Pirate**, **Blues Café** and **Péniche Makara**, to name but a few, are all moored by Quai de la Gare near the Bibliothèque. ❑

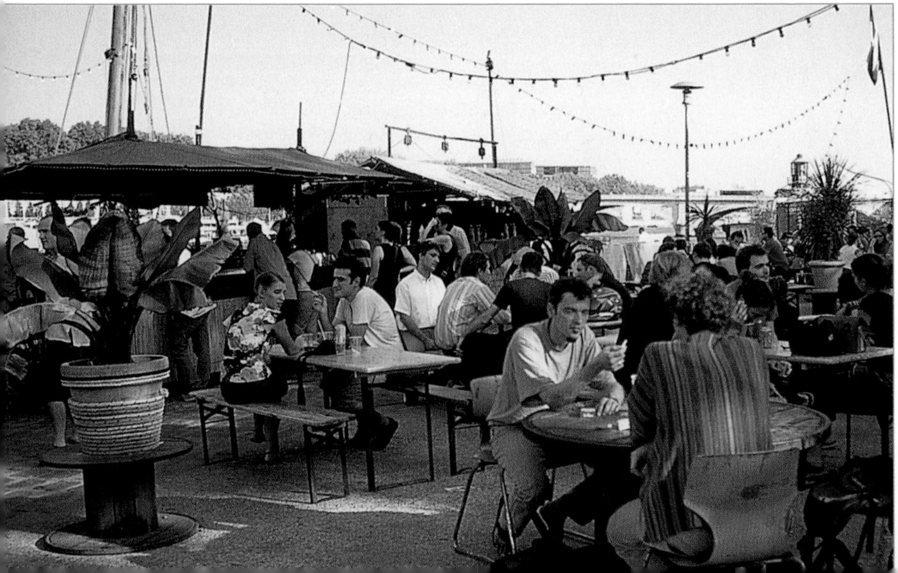

Recommended Restaurants, Bars and Cafés on pages 216–7

Paris Schooling

"Paris was where the 20th century was," said Gertrude Stein, and for a time all the fads and fashions, the art and ideas of modernity came together in Montparnasse

Today the name "Ecole de Paris" still conjures up the incredible artistic momentum of Paris between the wars, the mood of intellectual ferment, of artistic and literary debate, and the arrival of cocktails, jazz and the tango. It was neither a school nor a movement, nor an organised group – rather it is a label that has come to designate those mostly foreign-born artists who congregated around Montmartre in the first years of the 20th century and, after World War I, in the cafés and studios of Montparnasse.

Paris was an intellectual and cultural magnet; a bold city, where academic tradition had been challenged by the Impressionists, Cézanne and the Fauves; a city open to avant-garde currents like Cubism, Expressionism and Dadaism. Paris was a magnet, too, for foreign artists in search of refuge or a new beginning, be they Jews escaping the ghetto, Russians fleeing the Revolution or Americans after adventure escaping from Prohibition.

Though not a style, the Ecole de Paris is associated with figuration, not abstraction, a form of expressionism and a certain relationship to the contemporary world, not Surrealism. At its centre were Chagall, Soutine, Modigliani, Foujita, Pascin, Kisling and Van Dongen. More peripheral figures include Picasso, Chana Orloff, Marie Vassilieff and Maurice Utrillo.

The Ecole de Paris, though, was as much to do with lifestyle as artistic style. Artists rented studios at La Ruche, Cité Falguière, Villa Seurat and countless other studio courtyards around Montparnasse. Exchanges also took place in the area's cafés and brasseries, such as Le Dôme, La Rotonde and the glamorous La Coupole.

The artists painted each other, but also writers, critics and poets like Apollinaire, Max Jacob, Gertrude Stein and Henry Miller. Their paintings captured drinkers, dancers and prostitutes, Parisian icons like the Eiffel Tower, and themes like clowns and the circus.

Curiously, though, the figure who best epitomised the spirit of artistic Montparnasse was not an artist, but model and muse Kiki de Montparnasse. Born Alice Prin in 1901, she arrived in Paris during World War I and became part of the artistic circle who met at La Rotonde. Painted by Soutine, Van Dongen, Kisling and Foujita with her characteristic black fringe, she also entered the Surrealist pantheon, as mistress and model of Man Ray; she starred in several of his experimental films and in his photo *Le Violin d'Ingres*. Beautiful, charming, outrageous, Kiki painted, danced, sang lewd songs at Le Jockey and published her memoirs at the age of 28.

Perhaps, then, one should take Ecole de Paris literally, that it is Paris the city, not any academy or teacher, that was the inspiration, as place of liberty, cultural mix and school of life.

These artists' work can be seen in museums including the Centre Pompidou, Musée d'Art Moderne de la Ville de Paris, Musée de l'Orangerie and the Musée d'Art et d'Histoire du Judaïsme. ❑

ABOVE: Art Deco brasserie La Coupole.
RIGHT: Picasso, a Montparnasse art scene regular.

BEST RESTAURANTS, BARS AND CAFÉS

Restaurants

Price includes dinner and a half-bottle of house wine:
€ = under €25
€€ = €25–40
€€€ = €40–60
€€€€ = more than €60

L'Assiette

181 rue du Château, 14th ☎ 01 43 22 64 86 ⏲ L & D Wed–Sun. €€ [p338, B4]
Lulu, the cigar-smoking owner, is a local star. Her strong personality, ultra-simple cooking and obsession with impeccably sourced ingredients have made this a mecca for gourmets in the know. Dishes lean towards the southwest and include foie gras, roast lamb, sausage from the Landes region and home-made caramel ice cream. Everything is cooked to perfection.

L'Avant-Goût

26 rue Bobillot, 13th ☎ 01 53 80 24 00 ⏲ L & D Tue–Sat. €€ [p339, C4]
Great value for money, the inventive cuisine of chef Christophe Beaufront draws an appreciative crowd. The house speciality is roast pork *pot-au-feu* or, in season, *sanglier* (wild boar). The wine list is intelligent and affordable. This is probably the neighbourhood's best restaurant, and everyone knows it, so book ahead. There's also a takeaway menu.

La Cagouille

10 place Constantin-Brancusi, 14th ☎ 01 43 22 09 01 ⏲ L & D daily. €€ (set menu) €€€ (à la carte) [p341, E4]
Gérard Allemandou learned to love seafood on the Atlantic coast where he grew up. Grilled, roasted or fried, his seafood has an exquisite flavour. His tasty specialities include red mullet in olive oil and black sea bream grilled with cumin. Service is attentive, the wine list extensive and desserts are good. In warm weather, go for the pleasant outdoor seating – it makes up slightly for the somewhat plain interior.

Chez Paul

22 rue de la Butte-aux-Cailles, 13th ☎ 01 45 89 22 11 ⏲ L & D daily. €€€ [p339, C4]
This cheerful, elegant bistro is the most upmarket of the cluster on the Butte-aux-Cailles, serving traditional French fare. Boudin noir and steak with marrowbone come with potato purée, and there's usually a good fish of the day. Great choice of *apéritifs*.

La Closerie des Lilas

171 boulevard du Montparnasse, 6th ☎ 01 40 51 34 50 ⏲ L & D daily (until 1.30am). €€ [p338, A4]
The historic brasserie retains its charm and offers richly satisfying

fare, though it does cash in on its reputation as a famous 1920s watering hole, favoured by the likes of Hemingway, Lenin and Modigliani. For dining, choose from the reliable brasserie or the expensive restaurant, which serves great French classics such as frogs' legs and crêpes Suzette.

La Coupole

102 boulevard du Montparnasse,14th 01 43 20 14 20 L & D daily (until 1am). €€ (set menu) €€€ (à la carte) [p341, E4]

This vast, legendary Art Deco brasserie remains an eternal favourite with Parisians as well as tourists. Waiters offer elegant service in a 1920s dining hall. Hot dishes can be hit and miss, but the oysters and shellfish platters are superb. The code's relaxed – you can dress up or wear jeans – and you can dance downstairs to a theme that changes nightly.

L'Entrepôt

7 rue Francis-de-Pressensé, 14th 01 45 40 60 70 non-stop daily. €€ [p338, B4]

This used to be a paper warehouse, but now it's a three-in-one: bar, restaurant and arthouse cinema. The dining side of the operation serves fairly standard brasserie fare like *magret de canard*, beef tartare or fillet of salmon, with choices like crème brûlée at dessert. The place also does live music at weekends.

Paradis Thaï

132 rue Tolbiac, 13th 01 45 83 22 26 L & D daily. €€ [p339, C4]

The exotic yet understated mood in this restaurant is set by the enormous elephant in the entrance. The discreet decor offsets beautifully presented Vietnamese and Thai specialities, and the varied menu indicates levels of spiciness.

LEFT: traditional wine bistro in Montparnasse.
ABOVE: the welcoming, exotic Paradis Thaï.

Le Parc aux Cerfs

50 rue Vavin, 6th 01 43 54 87 83 L & D daily. €€ (set menu) €€€ (à la carte) [p341, E3]

This former artist's atelier has a cosy mezzanine and an interior courtyard that's a delight in summer. The Mediterranean menu is short but full of flair, and there's an excellent wine list. The ice creams are home-made.

Le Select

99 boulevard du Montparnasse, 6th 01 45 48 38 24 non-stop daily. €€€ [p341, E3]

No shortage of history or artistic associations at this Montparnasse stalwart: Hemingway, Cocteau, Man Ray and all used to frequent the place. Local intellectuals still hang out at the bar. The food, for what you get, is no bargain, but there's a very good choice of cocktails and spirits, especially whiskies.

Wadja

10 rue de la Grande-Chaumière, 6th 01 46 33 02 02 L & D Mon–Sat. € (set menu), €€€ (à la carte) [p338, A4]

The friendly owner serves up a market-fresh menu with personally chosen wines in a dining room that hasn't lost its 1930s atmosphere. A la carte takes over in the evening, with imaginative starters and hearty meat or fish mains. The daily menu is less expensive.

Bars and Cafés

Café de l'Atelier
95 boulevard du Montparnasse, 6th. Tel: 01 45 44 98 81. Non-stop daily. [p341, E3]
This pleasant café has a youthful crowd, friendly staff, a useful terrace (with heaters when required) and a range of snacks. The fact that it's open round the clock is an added bonus.

Les Tontons
38 rue Raymond-Losserand, 14th. Tel: 01 43 21 69 45. Non-stop Mon–Sat. [p338, A4]
This pleasant café boasts late opening hours and a traditional zinc counter. Its food offerings have a regional theme – the southwest – and run to large salads and 10 different varieties of tartare. The two owners are fans of French gangster movie *Les Tontons Flingueurs* (1963), hence the name of the place and all the posters and other memorabilia.

THE EIFFEL TOWER AND LES INVALIDES

Vital Paris experiences: the views from the top of its great iron tower, and in the dark depths of its sewers. At ground level, there are gracious boulevards, imperial splendour at Les Invalides and a grand art buffet: Impressionists at Musée d'Orsay, exotic artefacts at Quai Branly and new creativity at Palais de Tokyo

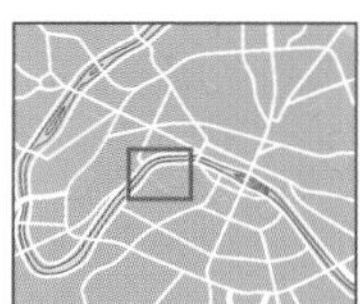

The Eiffel Tower looms up above the Seine like a giant playing hide-and-seek among the grand apartment blocks of the 7th *arrondissement*. At its foot is the **Champ de Mars**. This stretch of parkland, once a military exercise ground, now teems with tourists all year round. Facing the tower at the southern end of the Champ de Mars is the **Ecole Militaire**, the military academy where Napoleon learned his trade. Glimpses through the shuttered security are rare, but occasional open doorways reveal fountains, statues and soaring stairways. To the east, the **Esplanade des Invalides** is another splendid carpet of green that rolls from the gleaming gilt-domed church of the **Hôtel des Invalides** to the Seine and the Pont Alexandre III.

A chilly elegance prevails in the wide boulevards that link these great monuments and green expanses, but drift away from the crowd-filled Champ de Mars and savour the gracious tree-lined streets bordered by *hôtels* (mansions), whose sumptuous apartments are occupied by senior civil servants, captains of industry and rich, retired Americans.

LEFT: the Eiffel Tower, world symbol of the French capital.
RIGHT: the 7th *arrondissement* hosts some of the city's most prized restaurants.

THE TROCADÉRO

Across the river lies the 16th *arrondissement*. This takes up a sizeable slice of western Paris and, like the 7th, it is full of smart residences occupied by wealthy inhabitants. Not for those in search of the arcane or the avant-garde, this is the bastion of BCBG (*bon chic, bon genre*), a never-never land of big hair, Burberry plaid, diamond rings, pedigree dogs and Berthillon ice cream. The reason most tourists and Parisians venture here is to visit one of the museums

Main attractions
- TROCADÉRO
- MUSÉE GUIMET
- MUSÉE D'ART MODERNE DE LA VILLE DE PARIS
- PALAIS DE TOKYO
- EIFFEL TOWER
- ECOLE MILITAIRE
- MUSÉE DU QUAI BRANLY
- LES EGOUTS (THE SEWERS)
- LES INVALIDES
- MUSÉE RODIN
- MUSÉE D'ORSAY

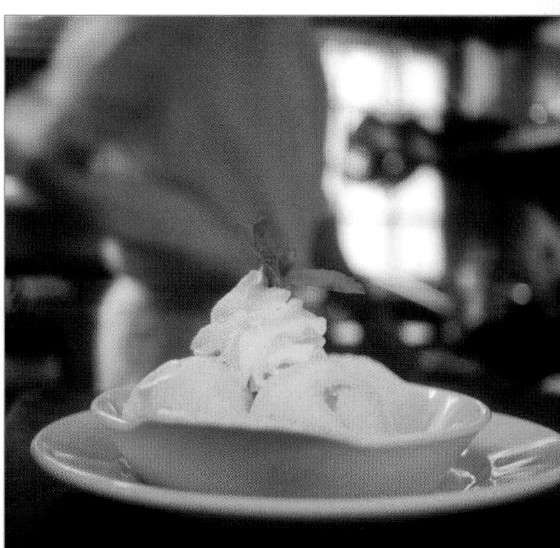

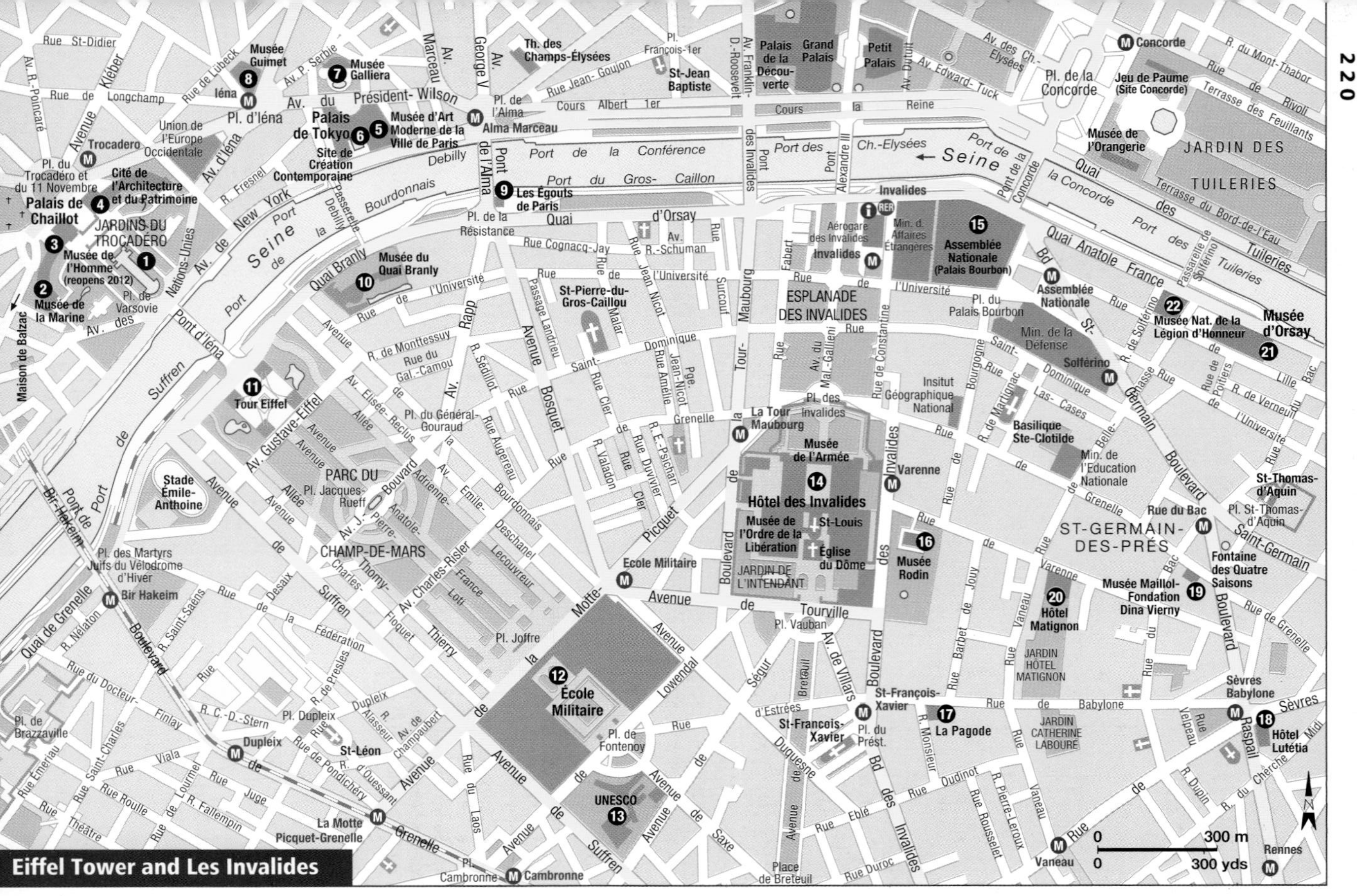
Eiffel Tower and Les Invalides
JARDIN DES TUILERIES
Musée de l'Orangerie
Jeu de Paume (Site Concorde)
Concorde
Pl. de la Concorde
Quai des Tuileries
Port des Tuileries
Port de la Concorde
Quai Anatole France
Musée d'Orsay
21
Musée Nat. de la Légion d'Honneur
22
Assemblée Nationale
Solférino
Min. de la Défense
Basilique Ste-Clotilde
Min. de l'Education Nationale
St-Thomas-d'Aquin
Fontaine des Quatre Saisons
Rue du Bac
Musée Maillol-Fondation Dina Vierny
19
ST-GERMAIN-DES-PRÉS
Boulevard Saint-Germain
Hôtel Lutétia
18
Sèvres Babylone
Raspail
Rennes
300 m
300 yds
20
Hôtel Matignon
JARDIN HÔTEL MATIGNON
JARDIN CATHERINE LABOURÉ
Vaneau
17
La Pagode
St-François-Xavier
16
Musée Rodin
Varenne
15
Assemblée Nationale (Palais Bourbon)
Pl. du Palais Bourbon
Min. d. Affaires Étrangères
Invalides
Aérogare des Invalides
Insitut Géographique National
ESPLANADE DES INVALIDES
14
Hôtel des Invalides
Musée de l'Armée
St-Louis
Église du Dôme
Musée de l'Ordre de la Libération
JARDIN DE L'INTENDANT
La Tour Maubourg
Pl. Vauban
Bd des Invalides
Av. de Villars
Avenue de Tourville
Avenue de Breteuil
Place de Breteuil
Avenue Duquesne
Avenue de Ségur
Avenue de Saxe
13
UNESCO
Pl. de Fontenoy
12
École Militaire
Ecole Militaire
Pl. Joffre
Cambronne
Pl. Cambronne
Avenue de Suffren
Avenue de la Motte-Picquet
Avenue Lowendal
Grand Palais
Petit Palais
Palais de la Découverte
Pont Alexandre III
Cours la Reine
Port des Ch.-Elysées
Seine
Av. Franklin-D.-Roosevelt
Pont des Invalides
St-Jean Baptiste
Th. des Champs-Élysées
Cours Albert 1er
Port de la Conférence
Port du Gros-Caillou
Quai d'Orsay
9
Les Égouts de Paris
Pont de l'Alma
Alma Marceau
Av. George V
Av. Marceau
St-Pierre-du-Gros-Caillou
Rue Cler
Rue Saint-Dominique
Rue de Grenelle
Avenue Bosquet
Av. Rapp
5
Musée d'Art Moderne de la Ville de Paris
6
Palais de Tokyo
Site de Création Contemporaine
7
Musée Galliera
Av. du Président-Wilson
10
Musée du Quai Branly
Quai Branly
PARC DU CHAMP-DE-MARS
11
Tour Eiffel
Pont d'Iéna
Port de Suffren
8
Musée Guimet
Iéna
Pl. d'Iéna
Trocadero
Cité de l'Architecture et du Patrimoine
4
JARDINS DU TROCADÉRO
1
Musée de l'Homme (reopens 2012)
3
Palais de Chaillot
2
Musée de la Marine
Pl. du Trocadéro et du 11 Novembre
Maison de Balzac
Av. R.-Poincaré
Stade Émile-Anthoine
Pl. des Martyrs Juifs du Vélodrome d'Hiver
Bir Hakeim
Pont de Bir-Hakeim
Quai de Grenelle
Boulevard de Grenelle
Dupleix
Pl. Dupleix
St-Léon
La Motte Picquet-Grenelle
Pl. de Brazzaville

Recommended Restaurants, Bars and Cafés on pages 232–3

around Place du Trocadéro, or to gaze at the magical views across the Seine to the Eiffel Tower.

Begin by crossing the Pont d'Iéna to the Trocadéro. From here, framed by the cascading fountains and gold statues of the **Jardins du Trocadéro** ❶, the Eiffel Tower can be seen at its most magnificent. Dominating the Place du Trocadéro is the **Palais de Chaillot**, built for the Paris International Exhibition of 1937. The imposing Pseudo-Classical palace was designed in the shape of an amphitheatre, with its wings following the original outline of the old Trocadéro, built for Paris's 1878 Exhibition. The building holds three museums and the Théâtre National de Chaillot, but major restoration is ongoing, and parts of the complex may be inaccessible at any time.

Musée de la Marine ❷

www.musee-marine.fr 01 53 65 69 69 Wed–Mon 10am–6pm charge Trocadéro

In the west wing, this museum charts the history of France as a seafaring nation. Hundreds of models, often of extraordinary craftsmanship, cover everything from historic battleships and three-masted schooners to langoustine-fishing boats and primitive canoes. A fine painting collection includes Vernet's series of the ports of France, but the centrepiece of the museum is the carved and gilded imperial barge built for Napoleon. Other displays include navigational instruments, sections on ship-building and rope-making, carved whale teeth and giant lighthouse lenses.

Musée de l'Homme ❸

www.mnhn.fr 01 44 05 72 72 Mon, Wed–Fri 9.45am–5pm, Sat, Sun 10am–6pm charge

In the same wing, the "Museum of Mankind" is somewhat reduced since its collection of tribal art was transferred to the Musée du Quai Branly *(see page 224)*. Currently under renovation, it is due to reopen in 2012.

Cité de l'Architecture et du Patrimoine ❹

www.citechaillot.fr 01 53 58 51 52 00 Mon, Wed, Fri, Sat, Sun 11am–7pm, Thur 11am–9pm charge Trocadéro

Located in the east wing, this museum and research centre hosts large-scale exhibitions on related topics. A state-of-the-art audio-visual centre is open to the public.

AROUND THE TROCADÉRO

Against the backdrop of the Palais de Chaillot, the terraces and grassy banks of the garden play host to flamboyant skateboarders and rollerbladers. At night, when the orna-

The imposing Art Deco Palais de Chaillot was built for the Paris International Exhibition of 1937 and is best viewed from the Eiffel Tower.

BELOW: view from the Eiffel Tower.

Maison Baccarat (11 place des Etats-Unis; tel: 01 40 22 11 00), the showcase of illustrious glass manufacturer Baccarat, is an *hôtel particulier* transformed by Philippe Starck into a cocoon of soft brushed concrete, crystal chandeliers and handmade carpets. As well as an elegant showroom, it contains the Cristal Room restaurant and the Galerie-Musée Baccarat, with a display of precious items made for world exhibitions and maharajahs.

RIGHT: 19th-century fashions from the Musée de la Mode. **BELOW:** carousel at the Trocadéro.

mental pool's huge fountains are lit up, the sight is spectacular.

West of Chaillot, villagey **Passy** is an upmarket residential area around busy shopping streets, on Rue de Passy and Rue de l'Assomption.

Maison de Balzac

47 rue Raynouard, www.balzac.paris.fr 01 55 74 41 80 Tue–Sun 10am–6pm free Passy

Wealthy Passy also hides the atmospheric house where the great writer Honoré de Balzac penned much of his massive *Comédie Humaine*, furnished as at the time and with a rich collection of Balzacian manuscripts and memorabilia, including the coffee pot that sustained his legendary 15-hour writing sessions.

PLACE D'IÉNA

Between the Trocadéro and the Champs-Elysées, this busy boulevard-hub is the site of an unusual mix of museums and culture centres.

Musée d'Art Moderne de la Ville de Paris 5

11 avenue du Président-Wilson, www.mam.paris.fr 01 53 67 40 00 Tue–Sun 10am–6pm free, charge for special exhibitions Iéna

To the east, another of the 1937 Exhibition buildings, the Palais de Tokyo, contains the city of Paris's own, underrated modern art collection. It gives a coherent survey of 20th-century art, especially relating to Paris, with strong holdings of the Fauvists, the *Ecole de Paris* *(see page 215)* and conceptual art from the 1970s. Its masterpieces include works by Picasso, Matisse (among them *La Danse*, 1932), Modigliani, Van Dongen and Soutine, and Raoul Dufy's gigantic mural *La Fée Electricité* (Electricity Fairy), a celebration of light and energy commissioned for the 1937 Exhibition; displayed in an oval room, it serves as a reminder of the building's original purpose as the Electricity Pavilion. The museum is well known for its temporary shows.

Palais de Tokyo – Site de Création Contemporaine 6

13 avenue du Président-Wilson, www.palaisdetokyo.com 01 47 23 54 01 Tue–Sun noon–midnight charge Iéna

Recommended Restaurants, Bars and Cafés on pages 232–3

In the east wing of the Palais, this state-funded contemporary arts centre, opened in 2002, is intended to serve as a laboratory for current art production. An adventurous, multi-disciplinary programme focuses on young artists through a dynamic mix of exhibitions, performances and workshops, and its fresh atmosphere, the hip "Tokyo Eat" restaurant-café, a stylish souvenir shop and the unique late-night opening hours have made it hugely popular.

Musée Galliera/Musée de la Mode de la Ville de Paris ❼

✉ 10 avenue Pierre 1er de Serbie, www.paris.fr/musees ☎ 01 56 52 86 00 ⏲ during exhibitions Tue–Sun 10am–6pm € charge Ⓜ Iéna

The imposing Italianate Palais Galliera is hard to miss. It houses the municipal collection of some 12,000 outfits and 60,000 accessories dating from the 18th century to the present day. To rotate these rich holdings, only a fraction of which can be displayed at a time, two exhibitions are held each year

focusing on a historic period, a theme or a designer.

Musée Guimet ❽

✉ 6 place d'Iéna, www.museeguimet.fr ☎ 01 56 52 86 00 ⏲ Wed–Mon 10am–6pm € charge Ⓜ Iéna

One of the world's finest museums of Asian art, the Guimet reopened in 2001 after five years of renovation. Begun as the private collection of industrialist Emile Guimet but later

ABOVE: Musée Guimet. **BELOW:** the Musée d'Art Moderne de la Ville de Paris.

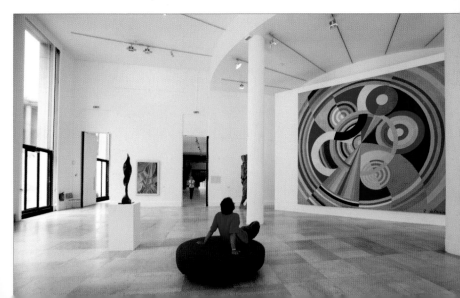

The branches of the city's sewers, which follow the road network almost exactly, are signposted with the same names (and the same blue-and-white plaques) as the streets above them. There are 2,050 km (1,274 miles) of sewers inside the Paris ringroad; the first public tours took place in 1867, during that year's Paris Exhibition.

taken over by the French state, the once-dusty museum has been enlarged and rejuvenated with spacious day-lit galleries that give its collections new visibility. The superb collection includes oriental art, statuary and textiles from China, Japan, India, Tibet, Nepal, Pakistan, Afghanistan, Korea and Vietnam – a reflection of France's colonial past. The prize exhibits are the Cambodian Buddhist sculptures from the temples of Angkor.

Across the Pont de l'Alma

Cross the Pont de l'Alma to discover two very different but equally fascinating museums.

Les Egouts de Paris – The Paris Sewers ❾

entrance by 93 quai d'Orsay, www.paris.fr/culture 01 53 68 27 81 Wed–Sat May–Sept 11am–5pm, Oct–Apr 11am–4pm charge RER Pont de l'Alma

For a surprisingly entertaining experience, descend into the bowels of Paris for an excursion into the sewer system, and a museum full of interesting facts about waste and water. Described by Hugo in *Les Misérables* as the "other Paris", this network of tunnels follows the well-known streets above ground. Accompanied by a film and, unsurprisingly, a strong odour, this is the alternative tour of Paris.

Musée du Quai Branly ❿

37 quai Branly, www.quaibranly.fr 01 56 61 70 00 Tue, Wed, Sun 11am–7pm, Thur, Fri, Sat until 9pm charge RER Pont d'Alma

Unlike his predecessor François Mitterrand, President Jacques Chirac was not known for his *grands projets*, but in his last years in office he sponsored this new museum of world cultures, in a multicoloured building by architect Jean Nouvel. It houses a fabulous collection of tribal art, including African, Aztec and Mayan artefacts, many formerly in the Musée de l'Homme or other museums but which can now be seen in a whole new light.

The Eiffel Tower

It's a short walk from the Musée du Quai Branly to Paris's trademark.

BELOW: the Musée du Quai Branly.

Recommended Restaurants, Bars and Cafés on pages 232–3

Tour Eiffel ⓫

www.tour-eiffel.fr
01 44 11 23 23 daily mid-June–Aug 9am–midnight, Sept–mid-June 9.30am–11pm charge
RER Champ de Mars-Tour Eiffel

When Gustave Eiffel's icon of iron girders was chosen as the centrepiece to the Exhibition of 1889, he claimed enthusiastically, "France will be the only country with a 300-metre flag-pole!" But his designs were met with a barrage of opposition. Opéra architect Charles Garnier and novelist Guy de Maupassant were the most vocal opponents; Maupassant organised a protest picnic under the tower's four legs – "the only place out of sight of the wretched construction".

However, the Parisian public loved their new tower, and only a few years later it was being lauded by writers and artists such as Apollinaire, Jean Cocteau, Dufy and Utrillo. Surviving a proposal for it to be dismantled in 1909, when the placing of a radio transmitter at the top saved the day, the tower is now swarmed over by some 6 million visitors a year.

The first two floors are negotiated on foot or by lift, and then another lift goes up to the top which, as well as a weather station and air navigation point, is an observation platform with space for up to 800 people at a time. The view is awesome. At night, the tower is transformed into a giant piece of diamond-studded jewellery, as 20,000 flashbulbs start firing on the hour to create a stunning five-minute display.

Along the Champ de Mars

Stretching beneath the Eiffel Tower are the ever-crowded gardens of the

ABOVE: view of Les Invalides from the Eiffel Tower.
BELOW LEFT: bistro La Fontaine de Mars is not too far from the tower.

Eiffel Statistics

At 321 metres (1,054 ft) high, including the masts, the Eiffel Tower was the tallest structure in the world until the Chrysler Building was constructed in New York in 1930. On hot days, the ironwork expands, enabling it to grow as much as an incredible 15 cm (6 inches).

A masterpiece of engineering, Gustave Eiffel's tower, world symbol of Paris, is held together with 2.5 million rivets, and the 10,100 tonnes of iron exert a pressure of 4 kg per sq cm (57 lb per sq inch), equivalent to the weight of a man sitting on a chair. Even in the strongest winds, the tower has never swayed more than 12 cm (4 inches). Up to 40 tonnes of paint are used when it is painted, every seven years. There are 360 steps to the first level, where there's an audio-visual presentation of the tower's history, and another 700 to the second. There's always a queue for the lifts, which travel 100,000 km (62,137 miles) a year. On the third level is Gustave Eiffel's sitting room. On a clear day panoramas of over 65 km (40 miles) can be seen.

After seven years of negotiation with the British government, Louis-Philippe, King of France, obtained permission to repatriate Napoleon's remains from St Helena.

Champ de Mars. For centuries this was a market garden supplying vegetables to Parisians, but after the Ecole Militaire was built in 1752 it became a parade ground, with capacity for 10,000 men. The first balloon filled with hydrogen rather than hot air was launched from here in 1783, and it was the venue for the first-anniversary celebration of the storming of the Bastille – a miserable Louis XVI was forced to attend.

RIGHT: no less than 12 kg (26 lb) of gold were needed when the Eglise du Dôme was regilded in 1989. **BELOW:** the interior of the dome was painted by Charles de la Fosse.

At the far end of the gardens is the imposing **Ecole Militaire** ⓬ (closed to the public). Louis XV commissioned the military college to help men of little means learn the art of soldiering, and a young Napoleon studied here for a year in 1784. The splendid 18th-century academy, designed by Jacques-Ange Gabriel, is still the foundation stone of French military expertise. The main facade, with its Cour d'Honneur enclosed by colonnades, borders Avenue de Lowendal.

UNESCO ⓭

7 place Fontenoy, www.unesco.org 01 45 68 03 59 visits by reservation free Ségur

Behind the university of war is the foundation for reconciliation and understanding, the headquarters of the United Nations cultural organisation. The graceful, Y-shaped building was designed by an alliance of American, French and Italian architects, and engineers led by Bauhaus member Marcel Breuer. Inside, 142 countries cooperate on educational, scientific and cultural projects. A tem-

Recommended Restaurants, Bars and Cafés on pages 232–3

ple of modern art, its decoration is equally cosmopolitan: Joan Miró ceramics, Henry Moore sculptures, an Alexander Calder mobile as well as a huge Picasso mural. The Japanese garden displays a spine-chilling relic: a stone angel found after the atomic bomb blast at Nagasaki in 1945.

LES INVALIDES ⓮

www.invalides.org 01 44 42 38 77 daily Apr–Sept 10am–6pm, Oct–Mar 10–5pm; closed 1st Mon of each month except July–Sept charge, includes Dôme and museums Invalides

The gleaming dome of the **Hôtel des Invalides** is a masterpiece of French Baroque architecture and one of Paris's most prominent landmarks. Behind it is a remarkable set of 17th-century buildings commissioned by Louis XIV to house and care for retired and wounded soldiers. It also served as the royal arsenal, and it was from here, in 1789, that revolutionaries comandeered 30,000 rifles for the storming of the Bastille. Napoleon, whose wars kept the hospital full, restored the institution to its former glory, making the church a necropolis and regilding its dome. The **Eglise du Dôme**, built as a royal chapel for Louis XIV, now contains Bonaparte's tomb. The emperor's body was returned to the city from St Helena in 1840, with much pomp and ceremony, and eventually laid to rest in the church crypt. His giant mausoleum is fittingly overblown.

Spread across either side of the Cour d'Honneur, the large **Musée de**

In 1784 Napoleon entered the Ecole Militaire as a cadet. He left as a sub-lieutenant a year later, with the recommendation: "He will go far, circumstances permitting."

LEFT: take time out from sightseeing with a light lunch at Sancerre (22 avenue Rapp). **BELOW:** the Bleuet de France organisation still collects funds for war veterans today.

FOOD

Every Thursday and Saturday the pleasant tree-lined Avenue de Saxe, south of the Ecole Militaire, plays host to the lovely Saxe-Breteuil market. The produce sold by the fruit and vegetable vendors, charcuterie and cheese specialists, fishmongers and olive stalls, is faultlessly fresh and well sourced.

BELOW RIGHT: Rodin's *The Thinker.*

l'Armée offers an extensive view of man's inhumanity to man and skill at warfare from the Stone Age to Hiroshima, with a terrifying selection of weapons and armour, and poignant displays on the two world wars. In a separate wing, the **Musée de l'Ordre de la Libération** commemorates the Resistance fighters who received the Order of Liberation, created by De Gaulle in 1940.

Stretching to the Seine, the grassy **Esplanade des Invalides** is much loved by strollers, joggers, dog-walkers and rollerbladers. On its west side is a series of *pétanque* courts, and nearby is a small airport coach terminal, by the Métro-RER station.

Around Les Invalides

Heading east along the Seine towards the Musée d'Orsay *(see page 231)*, you immediately pass the august colonnades of France's parliament, the **Assemblée Nationale (Palais Bourbon)** ⓯ (www.assemblee-nationale.fr; tel: 01 40 63 60 00, ring for details of guided tours). The extravagant Neo-Grecian columns facing the river were grafted onto the earlier 18th-century palace by Napoleon, to complement his Madeleine across the river, and they now shelter an armed guard in charge of protecting the 491 *députés* (Members of Parliament).

Musée Rodin ⓰

✉ Hôtel Biron, 79 rue de Varenne, www.musee-rodin.fr ☎ 01 44 18 61 10 ⓒ Tue–Sun Apr–Sept 9.30am–5.15pm, Oct–Mar 9.30am–4.15pm Ⓢ charge Ⓜ Varenne

Just next to Les Invalides stands the **Hôtel Biron**, a charming 18th-century *hôtel particulier* that's now for ever linked to its most famous occupant. Auguste Rodin's first critically acclaimed sculpture was *The Age of Bronze* (1877), depicting a naked youth caressing his hair, modelled by a Belgian soldier. The establishment was shocked, maintaining that the statue was too lifelike to be regarded as art. A card stuck to the work at the Paris salon read: "Beware – moulded from the body of the model." Eventually, the French gov-

Solid Genius

Auguste Rodin was born in the Quartier Latin in 1840, and grew up wandering the markets of Rue Mouffetard *(see page 197)*. Trained at the Petite Ecole from age 14, but rejected by the Ecole des Beaux-Arts, he worked as an assistant for ornamental artists and the sculptor Carrier-Belleuse, training himself while visiting the zoo at the Jardin des Plantes and horse markets on Boulevard St-Michel for inspiration. A trip to Italy in 1876, where he discovered Michelangelo, transformed his career. Further stimulus came from his incessant love affairs, interrupted only for a while when he took holy orders as a reaction to the death of his sister in a convent, after she had been rejected in love by one of his own close friends. Chastity did not suit him, though, and he soon returned to his mistresses and his art. Among his masterpieces are *The Kiss, The Thinker, The Burghers of Calais* and the unfinished *Gates of Hell,* on which he worked from the 1880s until his death in 1917.

Map on page 220

Recommended Restaurants, Bars and Cafés on pages 232–3

ernment bought the statue, and Rodin's reputation was confirmed.

Rodin came to live in the Hôtel Biron in 1908, and stayed here until his death in 1917. He paid his rent with his best works, which form the basis of the museum's exquisite collection. Here you can admire *The Kiss* (removed from the Chicago World Fair of 1893 for being too shocking), *The Thinker* (reputedly Dante contemplating the Inferno), *The Burghers of Calais*, *The Hand of God* and many other works.

Recently restored to their white marble finish, the statues ripple with life. Bronze casts of many of Rodin's major works are displayed outside in the beautiful rose garden, amid the lawns, hedged enclosures, pools, mature trees and topiaried yews, providing a context for the studies and smaller works around the house. Also in the garden is one of Paris's most atmospheric museum cafés.

Included in the exhibition are works by Camille Claudel, the most famous of Rodin's mistresses and a gifted artist in her own right.

Faubourg St-Germain

The area lying east of Les Invalides is well worth exploring, an elegant, aristocratic extension of St-Germain-des-Prés built up in the 18th century. Begin with Paris's most interesting cinema and tea house, **La Pagode** ⓱ in Rue de Babylone. The tea is strong, the gardens tropical and the films up to date, and the building itself is simply stunning, a 19th-century replica of a Far Eastern

ABOVE: convivial eating in the Faubourg St-Germain.
BELOW: the beautiful back garden of the Musée Rodin.

The Musée du Vin (Rue des Eaux, 16th; tel: 01 45 25 63 26), with its inappropriate address, is a sweet little museum devoted to all things related to the vine: tools, bottles, corkscrews and more. Visits conclude, naturally, with a glass of wine.

BELOW: some of the Musée d'Orsay's finest works: *L'Absinthe* by Edgar Degas (detail) and Renoir's *Danse à la Campagne*.

pagoda whose main auditorium is lined with golden dragon motifs.

When the nobility moved out of the Marais in the 18th century, the rich and famous built new town houses across the river from the Tuileries. Beautifully preserved, they are now mostly shut away behind heavily secured gates, since only French ministries and foreign governments can afford the rent. On Boulevard Raspail (at No. 45) stands the **Hôtel Lutétia ⓲**, its extravagant statued facade fronting a de luxe, four-star hotel where Charles de Gaulle enjoyed his first night of married life. When the hotel was requisitioned by the Gestapo in 1940, the owner bricked up the vintage wine cellar and, even though the hotel staff were interrogated to reveal the whereabouts of the *cave*, no one talked.

Continue walking along Boulevard Raspail towards the Seine until you come to Rue de Grenelle on the left, a narrow street stacked with beautiful buildings, including the Swiss and Dutch embassies, the Ministry of Education and the National Geographic Institute.

Musée Maillol – Fondation Dina Vierny ⓳

61 rue de Grenelle, www.museemaillol.com 01 42 22 59 58 Wed–Mon 11am–6pm charge Rue du Bac

The Hôtel Bouchardon is a distinguished 18th-century residence where the poet Alfred de Musset lived between 1824 and 1839, before going on an oriental voyage of discovery with George Sand. Since 1995 it has housed this museum displaying the works of sculptor Aristide Maillol, along with art by contemporaries Cézanne and Degas, drawings by Matisse, multiples by Duchamp, and works by Russian and Naïve artists. Dina Vierny, its founder and owner, was an art dealer and model for Maillol, whose sculptures adorn the Tuileries.

Rue de Varenne, one street over, has a collection of fine old houses, the most famous being the Paris residence of the French Prime Minister, **Hôtel Matignon ⓴**, which has the biggest private garden in the city.

Recommended Restaurants, Bars and Cafés on pages 232–3

MUSÉE D'ORSAY 21

www.musee-orsay.fr 01 40 49 48 14 Tue–Sun 9.30am–6pm, Thur until 9.45pm charge RER Musée d'Orsay

No visit to Paris is complete without a pilgrimage to this spectacular former railway station, crammed full of the finest art spanning the period from 1848 to World War I. Built in two years in 1898–1900, it was almost torn down to make way for a hotel in 1970. Prompted by public outcry, the government fulfilled the prophecy of painter Edouard Détaille, who said at the opening ceremony in 1900 that the station would make a better museum. Its glass-and-iron construction was a triumph of modernity, rivalling Eiffel's tower, while the facade reflected the Louvre across the river. Redesigned as a museum by Italian architect Gae Aulenti, it opened in 1986.

The museum is arranged on five levels around a vast central aisle, a grand setting for sculpture by artists such as Rudé, Cavalier and Guillaume. The best pieces are by Carpeaux, the Second Empire's foremost sculptor, including his controversial *La Danse* for the Opéra Garnier.

Other artworks are displayed in chronological order; starting on the ground floor, there are famous works by Ingres (notably *La Source*), Romantic painting by Delacroix, like the colourful *La Chasse aux Lions (Lion Hunt)*, and Manet's nude *Olympia* (1863), pronounced pornographic at the 1865 Paris salon and considered the first "modern" painting.

The museum's biggest draw, its Impressionist paintings, hang on the crowded top floor, bathed in soft light from the glass-vaulted roof. The galleries are full of paintings by Monet, Manet, Renoir, Pissarro, Degas, Cézanne and Van Gogh. At the end is a small café with great views of Paris.

On the mezzanine are works by the Nabis painters, Vuillard, Bonnard and Denis. There is also a fine collection of Art Nouveau decorative arts, with furniture by Guimard and Van der Velde and a wood-panelled salon by Alexandre Charpentier.

Next door, the **Musée National de la Légion d'Honneur** 22 (www.legiondhonneur.fr; tel: 01 40 62 84 25; Tue–Sun 11am–6pm; charge), with a pleasant courtyard, tells the story of France's most celebrated award. ❑

The smart 16th arrondissement is the domain of the wealthy. Passy and Auteuil, in its southern half, were spa towns in the 17th century; Passy still has a villagey air, but has a few busy shopping streets; Auteuil, less commercial, has many grand residences.

LEFT: the exquisite clock inside the Musée d'Orsay is a reminder of its past as a railway station.

Fair's Fair

Paris owes many famous buildings and monuments – even its most famous, the Eiffel Tower – to the series of World Fairs, *Expositions universelles*, it staged in the 19th and 20th centuries. The first Trocadéro was built for the Exhibition of 1878, and demolished to make way for the Palais de Chaillot, centrepiece of the city's last big fair in 1937, an event that also produced the Palais de Tokyo. Other durable constructions are the Grand and Petit Palais, built for the *Exposition* of 1900 – as was Pont Alexandre III and the Gare d'Orsay, now the Musée d'Orsay.

World Fairs were grand jamborees of national pride, a chance to show the world a catalogue of French triumphs in technology and the arts. The idea came from London, with the Great Exhibition of 1851, but Paris took to it with verve, staging its first fair in 1855; the second, in 1867, gave its patron Napoleon III great popular prestige. The 1937 fair was very different, a symbolic face-off between Nazi Germany and Soviet Russia, whose grandiose pavilions were opposite each other. Notably, the Spanish pavilion featured Picasso's famous *Guernica* – while the Exhibition jury awarded a Grand Prix to Hitler's architect Albert Speer, for his design for the Nazi rally grounds at Nuremberg.

BEST RESTAURANTS, BARS AND CAFÉS

Restaurants

Price includes dinner and a half-bottle of house wine:
€ = under €25
€€ = €25–40
€€€ = €40–60
€€€€ = more than €60

L'Affriolé

17 rue Malar, 7th ☎ 01 44 18 31 33 Ⓛ L & D Mon–Fri. **€€** [p335, C4]
One of the most appealing bistros in the area, with colourful mosaic tables and decorated with traditional *objets de cuisine*. The menu is seasonal and changes daily, and dishes are artfully presented with little *amuse-bouches* (appetisers). Reservations recommended.

L'Ami Jean

27 rue Malar, 7th ☎ 01 47 05 86 89 Ⓛ L & D Tue–Sat. **€€** [p335, C4]
Chef Stéphane Jégo has taken over this long-standing Basque restaurant, and he sends out some fine food from his kitchen: dishes like veal shank with the bones removed and served with onions and broad beans, or salted cod that's drizzled with a nice vinaigrette.

L'Arpège

84 rue de Varenne, 7th ☎ 01 45 51 47 33 Ⓛ L & D Mon–Fri. **€€€€** [p341, D1]
Chef Alain Passard, one of the heavyweight stars of French cuisine and an accomplished musician, hit the headlines when he turned his haute cuisine restaurant vegetarian, though he has since started serving seafood and poultry again. Much of the produce comes from his own kitchen garden. Beetroot baked in Guérande sea salt and the 12-flavours tomato confit dessert are among his famed inventions. The wine list hits the stratosphere. There's also a *prix fixe* lunch menu.

L'Atelier de Joël Robuchon

5 rue de Montalembert, 7th ☎ 01 42 22 56 56 Ⓛ L & D daily. **€€€€** [p338, A2]
Superchef Robuchon came out of retirement to open this de luxe "snack bar". The restaurant is built around an open kitchen, so you can watch the masters at work, and the atmosphere is slick, like that of a bar. It's out with long sophisticated menus, and in with the tapas principle, involving small portions of outstandingly creative dishes (order as many as your appetite or budget will allow). Reservations or first seatings only (11.30am and 6.30pm).

Au Bon Accueil

14 rue Montlessuy, 7th ☎ 01 47 05 46 11 Ⓛ L & D Mon–Fri. **€€** (set menu) **€€€** (à la carte) [p340, C1]
The Eiffel Tower can be seen looming from the pavement tables of this neighbourhood favourite. Inside is a sleek, contemporary dining room. The daily menu is based on market-fresh produce and the *prix fixe* menu is great value. The wine list is excellent (if expensive).

Chez Les Anges

54 boulevard de la Tour-Maubourg, 7th ☎ 01 47 05 89 86 Ⓛ L & D Mon–Fri. **€€** (set menu) **€€€** (à la carte) [p341, D1]
The decor is sleek and modern at this revamped restaurant, whose food changes with what the markets have to offer. The short set menu is a bargain, and à la carte options include red tuna tart with tomato fondue to start with and Bresse chicken as a main.

L'Esplanade

52 rue Fabert, 7th ☎ 01 47 05 38 80 Ⓛ L & D daily (until 1am). **€€€** [p335, D4]
This bar-restaurant has it all: breathtaking views of Les Invalides from the terrace, opulent decor

LEFT: the unbeatable L'Atelier de Joël Robuchon, for fabulous food by one of France's top chefs. **RIGHT:** friendly dining at Le 20 de Bellechasse.

by Jacques Garcia, a fashionable crowd and good, if expensive contemporary food.

La Fontaine de Mars

129 rue St-Dominque, 7th
01 47 05 46 44 L & D daily. €€€ [p340, C1]
The menu changes depending on the market, but southwest fare takes pride of place at this 1930s neighbourhood bistro. The house speciality, *cassoulet au canard confit*, is the real thing and so is the *île flottante*.

Tokyo Eat

Palais de Tokyo, 13 avenue du Président-Wilson, 16th
01 47 20 00 29 L & D Tue–Sun. €€€ [p334, B4]
The restaurant inside the Palais de Tokyo art gallery is an airy space with open kitchen, artist-customised chairs and funky lighting. The food, which skips from global satays, tandooris and unusual carpaccios to old faves like roast chicken, is generally OK, drawing the bright young things of western Paris as well as the art world. In fine weather, the restaurant migrates outside onto the terrace.

Le Vin de Bellechasse

20 rue de Bellechasse, 7th
01 47 05 11 11
L & D Mon–Fri. €€–€€€ [p341, E1]
A lovely restaurant with red *banquettes* and caricatures of loyal clients and stars on the wall. The menu and the wine list are well priced, and the setting is both intimate and lively. A popular locale among low-key fashion types and other creative or literary souls.

Bars and Cafés

Bellota-Bellota

18 rue Jean-Nicot, 7th. Tel: 01 53 59 96 96. Tue–Sat 11am– 11pm. [p335, C4]
A gem of a tapas bar specialising in the fine Iberian ham after which it is named, as well as Spanish cheeses, wine and seafood. Great for grazing or a light, romantic dinner. You can stop in and dine at the bar if you're early; otherwise reserve one of the handful of tables.

Le Café Constant

139 rue St-Dominique, 7th. Tel: 01 47 53 73 34. Tue–Sun 8.30am–10.30pm. [p340, C1]
It's a buzzy place, this café – hardly surprising given the quality of the food and the light price tag. There's a blackboard menu that changes regularly, lining up dishes like salmon-folded poached eggs with salad or steak tartare that's been cooked under the grill. Nice wines, too.

Le Café du Marché

38 rue Cler, 7th. Tel: 01 47 05 51 27. Non-stop Mon–Sat. [p341, C1]
Rue Cler is a market street, hence the name of this ever popular café – ideal for a break in the middle of a bit of shopping, which is exactly what most of the clientele are doing. The house wine, served by the carafe, is as good as the food.

The Eiffel Tower

It's the thing that, more than any other, says "Paris" – a true icon that was originally intended to stand for a mere 20 years

It's the most famous monument in the world – or at least, a member of a very select club: only the Pyramids and the Statue of Liberty (whose framework was also designed by Eiffel) enjoy similar renown. Built for the 1889 Exposition Universelle, it took over two years to build; it remained the world's tallest building until 1930, when it was overtaken by the Chrysler Building in New York (though the tower gained another 20 metres in 1957, with the addition of television aerials). Not everyone liked it at first, but today the tower is the most visited attraction in Paris. It has three platforms open to the public, at 57, 115 and 276 metres from the ground; and two restaurants, the Altitude 95 on the first level, and the haute cuisine Jules Verne on the second.

Above: this stamp dates from 1939 and commemorates the 50th anniversary of the Eiffel Tower.

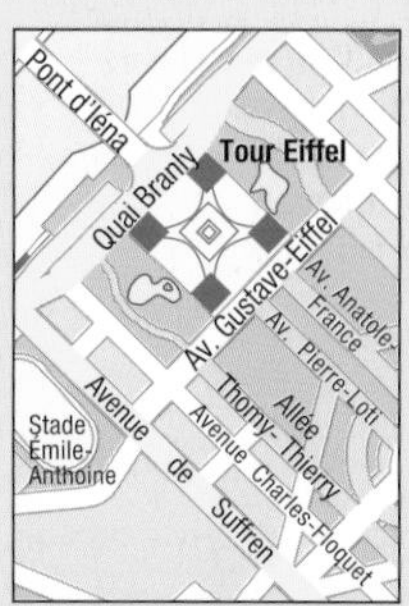

Essential info

www.tour-eiffel.fr
01 44 11 23 23
daily mid-June–Aug 9am–midnight, Sept–mid-June 9.30am–11pm
charge
RER *Champ de Mars-Tour Eiffel*

Above: the Eiffel Tower took two years to build. The first man to climb it was the Prince of Wales (later Edward VII).

Below: three large lifts operate between the ground and the second level; four smaller cabins then take visitors to the top.

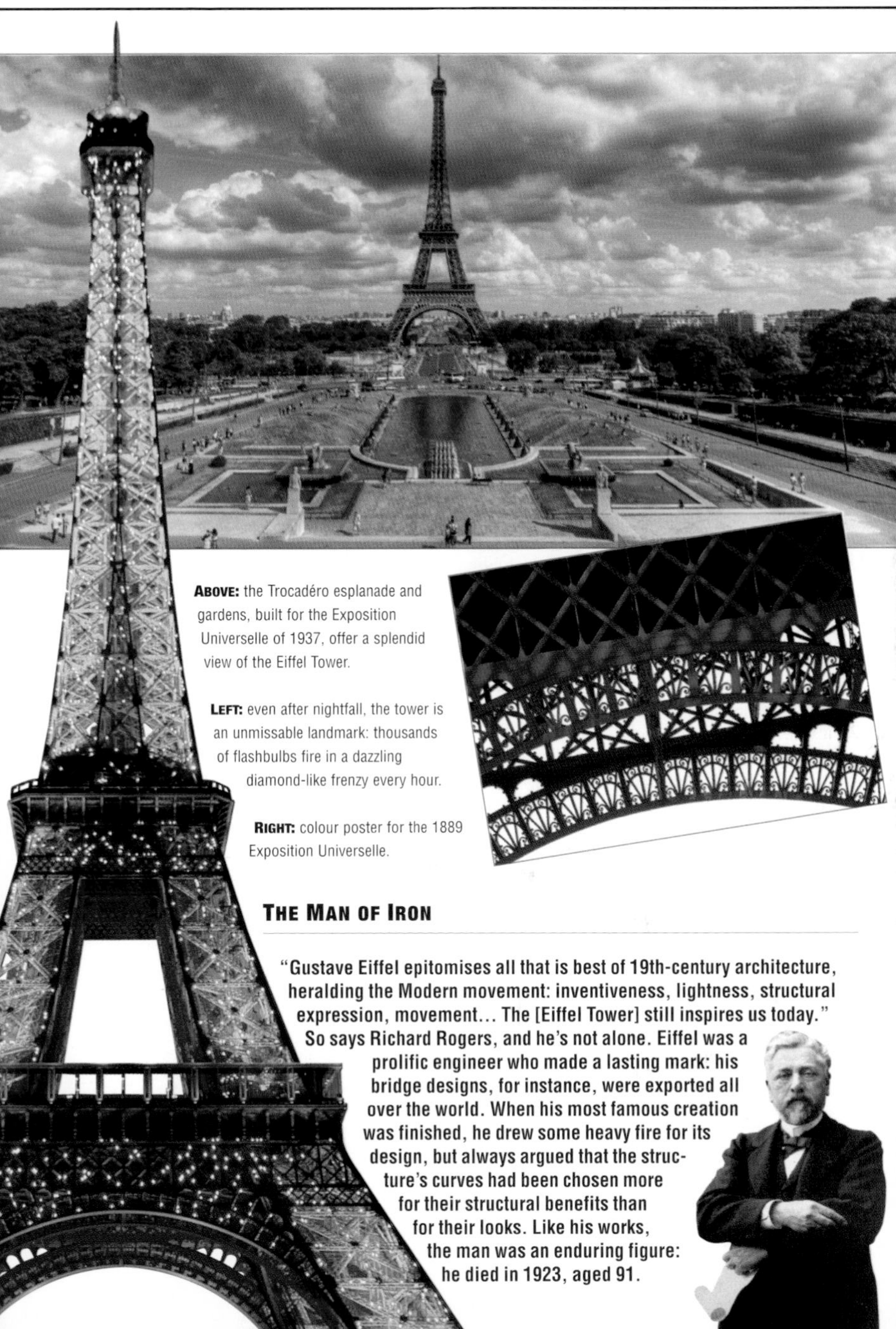

ABOVE: the Trocadéro esplanade and gardens, built for the Exposition Universelle of 1937, offer a splendid view of the Eiffel Tower.

LEFT: even after nightfall, the tower is an unmissable landmark: thousands of flashbulbs fire in a dazzling diamond-like frenzy every hour.

RIGHT: colour poster for the 1889 Exposition Universelle.

THE MAN OF IRON

"Gustave Eiffel epitomises all that is best of 19th-century architecture, heralding the Modern movement: inventiveness, lightness, structural expression, movement… The [Eiffel Tower] still inspires us today." So says Richard Rogers, and he's not alone. Eiffel was a prolific engineer who made a lasting mark: his bridge designs, for instance, were exported all over the world. When his most famous creation was finished, he drew some heavy fire for its design, but always argued that the structure's curves had been chosen more for their structural benefits than for their looks. Like his works, the man was an enduring figure: he died in 1923, aged 91.

Musée d'Orsay

The national museum of 19th-century art is best-known for its French Impressionist paintings, but its collection also contains key pieces from other artistic movements

When the Gare d'Orsay was built to coincide with the Exposition Universelle of 1900, painter Edouard Détaille said it looked like a palace of fine art – and that, just over eight decades later, is exactly what it became. For all that, the Musée d'Orsay is the museum that very nearly didn't happen. It was no longer a railway station by 1950 (its platforms were too short for modern trains) and was lined up for demolition. However, after a short spell as a theatre, President Giscard d'Estaing had it turned into a museum devoted to art – painting, sculpture and decorative works – from the period between 1848 and 1914, and since then it has been one of the city's three most important museums. The building itself is an impressive sight.

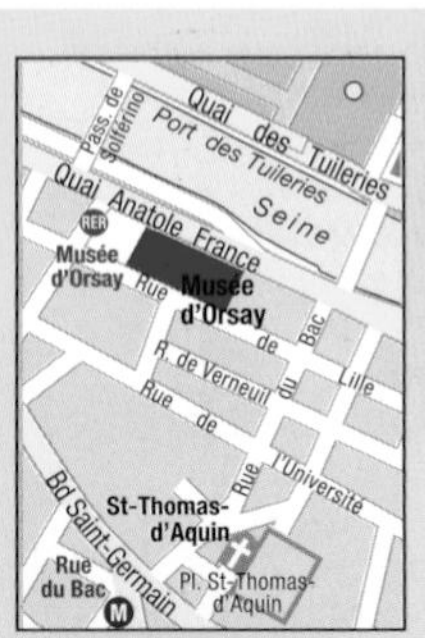

Essential info

www.musee-orsay.fr
01 40 49 48 14
Tue–Sun 9.30am–6pm, Thur until 9.45pm
charge
RER Musée d'Orsay

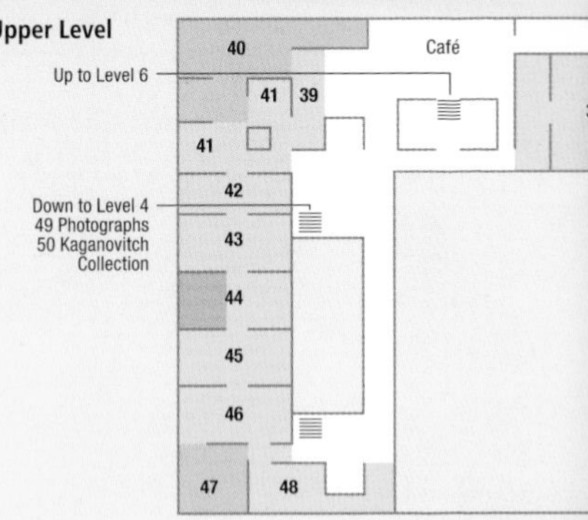

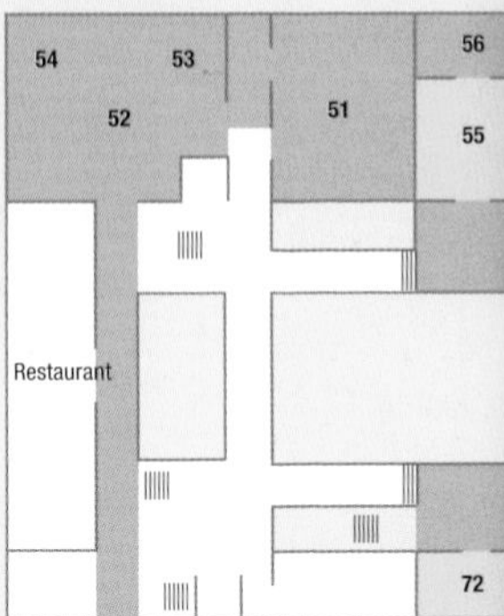

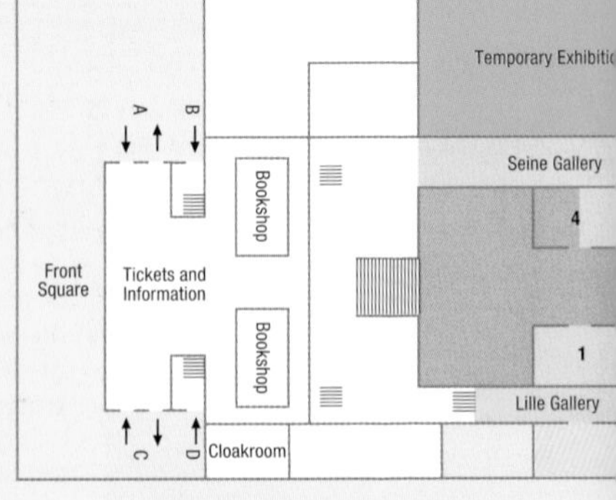

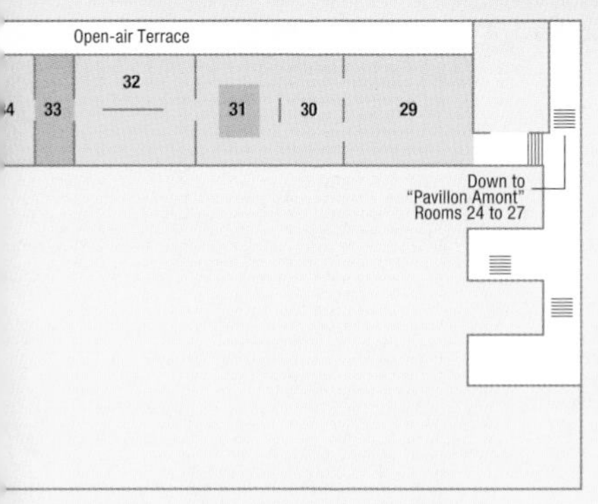

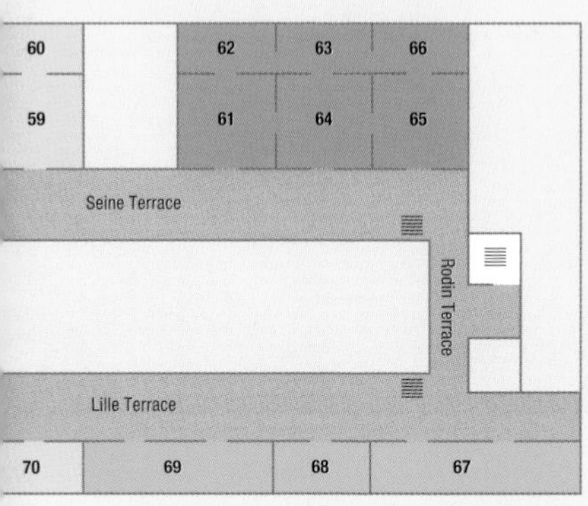

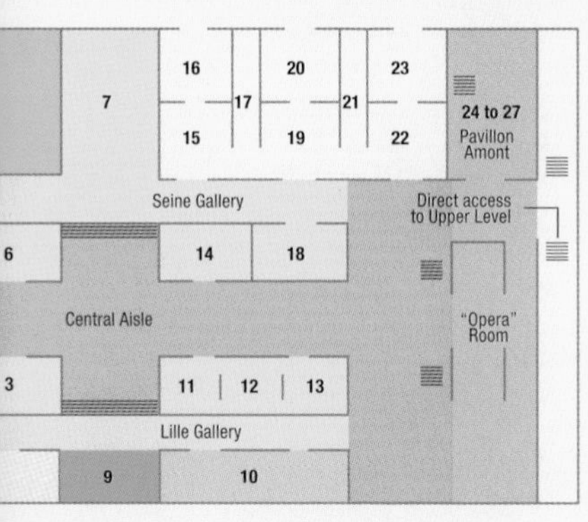

Sculpture

Painting

Architecture

Decorative Arts

Exhibitions

Drawings and Pastels

Photography

THE HIGHLIGHTS

The Musée d'Orsay follows a chronological route, from the ground floor to the upper level and then to the mezzanine, thereby showing links between the Impressionist painters and their forerunners.

Ground Floor

In the central sculpture aisle, François Rude's monument *Napoleon Waking up to Immortality* is a masterpiece of Romantic grandeur; late neoclassical exercises by Pradier (including *Sapho*, pictured), Cavelier and Guillaume echo antique sculpture; Mercié's *Young David* looks to the Renaissance. To the rear of the aisle is a superb model of the Opéra Garnier. The decorative arts galleries on the ground floor and mezzanine parallel developments in fine art: on the lowest level, don't miss the wardrobe by Diehl and Brandoly. The ground floor also has a number of paintings: Cabanel's sentimental *Birth of Venus*; the scandalous *Olympia* by Manet; Daumier's expressive *Crispin et Scapin* and his 24 painted clay heads, *Célébrités du Juste Milieu*, and Ingres's *La Source*, are also worth looking out for on this floor.

Middle Level

The opulent Salle des Fêtes houses academic marble sculpture, as well as Fantin-Latour's famous group portraits *Table Corner* and *A Studio in the Batignolles Quarter*, and Vuillard's painting, *In Bed*.

BELOW: based on a painting by Titian, Edouard Manet's *Olympia* caused a scandal when exhibited in 1865 – not least for the full-on gaze the subject (clearly a prostitute) aims at the spectator.

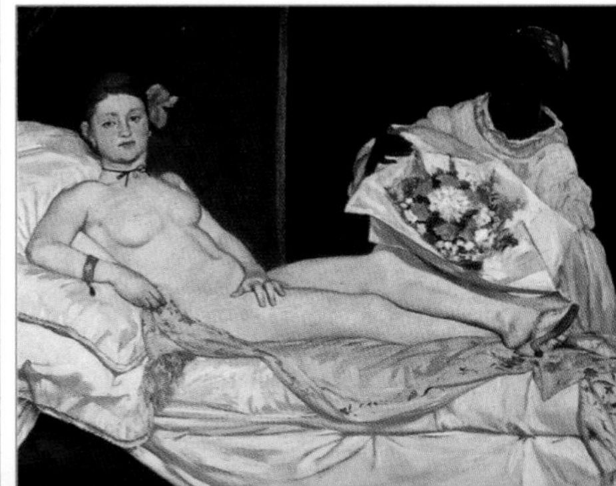

Above: Monet's famous painting *The Poppies* is one of the Impressionist movement's keystones, and one of the most widely reproduced works of art of all time. It was painted in the summer of 1873 at Argenteuil, a few miles west of the capital.

Above: the Gare d'Orsay was converted into a museum between 1977 and 1986. From the museum's upper level, visitors get a strong sense the original railway station layout: the platforms ran either side of wha now the central sculpture aisle. The vast, curved glass-and-iron roof is shown to advantage, as is the elaborate decoration over the side arche The glorious gilded clock at the far end is original.

Below: between 1888 and 1889, Van Gogh painted two versions of *L'Arlésienne* – a portrait of Mme Ginoux, owner of the Café de la Gare in Arles. This is likely to be the first; the second is in the Metropolitan Museum of Art in New York.

Right: Hippolyte Moulin's *Secret from on High* (1879) depicts a life-size nude Mercury (Hermes) whispering a secret to a herm, knowing that it will never repeat what he tells it.

THE HIGHLIGHTS (CONTINUED)

Upper Level

Most visitors come to see the Impressionist and Post-Impressionist paintings in the Galerie des Hauteurs. In the first room (29) is Manet's masterpiece *Le Déjeuner sur l'Herbe*; his pastels are exhibited in rooms 37 and 38. Monet and Renoir (rooms 32, 34, 39) stuck closest to the Impressionist ideal of pure colour and modelling through light, while Van Gogh (room 35) sought expression through colour and brushstrokes, as in the uneasy, blue *Self-Portrait*. Cézanne (room 36) originally exhibited with the Impressionists, but differed from them in his search for underlying structure. Don't miss the two large panels by Toulouse-Lautrec depicting his favourite models, dancers and personalities. In room 44 are later works by Gauguin, painted in the Pacific.

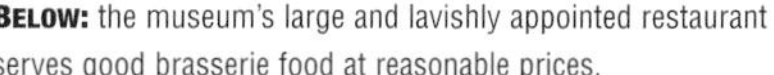

BELOW: the museum's large and lavishly appointed restaurant serves good brasserie food at reasonable prices.

ABOVE: the 1864 painting *Crispin et Scapin*, one of the greatest works by the great satirical artist Honoré Daumier, depicts a performance of 17th-century playwright Molière's play *Les Fourberies de Scapin*.

PARIS PARKS

Paris may often have seen itself as the quintessential city, but even born-and-bred Parisians feel a yearning for open spaces – and in the past few decades highly inventive, all-new parks have been added alongside the city's charming gardens and historic woodland

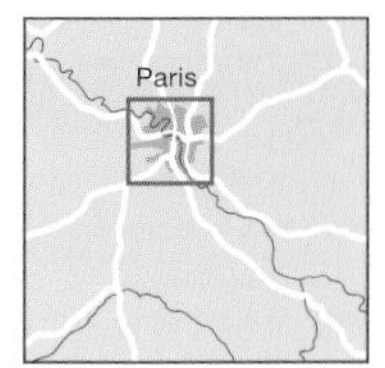

In 1759 Voltaire wound up his famous novel *Candide* with the line "We must cultivate our garden", but it was not until the 19th century that Paris began to make parks and gardens a touchstone for the health of the capital. While the 1980s may be remembered as the decade of the *grands projets* and monumental building, the 1990s and the new millennium have seen the city's parks and gardens flourish. Politicians have realised that improving the urban environment is a vote-winner, and thus derelict industrial sites are flowering and blossoming into suburban parks with a fervour not seen since Haussmann's day. More than ever, Parisians are looking to their green spaces as an escape from the increasing congestion and stress of urban living.

BOIS DE BOULOGNE ❶

Porte Maillot, Porte Dauphine, Porte d'Auteuil, Les Sablons

Past the *Périphérique* ringroad to the west of Paris, the Bois de Boulogne is one of the reasons why the 16th *arrondissement* alongside it is preferred by the wealthy as a place to live – Avenue Foch, perhaps the most expensive residential street in the capital, leads straight to its park gates. Cradled by an elbow of the Seine, this 860-hectare (2,125-acre) expanse of woods and gardens has been the Sunday afternoon playground for generations of Parisian families. Historically, it has also had a reputation for love, as successive kings used to house their mistresses here, and after Louis XIV opened the woods to the

On 19 October 1906, the Bois de Boulogne was the setting for France's first powered flight, when Brazilian aviator Alberto Santos-Dumont flew 60 metres (200 ft) in his box biplane 14bis.

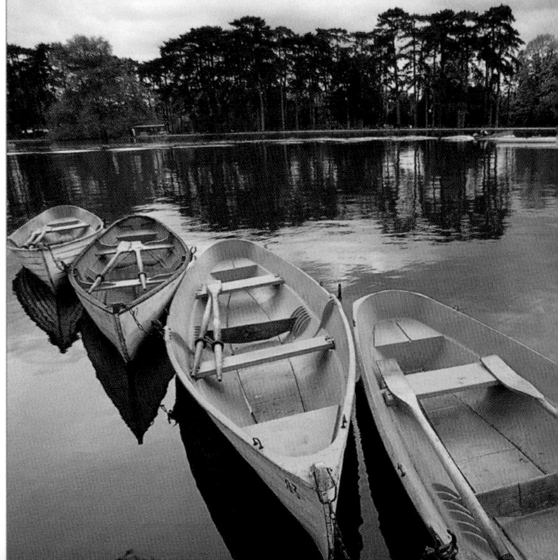

PRECEDING PAGES: blue skies reflected in La Geode in the Parc de la Villette.
LEFT: the Parc de Bagatelle, inside the Bois de Boulogne, in all its autumnal glory.
RIGHT: boating lake in the Bois de Boulogne.

TIP

Every June and July, the lovely Orangerie de Bagatelle, in the Bois de Boulogne, hosts candlelit recitals of the music of Chopin. For information, tel: 01 45 00 22 19 or see www.frederic-chopin.com

public in the 17th century, it was noted that "marriages from the Bois de Boulogne do not get brought before the Right Reverend".

In 1852, Napoleon III had the surrounding wall of the royal hunting ground, built by Henri II, demolished and the park remodelled following the example of Hyde Park in London. Today it offers gardens, wild woods, horse racing at two of France's most famous racecourses, Longchamp and Auteuil, a sports stadium, boating, museums, restaurants and theatre.

Discovering the Bois

A good place to begin exploring the Bois is the beautiful Art Nouveau Métro stop at **Porte Dauphine**, and the best way is by bicycle, which can be rented (May–Sept daily, Oct–Apr Sat–Sun) near the Pavillon Royal, off Route de Suresnes. A network of cycle paths and nature trails criss-crosses the woods, giving easy access to the vast park and its lakes and waterfall. Note that walking around the park at night is a risky undertaking.

On the northern edge is the **Jardin d'Acclimatation** (www.jardindacclimatation.fr; tel: 01 40 67 90 82; daily 10am–6pm, June–Sept until 7pm; charge), an amusement park for children, with a hall of mirrors, zoo, go-kart racing, a wooden fort, theatre and puppet show (Wed, Sat–Sun at 3pm and 4pm). There is also the **Musée en Herbe** (tel: 01 40 67 97 66; Sun–Fri 10am–6pm, Sat 2–6pm), which organises art exhibits and workshops for future Picassos.

Further west, the **Parc de Bagatelle** (charge) surrounds a small château built by the Count of Artois, later Charles X, who bet Marie-Antoinette he could build a house in three months. The bet was won at great cost, hence the ironic name *bagatelle* (meaning "paltry sum"). The gardens are magnificent, with 8,000 roses blooming from June to October, a walled iris garden flowering in May and a display of water lilies in August. Art exhibitions and classical concerts are held in the Trianon and Orangerie during the summer season.

In the centre of the Bois is the **Pré Catalan**, most romantic spot in western Paris. In spring, narcissi, tulips and daffodils carpet the manicured

BELOW: the pink facade of the exquisite Château de Bagatelle.

lawns, bathing the foot of the colossal copper beech, over 200 years old, whose branches span over 500 metres/yds. **Le Pré Catalan** restaurant offers sumptuous fare in elegant Belle Epoque surroundings.

Nearby, the **Jardin Shakespeare** (tel: 01 44 19 95 33; daily for guided tours 3–3.30pm, 4–4.30pm; charge; no credit cards) is planted with flowers, trees and shrubs that feature in Shakespeare's plays: there's *Macbeth's* heather, Mediterranean herbs from *The Tempest* and Ophelia's stream. In summer, open-air productions of the Bard's plays (usually in French) are presented in the leafy theatre.

Musée Marmottan ❷

2 rue Louis Boilly, www.marmottan.com 01 44 96 50 33 Tue–Sun 11am–6pm charge La Muette

Just inside Passy by the eastern border of the park is this dazzling little museum, with 65 paintings by Monet that were donated by his son Michel in 1971, among them his celebrated *Impression Soleil Levant* (1872), which gave its name to the Impressionist movement. Once home to avid art collector Paul Marmottan, this beautiful 19th-century mansion also exhibits works by Pissarro, Renoir, Gauguin and Berthe Morisot, as well as a superb collection of First Empire furniture.

ABOVE: the Bois de Boulogne boasts an array of plants, trees and flowers.

Paris Parks

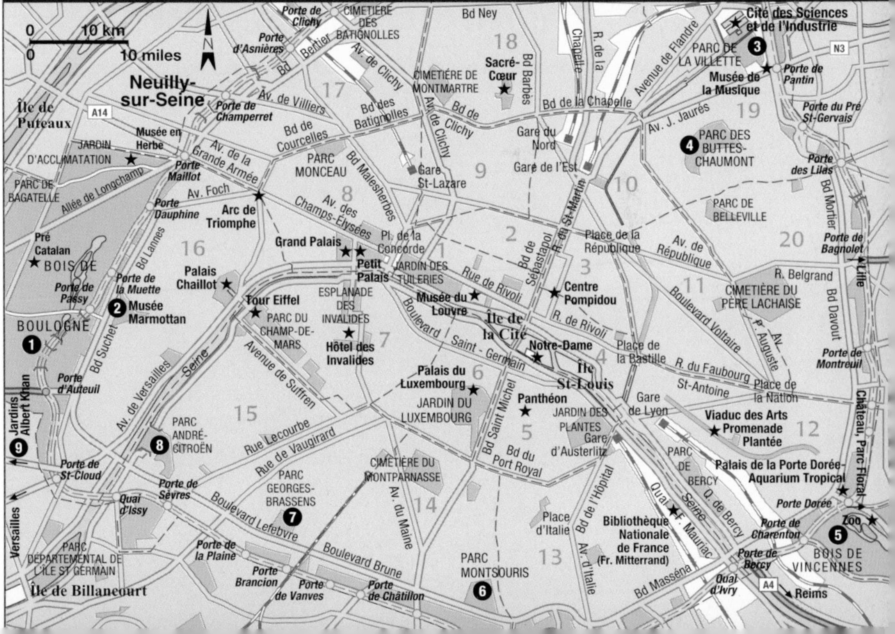

From mid-July to the end of August every year, the Parc de la Villette stages a popular free film season, Le Cinéma en Plein Air; seating is on one of the park's big lawns, and the huge screen is inflatable. The park also holds a 10-day jazz festival each September. For information about both events, tel: 01 40 03 75 75 or log on to www.villette.com.

PARC DE LA VILLETTE ❸

Porte de Pantin, Porte de la Villette

In northeast Paris, nestling against the *Périphérique*, this multi-purpose park and leisure area was one of the most spectacular 1980s *grands projets*. Built on the site of a huge abattoir, rendered obsolete by improved refrigeration techniques and poor design (the cows could not even get up the steps), its 55 hectares (136 acres) of futuristic gardens surround a colossal science museum, the **Cité des Sciences et de l'Industrie** (www.cite-sciences.fr; tel: 01 40 05 70 00; Tue–Sat 10am–6pm, Sun until 7pm; charge). It's not a museum for academics: exhibits are interactive, with buttons, levers, keyboards and screens to keep mind and body alert. There's even a Mirage jet fighter to inspire budding aviators.

Begin at *L'Univers*, with a spectacular planetarium and explanation of the inexplicable Big Bang. *La Vie* is an eclectic mix of medicine, agriculture and economics. *La Matière* reproduces a nuclear explosion and lets you land an Airbus 320, and *La Communication* has displays of artificial intelligence, three-dimensional graphics and virtual reality.

La Géode (www.lageode.fr; tel: 01 40 05 12 12; Mon 10.30am–6.30pm, Tue–Sun 10.30am–8.30pm; charge) is a giant silver ball housing an IMAX cinema; there is also **L'Argonaute**, a retired submarine, and **Cinaxe** (charge), a flight simulator-cum-cinema, which is definitely not for the queasy. The refurbished **Planétarium** (charge) boasts digital projectors that bring new visual panache to its virtual journeys through space.

RIGHT: kids will love La Villette.
BELOW: the Cité des Sciences et de l'Industrie complex.

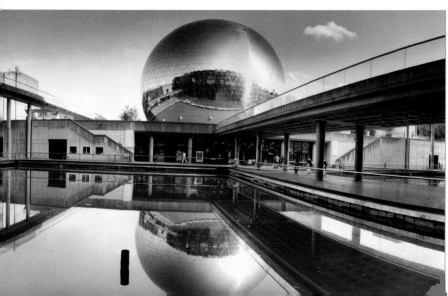

Map on page 245

Music and *Folies*

The former cattle market now houses a cultural and conference centre in the immense 19th-century **Grande Halle**. Next to it, the **Cité de la Musique** (www.cite-musique.fr; tel: 01 44 84 45 00; Tue–Sat noon–6pm, Sun 10am–6pm; charge) is an edifice of sharp angles designed by Christian de Portzamparc, which includes the **Musée de la Musique**. It charts the development of classical, jazz and folk music, and houses an impressive collection of over 4,500 musical instruments. Portzamparc also designed the music and dance conservatory, another part of the Cité, east of the Grande Halle. The Cité's large auditorium hosts concerts by some of the world's most illustrious visiting performers, and nearby is the **Zénith**, one of Paris's biggest rock and pop venues.

The gardens of La Villette are the biggest built in Paris since Haussmann's time. Designed by Bernard Tschumi and opened in 1993, they comprise several thematic areas, such as the **Jardin des Frayeurs Enfantines** (Garden of Childhood Fears), with a huge dragon slide, and the **Jardin des Vents** (Garden of Winds), home to multicoloured bamboo plants. Abstraction continues in the form of Tschumi's *folies*: red, angular tree houses – minus the trees – that are scattered throughout the park, each with a special function, such as play area, workshop, day-care centre or café. After dark, blue strip lighting gives the gardens a strange, otherworldly aspect.

ABOVE: fun and games at the Cité des Sciences. **BELOW LEFT AND RIGHT:** Cité de la Musique exhibits.

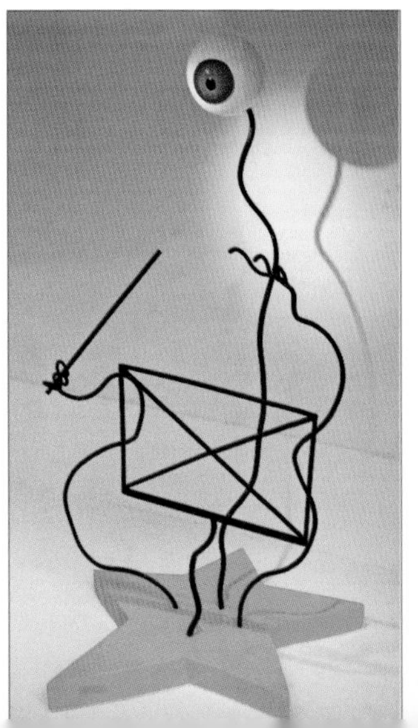

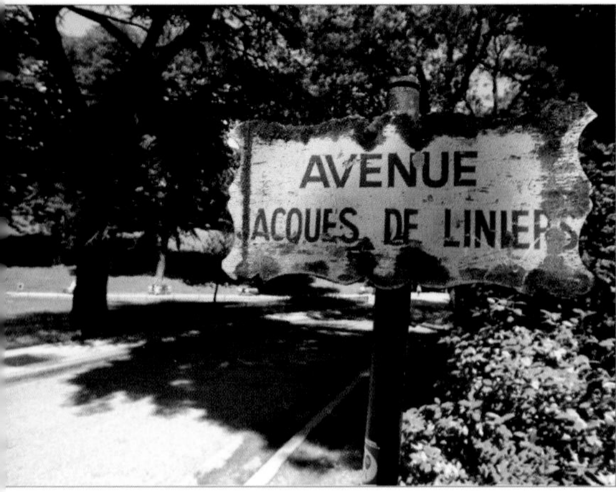

ABOVE: Parc de Buttes-Chaumont.

PARC DES BUTTES-CHAUMONT ❹

daily 7.30am–dusk Botzaris, Buttes-Chaumont

South of La Villette towards Belleville, this charmingly eccentric park was built by Haussmann in the 1860s on the site of a rubbish dump and gypsum quarry. The uneven ground provided a perfect setting for some wooded, rocky landscaping, and a lake was created around an artificial 50-metre (165-ft) "mountain", capped by a Roman-style temple, with a waterfall and a cave containing artificial stalactites. It's a little like a picturesque fantasy, and children love to explore here. Ice-skating, boating and donkey rides are also on offer down below, and the puppet show or "Guignol" in the open-air theatre has been a popular attraction for over 150 years.

Green-Fingered Emperor

It was Napoleon III who gave Paris its first public gardens; before that, the only landscaped green spaces in the city were owned by noblemen, who sometimes let ordinary citizens have the use of them, and sometimes didn't. His motives had as much to do with a desire to improve the city's hygiene as with philanthropy. The Parcs et Plantations department, created by Haussmann to carry out the emperor's gardening zeal, created the majority of the parks and gardens visible in the city today: some 1,834 hectares (4,532 acres) in all. Napoleon took a close interest in the work; he had acquired a taste for English landscape gardening styles during his years of exile in London, and he oversaw the laying out of the Bois de Boulogne personally. Other notable green spaces landscaped during his rule included the Bois de Vincennes, the Parc de Montsouris and, one of the greatest triumphs of the Parcs et Plantations designers, the Parc des Buttes-Chaumont.

BOIS DE VINCENNES ❺

Château de Vincennes, Porte de Charenton, Porte Dorée

On the southeast edge of Paris lies this expanse of wood and parkland, another former royal hunting ground, which Philippe-Auguste enclosed in the 12th century with a 12-km (7-mile) wall to protect its forests from poachers. Renowned for its château, racecourse and zoo, the Bois de Vincennes has other modern attractions such **La Cartoucherie**, which was once an ancient arsenal, but now a complex of theatres where plays are staged by some of France's most avant-garde companies, including the Théâtre du Soleil.

Château de Vincennes

www.chateau-vincennes.fr 01 48 08 31 20 May–Aug 10am–6pm, Sept–Apr 10am–5pm charge

King Charles V built much of this medieval fortress in the 1360s, and Henry V of England died here in 1422. Over the centuries it has had many uses: it has served as a prison – incarcerating among others the philosopher Diderot and Revolutionary Mirabeau – a porcelain factory and, under Napoleon I, an arsenal. Napoleon III began a restoration programme, but the château was severely damaged by the Germans in 1944. Restoration is now complete, and there is a museum in the 14th-century keep.

Parc Floral de Paris

www.parcfloraldeparis.com
01 49 57 24 84 daily 9.30am–dusk charge

Just south of the château, this park within the Bois is a favourite with families, who wander the Vallée des Fleurs, in bloom all year round, the pine wood and the water garden, and take advantage of the adventure playground. At weekends in summer it puts on an excellent season of jazz and classical concerts by the lake, which are free for visitors already inside the park.

Parc Zoologique de Paris

01 44 75 20 00 Mon–Sat 9am–6pm, Sun 9am–6.30pm
charge

On the western side of the Bois is Paris's main zoo, although it is currently closed for renovation. It was all the rage when it opened in 1934, because its animals roamed free. Each enclosure is different, inspired by the animals' natural environment, and a giant artificial mound is home to 60 species of animals, including monkeys, gazelles and goats.

Palais de la Porte Dorée – Aquarium Tropical

www.palais-portedoree.org
01 44 74 84 80 Tue–Fri 10am–4.45pm, Sat–Sun 10am–8.15pm
charge

A few minutes' walk from the zoo is the city's aquarium, which has tropical fish and also a crocodile pit, in the basement. The Palais is a masterpiece of Art Deco design, built as a "Museum of the Colonies" at the height of the colonial era; its sculpted facade celebrates the *"Gloire"* of the French Empire in Africa, Asia and the South Pacific. It was formerly also home to a museum of tribal art, but this collection has been absorbed by the newly opened **Musée du Quai Branly** *(see page 224)*. The Palais also hosts architecture shows, and is due to be refurbished to contain a new museum of immigration.

The "Chaumont" in Buttes-Chaumont is a corruption of monts chauves, *which means bald mountains. The park created there under Napoleon III was, in the 20th century, highly popular with the Surrealists: André Breton and Louis Aragon averred that it was the home of the "city's subconscious", and regularly used to stroll there in the evening.*

BELOW: baby giraffe at the Parc Zoologique de Paris.

A favourite call-in for regular visitors to the book market in Parc Georges-Brassens is Au Bon Coin, an atmospheric traditional café just outside the park at 85 rue Brancion, where book-lovers meet up to compare their latest finds.

BELOW: scenic Bois de Vincennes.

New-Age Experiments and Oriental Gardens

Parc Montsouris ❻

Porte d'Orléans, RER Cité Universitaire

In the south of Paris, this 19th-century park is made up of 16 hectares (40 acres) of gently undulating grass and trees. It was much loved by Cubist Georges Braque and the exiled Lenin, who both used to live close by. On the day the park opened in 1878, the lake suddenly and inexplicably drained dry, and its engineer committed suicide.

Parc Georges-Brassens ❼

Porte de Vanves

The far-flung southwest of Paris is the capital's most populated district and home to two of its newest parks. Parc Georges-Brassens was opened in 1982 on the site of another old abattoir, and is now a child's playground paradise, with playhouses, rock piles, rivers and mini-lakes. It includes a garden designed for the blind: close your eyes, follow the trickling of fountains and smell the fragrant foliage. Braille signs give relevant information on herbs and shrubs. Along Rue des Morillons there are also 700 vines, which produce a few hundred bottles each year of the red Clos des Morillons (full-bodied, fine bouquet). It is sold at the wine shop **Le Repaire de Bacchus** at 75 rue des Morillons, and proceeds go to charity. At weekends, the ancient market halls host a giant antiquarian book market.

Parc André-Citroën ❽

Balard, Javel-André Citroën, RER Boulevard Victor

Further west on the banks of the Seine, the once-derelict site of the Citroën car factory has been turned into this stunning modern park, designed by Gilles Clément and Alain Prévost, where futuristic formal gardens mix with spacious lawns and a wild garden; two huge glasshouses glisten next to the esplanade, and children leap in and out of spurting fountains.

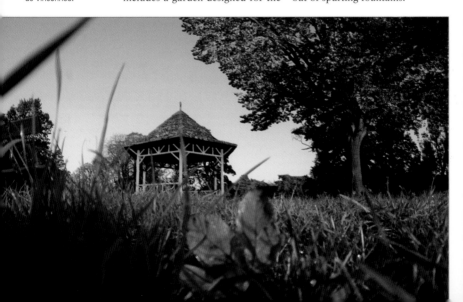

Map on page 245

Beyond the glass greenhouses lie two themed gardens – one "black" and one "white" – and on the park's northeast side a series of six more colourful gardens have been planted to a different colour scheme – gold, silver, red, orange, green and blue. Each garden is linked to a metal, a planet, a day of the week, and a sense: thus gold is linked to the sun, Sunday and the intangible sixth sense. The tethered **Eutelsat** hot-air balloon (charge) lifts 135 metres (440 ft) into the air at weekends to give visitors a stunning panoramic aerial view over the capital.

Jardins Albert Kahn ❾

✉ 14 rue du Port, Boulogne-Billancourt, www.albert-kahn.fr ☎ 01 55 19 28 00 🕒 Tue–Sun May–Sept 11am–7pm, Oct–Apr until 6pm € charge 🚇 Boulogne-Pont St-Cloud

More traditional horticulture is found beyond the city limits in the suburb of Boulogne-Billancourt, where the legacy of financier Albert Kahn (1860–1940) takes the form of an extraordinary park, created between 1895 and 1910. Japanese, English and French gardens lie alongside an Alpine forest and North American prairie. The grass is cut at different levels, from "beatnik" style to "sailorboy". Kahn called the gardens "the plant expression of my thoughts concerning a reconciled world", an idea complemented by 72,000 photographs of world landscapes taken between 1910 and 1931, and exhibited on permanent rotation. ❑

ABOVE: playing boules in the Jardin du Luxembourg *(see pages 208–9)*. **BELOW:** the Japanese garden in Jardins Albert Kahn.

LA DÉFENSE

West of the capital, just outside the city ringroad, is a brave new world of glass-faced skyscrapers and architectural daring

La Défense was a business district from the outset, and its visitor attractions are understandably few: a shopping mall, a new multiplex cinema and little else. That said, it's worth visiting for the buildings themselves: from the 1950s, when the first landmark edifice went up (the vast, parachute-shaped CNIT), La Défense has been an architectural playground. The latest, 2006's curve-sided Tour Exaltis, is a typically unorthodox addition.

BELOW: the Grande Arche de La Défense, the district's focal and most dramatic building, was completed in 1989.

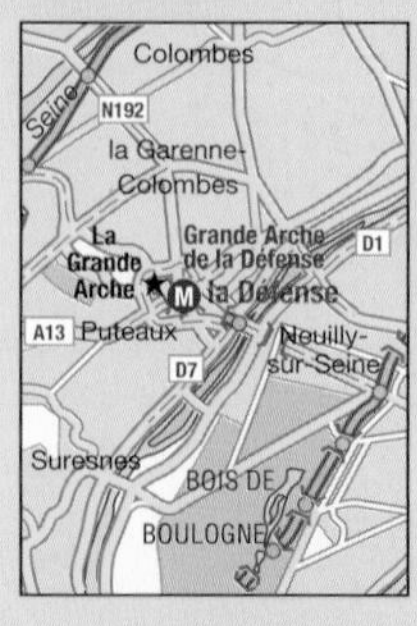

Essential info

www.grandearche.com
01 49 07 27 27
daily Apr–Aug 10am–8pm, Sept–Mar 10am–7pm
charge
La Défense

ABOVE: a glass-walled lift shoots up a glass tube through a canvas "cloud" and into the roof of the Grande Arche, from where visitors can enjoy stunning views over the Bois de Boulogne and Paris.

ABOVE: the Quatre Temps shopping mall is the outlet for clothes, electronics and food; ongoing renovation is improving it dramatically.

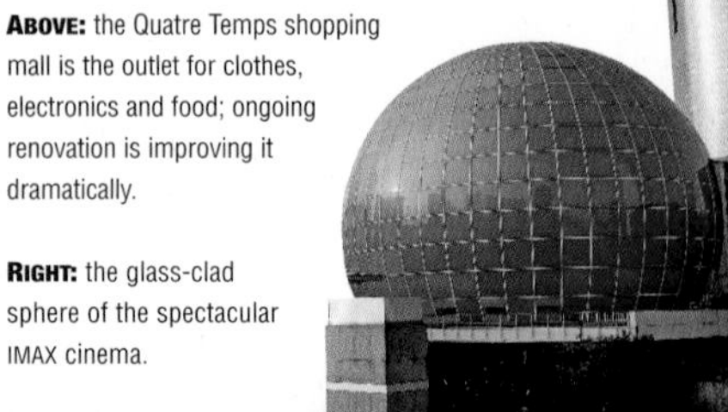

RIGHT: the glass-clad sphere of the spectacular IMAX cinema.

SKYSCRAPERS, CAMERA, ACTION!

With such a striking alternative to the classic Paris topography right on their doorstep, it's surprising that relatively few French film-makers have brought their cameras to La Défense: this is, after all, the nearest thing France has to Manhattan. When it does come to the screen, the district's emphatically 21st-century urban scenery is used either for sheer dramatic impact, or as visual shorthand for the soullessness of modern life, as in Bertrand Blier's social satire *Buffet Froid*. With similar intentions, Jacques Tati set his 1967 comedy *Play Time* (pictured) in a concrete jungle clearly intended to represent La Défense – although it was all built on a studio back lot in Joinville, some distance from Paris. Cast and crew nicknamed it Tativille.

LEFT: La Défense isn't only concrete and glass – there are fountains, gardens and sculptures by artists including Miró. The huge central esplanade, shown here, brings welcome light and space.

BELOW: the extensive use of glass on many of the buildings at La Défense fosters a certain futuristic feel – and the multiple reflections make for some interesting photo opportunities.

DISNEYLAND PARIS

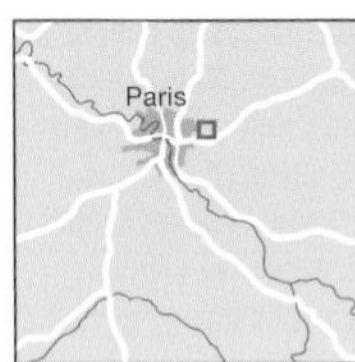

A fairytale castle, classic Disney fantasy and eye-popping rides, plus a full-scale hands-on movie studio, crashing cars and state-of-the-art special effects – Walt's vast dreamworld promises fast fun for the entire family

With twice as many visitors a year as the Eiffel Tower or the Louvre, **Disneyland Paris** ❶ (www.disneylandparis.com; tel: 08 25 30 02 22; for more details, *see page 255*) is the most popular tourist attraction in Europe. Located at Marne-la-Vallée, 32 km (20 miles) east of Paris, on an 83-hectare (205-acre) site, this is, as Disney put it, the land "where dreams come true".

According to the Disney marketing machine, Disneyland Paris was something of a homecoming – Walt's family originally came from Isigny-sur-Mer in Normandy, and their name d'Isigny (from Isigny) became Disney in America. But generous financial incentives from the French government rather than family history were behind the final decision to bring Disneyland to Europe.

BELOW: Goofy and his friends are always happy to strike a pose.

This complex is in fact properly named **Disneyland® Resort Paris**, and it has three parts: the main park, the hotels and shops of **Disney Village** and, the most recent addition, **Walt Disney Studios**, a self-contained park that offers a behind-the-scenes look at the history of animation, film and television. But it doesn't end there. If present plans are maintained, the whole site will not be fully developed until 2017, by which time there will be another new golf course and 13,000 more hotel rooms.

GETTING YOUR BEARINGS

Disneyland Paris theme park is divided into five main areas, or "lands", each with attractions, restaurants and shops on a particular theme – the same floor plan as in other Disneylands in California, Florida and Tokyo. Designed by "Imagineers", the artistic and mechanical wizards who spend their lives thinking up weird and wonderful attractions, this is Disney's most technologically advanced park, benefiting from state-of-the-art robotics and audio-animatronics, so that life-size, lifelike figures speak, sing and dance with gusto.

Decide what you want to do in order of priority, and get there early, as queues at popular rides soon get pretty long – up to 45 minutes. Heading round the park in an anticlockwise direction cuts down crowds, as the circular train chugs clockwise.

Main Street USA

Once through the Victorian turnstiles you enter this trademark Disney souvenir and shopping area, replicating one idea of 19th-century, small-town America. **City Hall**, on the left, is the central information centre and contact point for lost children and property. Here, too, is **Main Street Station**, from where the Disneyland train circles the park. The station is often quite crowded, so it's a good idea to board the train at one of the other stations en route, such as Frontierland.

The bandstand in Main Street square is the best place to view the parades which traverse the park at least once every day, passing around the bandstand and out through the large green gates. The Disney Cinema Parade is usually at 1.30pm, the Once Upon a Dream Parade is at 4pm, and on summer nights there's the Electrical Parade, with illuminated floats lit up by a million light bulbs. Each evening, the bandstand is also the best spot from which to view **Candleabration**, a dazzling sound-and-light spectacular created to mark the park's 15th anniversary.

Frontierland

To the left of Main Street, Frontierland evokes dreams of the Wild West (at least that's the idea). Its centrepiece, **Big Thunder Mountain**, is a towering triumph of red rock reminiscent of a Western movie. The small town of Thunder Mesa surrounding the mountain represents a pioneer settlement, including Cavalry Fort and Lucky Nugget Saloon, where Miss Lil entertains on a vaudeville stage. **Phantom Manor**, home to some spectacular animatronics, provides a high-tech rollicking ride through a haunted house. The house itself was copied from Norman Bates's abode in Hitchcock's *Psycho*. Inside are singing cowboy skeletons and holographic ghosts.

The **Rivers of the Far West**, an artificial lake in the middle of Frontierland, can be enjoyed by Mississippi paddle steamer, keelboat or Indian

ABOVE: fairytale castle.

Disneyland Made Easy – the Facts

Disneyland Paris is open every day of the year. Times vary slightly, but in general from Sept–mid-July the main park is open 10am–7pm, Walt Disney Studios 10am–6pm, often with later hours at weekends; mid-July–Aug, the main park opens daily 10am–11pm, the Studios 10am–7pm. For all details, including bookings, current prices and places where you can buy tickets, tel: 08 25 30 02 22 or visit www.disneylandparis.com.

A standard Disney ticket is valid for one day's entry to either the main park or Walt Disney Studios. A better option is a **Hopper Ticket**, which gives unlimited entry to both parks for two or three days. They do not have to be used on consecutive days, and are valid for one year. Staying in one of the Resort hotels can also cut costs, as meals and unlimited park entry can be included in the package. For information on how to get to Disneyland Paris, *see page 257*.

canoe. The Indian canoe station, verdant and full of birdsong (taped, but it fools the real birds) is a tranquil contrast to the roller-coaster ride. Also in Frontierland you'll find the Pocahontas Indian Village, inspired by the Disney film of the same name.

ABOVE: the Mad Hatter's Tea Cups ride. **BELOW RIGHT:** the magic of Disney.

Adventureland

Paths lead on to Adventureland: sparse scrub gives way to bamboo and flowers, and the twang of guitar fades into the beat of African drums. Here is another unforgettable attraction, **Pirates of the Caribbean** (queues generally move fast). As you descend, the air cools, water drips and the darkness is punctuated only by flickering firelight. The water ride, through tropical swamp to the open sea, is orchestrated by jovially barbaric Disney workers. For the six-minute journey you are spellbound by animated pirates invading a treasure-rich port – here, a singing donkey, there, an inebriated pig that taps its trotters in time to the music.

Rival to Big Thunder Mountain, the first-ever 360-degree looping roller-coaster created by Disney is **Indiana Jones and the Temple of Peril**, near Explorers' Club Restaurant. Hold on to your stomach as the ore-carts plunge through rainforest and turn upside down above a mock archaeological dig inspired by the Indiana Jones saga. As with other top rides, get here early.

Elsewhere, Adventureland offers the ultimate treehouse, **La Cabane des Robinson**, home of the Swiss Family Robinson; an **Adventure Isle** based

Disney Village

Open every day, for several hours after the main park and Walt Disney Studios have closed – so that visitors needn't fear having nothing to do once they've left their last ride – the "Village" between the park and the hotels buzzes with shops, restaurants, nightclubs and a huge cinema complex. Family entertainment takes the form of **Buffalo Bill's Legend**, a 90-minute Wild West show with Indian chiefs, buffaloes and carousing cowboys.

For places to eat, the **LA Bar and Grill** offers a pizza terrace and Beach Boys music as a mood-setter; **Key West** serves seafood dishes at the sign of the life-size shark, while upstairs you can sip a Cyclone Special under an alligator at the **Hurricane Disco**. Slightly more low-key, **Annette's Diner** is well priced and entertaining, and fills up early with young families. Taking the theme of an American 1950s diner, it serves burgers, fries and beer, brought by roller-skating waiters. The mood continues in **Rock 'n' Roll America**, a 1950s dance hall. Across the strip, **Billy Bob's** presents simple chicken dishes with a background of bluegrass tunes. The area around the lake is more sedate and more expensive, and appeals to couples on a romantic night out.

on *Treasure Island*, with rope bridge and Ben Gunn's cave; and **Captain Hook's Pirate Ship** which, with Skull Rock, acts as a playground.

Fantasyland

The most popular land for younger children, with Disney's emblem **Le Château de la Belle au Bois Dormant** (Sleeping Beauty's Castle), centrepiece of the park, where Sleeping Beauty's tale is told through rich tapestries and stained-glass windows. Underneath lies **La Tanière du Dragon** (The Lair of the Dragon), hiding a 27-metre (88-ft) -long creature that roars, curls its claws and hisses smoke. Next door, **Blanche-Neige et les Sept Nains** (Snow White and the Seven Dwarfs) leads children through the classic fairytale in cars from the dwarfs' mine, and terrifies them with a holographic floating witch's head.

Peter Pan's Flight is another one to visit early in the day, before the tour buses arrive; here you can take a pirate galleon into the skies above London, as far as Never-Never Land. More sedate amusement is found in **It's a Small World**, a cheerful puppet kingdom of singing children, a real Disney classic.

Discoveryland

The futuristic high-tech experiences in Discoveryland are great for older kids. **Space Mountain** is a roller-coaster ride into outer space inspired by Jules Verne's *From the Earth to the Moon*, and **Star Tours** offers a trip with George Lucas's *Star Wars* characters. To get there, you walk past hard-working robots complaining about the trials of life. On the ride itself, the five minutes spent in the flight simulator are riveting as the spaceship crashes through meteors and engages in a laser battle. For a voyage through time in 10 minutes join the robotic timekeeper at the **Visionarium**, where a 360-degree screen offers a panoramic view of Europe, from the Swiss Alps to Gérard Depardieu's nose. The view of Paris circa 2200 is the best feature.

Discoveryland also has a recently added attraction, **Buzz Lightyear Laser Blast**, based on the *Toy Story* films and launched in 2006. Allow plenty of time for queuing: it's rather like a giant video game, in which participants use their laser pistols to shoot down baddies, all under the guidance of Buzz. A photo is taken of players as they end the ride, with their score printed in the corner.

WALT DISNEY STUDIOS PARK

Walt Disney Studios, built alongside the main park, is a new park of rides and attractions inspired by the world of cinema, opened in 2002. The park is supposedly arranged around a working film studio, and guests learn about the movie-making process and can step into the action themselves. Instead of "Lands", this park is made up of four zones.

Front Lot

As you walk through the majestic Studio Gates, the first thing you see

TIP

Disneyland is easy to reach from central Paris, via RER line A4 to Marne-la-Vallée-Chessy (from Châtelet-Les Halles). The trip takes about 35 minutes. A combined RER and single Disney ticket (but not Hoppers) is available from many RER stations and tourist offices. Disneyland Paris also has its own train station, with direct Eurostar services from London and fast TGV connections from Roissy airport and many other destinations.

BELOW: Donald is one of the stars of the daily Once Upon a Dream parade.

When you get to the park (as early as possible!) go straight to the **Fastpass** desks by the most popular rides, such as Space Mountain or Buzz Lightyear Laser Blast. For no extra charge, Fastpass allows you to book a time for the ride later in the day; so when you go back at the right time, you don't have to queue. Resort hotel guests also cut queues, as they can enter the parks an hour early.

are palm trees, a Mickey Mouse "Sorcerer's Apprentice" water fountain and a 33-metre (110-ft) water tower, the traditional symbol of a Hollywood film studio. Strolling down the 1940s Hollywood Boulevard and watching starlets in veiled hats pose for the cameras, you soon realise this is all an elaborate set, complete with hundreds of movie props. Don't be surprised when "producers" try to recruit you as an actor.

Toon Studio

This is Disney's homage to the art of film animation – from its origins in Europe to the greatest animated pictures of the 21st century. A movie highlighting moments from Disney's cartoon classics is followed by a cartooning demonstration, and guests can try out their own animation skills at interactive play stations.

Animagique is a colourful show in the tradition of Czech "black light" theatre, bringing to life scenes from pictures like *The Lion King* and *Pinocchio*. The genie from *Aladdin* invites kids of all ages onto a film set called **Flying Carpets over Agrabah** – the mayhem begins when the actor-turned-director tries to organise a film shoot, with guest-actors whizzing round a giant lamp on magic carpets. For the resort's 15th anniversary this zone has also been expanded with two high-excitement new attractions: **Crush's Coaster**, a spinning roller-coaster based on the film *Finding Nemo*, and **Cars Race Rally**, an interactive ride based on the film *Cars*.

BELOW: the dam bursts in Catastrophe Canyon.

Production Courtyard

Heartbeat of the studio production facilities, with productions and shows almost every day. The **Walt Disney Television Studios** is the European home of Disney Channel. You get a glimpse of a busy production facility, and there's even a chance guests may be chosen to appear in one of the shows. Combining live performers and special effects, **CinéMagique** is a magical journey through 100 years of the moving image.

The **Studio Tram Tour** takes you on a tour of the studios, offering a peek behind the scenes at sets, movie props, special effects, decor and costumes. When the tram visits **Catastrophe Canyon**, a dam bursts, releasing a deluge of recycled water.

The Twilight Zone **Tower of Terror** takes you on a gravity-defying 13-storey drop and will delight all thrill seekers. Kids will enjoy a live encounter with **Stitch**.

Back Lot

This is home to some of the biggest thrills – the special effects facility, recording stages and the stunt workshops. The **Rock 'n' Roller Coaster**, starring Aerosmith, gives you the chance to "ride the music" in a sight-and-sound spectacular, featuring hairpin turns, loops and heart-stopping drops (it is too scary for small children). **Armageddon** takes guests on a voyage through the history of special effects, and into a full-sized set of a Mir Russian space station (from the

Map on page 265

Bruce Willis sci-fi hit *Armageddon*). Wind tunnels howl, meteors crash and guests dodge fireballs until an explosion in the heart of the ship brings the action to a climax.

Highlight of the Back Lot is the **Stunt Show Spectacular**. This live-action show trashes cars, motorcycles and jet-skis in a crescendo of movie stunts performed in a Mediterranean village seaside set.

WHERE TO STAY

The wider resort – **Disney Village** and the hotels – is a celebration of "Americana". **Hotel Cheyenne** is the most imaginative: a film-set Western hotel, with saloon, sheriff's jail and wooden-planked stores. At the other "moderately priced" hotel, **Santa Fe**, Clint Eastwood grimaces down from a mock drive-in movie screen above the reception. The hotel style recalls Mexican villages.

The more expensive **Sequoia Lodge** and **Newport Bay Club** hotels overlook Lake Disney. One recalls Hitchcock's *North by Northwest* in its pine surroundings, and the other is a New England mansion. Across the lake, **Hotel New York** offers luxury rooms in a Manhattan-style skyscape designed by Michael Graves.

The jewel of the resort's hotels is naturally the four-star **Disneyland Hotel**, its Victorian style whispering 19th-century elegance. In a forest 5 km (3 miles) from the main park is **Davy Crockett Ranch**, with 97 camping and caravan places, 498 fully equipped cabins in "pioneer village" style and sports facilities. ❑

ABOVE: riding on the Flying Carpets over Agrabah.
BELOW: the four-star Disneyland Hotel.

TRIPS OUT OF TOWN

Within easy reach of Paris can be found the grand palaces beloved of Louis XIV and Napoleon, medieval gems such as Chartres or St-Denis, and the natural world that has inspired so many artists, at Barbizon and Monet's fabulous garden at Giverny

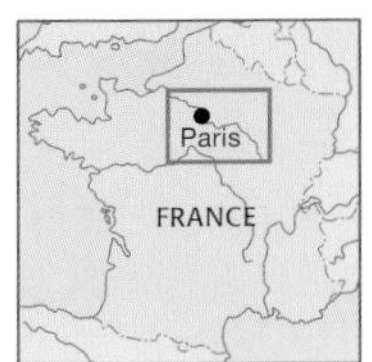

Many of the fascinating places beyond the city limits are just a train ride away. Alternatively, you can hire a car *(see page 283)* to venture off the beaten track – your meanderings may lead to quaint old *auberges* serving hearty evening meals by the fire or lunch on a riverside terrace. If time is limited, then a trip to Versailles or **Disneyland Paris** ❶ *(see page 254)* is an obvious choice, but you could take a day or two to visit towns such as Rouen or Chartres further away, stopping at sights along the way. The forests of the Ile-de-France and surrounding regions are dotted with châteaux and monuments.

SNCF trains are generally fast and efficient, and, on arrival at your destination, you'll find the needs of visitors well catered for, with a plentiful supply of maps and information on tourist sights, hotels, restaurants and taxis. Some places, such as St-Denis, St-Germain-en-Laye and Versailles itself, are stops on Paris's speedy RER suburban train network *(see page 281)*. Tours to all the main destinations are also available from hotels and many agencies in Paris.

PRECEDING PAGES: Monet's lily pond at Giverny. **LEFT:** view of the gardens at Château de Versailles. **RIGHT:** ornate lampstands inside Château de Versailles.

THE SHORTEST HOPS

Château de Versailles ❷

www.chateauversailles.fr 01 30 83 78 00 Tue–Sun Apr–Oct 9am–6pm, Nov–Mar until 5pm; other parts of the estate have separate opening times charge RER C5 to Versailles-Rive Gauche

The RER line C5 from St-Michel-Notre-Dame will drop you very near the Sun King's magnificent château and gardens. You will have to pick

Main attractions

CHÂTEAU DE VERSAILLES
CHÂTEAU DE MALMAISON
CHÂTEAU DE ST-GERMAIN-EN-LAYE
BASILIQUE DE ST-DENIS
CHANTILLY
VAUX-LE-VICOMTE
CHÂTEAU DE FONTAINEBLEAU
CHARTRES
ROUEN
FONDATION MONET, GIVERNY

During the Revolution, the tombs in St-Denis (above) *were vandalised and the royal bodies thrown into a pit. However, they were secretly rescued and finally returned to their original resting places in restored tombs by Louis XVIII in 1816.*

BELOW: boating at Versailles.

and choose what you most want to see, as you need much more than a day to take in everything.

Apart from the main palace there is the **Grand Trianon** in the north of the park, the **Petit Trianon** and the nearby **Hameau de la Reine**, Marie-Antoinette's fantasy farmhouse, where she played at being a shepherdess. In the vast gardens (open daily dawn until dusk), the fountains dance to music every Saturday and Sunday afternoon from April to September (extra charge), while on most Saturdays in July and August the gardens stay open at night for a superbly lit repeat performance, the dazzling *Grandes Eaux Nocturnes*.

Musée National de Céramique – Sèvres ❸

www.musee-ceramique-sevres.fr 01 41 14 04 20 Wed–Mon 10am–5pm charge Pont de Sèvres

Half a day will suffice for a visit to Sèvres, set on the edge of the lovely wooded Parc de St-Cloud, laid out by Le Nôtre around a château that no longer exists. The suburb has been famous for its porcelain for more than 200 years, and the ceramics workshops, set in a wooded park, now contain this beautiful museum.

Château de Malmaison ❹

www.chateau-malmaison.fr 01 41 29 05 55 Apr–Sept Mon–Fri 10am–5.45pm, Sat–Sun 10am–6.15pm, Oct–Mar Mon–Fri 10am–12.30pm, 1.30–5.15pm, Sat–Sun 10am–2.30pm, 1.30–5.45pm charge RER A to La Défense, bus 258

Further west in Rueil-Malmaison, this château was the favourite home of Napoleon Bonaparte's first wife, Empress Joséphine, and he allowed her to live on here after their divorce; she died here in 1814. Before the break-up, Napoleon used to retreat here between battles. Along with the neighbouring little **Château de Bois-Préau**, it forms an important museum of the First Empire, with period interiors that include Joséphine's bedroom and other Napoleonic memorabilia. The magnificent rose garden looks much as it did in Joséphine's day.

Château de St-Germain-en-Laye – Musée des Antiquités Nationales ❺

www.musee-antiquitesnationales.fr 01 39 10 13 00 Wed–Mon 10am–5.15pm charge RER A1 to St-Germain-en-Laye

The wealthy suburb of St-Germain-en-Laye has perched above Paris since the 12th century, and was once a royal retreat. Its château, which has a lovely Gothic chapel, was rebuilt for François I (his royal salamander and "F" can be seen in the courtyard). Inside, you won't find period furnishings or portraits, but a museum of prehistoric and ancient times. The terrace gardens overlooking the Seine were designed by Le Nôtre and inspired Impressionist painter Alfred Sisley (1839–99).

ABOVE: Le Nôtre's manicured gardens are dotted with elegant sculptures.

Basilique de St-Denis ❻

www.monum.fr 01 48 09 83 54 daily 10am–5.15pm, Apr–Sept until 6pm charge Basilique-St-Denis

Less than 4 km (3 miles) north of Paris stands the final resting place of France's kings and queens. Revered as an early masterpiece of Gothic architecture, the basilica

Trips Out of Town

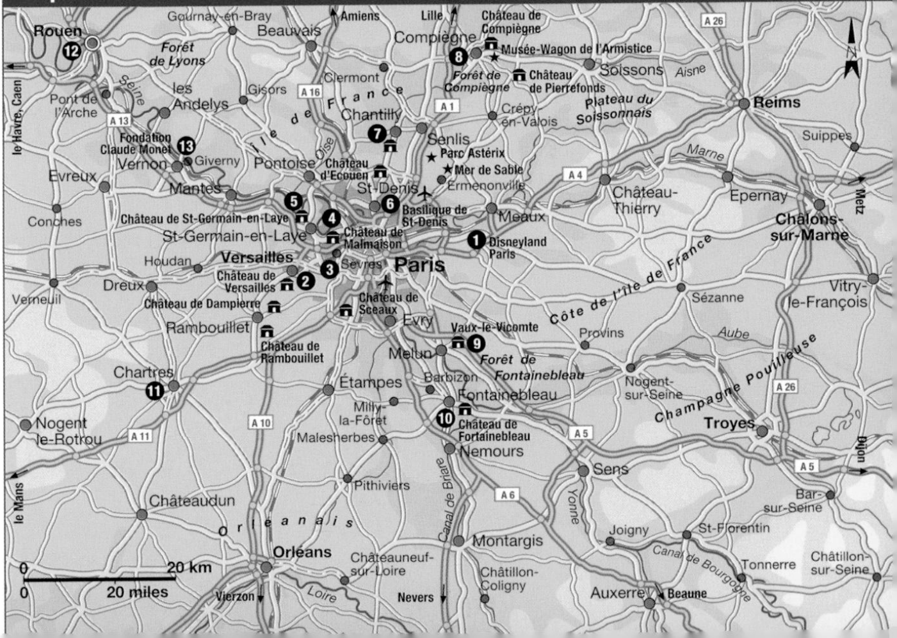

ABOVE AND BELOW: fine silverware and the duchess's blue bedroom in the Château de Chantilly.

was mainly built by the charismatic Abbot Suger, close friend of Louis VII, in the 12th century on the site of an abbey church. According to legend, this is the spot reached by St Denis, first bishop of Lutetia, when he walked out of Paris carrying his head, after being beheaded on Montmartre. Monarchs from as far back as Dagobert I (628–37) are buried here, and the medieval and Renaissance tomb sculptures are some of the finest in France.

NORTH TO CHANTILLY AND COMPIÈGNE

Chantilly, about 50 km (30 miles) away from Paris, is famous for horse racing, but also has a sumptuous palace, a magnificent park created by Le Nôtre and the splendidly palatial 18th-century **Grandes Ecuries**, stables built by Prince Louis-Henri de Bourbon, who believed that he would be reincarnated as a horse.

The Château de Chantilly ❼

www.chateaudechantilly.com 03 44 27 31 80 Apr–Oct daily 10.30am–5pm, Nov–Mar Wed–Mon 10am–5pm charge SNCF from Gare du Nord

This fairytale castle is nestled in a forest grove, its white walls topped by a blue-slate roof, and wild ducks bustling around the moat. Inside, the **Musée Condé** holds works by Botticelli, Raphael, Giotto and Holbein.

You don't have to be a horse-racing enthusiast to enjoy the **Musée Vivant du Cheval** (www.museevivantducheval.fr; tel: 03 44 27 31 80; Wed–Mon Apr–Oct 10am–6pm,

Map on page 265

Nov–Mar 10.30am–5pm; charge), under the impressive dome of the Grandes Ecuries, with various breeds on show and many exhibition rooms – these stables once housed 240 horses and 500 dogs. Riding displays are held on the first Sunday of each month. The Chantilly racecourse is the most fashionable in France, and high society gathers here in June for the prestigious flat-racing trophies.

Compiègne and its forest

The town of **Compiègne** ❽, 30 km (20 miles) northeast of Chantilly and 80 km (50 miles) northeast of Paris (SNCF from Gare du Nord), sits between the Oise River and one of France's largest forests. Its Hôtel de Ville has the oldest bell in the country in its clock tower, and *picantins* (little figures) strike every hour. The **Château de Compiègne** (www.musee-chateau-compiegne.fr; tel: 03 44 38 47 02; Wed–Mon 10am–6pm; charge) was once the favourite residence of Napoleon III and has three museums (one of vintage cars).

If you enjoy walking, make your way on foot to **Les Beaux Monts**, just outside the town, for a spectacular view of the château and the Oise. From here, a circular walk, lasting between one and two hours, has been marked out, guiding you through the beautiful **Forêt de Compiègne**, an ancient royal hunting forest full of old oaks and beech trees. By car or SNCF bus from Compiègne station, you can also visit the **Musée-Wagon de l'Armistice** (www.mairie-compiegne.fr; tel: 03 44 85 14 18; Wed–Mon Apr–mid-Oct 9am–12.30pm and 2–6pm, mid-Oct–Mar 9am–noon and 2–5.30pm; charge) in the Clairière de l'Armistice (Armistice Clearing), where the 1918 Armistice between Germany and the Allies was signed, and where Hitler humiliated the French by making them surrender in the same place on 22 June 1940.

On the eastern edge of the forest is Napoleon III's hunting lodge, the **Château de Pierrefonds** (www.monum.fr; tel: 03 44 42 72 72; May–Aug daily 9.30am–6pm, Sept–Apr Tue–Sun 10am–1pm, 2–5.30pm; charge). Entirely reconstructed in

"Why have I been taken to Versailles seven times and never here?" A famous statement made by President of the United States Richard Nixon, during his official visit to Chantilly in 1968.

BELOW: the charming Château de Chantilly is surrounded by a moat.

The monogram of King François I at the Château de Fontainebleau.

the 19th century in Romantic medieval style by Viollet-le-Duc, with drawbridge, moat and towers, it is a remarkable architectural oddity. Inside, the fanciful architect allowed his imagination free rein.

SOUTHEAST TO FONTAINEBLEAU

Vaux-le-Vicomte ❾

www.vaux-le-vicomte.com 01 64 14 41 90 late Mar–early Nov daily 10am–6pm, gardens open some weekends Nov–Mar charge SNCF from Gare de Lyon to Melun

RIGHT: a curious visitor.
BELOW: the Château de Fontainebleau seen from the Etang des Carpes.

Some 40 km (25 miles) south of Paris outside Melun is this luxurious 17th-century château, built by Louis XIV's powerful treasurer Nicolas Fouquet, a devoted patron of the arts. The impeccable house, along with a beautiful garden *à la française* – the first created by Le Nôtre – was his undoing: jealous advisers whispered to the king that Fouquet had paid for it with treasury funds. After a grand house-warming party for the young monarch, Fouquet was imprisoned at Vincennes, and the upstaged Louis set out to build something even more splendid – Versailles – using the very same architect and designers.

The château and grounds provide an intriguing visit. One room traces the history of its owners, others are decorated in sumptuous period style, with coffered, painted ceilings and Gobelins tapestries, and the kitchen equipment is fascinating. The candle-lit tour on Saturday evening (May to mid-Oct 8pm–midnight) gives an added atmospheric dimension.

Château de Fontainebleau ⑩

www.musee-chateau-fontainebleau.fr 01 60 71 50 70 Wed–Mon June–Sept 9.30am–6pm, Oct–May until 5pm charge SNCF from Gare de Lyon to Fontainebleau-Avon, then bus

Melun sits on the edge of the **Forêt de Fontainebleau**, which was once a royal hunting ground and is now the haunt of cyclists, mushroom hunters, birdwatchers, picnickers and rock climbers, attracted by the giant rock formations. The town of Fontainebleau lies just 15 km (9 miles) away, and is dominated by the first of France's purpose-built royal châteaux, residence of French sovereigns from François I to Napoleon III. Each one added something to the palace, creating a mixture of styles, but Napoleon I outdid them all by building an ornate throne room – his *grands appartements* are definitely worth seeing.

The artists' village: Barbizon

Barbizon, 7 km (4 miles) away on the eastern edge of the forest, is a village that has attracted landscape painters since the 1840s, when Théodore Rousseau (1812–67) and Jean-François Millet (1814–75) fled to the woods to escape the Industrial Revolution and rediscover nature. The Office du Tourisme is set in Rousseau's former house, and his workshop is now a museum to the **Ecole de Barbizon** (tel: 01 60 66 22 27; Wed–Mon 10am–12.30pm and 2–5.30pm; charge).

ABOVE: the rear facade of Vaux-le-Vicomte, complemented by Le Nôtre's elegant French-style gardens.
BELOW: the Château de Fontainebleau library.

ABOVE: the apse in Chartres cathedral.

SOUTHWEST TO CHARTRES

A trip to **Chartres** ⓫ – 89 km (55 miles) from Paris – can be taken slowly, stopping off at the châteaux of **Dampierre** and **Rambouillet** *(see below)* on the way, or you can go straight there by train (SNCF from Gare Montparnasse). The two spires of the magnificent Gothic cathedral (www.chartres-tourisme.com; tel: 02 37 18 26 26; daily 8am–7.30pm; entrance charge for towers) soar above the surrounding fields. Originally Romanesque, the cathedral dedicated to the Virgin Mary was destroyed by fire in 1194, but everyone from peasant to lord contributed straightaway to the rebuilding, with labour or money. The famous rose windows, together with 170 more of Europe's finest original stained-glass windows, fill the cathedral with changing colours. Behind the cathedral is the **Musée des Beaux-Arts** (tel: 02 37 90 45 80; Nov–Apr Mon, Wed–Sat 10am–noon and 2–5pm, Sun 2–5pm, May–Oct until 6pm; charge), with Renaissance and 18th-century paintings and some fine tapestries.

The **Maison de l'Archéologie** (1 rue de l'Etroit Degrè; tel: 02 37 30 99 38; July–Sept Tue–Sun 2–6pm, Oct–May Wed and Sun 2–5pm), tells the story of the excavated Gallo-Roman city. Along the banks of the Eure, a path passes typical medieval washhouses and takes you past the Benedictine church of **St-Pierre** to the remains of the old city wall.

WEST TO MONET'S GIVERNY

For a longer break from Paris, head for **Rouen** ⓬, France's third-largest city, on the Seine about 110 km (70 miles) along the N13 from Paris (or by SNCF from Gare St-Lazare). Once the capital of Normandy, Rouen has a wealth of picturesque timber-frame houses, narrow streets and many of France's finest Gothic buildings, both civic and religious, despite the damage it suffered during World War II. The city is centred around the impressive, soaring Gothic cathedral, which was much loved and much painted by Claude Monet. Joan of Arc was burned at the stake in the city in 1431, after a trial conducted by the bishop of Beauvais, who was in cahoots with the English occupiers, on a site that is now one of Rouen's liveliest squares.

Châteaux around Paris

The Ile-de-France region is rich in châteaux, many built in the wake of the Sun King's extravagance at Versailles. The **Château de Sceaux** (tel: 01 41 87 29 50), 7 km (4 miles) south of Paris, was built in 1670 for Fouquet's successor Colbert, with a beautiful park and gardens by Le Nôtre. Rebuilt in 1856, it now hosts the Musée de l'Ile-de-France. More Le Nôtre gardens are found at the **Château de Dampierre** (tel: 01 30 52 53 24), 35 km (22 miles) southwest, which has a touch of Versailles about it. The president's summer residence, **Rambouillet** (tel: 01 34 83 00 25), 15 km (9 miles) further on, was once a feudal castle and is open when the president is away. The **Château d'Ecouen** (tel: 01 34 38 38 50), 19 km (11 miles) north, is a masterpiece of Renaissance architecture, now the Musée National de la Renaissance, with the finest tapestries in France. **Maisons** (tel: 01 39 62 01 49) at Maisons-Laffitte, near St-Germain-en-Laye, is a small gem designed in 1641 by François Mansart for René de Longueil, future finance minister of Louis XIV.

Map on page 265

The road to Rouen passes not far from **Giverny**. Set on a hillside just above the Seine, this small village is where Claude Monet lived and worked for 43 years until his death in 1926, at the age of 86.

Fondation Claude Monet ⓭

www.fondation-monet.com
02 32 51 28 21 Apr–Oct Tue–Sun 9.30am–6pm charge
SNCF from Gare St-Lazare to Vernon 6 km/3 miles away, then bus

Monet's house is now a museum and memorial beautifully restored and redecorated in the same colours the painter loved. The gardens that the father of Impressionism designed and drew inspiration from are a living work of art – at their colourful best during May, June and July – with the Japanese bridge and the famous waterlilies on the pond. Arrive early, though, to try to avoid the crowds, and if possible go on a weekday.

Only copies of Monet's works are on display at Giverny but, nearby, the **Musée d'Art Américain** (www.maag.org; tel: 02 32 51 94 65; Apr–Oct Tue–Sun 10am–6pm; charge), built in celebration of the American Impressionists who settled in Giverny in Monet's time, puts on temporary exhibitions of American art and American artists who worked in France.

You can also head for the **Forêt de Lyons**, northeast of Giverny (buses run from Rouen and Vernon). The centennial beech trees make a walk or cycle ride a particular pleasure, with fine views of Norman villages and their half-timbered houses. ❑

ABOVE: Claude Monet in his garden at Giverny (*c.*1920).
BELOW: his famous *Japanese Bridge*.

VERSAILLES

Paris was not always the capital of France – for a while, the country was run from a sumptuous palace at Versailles, to the southwest of the city

The Château de Versailles is the ultimate expression of the French monarchy's power and ostentation prior to the Revolution. Built in 1624 as a hunting lodge for Louis XIII, the building was developed (as was the land surrounding it) by Louis XIV, who employed the celebrated creative trio of Le Vau, Le Nôtre and Le Brun, as well as the no less illustrious architect Mansart. Versailles became the capital of France, and, by 1774, following alterations by Louis XV and XVI, the palace had 2,143 windows and 67 staircases, and was home to 10,000 courtiers and servants. The gardens were designed by Le Nôtre on the same grand scale as the château itself, and adorned with statues and fountains. The name Versailles evokes not only a building, but also the world of the Sun King's court.

ABOVE: this beautiful gilded clock face is one of many Versailles adornments with the Sun King's effigy.

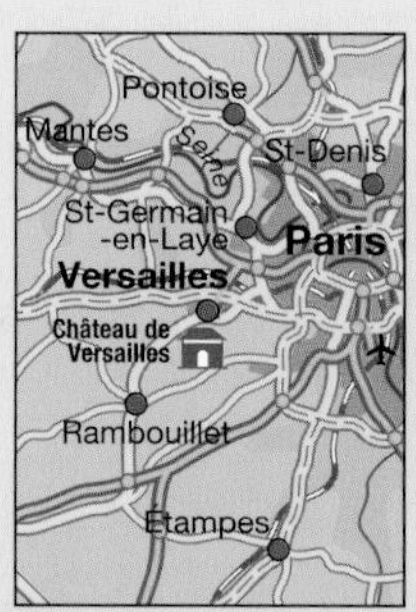

Essential info

www.chateauversailles.fr
01 30 83 78 00
Château: Tues–Sun Apr–Oct 9am–6.30pm, Nov–Mar until 5.30pm
charge
RER C5 to Versailles-Rive Gauche

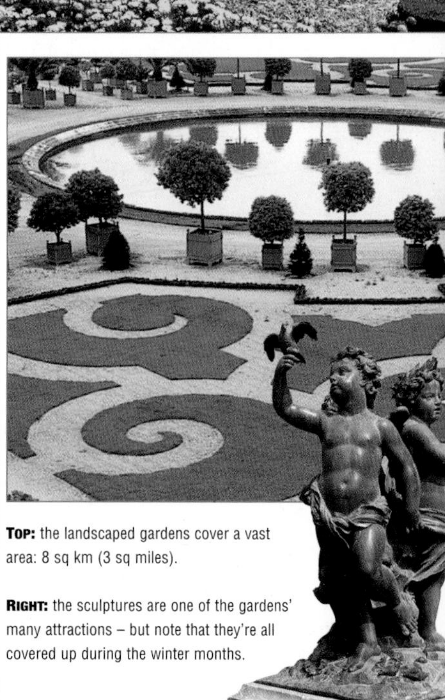

TOP: the landscaped gardens cover a vast area: 8 sq km (3 sq miles).

RIGHT: the sculptures are one of the gardens' many attractions – but note that they're all covered up during the winter months.

THE SUN KING

Louis XIV, later known as the Sun King, came to the throne at the age of five, in 1643, and his reign lasted 72 years – the longest in the history of France. It was a golden age of literature and art, and of French international expansion: Louis waged an aggressive foreign policy, built up a navy and reorganised the army into the most formidable fighting force on the Continent. His energy was prolific, and he served as his own prime minister – hence his famous comment *"L'Etat, c'est moi"* ("I am the state"). But for all the show of luxury and accomplishment, he was far from a benevolent monarch: in 1685 he revoked the Edict of Nantes, which brought about the bloody persecution of Protestants. He was succeeded by his grandson, Louis XV.

ABOVE: there's an extra charge to enter the gardens on Saturdays and Sundays between April and September, when the fountains come to life and 17th-century music plays over the flower beds and pathways. But although it's fabulous to see the gardens in such watery splendour, Sunday is the worst day to visit the inside of the château, as it can become unbearably overcrowded.

ABOVE: the view northwest from the château along the gardens' central aisle. The fountain in the foreground is the centrepiece of the Bassin d'Apollon (Apollo's Pond).

BELOW: the scale and glory of the château are apparent right from its main entrance – the Cour de Marbre (Marble Courtyard).

The Unlucky Queen

Marie-Antoinette has always had a bad press. On the one hand, there's the apparent heartlessness of her almost certainly fictitious comment "Let them eat cake"; on the other, the frivolity of her antics at her model farm, Le Hameau de la Reine, where she and her servants dressed as farm hands and milked carefully washed cows and goats into Sèvres porcelain buckets. What's more, she was Austrian, a lifelong handicap in the French court. For many courtiers, the unfortunate queen could do nothing right; Versailles was a vipers' nest of intrigue, and she was continually criticised – unfairly for the most part. Losing her life on the guillotine in 1793 was the crowning misfortune.

Above: as Premier Peintre, or Chief Painter to the King, Charles Le Brun (1619–90) directed the team of artists who decorated the ceilings at Versailles.

Right: the magnificent Baroque Royal Chapel, adorned with carved white marble, gilding and murals. The royal family worshipped from the gallery.

Below: the freshly restored and impossibly lavish Hall of Mirrors. The unification of Germany was ratified here in 1871, as was the Treaty of Versailles in 1919.

Above: the Hameau de la Reine ("Queen's Hamlet") was built in 1783 at the request of Marie-Antoinette, who wanted a refuge from the routines of the château. It was a working farm, with orchards and fields that produced food for the royal table.

THE HIGHLIGHTS

The château's main tour, plus the gardens, can be covered in a day; but to savour fully the wealth of historic and architectural heritage, allow two days.

The Main Tour

The main part of the château, which can be accessed without a guide, includes the lavish State Apartments of the King and Queen *(Grands Appartements)*, notably the King's State Bedroom. Also included is the Queen's bedchamber and the vast Hall of Mirrors. Other highlights of the main tour include, in the Hercules Room, François Lemoyne's fresco *The Apotheosis of Hercules*, and, in the Battle Gallery near the end, a copy of David's colossal *The Crowning of the Empress Joséphine at Notre-Dame*. For an extra fee, access is granted to Louis XIV's private bedroom and the apartments of the dauphin and dauphine.

The Trianons and Hameau

The single-storey, Italianate Grand Trianon was built for Louis XIV as a miniature palace in which he could escape the formality of the château. The Petit Trianon was built as a retreat for Louis XV and his mistresses. A cluster of thatched cottages, the Hameau ("Hamlet") is associated with Marie-Antoinette (left); they were the queen's fairytale farm and dairy, but renovation makes them inaccessible until mid-2008.

BELOW: the King's State Bedroom, created in 1701 – a place for day-to-day business, not sleep.

TRO

INSIGHT GUIDES

PARIS

Travel Tips

Transport

Getting There and Getting Around

Paris must be one of the easiest cities in the world to explore. Its traffic may seem daunting at times, but historic Paris – within the ring of the *Boulevard Périphérique* – is a compact city, with intimate *quartiers* that invite you to get to know them on foot. If you need a rest or to get somewhere fast, you're never far from a station of the Métro or the RER suburban railway, which offer low fares and a shared, easy-to-use ticket system. For further details, check the tourist office website, www.parisinfo.com.

Getting There

By Air

Most major international airlines fly regularly to Paris's Roissy-Charles de Gaulle airport (Paris-CDG), northeast of the city. Air France naturally has the largest number of flights from North America and within Europe. British Airways and British Midland have frequent flights from various UK airports, and the low-cost airlines easyJet, Flybe and bmibaby also fly to Charles de Gaulle from airports around the UK, including Belfast.

Travellers from the US and Canada can fly direct to Paris-CDG or to the larger provincial cities such as Nice and Lyon on Air France, Air Canada and many US airlines. Note, though, that a flight to London and then a train or local low-cost flight to Paris may prove cheaper.

Many French domestic and some international flights use Orly airport, in the south of the city. Low-cost operator Ryanair flies to Beauvais, 88 km (55 miles) north of Paris, from Glasgow, Dublin and Shannon.

A big range of fare options can be found on the Internet. For flights originating in the UK, check out Cheap Flights (www.cheapflights.co.uk) or the Travel Supermarket (www.travelsupermarket.com); from North America, try www.best-fares.com or www.eurovacations.com. In France, Nouvelles Frontières (www.nouvelles-frontieres.fr) or Last minute (www.last-minute.com) offer competitive fares on both scheduled and charter flights, and Opodo (www.opodo.com) is a pan-European alliance of several major airlines that offers a broad range of fares.

Students and anyone under 26 can also get discount flights through specialist travel agencies. In the UK, try STA Travel, with over 65 branches, tel: 0871 230 0040, www.statravel.co.uk; in the US, STA Travel also has branches across the country, tel: 1 800 781 4040, www.statravel.com.

By Sea or Tunnel

Ferries

Ferries from the UK, Ireland and the Channel Islands to France have cut prices since the Channel Tunnel opened. Catamaran-style "fast ferries" offer the quickest service, but are sometimes cancelled if the sea is really rough. Boulogne, Calais and Le Havre all have motorway links to Paris. Trains meet connecting ferries at Dover, Calais and some other Channel ports.

The following companies operate from the UK and Ireland:

Brittany Ferries, tel: 0871 244 0744 (UK), 08 25 82 88 28 (France), www.brittany-ferries.com. Portsmouth to Caen, Cherbourg and St-Malo: Poole to Cherbourg, and Plymouth and Cork to Roscoff.

Airlines

Air Canada: tel: 0871 220 1111 (UK), 1 888 247 2262 (Canada/US), 08 25 88 08 81 (France), www.aircanada.ca
Air France: tel: 0871 663 3777 (UK), 800 237 2747 (US), 08 20 32 08 20 (France), www.airfrance.com
American Airlines: tel: 020 7365 0777 (UK), 800 433 7300 (US), 01 55 17 43 41 (France), www.aa.com
British Airways: tel: 0844 493 0787 (UK), 800 247 9297 (US), 08 25 82 54 00 (France), www.ba.com
British Midland: tel: 0870 607 0555 (UK), 800 788 0555 (US), 01 41 91 87 04 (France), www.flybmi.com
Continental Airlines: tel: 0845 607 6760 (UK), 800 523 3273 (US), 01 71 23 03 35 (France), www.continental.com
Delta Airways: tel: 0845 600 0950 (UK), 800 241 4141 (US), 08 11 64 00 05 (France), www.delta.com
United Airlines: tel: 0845 844 4777 (UK), 800 538 2929 (US), 810 727 272 (France), www.united.com

Budget Airlines
bmibaby: tel: 0905 828 2828 (UK), 00 44 870 126 6726 (UK no., for calls from France), www.bmibaby.com
easyJet: tel: 0905 821 0905 (UK), 08 26 10 26 11 (France), www.easyjet.com
flybe: tel: 0871 700 2000 (UK), 00 44 1392 268513 (UK no, for calls from France), www.flybe.com
Ryanair : tel: 0871 246 0000 (UK), 0818 30 30 30 (Ireland), 08 92 23 23 75 (France), www.ryanair.com

Condor Ferries, tel: 01202 207216 (UK), 08 25 13 51 35 (France), www.condor-ferries.co.uk. Weymouth to St-Malo and Portsmouth to Cherbourg, via the Channel Islands.
Irish Ferries, tel: 0818 300 400 (Ireland), 01 70 72 03 26 (France), www.irishferries.com. Services from Rosslare to Cherbourg and Roscoff.
LD Lines, tel: 0844 576 8836 (UK), 08 25 30 43 04 (France), www.ldlines.com. Portsmouth and Newhaven to Le Havre.
Norfolk Line, tel: 0844 847 5042 (UK), 03 28 59 01 01 (France), www.norfolkline.com. Dover to Dunkerque.
P&O Ferries, tel: 08716 645645 (UK), 08 25 12 01 56 (France), www.poferries.com. Sails from Dover to Calais.
SeaFrance, tel: 0871 423 7119 (UK), 03 21 17 70 26 (France), www.seafrance.com. Frequent sailings from Dover to Calais.
Transmanche Ferries, tel: 0800 917 1201 (UK), 08 00 65 01 00 (France), www.transmancheferries.com. Newhaven to Dieppe.

The Channel Tunnel

The alternative to ferries for those driving from the UK, **Eurotunnel** takes cars and passengers from Folkestone to Calais on a drive-on, drive-off service, known as *Le Shuttle*, taking 35 minutes platform to platform and about an hour from motorway to motorway. Payment is made at toll booths, which accept cash or credit cards, and the price applies to the car, regardless of the number of passengers. You can book in advance via tel: 0870 535 3535 (UK), 08 10 63 03 04 (France), or www.eurotunnel.com, or simply turn up and take the next available service. Unlike the ferries, *Le Shuttle* is never affected by bad weather, and runs 24 hours a day, all year, with from two to five departures an hour, depending on the season and time of day.

By Rail

The fast, frequent train service from London St Pancras to Paris (Gare du Nord), runs about 16 times a day, and takes 2 hours 25 minutes. Some trains stop at Ashford in Kent (two hours from Paris). For reservations, contact Eurostar, tel: 0870 518 6186 (UK) or 01 70 70 99 49 (France) or www.eurostar.com. There are frequent fare offers, and lower fares for children aged 4–11; those under 3 travel free but are not guaranteed a seat.

Paris has six mainline railway stations, with lines radiating across France and Europe. Each connects with several Métro or RER lines, and all have left-luggage facilities *(consignes)* and coin-operated lockers *(consignes automatiques)*.The SNCF's *Train à Grande Vitesse* (TGV) high-speed trains offer fast, comfortable services from Paris to cities around France and other European countries. They are not cheap, so it pays to travel off-

ABOVE: Gare du Nord station is the starting point for many day trips.

peak: you must reserve TGV tickets in advance, and can obtain additional discounts if you book 30 days in advance. Information and reservations are available outside France from **Rail Europe**, (UK) tel: 0844 848 4064, www.raileurope.co.uk, or (US) tel: 1 800 622 8600, www.raileurope.com. You can also contact **French Railways (SNCF)** direct, tel: 08 92 35 35 35 (France), www.sncf.com.

Note that before boarding an SNCF train you must have your ticket date-stamped *(composté)* for it to be valid. Simply insert your ticket in the orange *composteur* machine at the platform entrance.

By Bus

Eurolines is a consortium of around 30 European coach companies, which has daily services from London (Victoria Coach Station) to Paris that represent one of the cheaper ways to get to the French capital. The ticket includes the ferry crossing (via Dover), and there are discounts available for under-26s and senior citizens, and passes that give unlimited travel for a month or longer. For more information, contact **National Express-Eurolines**, tel: 0871 781 8181 (UK), www.nationalexpress.com, or **Eurolines France** at Gare Routière-Coach Station Galliéni, 28 avenue du Général de Gaulle, Porte de Bagnolet (Métro Galliéni), tel: 08 92 89 90 91, www.eurolines.com.

GETTING AROUND

From the Airports

FROM ROISSY-CHARLES DE GAULLE

Train

Trains are the quickest and most reliable way to get to central Paris. RER line B trains go direct from Terminal 2; from Terminal 1 there is a free connecting shuttle bus *(navette)*. Trains run every 15 minutes between about 5am and 11.50pm, calling at Gare du Nord and Châtelet-Les Halles, the hub of the Métro network. The average journey time is about 45 minutes.

Bus

The Roissybus runs between the airport and Rue Scribe, near Place de l'Opéra. It runs every 15 minutes from 5.45am to 11pm and takes between 45 minutes and an hour. Alternatively, there are Air France buses direct to northwest Paris (Porte Maillot and Charles de Gaulle-Etoile), every 12 minutes, 5.45am–11pm, and to southern Paris (Gare de Lyon, Gare Montparnasse), every 30 minutes, 7am–9pm. For recorded information on Air France buses in English, French, German or Italian, tel: 08 92 35 08 20. All bus services call at both airport terminals.

BETWEEN AIRPORTS

RER line B runs from Roissy-Charles de Gaulle to Antony station, from where the fast Orlyval shuttle trains run to Orly airport. An Air France bus also links Roissy-Charles de Gaulle and Orly every 30 minutes, from 6am to 10.30pm (less frequently at weekends).

Taxi

By far the most expensive, but unquestionably the easiest way to get to Paris from the airport. This can take from 30 minutes to over an hour, depending on traffic. The cost is shown on the meter, but remember that a supplement will be charged if you put more than one item of luggage in the car's boot.

FROM ORLY

Train

Shuttle trains run from the two Orly terminals (Orly-Sud and Orly-Ouest) to the Aéroport d'Orly rail station, on RER line C, which stops at Gare d'Austerlitz, St-Michel-Notre-Dame and the Musée d'Orsay. It runs every 15 minutes from 5am to 1.30pm and takes approximately 45 minutes to Gare d'Austerlitz.

The more expensive Orlyval (www.orlyval.com) automatic train runs to Antony station on RER line B, which has frequent trains to Châtelet-Les Halles and Roissy-Charles de Gaulle airport. It runs about every 5–8 minutes from 6am to 11pm daily, and takes

35 to 50 minutes depending on the final destination.

Bus

Air France buses run from both Orly terminals to Invalides and Gare Montparnasse, every 20 minutes, 6am to 11pm, and take 30 minutes. Tickets are available from the Air France terminus.

The Orlybus also runs from both terminals to Place Denfert-Rochereau. There are services every 10–12 minutes, from 6am to 11.30pm every day.

Taxi

Taxis are available outside the terminal buildings at any time. The journey from Orly to the city centre takes 20–40 minutes, depending on the traffic.

Public Transport

Métro and RER

Run by the Régie Autonome des Transports Parisiens (RATP), the Paris Métro is one of the world's oldest subway systems. Used by around 9 million people every day, it is quick and efficient.

The Métro operates from 5.30am, with the last train leaving end stations at around 12.30am (2.15am on Saturdays and public holidays). You can pick up a comprehensive map free at any Métro station. The lines are identified by numbers, colours and the names of their final station, so Line 4 running north is shown as *Direction Porte de Clignancourt*, while going south is *Direction Porte d'Orléans*. Follow the orange *correspondance* signs to change Métro lines.

The Métro operates in conjunction with the RER (suburban regional express train networks), which has five main lines: A, B, C, D and E, that run out into the suburbs. RER trains run daily about every 12 minutes from

5.30am to midnight (1am Friday–Saturday). They have fewer stops than the Métro in central Paris, and so can be significantly faster.

Buses and Trams

Taking the bus is a pleasant way to see the city, but is much slower than the Métro because of often heavy traffic. The same tickets are used as for the Métro and RER, but you must remember to punch single tickets (though not travel cards) in the *composteur* machine by the entry doors and behind the driver every time you board a bus.

Buses don't automatically halt at every bus stop, so when you want to get off press one of the request buttons, and the *arrêt demandé* (bus stopping) sign will light up. Each bus has a map of its route posted at the front and back and at every bus stop. Most routes run from 6.30am to 8.30pm Monday to Saturday, although some routes continue until 12.30am, and some routes run all day on Sunday.
From 12.30am to 5.30am nightly over 40 *Noctilien* night bus routes operate around Paris and its region, including one that makes a circuit around the main railway stations. Tickets are the same as for daytime services. Full details

BELOW: busking on the Paris Metro.

TAXIS

Taxis are readily available at airports and railway stations. In the city itself there are almost 500 taxi ranks, but be careful to hail only a genuine taxi – one with a light on the roof – as other operators may charge exorbitant fares. The white light will be on if a cab is free, while a glowing orange light means that the taxi is occupied.

Paris taxis operate on three fare rates at different times:
- **Tariff A** 10am–5pm Monday to Saturday, in the city.
- **Tariff B** 5pm–10am Monday to Saturday, 7am–midnight Sunday, and 7am–7pm daily in the suburbs (all areas outside the *Boulevard Périphérique*).
- **Tariff C** midnight–7am Sundays in the city, and 7pm–7am in the suburbs.

The website www.taxi-paris.net provides comprehensive information on Paris's cabs. The following companies take phone bookings 24 hours a day:
Alpha: 01 45 85 85 85
G7: 01 47 39 47 39
Taxis Bleus: 08 91 70 10 10
Charles de Gaulle airport taxis: 06 07 60 49 14

If you have a complaint about a taxi, send it (with the cab licence number) to: Service des Taxis, Préfecture de Police, 36 rue des Morillons, 75015, tel: 01 55 76 20 05.

Above: Tram line T3 – the only line so far inside the city limits.

of night buses can be found on www.noctilien.fr.

Another service is the *Balabus*, a special sightseeing bus that runs up and down from Gare de Lyon to La Défense, passing many of Paris's major attractions. It runs only on Sundays and on public holidays between 11 April and 26 September, from 12.30 to 8pm. The tour lasts about 50 minutes, and tickets are the same as for regular buses. Look out for bus stops marked *Balabus* or *Bb*.

Paris also has a Tramway system, which was reintroduced in 1992, the city's original tram network having closed in 1938. There are four lines in the Paris suburbs: T1 from Gare St-Denis to Noisy-le-Sec in the north, T2 from La Défense to Issy-Val de Seine, T3 flanking the southern *Périphérique* from Pont du Garigliano to Porte d'Ivry, and T4, between Bondy RER and Aulnay-sous-Bois.

Tickets and Fares

The Métro, RER, city buses and trams all use the same tickets (€1.60 for a single fare). A book or *carnet* of 10 tickets offers a considerable saving at €11.60.

Boat and Bus Tours

For river buses, *bateaux mouches* boat cruises along the Seine and sightseeing tours of Paris by coach, *see page 317.*

Single tickets and *carnets* can be bought at Métro stations, tourist offices, tobacco shops, news-stands and some other shops. Only single tickets can be bought on board buses, so to use another ticket type you must buy it in advance at one of the other ticket outlets. With one ticket you can make a journey of any distance within fare zones 1 and 2, which includes the whole of central Paris and the Métro system, no matter how many times you change lines or whether you use the RER. However, every time you board a bus you must use a new single ticket.

All public transport in Paris is free for children under 4, and half-price for those aged 4–11.

A range of travel passes provide good-value, time-saving alternatives to buying single tickets or *carnets*. The most popular is the *Paris Visite* card, giving unlimited travel for one, two, three or five consecutive days on the Métro, buses and railways in Paris and the Ile de France. The cards are valid for a combination of fare zones, beginning with zones 1–3 (all of central Paris), approximate prices for which are €9, €14, €19 and €28 for adults, or €4.50, €7, €10 and €14 for children aged 4–11). *Paris Visite* holders also obtain discounts at several attractions, shops and restaurants. Cards can be bought from Métro, RER and SNCF stations and several other outlets; for full current details, check www.parisvisite.com.

Another option is the *Mobilis* card, which gives unlimited travel for one day on the Métro, buses, RER and other local networks, without the other benefits of the *Paris Visite*. It can be bought at all the usual ticket outlets and from all Métro stations; prices range from €5.50 for zones 1 and 2 to €18.70 for all 8 zones. *Mobilis* cards are not valid for trips to either Paris airport.

Note that *Paris Visite* and *Mobilis* cards are valid for one calendar day (or series of them), not for 24 hours from the time you buy them, so to take full advantage it's best to start using them first thing in the morning.

For anyone spending longer in Paris the most useful option is the *Carte Orange* travel pass, which gives unlimited travel on all services in the zones of your choice for a month (*Mensuelle*, approximately €56, zones 1–2) or a week (*Hebdomadaire*, €17). To buy either you need to take a passport

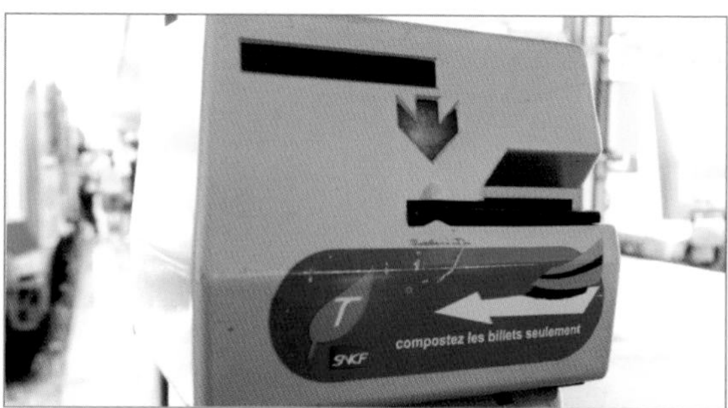

photograph to any Métro or SNCF station, and must fill in a brief form and sign your name on the card. There are also special youth and senior travel cards. For further information on all Paris transport services and fare options, check www.ratp.fr or www.parisinfo.com.

Private Transport

Driving in Paris requires confidence and concentration. In fact, the best thing to do with a car in the city is to leave it in a car park and take public transport.

If you do intend to drive, here are a few guidelines. Seat belts are obligatory in the front and back of the car, and the speed limit in town is 50 kph (30 mph). Do not drive in bus lanes at any time, and at unmarked junctions give priority to vehicles approaching from the right. This applies to some roundabouts, where cars on the roundabout stop for those coming onto it. Helmets are compulsory for motorbike riders and passengers. Street parking is very difficult to find; most spaces are metered Monday–Saturday 9am–7pm (paid for not with coins but a *Paris Carte*, currently €10 or €30, purchased

from a *tabac*) and the maximum stay is two hours. Most car parks are underground; see www.parkingsdeparis.com. Illegally parked cars may be towed away. Do not leave any possessions on show, as theft from cars is common.

Petrol can be hard to find in the city centre, so if your tank is almost empty head for a *porte* (exit) on the *Périphérique* (the multi-lane ringroad), where there are petrol stations open 24 hours a day all year round.

Drivers are liable to on-the-spot fines for speeding or drunk driving. The limit in France is 50mg/litre of alcohol in the blood (equivalent to about two glasses of wine) and is strictly enforced.

Car Hire

Some fly/drive packages are good value, if you are on a short visit. The SNCF offers a good deal on its combined train/car hire bookings *(train + auto)*. Weekly rates always work out better than daily rentals, and it will often be cheaper to hire a vehicle online from the UK or the US before leaving for France. The minimum age for hiring a car varies from 21 to 23, depending on the company. The hirer must have held a full licence for at least a year, and must have a credit card.

Central reservation services of major car hire firms are:
Auto Europe, (UK) www.auto-europe.co.uk, (US) www.autoeurope.com. Online bookings in France and across Europe, at competitive rates.
Avis, tel: 0821 230 760, www.avis.fr.
easycar, www.easycar.com
Europcar, tel: 08 25 35 83 58, www.europcar.fr.
Hertz, tel: 0825 001 185, www.hertz.fr.

Bicycles

If you know Paris reasonably well and have nerves of steel, a bicycle is an excellent way to explore. You can hire bicycles from:
Paris-Vélo, 2 rue du Fer à Moulin, 5th, tel: 01 43 37 59 22, www.paris-velo-rent-a-bike.fr.
Paris à Vélo c'est Sympa, 22 rue Alphonse-Baudin, 11th, tel: 01 48 87 60 01, www.parisvelosympa.com.

Vélib (www.velib.paris.fr) is Paris's new bike transit system. You can pick up and drop off your bike at 750 locations throughout the city. Bikes are available round the clock with a credit card.

Hitchhiking

It can be difficult to get a lift out of the Channel ports, so take a bus or train for the first leg of the journey. Hitching is forbidden on *autoroutes* (motorways), but waiting at toll booths is allowed.

Allostop aims to connect hitch hikers with drivers. You simply pay a registration fee and a contribution towards the total petrol cost. Tel: 01 53 20 42 42, or visit www.allostop.net.

ACCOMMODATION

SOME THINGS TO CONSIDER BEFORE YOU BOOK THE ROOM

Paris is renowned for the diversity of its hotels, from small, family-run guesthouses to ultra-chic hideaways and utterly luxurious palace hotels. All French hotels are officially classified with from one to five stars, for the very top hotels, but these star ratings are based on quite arbitrary criteria and so are not a reliable guide to a hotel's real quality: it pays to take other factors into consideration. A complete listing of all hotels in Paris is available from tourist offices.

Booking and Prices

It is always advisable to reserve accommodation in advance, either direct with the hotel, through a booking service or via the Paris Tourist Office *(see Internet on page 313 and Tourist Offices on page 317)*. Tourist offices will also book your first night's accommodation if you arrive in person without a room, for a small fee. One private reservation service is: **Prestotel,** 1 rue Condorcet, 9th, tel: 01 45 26 22 55, fax: 01 45 26 05 14.

Hotel prices are not subject to controls and can change without notice, so check when booking. The majority of hotels also vary prices by season; low season is generally November to March, high season April to October, but this can vary, as many hotels are particularly busy (and so have higher rates) during certain winter trade fairs and fashion weeks. State your arrival time if you book online or by phone, or your room will not be held after 7pm.

Holiday Flats

The companies below let apartments to tourists, ranging from bedsits to five-bedroom flats.

At Home in Paris, 15 rue Friedland, 8th, tel: 01 42 12 40 40, www.at-home-in-paris.com.

Citadines, tel: 08 25 33 33 32, www.citadines.com. Aparthotels: studios and one-bed flats, with kitchenettes and living area, but also reception and business services. Stays from one night; 16 locations around Paris.

France Ermitage, 5 rue Berryer, 8th, tel: 01 42 56 23 42, www.france-ermitage.com.

Bed & Breakfast

Alcôve & Agapes, Le Bed & Breakfast à Paris, 8bis rue Coysevox, 18th, tel: 01 44 85 06 05, www.bed-and-breakfast-in-paris.com. Has 125 homes on its register; hosts range from artists to grandmothers. €75–195.

Good Morning Paris, 43 rue Lacépède, 5th, tel: 01 47 07 28 29, www.goodmorningparis.fr. Over 100 b&b rooms throughout the city; prices range from €56 for one person, and €69 for two.

Hostels

Holders of accredited Youth Hostel cards can stay in Paris hostels for approximately €20 per night (non-members can often use them too, for a slightly higher charge). These hostels are run by two organisations:

Fédération Unie des Auberges de Jeunesse (FUAJ), 27 rue Pajol, 18th, tel: 01 44 89 87 27, www.fuaj.fr. Affiliated to the International Youth Hostel Federation.

Ligue Française pour les Auberges de Jeunesse (LFAJ), 67 rue Vergniaud, 13th, tel: 01 44 16 78 78, www.auberges-de-jeunesse.com.

An International Youth Hostels Guide is available from the (UK)

Youth Hostel Association, tel: 01629 592700, www.yha.org.uk; (US) **Hosteling International-USA**, tel: 301 495 1240, www.hiayh.org.

There are also non-affiliated hostels, listed under *Young Paris* on www.parisinfo.com. **MIJE**, tel: 01 42 74 23 45, www.mije.com, has three excellent-value "youth hotels", and **Ethic-Etapes**, tel: 01 40 26 57 64, www.ethic-etapes.com, also provides youth accommodation, often combined with courses and activities.

Youth Hostels

Auberge Jules Ferry, 8 boulevard Jules-Ferry, 11th, tel: 01 43 57 55 60, www.fuaj.org. Conveniently located by the Bastille.
Auberge Internationale des Jeunes, 10 rue Trousseau, 11th, tel: 01 47 00 62 00, www.aijparis.com. Also close to the Bastille.
Centre International de Paris/Louvre (BVJ), 20 rue Jean-Jacques Rousseau, 1st, tel: 01 53 00 90 90, www.bvjhotel.com. A large hostel that is well situated for visiting the Louvre.
Le Fauconnier, 11 rue du Fauconnier, 4th, tel: 01 42 74 23 45, www.mije.com. A renovated 17th-century building in the Marais.
Le Fourcy, 6 rue de Fourcy, 4th, tel: 01 42 74 23 45, www.mije.com. Very attractive MIJE hotel in the historic heart of the Marais.
Maubuisson, 12 rue des Barres, 4th, tel: 01 42 74 23 45, www.mije.com. Impressive medieval building near the Hôtel de Ville.

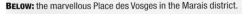

ACCOMMODATION LISTINGS

ILE DE LA CITÉ, ILE ST-LOUIS AND THE MARAIS

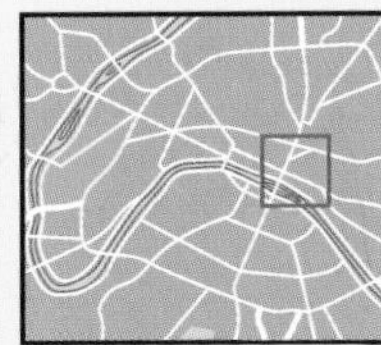

Hôtel de la Bretonnerie
22 rue St-Croix-de-la-Bretonnerie, 4th
Tel: 01 48 87 77 63
[p339, D2]
www.hotelbretonnerie.com
Historic features abound in this delightful Marais hotel set in a 17th-century *hôtel particulier*. The rooms and seven suites are all furnished with lavish fabrics and rich colours; some have wooden beams and romantic four-poster beds. **€€€**

Hôtel des Deux-Iles
59 rue St-Louis-en-l'Ile, 4th
Tel: 01 43 26 13 35
[p339, C3]
www.deuxiles-paris-hotel.com
A peaceful and attractive hotel in a 17th-century mansion house in the Ile St-Louis. Some rooms have views over a pretty courtyard. **€€€**

Grand Hôtel Jeanne d'Arc
3 rue de Jarente, 4th
Tel: 01 48 87 62 11
[p339, D2]
www.hoteljeannedarc.com
This affordable little place has bedrooms in bright colours which are all quite large, clean and comfortable for the price. Good location, near Place du Marché-Ste-Catherine. **€€**

Hôtel du Jeu de Paume
54 rue St-Louis-en-l'Ile, 4th
Tel: 01 43 26 14 18
[p339, C3]
www.jeudepaumehotel.com
There's history in spades at this charming hotel on the Ile St-Louis: the breakfast room was a real tennis court in the time of Louis XIII. Rooms are simple but elegant, with walls lined with Pierre Frey fabrics; you get to them via a dramatic glass lift. **€€€€**

Hôtel Lutèce
65 rue St-Louis-en-l'Ile, 4th
Tel: 01 43 26 23 52
[p339, C3]
www.paris-hotel-lutece.com
The Lutèce has the same owners as the Hôtel des Deux-Iles, and is similarly charming, rich in 17th-century beams and stonework.

BELOW: the marvellous Place des Vosges in the Marais district.

PRICE CATEGORIES

Price ranges, per double room, are as follows:
€ = €30–55
€€ = €55–100
€€€ = €100–200
€€€€ = €200–300
€€€€€ = over €300

The wood-panelled sitting room has a superb fireplace, and rooms are decorated in warm colours. **€€€**

Murano Urban Resort
13 boulevard du Temple, 3rd
Tel: 01 42 71 20 00
[p339, D1]
www.muranoresort.com
This high-tech designer hotel on the edge of the Marais boasts a huge Chesterfield in the salon, futuristic bedrooms and a Mediterranean restaurant. Two suites have their own private pools on the balcony, and there's an opulent spa. **€€€€**

Pavillon de la Reine
28 place des Vosges, 3rd
Tel: 01 40 29 19 19
[p339, D2]
www.pavillon-de-la-reine.com
Arguably the smartest hotel in the Marais, in an imposing mansion in a lovely location on Place des Vosges. It has 55 rooms furnished with Louis XIII-style antiques; some overlook the beautiful Pavillon de la Reine courtyards. **€€€€€**

Hôtel du Petit Moulin
29 rue du Poitou, 3rd
tel: 01 42 74 10 10
[p339, D1]
www.hoteldupetitmoulin.com
This fashionable hotel in the Marais was designed by Christian Lacroix using sumptuous fabrics and screen-printed *trompe l'œil* to create comfort and individuality. The reception occupies an old bakery, still with its painted glass ceiling panels, while the bar marries zinc counter, murals and pop colours. **€€€**

Hôtel de la Place des Vosges
12 rue Birague, 4th
Tel: 01 42 72 60 46
[p339, D2]
www.hotelplacedesvosges.com
Carefully renovated former stables with only 16 rooms, making the hotel intimate but comfortable. It's popular, so book ahead. Note that the lift only goes as far as the fourth floor. **€€€**

Hôtel Saint-Louis Marais
1 rue Charles V, 4th
Tel: 01 48 87 87 04
[p339, D3]
www.saintlouismarais.com
A small, comfortable hotel with an impressive reception area. It offers 16 recently renovated, snugly-sized rooms, all with 17th-century beams. **€€€**

Beaubourg, Les Halles, Louvre and Tuileries

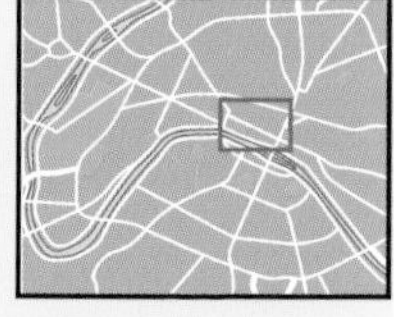

Hôtel Andrea
3 rue St-Bon, 4th
Tel: 01 42 78 43 93
[p338, C2]
This modest hotel set in an early 19th-century building is handily situated just off the Rue de Rivoli. 32 rooms. **€€**

Hôtel Brighton
218 rue de Rivoli, 1st
Tel: 01 47 03 61 61
[p338, A1]
www.esprit-de-france.com
Recently restored, this hotel has several rooms that overlook the Jardin des Tuileries, and a reception area awash with gilt, marble and glass chandeliers. Rooms are large and decorated with a mix of traditional quality fabrics, careful lighting and sober furniture and artworks. The rooms with the fine views are understandably popular, so book well ahead. **€€€**

BELOW: the luxurious Hôtel Meurice.

Hôtel Britannique
20 avenue Victoria, 1st
Tel: 01 42 33 74 59
[p338, C2]
www.hotel-britannique.fr
A comfortable hotel near the Ile de la Cité, furnished with inviting leather sofas in the sitting room. Courteous service. 40 rooms. **€€€**

Le Duo
11 rue du Temple, 4th
Tel: 01 42 72 72 22
[p339, C2]
www.duoparis.com
The former Hôtel Axial Beaubourg has (under the same management) expanded into the building next door and become Le Duo, a stylish boutique hotel. Rooms are a mix of ancient and modern: eminently 21st-century colours and fabrics and state-of-the-art technology are combined with stout old wooden beams in the ceilings. Wonderfully handy for the Marais and the Centre Pompidou. **€€€**

Hôtel Edouard VII
39 avenue de l'Opéra, 2nd
Tel: 01 42 61 56 90
[p336, A4]
www.edouard7hotel.com
Historic hotel on one of the most beautiful avenues in Paris, Avenue de l'Opéra, close to the Opéra Garnier and the Louvre. The hotel features the Angl'Opéra restaurant. **€€€€€**

Hôtel Madeleine Opéra
12 rue Greffulhe, 8th
Tel: 01 47 42 26 26
[p336, A3]
www.hotel-madeleine-opera.com
An excellent-value hotel – and if the entrance,

two centuries old, looks like a shop, that's because this is what it once was. It's well located; rooms are small and their decor and fittings are fairly simple, but it's all clean, trim and pretty. There's no restaurant, but breakfast can be served in your room (for an extra charge). **€€**

Hôtel Meurice
228 rue de Rivoli, 1st
Tel: 01 44 58 10 10
[p338, A1]
www.meuricehotel.com
Elegant, 18th-century-style salons and a Michelin-starred restaurant are among the many assets of this historic *grand hôtel*. The 152 soundproofed, air-conditioned rooms and 28 suites are located under the Rue de Rivoli arcades, and many have great views over the beautiful Jardin des Tuileries; the top-floor suite is the ultimate in luxury, with its own terrace with panoramic views over Paris. **€€€€€**

Hôtel Normandy
7 rue de l'Echelle, 1st
Tel: 01 42 60 61 08
[p338, A1]
www.hotel-normandy.com
Between the Louvre and the Opéra, the Normandy offers traditional comfort; 115 well-appointed rooms, a bar and a restaurant. **€€€€€**

Hôtel de Rouen
42 rue Croix-des-Petits-Champs, 1st
Tel/fax: 01 42 61 38 21
[p338, B1]
www.hotelderouen.net
Small, cosy hotel with 22 rooms; an excellent spot near the Louvre and all the sights of central Paris, and good value for money. **€**

Hôtel Saint-Merry
78 rue de la Verrerie, 4th
Tel: 01 42 78 14 15
[p338, C2]
www.hotel-saintmerry.com
This is probably the most original hotel in Paris. The Saint-Merry was once a 17th-century presbytery, and its 11 rooms are decorated accordingly, with mahogany church pews, iron candelabra and, in one, a carved-stone flying buttress. The phone booth is in a confessional; the windows are, of course, stained glass. Affable Mr Crabbe, the owner, has devoted 35 years to renovating this Gothic masterpiece. Note, though, that another feature of this venerable building is that it does not have a lift. **€€€**

Hôtel Tiquetonne
6 rue Tiquetonne, 2nd
Tel: 01 42 36 94 58
Fax: 01 42 36 02 94
[p338, C1]
Nicely situated in an old part of Paris close to Les Halles, the Tiquetonne is popular and well maintained, with 47 sizeable en suite double rooms. Closed in August. **€**

Hôtel Vivienne
40 rue Vivienne, 2nd
Tel: 01 42 33 13 26
[p336, B3]
www.hotel-vivienne.com
Good-value hotel close to the Bourse and well located for the Louvre, the Madeleine and the most popular shopping areas, with 44 pretty and comfortable rooms. **€€**

Grands Boulevards and Champs-Elysées

Hôtel Banville
166 boulevard Berthier, 17th
Tel: 01 42 67 70 16
[p334, A1]
www.hotelbanville.fr
Close to L'Etoile and Porte Maillot, this family-run hotel is sleek and cosy. Its 38 rooms have chic marble bathrooms, and some have terraces looking towards the Eiffel Tower. Wi-Fi access in the lobby. **€€€€**

Price Categories

Price ranges, per double room, are as follows:
€ = €30–55
€€ = €55–100
€€€ = €100–200
€€€€ = €200–300
€€€€€ = over €300

Berne Opéra
37 rue de Berne, 8th
Tel: 01 43 87 08 92
[p335, E1]
www.hotel-berne-opera-paris.federal-hotel.com
Set in a quiet street near the Opéra, this is a comfortable and pleasant mid-range hotel of 36 rooms with good modern facilities, and it welcomes young families. **€€€**

Bradford Elysées
10 rue St-Philippe-du-Roule, 8th
Tel: 01 45 63 20 20
[p335, C2]
www.astotel.com
Large and airy rooms by the Champs-Elysées make it a pleasure to stay in this elegantly furnished, initimate 1900s hotel. There are 50 rooms, and the hotel has air-conditioning, a bar and good facilities for children, too. **€€€€**

Le Bristol
112 rue du Faubourg St-Honoré, 8th
Tel: 01 53 43 43 00
[p335, D2]
www.lebristolparis.com
This is a discreetly upmarket 1920s hotel with period furniture in all 195 rooms. Lovely gardens complete an extremely pleasant experience; expensive, but worth it. **€€€€€**

Hôtel Chopin
46 passage Jouffroy, 9th
Tel: 01 47 70 58 10
[p336, B3]
www.hotelchopin.fr

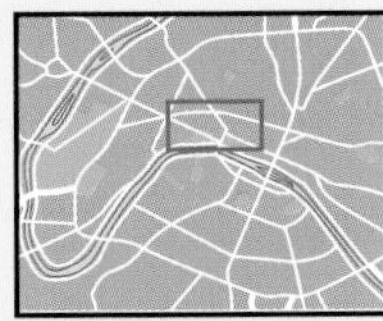

There are few hotel entrances as atmospheric as this one, at the end of a glass-roofed 19th-century shopping arcade. Staff are helpful and friendly, and the rooms, though on the small side and perhaps slightly overloaded with salmon-pink decor, are clean, comfortable and quiet. It's great value, and popular, so make sure to book well ahead. **€€**

ABOVE: the Hôtel Ritz, on the glamorous Place Vendôme.

Hôtel de Crillon
10 place de la Concorde, 8th
Tel: 01 44 71 15 00
[p335, E3]
www.crillon.com
Perhaps the grandest of all the grand hotels in the capital, and probably the best-known, the Crillon enjoys a truly stunning location in one of the magnificent mansions that preside over the Place de la Concorde, built by Jacques-Ange Gabriel for Louis XV in the 1750s. With rooms in a suitably *ancien régime* style, adorned with plentiful amounts of real marble and gold leaf, it's frequented by film stars, heads of state and the very, very rich; the grand building – Marie-Antoinette used to have singing lessons here – is also home to the Michelin-starred Ambassadeurs restaurant. **€€€€€**

Hôtel Daniel
8 rue Fréderic Bastiat, 8th
Tel: 01 42 56 17 00
[p335, C2]
www.hoteldanielparis.com
One of Paris's newest hotels, and one of its most luxurious: the Daniel is only the second Relais & Châteaux establishment in Paris, and it's a lovely romantic marvel, five minutes from the Champs-Elysées. Top floor rooms have balconies and wonderful views; all are sumptuously decorated. It's expensive, but the gourmet restaurant, Le Lounge, is as impressive as the rest of the hotel. **€€€€**

Fouquet's Barrière
46 avenue George V, 8th
Tel: 01 40 69 60 00
[p334, C2]
www.fouquets-barriere.com
With its metal-clad entrance, this brand-new luxury hotel next door to the iconic brasserie Fouquet's puts its exclusive cards on the table from the off. Inside, the full-on modern luxury continues with decor by fashionable designer Jacques Garcia, marble bathrooms, a spa and more. Of the 107 rooms, 40 are suites. **€€€€€**

Four Seasons George V
31 avenue George V, 8th
Tel: 01 49 52 70 00
[p334, C3]
www.fourseasons.com
The opulently furnished rooms here have lavish marble bathrooms, and guests can also count on a restaurant, a top-class wine cellar and a health club among its many facilities. The George V is supremely elegant, stylish and extremely exclusive. **€€€€€**

Hotel François 1er
7 rue Magellan, 8th
Tel: 01 47 23 44 04
[p334, C3]
www.hotelfrancoispremier.com
Nicely located for shopping sprees on Avenue Montaigne, the François 1er is a classy, calm boutique hotel with five categories of room, from *classique* to suite. A lot of care has gone into the choice of the Belle Epoque fabrics and furniture, and there's a lot of dark wood in the rooms and public areas (the bar is almost nothing but dark wood). The hotel is Wi-Fi capable. **€€€€€**

Hôtel Keppler
10 rue Keppler, 16th
Tel: 01 47 20 65 05
[p334, B3]
www.keppler.fr
Long popular with tourists and business travellers, with balconies overlooking this smart neighbourhood near L'Etoile, the Keppler has recently been given a complete overhaul to make it a chic style hotel, with up-to-the-minute electronics and entertainment facilities in all of its 49 rooms. There's also a winter garden and a spectacular glass roof. **€€€€€**

Hôtel Mansart
5 rue des Capucines, 1st
Tel: 01 42 61 50 28
[p335, E3]
www.esprit-de-france.com
Named in honour of Jules Hardouin-Mansart, architect to Louis XIV, and good value for this location, just off über-chic Place Vendôme. The lobby has abstract murals inspired by designs for French formal gardens, and the spacious, high-ceilinged rooms are furnished with antiques and oil paintings: the duplex Vendôme suite looks out over the square itself. **€€€**

PRICE CATEGORIES

Price ranges, per double room, are as follows:
€ = €30–55
€€ = €55–100
€€€ = €100–200
€€€€ = €200–300
€€€€€ = over €300

Plaza-Athénée
25 avenue Montaigne, 8th
Tel: 01 53 67 66 65
[p335, C3]
www.plaza-athenee-paris.com
This palatial hotel, featuring lavish Versace decor, offers 190 soundproofed rooms, a disco, a restaurant and suites furnished in Louis XVI or Regency style. Super-chef Alain Ducasse is in charge of the fabulous restaurant *(see page 154)*. If you can't stretch to the price of a room, treat yourself to a cocktail in the fashionable bar. **€€€€€**

Hôtel Ritz
15 place Vendôme, 1st
Tel: 01 43 16 30 30
[p335, E3]
www.ritzparis.com
The Ritz offers pure, unashamed luxury in one of the finest squares in the capital. Sadly, it is now often remembered as the setting for the last supper eaten by Princess Diana and Dodi al-Fayed (son of the owner). Beyond most budgets, but for a taste of luxury, have a cocktail in the elegant Hemingway Bar. **€€€€€**

Hôtel de Sers
41 avenue Pierre 1er de Serbie, 8th
Tel: 01 53 23 75 75
[p334, C3]
www.hoteldesers.com
The Sers combines modern style and comfort with the classic service of a traditional small French hotel. It has brushed-concrete floors downstairs, an interior courtyard with perpetually changing coloured light washes, modern furniture and very sleek bathrooms, but young architect Thomas Vidalenc has cleverly warmed up the minimalism with lots of lilac and crimson in carpets and curtains, as well as a witty nod to its Belle Epoque origins in the gallery of portraits in the hallway. **€€€€€**

Le Sezz
6 avenue Frémiet, 16th
Tel: 01 56 75 26 26
[p340, A1]
www.hotelsezz.com
Le Sezz opened for business in 2005: behind its antique facade it's a seriously glam boutique hotel designed by hot furniture designer Christophe Pillet, which means one-way mirror-partitions between bedrooms and bathrooms, oversized soaking tubs, large shaggy rugs in red or green, dark concrete-like walls and a plethora of straight lines. **€€€€€**

Hôtel de la Trémoille
14 rue de la Trémoille, 8th
Tel: 01 56 52 14 00
[p334, C3]
www.hotel-tremoille.com
This discreetly elegant hotel has been thoroughly modernised yet retains its sense of Parisian style – 19th-century panelling, mouldings and fireplaces meet contemporary lighting and fabrics, and the comforts of air-conditioning, Internet access and so on. There's a fitness room and spa facilities in the basement. It's a calm hideaway, and you can even have your breakfast dispatched to you in privacy through a hatch by the door. Attached is the similarly elegant Senso bar and restaurant. **€€€€€**

Montmartre, Bastille and East Paris

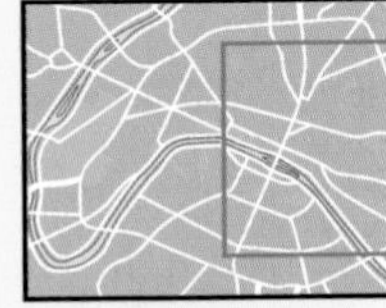

Hôtel Amour
8 rue de Navarin, 9th
Tel: 01 48 78 31 80
[p336, B2]
www.hotelamour.paris.fr
One of the biggest recent stories on the Paris hotel scene, this "art hotel" is the brainchild of the duo behind trendy nightclubs Le Baron and Paris-Paris, artists André and Lionel. Rooms are individually decorated: seven of the 20 contain artists' installations, and two have private bars and big terraces. Perhaps surprisingly, it's also friendly and reasonable value. Located in the Pigalle district, it attracts a fashionable clientele. **€€€**

Hôtel Apollo
11 rue de Dunkerque, 10th
Tel: 01 48 78 04 98
[p337, D2]
www.hotel-apollo-paris.com
A traditional railway hotel opposite the Gare du Nord, this is a pleasant surprise for this location. Rooms are comfortable in an old-fashioned way, and the windows are double glazed. **€€**

Hôtel Beaumarchais
3 rue Oberkampf, 11th
Tel: 01 53 36 86 86
[p339, E1]
www.hotelbeaumarchais.com
A fun, good-value designer hotel located in the trendy Oberkampf district, with plenty of nightlife nearby. The rooms are painted in bright, primary colours. There's a terrace for breakfast in summer, and private parking (for a separate charge); 31 rooms. **€€€**

Hôtel Garden St Martin
35 rue Yves-Toudic, 10th
Tel: 01 42 40 17 72
[p337, D3]
Situated near the Canal St-Martin, a little off the beaten track, this is a value-for-money hotel with a small garden terrace and even smaller lift. All the rooms are clean and compact. **€€**

Holiday Inn Paris – Gare de l'Est
5 rue du 8 mai 1945, 10th
Tel: 01 55 26 05 05
[p337, D3]
www.holidayinn.com
Reminiscent of the grand age of stream, this great railway hotel has an old style charm and class mixed with modern luxury and sleek design. There are 200 rooms. Formerly the Mercure Terminus Est. **€€€**

Kube Rooms & Bars
1–5 passage Ruelle, 18th
Tel: 01 42 05 20 00
[p337, D1]
www.kubehotel.com
The name alone tells you you're dealing with somewhere trendy. This younger sibling of the

ABOVE: typical apartments in bohemian Montmartre.

Murano in the Marais *(see page 286)* lives up to expectations with details like beds lit from underneath and fingerprint access to the 41 rooms. The Ice Kube vodka bar on the top floor, with DJs performing every night, is the talk of the town: its bars and glasses are carved from solid ice, and you have to don special coats to drink there. **€€€€€**

Le Pavillon Bastille
65 rue de Lyon, 12th
Tel: 01 43 43 65 65
[p339, E3]
www.paris-hotel-pavillon bastille.com
Classy, contemporary hotel situated behind an attractive courtyard opposite the Opéra Bastille. Decor is modern and well kept, and facilities and services such as Wi-Fi are excellent. Popular with business people. **€€€**

Regyn's Montmartre
18 place des Abbesses, 18th
Tel: 01 42 54 45 21
[p336, B1]
www.regynsmontmartre.com
Straightforward budget hotel in the heart of Montmartre, opposite Abbesses Métro station. Some of its rooms have great views. Relaxed and cosy atmosphere. **€€**

Hôtel Royal Fromentin
11 rue Fromentin, 9th
Tel: 01 48 74 85 93
[p336, A1]
www.hotelroyalfromentin.com
A hotel not far from Pigalle with its own special touches typical of the neighbourhood: the lobby was formerly a cabaret dating from the 1930s, the Dom Juan, and it still has the original wood panelling and some appropriate cabaret paraphernalia. Several of its 47 rooms have views of the Sacré-Cœur; the decor is bright but fairly traditional, and rooms are spacious and clean. There's a vintage glass lift, too. **€€€**

Hôtel Saint-Louis Bastille
114 boulevard Richard-Lenoir, 11th. Tel: 01 43 38 29 29
[p339, E1]
www.saintlouisbastille.com
Recently renovated, this affordable hotel is a perfect base for the dedicated bar-hopper, as it's on the corner of rue Oberkampf, still one of the liveliest nightlife hubs in the city. Five of the 27 rooms are singles; the decor is unremarkable, but rooms do have air-conditioning and Wi-Fi (both unusual at this price range); breakfast is served in a vaulted basement. **€€**

Terrass
12–14 rue Joseph-Maistre, 18th. Tel: 01 46 06 72 85
[p336, A1]
www.terrass-hotel.com
The main attraction of this Montmartre hotel is the view from the rooftop restaurant – it is superb, taking in the whole of Paris. It's a favourite with some celebrities, who favour the hotel's plush suites. The rest of the rooms are comfortable if unremarkable. Cosy bar area with a roaring fire in winter months. **€€€€**

Timhôtel Montmartre
11 rue Ravignan, 18th
Tel: 01 42 55 74 79
[p336, B1]
www.timhotel.com
A reliable chain that has several hotels around the capital, including those at Place d'Italie, St Lazare, the Louvre and on the Boulevard de Clichy. All the Timhôtels are quite modern, well equipped and individually decorated, and decent value. This one in Montmartre is located in an attractive, tree-lined square with a fountain. **€€€**

PRICE CATEGORIES

Price ranges, per double room, are as follows:
€ = €30–55
€€ = €55–100
€€€ = €100–200
€€€€ = €200–300
€€€€€ = over €300

LATIN QUARTER AND ST-GERMAIN-DES-PRÉS

Hôtel d'Angleterre
44 rue Jacob, 6th
Tel: 01 42 60 34 72
[p338, A2]
www.hotel-dangleterre.com
This was once the home of the British Ambassador, and was the site on which the US Treaty of Independence was drawn up in 1783. Elegant yet relaxed and very comfortable, it is located in a smart corner of the Left Bank. There are 27 good-sized rooms, all en suite. €€€

Aramis Saint-Germain
124 rue de Rennes, 6th
Tel: 01 45 48 03 75
[p338, A4]
www.hotel-aramis.com
Affiliated to the Best Western group, the Aramis offers 42 attractive and comfortable rooms, with well-equipped bathrooms, TV and other facilities. Some rooms have air-conditioning. It's well located, not far from the Jardin du Luxembourg. €€€

Les Argonautes
12 rue de la Huchette, 5th
Tel: 01 43 54 09 82
[p338, B3]
www.hotel-les-argonautes.com
A comfortable, friendly budget hotel in the bustling heart of the Latin Quarter near the Théâtre de la Huchette and only a short walk from Notre-Dame. €€

Le Clos Médicis
56 rue Monsieur-le-Prince, 6th
Tel: 01 43 29 10 80
[p338, B4]
www.closmedicis.com
This stylish boutique hotel in an 18th-century *hôtel particulier* near the Jardin du Luxembourg offers chic bedrooms, antique tiles in the bathrooms, fabulous flower arrangements, an open fire in the lounge in winter and helpful staff. There's also a courtyard garden. €€€

Hôtel Familia
11 rue des Ecoles, 5th
Tel: 01 43 54 55 27
[p339, C4]
www.familiahotel.com
An excellent location, within a few minutes' walk of the islands and St-Germain-des-Prés. Fifth- and sixth-floor rooms have a view of Notre-Dame. The many returning guests appreciate the hospitable Gaucheron family, who live on the premises and take great pride in every detail of the hotel. €€

Hôtel du Globe
15 rue des Quatres-Vents, 6th
Tel: 01 43 26 35 50
[p338, B3]
www.hotel-du-globe.fr
Occupying a 17th-century building in St-Germain, the dinky Globe (14 rooms) was comprehensively renovated just a few years back, but retains period furniture (and a suit of armour) in its public areas and rooms with time-worn, bare stone walls. A nice use of bright colours adds to the romance of the setting. Staff are friendly and very helpful. €€€

Hôtel des Grandes Ecoles
75 rue du Cardinal-Lemoine, 5th
Tel: 01 43 26 79 23
[p338, C4]
www.hotel-grandes-ecoles.com
At first glance, you might think you were in the French countryside; there are 50 large rooms around a cobbled courtyard, and a garden of old trees and trellised roses. It's a short uphill walk from the Métro, but you are still close enough to everything you may want to visit, including the Place de la Contrescarpe and Rue Mouffetard. A cult address, so reserve well ahead. €€€

Grand Hôtel de l'Univers
6 rue Grégoire-de-Tours, 6th
Tel: 01 43 29 37 00
[p338, B3]
www.hotel-paris-univers.com
Bare stone walls, wooden beams and high ceilings abound at this hotel, in a 15th-century building. Decor in the rooms is either cheerful or a little loud, depending on your tastes. In August, if you stay for three nights you get the fourth for free. The nearby Hôtel St-Germain-des-Prés (36 rue Bonaparte, tel: 01 40 46 83 63) is run by the same management. €€€

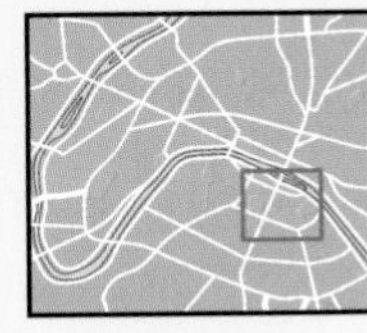

L'Hôtel
13 rue des Beaux-Arts, 6th
Tel: 01 44 41 99 00
www.l-hotel.com
[p338, A2]
This legendary hotel has been redecorated by Jacques Garcia, but retains something of its old sense of decadence in the extravagant decor, cellar *fumoir* and mini swimming pool. The Mistinguett suite still has the music-hall star's Art Deco mirror bed; other rooms are plushly Napoleonic, while the bedroom where Oscar Wilde died is perfect for preening, with its peacock-patterned walls. €€€€€

BELOW: cosy, ethnic hotels are a popular choice.

ABOVE: charming St-Germain two-star hotel.

Left Bank St Germain
9 rue de l'Ancienne-Comédie, 6th.
Tel: 01 43 54 01 70
www.paris-hotels-charm.com
[p338, B3]
Charming hotel five minutes' walk from the Seine, and only 10 minutes from the Louvre and Notre Dame. Cosy rooms with classic décor. **€€€€**

Hôtel Lenox
9 rue de l'Université, 7th
Tel: 01 42 96 10 95
[p338, A2]
www.lenoxsaintgermain.com
This trendy hotel is decorated in Art Deco style and is very popular among creative types such as photographers, artists and dress designers. There's a bar, and the rooms are spotless. It's very popular, so you should reserve well in advance if you can. **€€€**

Hôtel La Louisiane
60 rue de Seine, 6th
Tel: 01 44 32 17 17
[p338, B3]
www.hotel-lalouisiane.com
The Art Deco Louisiane is a relic of St-Germain's artistic, literary and jazz past. Many big American jazzmen have stayed here: Miles Davis, John Coltrane to name but two; then it was Jim Morisson's turn and, more recently, Quentin Tarantino. Facilities are basic, but people come here for the feel of the place and the lively setting overlooking Rue de Buci street market. **€€**

Hôtel Lutetia
45 boulevard Raspail, 6th
Tel: 01 49 54 46 46
[p338, A2]
www.lutetia-paris.com
An early Art Deco palace conveniently situated in the heart of the bustling St-Germain-des-Prés and once frequented by such literary luminaries as Dorothy Parker, Ernest Hemingway and F. Scott Fitzgerald. A monument to the Jazz Age, it has been finely renovated and still has enough chic-appeal to attract a few famous faces: Catherine Deneuve is a regular visitor. **€€€€€**

Hôtel des Mines
125 boulevard St Michel, 5th
Tel: 01 43 54 32 78
[p338, B4]
www.hoteldesminesparis.com
In the heart of Paris and a few minutes' walk from the Jardin du Luxembourg. Simple design and comfortable rooms. Triple and quadruple rooms make it ideal for families. Excellent value for money. Personalised and warm welcome. **€€€**

Hôtel Montalembert
3 rue de Montalembert, 7th
Tel: 01 45 49 68 68
[p338, A2]
www.montalembert.com
The Montalembert has an ornate Beaux-Arts-style exterior and stylish rooms furnished with antiques. The attic suite is Terence Conran's pied-à-terre. **€€€€€**

Hôtel de Saint-Germain
50 rue du Four, 6th
Tel: 01 45 48 91 64
[p338, A3]
www.hotel-de-saint-germain.fr
In an excellent location on the Left Bank, with 30 comfortable, bright rooms. There are also five family rooms. Wi-Fi access. **€€€**

Hôtel des Saints-Pères
65 rue des Saints-Pères, 6th
Tel: 01 45 44 50 00
[p338, A3]
www.esprit-de-france.com
The Saints-Pères occupies a 17th-century building, with a lovely little garden and a swish little bar. If you can, book room 100, which has a fine 17th-century ceiling by painters of the Versailles school; other rooms are a nice mix of modern and traditional touches. There's also a duplex suite with the bathroom on the upper level. **€€€**

Hôtel de la Sorbonne
6 rue Victor-Cousin, 5th
Tel: 01 43 54 58 08
[p338, B4]
www.hotelsorbonne.com
39 tidy rooms decorated in no-fuss fashion, just a pigeon's hop from the Jardin du Luxembourg. The bathrooms are on the small side but they are new. Very reasonable prices (book online for the best deals) make this a good bet. **€€€**

La Villa
29 rue Jacob, 6th.
Tel: 01 43 26 60 00
[p338, A2]
www.villa-saintgermain.com
A clean, sleek, modern hotel in the beating heart of St-Germain-des-Prés. It has all the mod cons (such as Wi-Fi) you might need, and the airy public areas are equipped with Art Deco-style lamps and furniture. Rooms are decorated with faux croc-skin bedheads and taffeta on the walls, and room numbers – nice touch, this – are beamed onto the floor in front of the door. **€€€€**

PRICE CATEGORIES

Price ranges, per double room, are as follows:
€ = €30–55
€€ = €55–100
€€€ = €100–200
€€€€ = €200–300
€€€€€ = over €300

MONTPARNASSE, THE EIFFEL TOWER AND INVALIDES

Hôtel Aviatic
105 rue de Vaugirard, 6th
Tel: 01 53 63 25 50
[p341, E3]
www.aviatic.fr
A little winter garden and a characterful lounge and reception area set the tone at this carefully put-together establishment. The breakfast room looks more like an old-fashioned bistro than part of a hotel, and rooms are decorated with objects picked up at flea markets. Book 45 days in advance and get a discount. **€€€**

Hôtel Duc de Saint-Simon
14 rue de St-Simon, 7th
Tel: 01 44 39 20 20
[p341, E1]
www.hotelducdesaintsimon.com
A sense of being very pleasantly removed from the city bustle is fostered by this hotel's lovely courtyard, and maintained by the lavish Belle Epoque decor and appointments inside. There are 34 rooms in three categories, all done out with panache, creating a distinctly romantic feel; four have lovely terraces above the hotel garden. **€€€€**

Hôtel Eiffel Rive Gauche
6 rue du Gros-Caillou, 7th
Tel: 01 45 51 51 51
[p340, C1]
www.hotel-eiffel.com
This is a nicely unusual hotel, in that the decor has a warm Provençal theme: lots of ochres and reds in rooms and common areas. Given its setting a short stroll from the Eiffel Tower, it's quite a bargain. **€€€**

Grand Hôtel Lévêque
29 rue Cler, 7th
Tel: 01 47 05 49 15
[p341, C1]
www.hotel-leveque.com
This hotel was renovated recently, and air-conditioning was installed. The rooms might be more reminiscent of international chains than a small Paris hotel, but they're large and airy enough, and the rates are good: they even have a few basin-only singles for the seriously money conscious. **€€**

Hôtel Istria St-Germain
29 rue Campagne-Première, 14th
Tel: 01 43 20 91 82
[p341, E4]
www.hotel-istria-paris.com
The "St-Germain" in the name is very cheeky – this is most definitely Montparnasse. Odd, too, that this charming hotel shouldn't play up its Montparnasse arts heritage – this is the place where Man Ray, Marcel Duchamp and poet Louis Aragon once lived, after all. Rooms (renovated since its artistic heyday) are well lit and soberly furnished, and there's a cosy cellar breakfast room. **€€**

Hôtel Mayet
3 rue Mayet, 6th
Tel: 01 47 83 21 35
[p341, D3]
www.mayet.com
This well-renovated little hotel on a quiet Montparnasse street still dotted with craftsmen's workshops proves that it is possible to find contemporary design on a budget. Bedrooms are compact but stylish in dark grey and red, and there's a comfortable salon with sofas and modern paintings. **€€€**

Saint-Thomas-d'Aquin
3 rue du Pré-aux-Clercs, 7th
Tel: 01 42 61 01 22
[p338, A2]
www.hotel-st-thomas-daquin.com
Close to the Eiffel Tower and the Musée d'Orsay, this hotel offers 21 rooms, each with TV and telephone. Good for those holidaying with pets, as animals are allowed. **€€€**

Le Walt
37 avenue de La Motte-Picquet, 7th
Tel: 01 45 51 55 83
[p341, C1]
www.inwoodhotel.com
This newish boutique hotel certainly has the glam factor: warm chocolate decor in the 25 rooms – some of which have views of the Eiffel Tower, and all of which have sleek glass-and-chrome bathrooms and large oil paintings over the bed – combine with wooden floors and a stylish little courtyard restaurant. **€€€€**

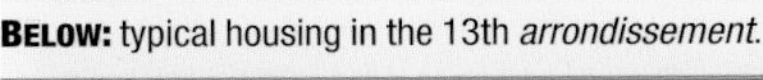
BELOW: typical housing in the 13th *arrondissement*.

ACTIVITIES

THE ARTS, NIGHTLIFE, FESTIVALS, PARIS FOR CHILDREN AND SPORTS

After days spent exploring the sights and scents of Paris, there's no need just to lie in your room. This is one of the great cultural capitals, hosting world-class music, theatre, opera and dance programmes. Main seasons tend to run from September to June, but year-round a vibrant range of festivals and commemorations adds colour to the cultural scene. Nightlife – like most things here – has a special Parisian style, and when you need to get some exercise, or to keep kids happy, you can do that, too.

THE ARTS

Theatre, Opera, Ballet and Concerts

There is a wonderful choice of theatre, concerts, ballet and opera in Paris – though drama in any language other than French is scarce. Some of the main venues are listed below. Look out also for adventurous contemporary dance companies, concerts and performances at the Centre Pompidou, the excellent classical music seasons at the Musée d'Orsay and Musée du Louvre, and the many music recitals in churches, especially during the Festival d'Art Sacré each December.

Centre National de la Danse
1 rue Victor-Hugo, 93507 Pantin.
Tel: 01 41 83 27 27
www.cnd.fr
A lavish new centre for contemporary dance, in Pantin on the northeast edge of the city.

Cité de la Musique
221 avenue Jean-Jaurès, 19th
Tel: 01 44 84 45 00
www.cite-musique.fr
Opened in 1995, this complex at La Villette includes a concert hall, information service, museum and bookshop dedicated to music.

Comédie Française
1 place Colette, 1st
Tel: 01 44 58 15 15
www.comedie-francaise.fr
This is France's principal national theatre, where works by such greats as Molière and Racine are performed. More recent plays, including those by Genet and Anouilh, are also shown here.

Opéra National de Paris
Palais Garnier:
place de l'Opéra, 9th
Opéra Bastille:
2bis place de la Bastille, 12th
Tel: 08 92 89 90 90
www.operadeparis.fr
Opera and ballet performances are staged in the sumptuous 19th-century surroundings of the Palais Garnier and in the modern Bastille building.

Théâtre du Châtelet
2 place du Châtelet, 1st
Tel: 01 40 28 28 40
www.chatelet-theatre.com.
Opera, classical concerts and occasional ballet.

Théâtre National de la Colline
15 rue Malte-Brun, 20th
Tel: 01 44 62 52 52
www.colline.fr
Modern theatre with a focus on contemporary playwrights.

Théâtre du Vieux Colombier
21 rue du Vieux Colombier, 6th
tel: 01 44 39 87 00
www.theatreduvieuxcolombier.com.
Small-scale productions of classical and modern drama from the Comédie Française troupe.

Théâtre de la Ville
2 place du Châtelet, 4th
Tel: 01 42 74 22 77
www.theatredelaville-paris.com
One of Paris's liveliest venues, hosting contemporary dance, classical, contemporary and world music, theatre and a wide range of international artists.

What's On and Where to Get Tickets

The listings magazines *L'Officiel des Spectacles* and *Pariscope* (www.premiere.fr) both appear every Wednesday with full details of cultural events and venues in and around the city. *Figaroscope*, the Wednesday supplement of *Le Figaro* national newspaper (www.figaroscope.fr), is another very useful source of entertainment information.

Music, theatre and tickets for a big range of other events in Paris can also be booked at discounted prices through various local websites; try www.billetreduc.com, www.ticketac.com or webguichet.com. All are in French only; normally, once you make the booking by credit card you will be sent an email or a text message to a mobile phone with a booking number, which you must show at the venue (about 30 minutes before the performance) to collect your tickets.

The Paris tourist office website provides a great deal of up-to-date information in several languages on what's on in the city in theatre, music, exhibitions and other attractions, together with news of upcoming programmes and festivals, on www.parisinfo.com.

Main ticket agencies

FNAC Billeterie, at FNAC stores: 1–7 Forum des Halles, rue Pierre-Lescot, 1st; 77–81 boulevard. St-Germain, 6th; 136 rue de Rennes, 6th; 74 avenue des Champs-Elysées, 8th; passage du Havre, 109 rue St-Lazare, 9th; 4 place de la Bastille, 12th; Centre Commercial Italie, 30 avenue d'Italie, 13th; 26–30 avenue des Ternes, 17th. Bookings can also be made online at www.fnac.com.

Virgin Megastore, 52 avenue des Champs-Elysées, 8th. Tickets can be bought by phone, tel: 01 49 53 50 00, online at www.virginmega.fr or in person, Mon–Sat 10am–midnight, Sun noon–midnight.

Kiosque Madeleine, Place de la Madeleine, 8th, and **Kiosque Montparnasse**, Parvis de la Gare Montparnasse, 14th; these kiosks sell tickets for perfomances the same day at half-price. Tue–Sat 12.30–7.45pm, Sun 12.30–3.45pm.

CROUS (Centre Régional des Œuvres Universitaires et Scolaires), 39 avenue Georges-Bernanos, 5th, tel: 01 40 51 36 00, www.crous-paris.fr. Reduced-price seats for students (with valid student cards).

BELOW: the Kiosque Montparnasse sells discounted tickets.

Museums

Most national museums charge an entrance fee, but are often free for under-18s, and municipal museums are free for all. Entrance at national museums is often cheaper on Sunday, and is free for all on the first Sunday of each month. There are also reductions at most museums for senior citizens and students with a valid student card.

If you plan to visit several museums during your stay, buying a *Paris Museum Pass* means you need queue only once to visit over 60 museums or monuments – including all the most famous ones – in Paris and the Ile-de-France region, and also saves a great deal of money on entrance prices. Tickets are available for two, four or six days, and cost around €30–€60 per person. They are sold at tourist offices and the participating museums. For full details, see www.parismuseumpass.com.

As a rule, national museums are closed on Tuesday, and municipal museums on Monday. Opening times at many museums vary on Sundays and public holidays. Most museums stay open throughout the day, but a few small ones close for lunch from noon–12.30pm to about 2.30pm.

Nightlife

Paris nightlife offers something for everyone, from elitist bars and clubs where you can do a bit of celebrity-spotting to underground cafés run by squatters. You can find jazz, salsa, tango, Congolese storytelling, shiatsu massages and, of course, traditional French *chansons*.

Cabarets

Chez Michou
80 rue des Martyrs, 18th
Tel: 01 46 06 16 04; www.michou.fr
Drag shows every night.

Le Crazy Horse
12 avenue George V, 8th
Tel: 01 47 23 32 32
www.lecrazyhorseparis.com
Sexiest and most skimpily dressed of the big cabarets.

Le Lido
116bis avenue des Champs-Elysées, 8th
Tel: 01 40 76 56 10
www.lido.fr
Traditional cabaret glamour, with countless costume changes, and three shows daily.

Moulin Rouge
82 boulevard de Clichy, 18th
Tel: 01 53 09 82 82
www.moulinrouge.fr
The original, still going strong with two shows a night; tourist prices, and a host of tour buses.

Nightclubs

Alcazar – Mezzanine
62 rue Mazarine, 6th
Tel: 01 53 10 19 99
www.alcazar.fr
A cool bar and even cooler DJs pull in a mixed crowd of Parisians and tourists.

Le Balajo
9 rue de Lappe, 11th
Tel: 01 47 00 07 87
Latin dance music and rock and roll, in an old Bastille dance hall. Thur and Sun afternoon and Tue, Thur–Sun evening.

Les Bains Douches
7 rue du Bourg-l'Abbé, 3rd
Tel: 01 53 01 40 60
www.lesbainsdouches.net
Former Turkish baths frequented by the smart set; some are there more for rubbernecking than dancing. Wed–Sat 11.30pm–5am.

Batofar
11 quai François-Mauriac, 13th
Tel: 09 71 25 50 61
www.batofar.org
Interesting live music and club events on a renovated lightship moored on the Seine.

Le Cab
2 place du Palais-Royal, 1st
Tel: 01 58 62 56 25
www.cabaret.fr
Trendily designed basement club and lounge by the Palais Royal that draws showbiz names and beautiful people.

Le Divan du Monde
75 rue des Martyrs, 18th
Tel: 01 42 52 02 46
www.divandumonde.com
Cheap and friendly, this former café (once frequented by Toulouse-Lautrec) is now a throbbing, eclectic club (R&B, jazz, trance, etc.); no elitist door policy, or a dress code. Thur–Sat from 7pm.

Elysée Montmartre
72 boulevard Rochechouart, 18th
Tel: 01 44 92 45 36
Fun for all ages, with theme evenings from rock and roll to salsa (check website or listings magazines for details on any specific evening).

Barrio Latino
46–8 rue du Faubourg St-Antoine, 12th
Tel: 01 55 78 84 75
www.buddhabar.com
Lavish 3,000-sq-metre (32,000-sq-ft) hacienda with an imposing staircase now listed as a historic monument. Gustave Eiffel designed the front of the building. The restaurant and the conservatory serve a rich variety of South American dishes. Bossa nova and salsa nights. Daily noon–2am.

La Java
105 rue du Faubourg-du-Temple, 10th. Tel: 01 42 02 20 52
www.la-java.fr
Latin American music in a Belleville dance hall, with live bands at weekends. See website or listings magazines for details of specific evenings.

La Locomotive
90 boulevard de Clichy, 18th
Tel: 01 53 41 88 89
www.laloco.com
Rough and ready, mainstream and enormous, this giant venue has

BELOW: on the decks at Batofar, housed in a renovated lightship.

three dance floors, and a location next door to the Moulin Rouge. Daily 11pm–dawn; during the week, it hosts live music.

Rex Club
5 boulevard Poissonnière, 2nd
Tel: 01 42 36 10 96
www.rexclub.com
A techno and house stalwart with one of the best sound systems in Paris, and big-name DJs.

Red Light
34 rue du Départ, 15th
Tel: 01 48 79 85 49
www.leredlight.com
House music and a mixed gay-straight clientele.

FESTIVALS AND EVENTS

A listing of all major events in Paris is available from the Tourist Office *(see page 317)*. Here are just some of the festivals and events that occur every year:

- **January** Fashion shows at Paris-Expo.
- **February–March** *Six Nations Rugby Tournament.* International rugby extravaganza running for three weekends.
- **late February–early March** *Salon de l'Agriculture.* Rural France comes to Paris in a huge agricultural and food fair.
- **late March–early May** *Foire du Trône.* France's biggest funfair; Pelouse de Reuilly, Métro: Porte Dorée.
- **late March–early April** Paris Film Festival, Champs-Elysées.
- **May** *Carré Rive Gauche.* Open days at the Left Bank antiques enclave.
- **May** *Paris Expo.* Extensive food, art and design exhibition.
- **late May–early June** French Tennis Open; Stade Roland-Garros, Métro: Porte d'Auteuil
- **June** *Fête de la Musique* (21 June). Huge street music festival; free concerts and dances all across Paris.
- **July** Bastille Day. Celebrations begin at the Bastille on the evening of 13 July; on the 14th, a military parade starts at 10am on the Champs-Elysées. Fireworks follow at the Trocadéro.
- **mid-July–mid-August** *Paris Quartier d'Eté.* Summer arts festival: contemporary dance, street theatre, world music and outdoor jazz provide cultural entertainment when the theatres and concert halls close down for the summer. *Paris-Plage.*The beach comes to Paris with sand, paddling pools, cafés and beach volleyball on the *quais* of the Seine. *See page 111. Cinéma en Plein Air.* Classic movies on a giant screen at the free outdoor film festival at La Villette.
- **September** *Journée du Patrimoine* (3rd weekend). Open day at otherwise off-limits government and private buildings. *Festival d'Automne* (until Dec). Annual festival of theatre, music and dance.
- **October** (1st Sat) *La Nuit Blanche.* Stay up all night for artistic happenings in museums and venues all over town.
- **November** The arrival of Beaujolais Nouveau is celebrated in bars and cafés (3rd Thursday of the month).
- **December** Notre-Dame is packed for the Christmas Eve service. On New Year's Eve, crowds fill the Champs-Elysées, and there's a giant fireworks display at Trocadéro.
- **mid December–late January** *Patinoire de Noël.* Ice-skating in a spectacular setting: the first floor of the Eiffel Tower.

BELOW: Fête de la Musique fun.

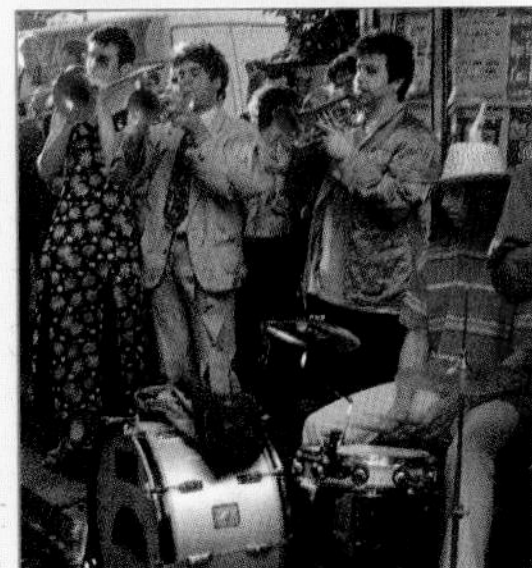

Pubs and Bars

Bar du Crillon
Hôtel de Crillon,
16 rue Boissy d'Anglas, 8th
Tel: 01 44 71 15 39
www.crillon.com
The bar in this supremely grand hotel is where Hemingway drank when he had the money. The turn-of-the-20th-century decor has been given a designer facelift by Sonia Rykiel.

Bar du Plaza
Hôtel Plaza Athénée
25 avenue Montaigne, 8th
Tel: 01 53 67 66 65
www.plaza-athenee-paris.com
Come here for the chic designer interior,the off-the-wall cocktails and to mix with the Gucci- and Prada-clad crowd.

La Belle Hortense
31 rue Vieille-du-Temple, 4th
Tel: 01 48 04 71 60
Wine bar and bookshop in the heart of the Marais.

Les Couleurs
17 rue St-Maur, 11th
Tel: 01 43 57 95 61
Arty hang-out near the Oberkampf drag where kitsch meets distressed chic (tacky mural, exposed brick, bare lightbulbs) and potent cocktails.

Kitty O'Sheas
10 rue des Capucines, 2nd
Tel: 01 40 15 00 30
www.kittyosheas.com
One of the first Irish pubs in Paris and now a venue for watching televised Irish and British football and rugby internationals. Live music some evenings. Daily 11am–2am.

La Flèche d'Or
102bis rue de Bagnolet, 20th
Tel: 01 44 64 01 02
www.flechedor.fr
A hip mecca for eastern Paris, the Golden Arrow occupies a former railway station. Free concerts on weeknights at 6pm.

The Frog & Rosbif
116 rue St-Denis, 2nd

Tel: 01 42 36 34 73
www.frogpubs.com
English pub serving cask ales, Guinness and lagers on tap.

Le Fumoir
6 rue de l'Amiral-de-Coligny, 1st
Tel: 01 42 92 00 24
www.lefumoir.com
The "smoking room" isn't very smoky, but does feel more like an elegant club than a bar. Regulars sit in plush leather chairs sipping *mojitos* (Cuban rum cocktails) while perusing the 3,000-plus library or the rack of newspapers.

Harry's Bar
5 rue Daunou, 2nd
Tel: 01 42 61 71 14
www.harrybar.fr
A Parisian landmark, said to be the birthplace of the Bloody Mary. F. Scott Fitzgerald was a regular in the 1920s.

The Honest Lawyer
176 rue de la Pompe, 16th
Tel: 01 45 05 14 23
www.honest-lawyer.com
A short walk from Place Victor-Hugo, this yuppie pub has three TVs, reasonably priced pub grub and a jazz brunch on Sunday.

The Lizard Lounge
18 rue du Bourg-Tibourg, 4th
Tel: 01 42 72 81 34
Students, anglophone au pairs and anglophile French perch at the undulating bar, or retreat to the intimate basement.

Mama Shelter
109 rue de Bagnolet, 20th
Tel: 01 43 48 48 48
www.mamashelter.com
Trendy place designed by Philippe Starck with a unique atmosphere. Right across from the pop rock venue La Flèche d'Or *(see page 297)*. Enjoy the refined cuisine of chef Alain Sanderens on the terrace next to the barbecue or a drink at the Island bar. Live world music Thur–Sat.

Rosebud
11bis rue Delambre, 14th
Tel: 01 43 35 38 54
The decor is a throwback to the 1930s, when the likes of Jean-Paul Sartre sometimes drank here. It draws an older crowd, including arty and media types.

Pub St Germain
17 rue de l'Ancienne-Comédie, 6th
Tel: 01 56 81 13 13

A mythical 1968 place, this pub has recently been renovated. It is now a large space over three floors. Chic and refined, and good for drinks and food alike. Daily non-stop.

Music Venues

Caveau de la Huchette
5 rue de la Huchette, 6th
Tel: 01 43 26 65 05
www.caveaudelahuchette.fr
Frequented by GIs in World War II, it now hosts a young clientele for cellar jazz. Sun–Wed 9.30pm–2.30am, Thur–Sat 9.30pm–6am.

La Chapelle des Lombards
19 rue de Lappe, 11th
Tel: 01 43 57 24 24
Lively music in a popular club. Tue–Sun 11.30pm–dawn.

La Cigale
120 boulevard de Rochechouart, 18th
Tel: 01 49 25 81 75
www.lacigale.fr
A popular club hosting up-and-coming bands.

New Morning
7–9 rue des Petites-Ecuries, 10th
Tel: 01 45 23 51 41
www.newmorning.com
For jazz aficionados.

Le Sunset/Sunside
60 rue des Lombards, 1st
Tel: 01 40 26 46 60
www.sunset-sunside.com
The Sunset offers two clubs in one: electric jazz and world music on the ground floor and acoustic jazz in the more intimate cellar.

Cinema

There are few better cities for movie-going than Paris, with a choice of films each week that's unmatched anywhere in Europe. There is a high concentration of modern multi-screen cinemas showing the latest films, but if you'd rather see world cinema or a French classic than the most recent Hollywood block-buster, there are plenty of good

ABOVE: the Gaumont Marignan cinema, on the Champs-Elysées.

retro and arthouse cinemas, too. To find out what's on, check *Pariscope*.

The majority of cinemas in central Paris show films in their original language with subtitles in French (these are marked "VO" – *version originale*), but once you get out of the city centre, mainstream films are usually dubbed into French (and marked "VF" – *version française*). Ticket prices are reduced by up to 30 percent on Monday and/or Wednesday.

Cinemas on the Champs-Elysées (8th *arrondissement*) and around Odéon in St-Germain-des-Prés (6th *arrondissement*) show recent releases in VO, as do the Latin Quarter arts cinemas (5th *arrondissement*) for old movies. The cinemas listed here (out of 400 screens across Paris) are particularly attractive, or present interesting programmes, usually in VO:

Le Champo
51 rue des Ecoles, 5th
Tel: 01 43 54 51 60
Ever-popular arthouse cinema in the Latin Quarter.

Le Cinéma des Cinéastes
7 avenue de Clichy, 17th
Tel: 01 53 42 40 20
Three screens for film buffs.

Cinémathèque Française
51 rue de Bercy, 12th
Tel: 01 71 19 33 33
www.cinematheque.fr
France's official film theatre has a great new home in Bercy, to cover the whole of world cinema.

Forum des Images
Forum des Halles, 1st
Tel: 01 44 76 62 00
www.forumdesimages.net
A film archive on Paris, and always intriguing film seasons.

Gaumont Marignan
27–33 avenue des Champs-Elysées, 8th
Tel: 08 92 69 66 96.
One of many multi-screen complexes on the Champs-Elysées.

La Géode
Parc de la Villette, 19th
Tel: 08 92 68 45 40, www.lageode.fr
An IMAX cinema housed inside a huge glittering dome. Mainly nature- or science-themed films.

Le Grand Rex
1 boulevard Poissonnière, 2nd
Tel: 08 92 68 05 96
Art Deco cinema; one big screen.

Max Linder Panorama
24 boulevard Poissonnière, 9th
Tel: 08 92 68 50 52
www.maxlinder.com
A panoramic screen and state-of-the-art acoustics in a 1930s setting – the best of both worlds.

La Pagode
57bis rue de Babylone, 7th
Tel: 01 45 55 48 48
A unique cinema experience: the latest films are shown in the tranquil setting of a mock-Japanese pagoda, complete with tearoom.

FOR CHILDREN

Most children are not really that interested in city sightseeing; Disneyland Paris *(see pages 254–9)* is what they are after, or failing that an afternoon in one of Paris's parks *(see pages 243–51)*. To find out details of other current activities and entertainments available in Paris that should appeal to children, such as plays, films, puppet shows and circuses, refer to *L'Officiel des Spectacles* and *Pariscope*.

In terms of accommodation, most hotels have family rooms. A cot *(lit bébé)* can often be provided for a small supplement, but ask first if booking in advance.

Taking your children out to a restaurant should not be a problem (but check beforehand with more upmarket places). French children are used to eating out from an early age and so are generally well behaved. Many restaurants offer a children's menu, with smaller portions; if not, they may split a *prix fixe* menu between two. With very young children, just ask

ABOVE: playing basketball in the Jardin du Luxembourg.

for an extra plate and give them food from your own. Alternatively, order a simple dish from the *à la carte* menu, such as an omelette or soup. With the bread that comes automatically to a French table, and ice cream or fruit to follow, most children will be well fed.

Puppet Shows

Théâtre de Marionnettes du Jardin du Luxembourg
Tel: 01 43 26 46 47 or 01 43 29 50 97 for a recorded message (in French) about current children's puppet shows.

SPORTS

Participant

You perhaps wouldn't go to Paris primarily in search of sports facilities or events (except for the Tennis Open in June), but the city does cater fairly well for the sports enthusiast. You can find information on sporting events in *Le Figaro* each Wednesday.

Cycling

The Bois de Boulogne and Bois de Vincennes offer good cycling, as do the Quais de Seine and the Canal St-Martin. Call the **Fédération Française de Cyclotourisme** (www.ffct.org) for your nearest cycling club, tel: 01 56 20 88 88.

Fitness Centres

Club Med Gym
17 rue du Débarcadère, 17th
Tel: 01 45 74 14 04
www.clubmedgym.fr
One of a chain of health clubs that offer step classes, weights, martial arts and sauna. Not all clubs have a pool, so check first.

Club Quartier Latin
19 rue Pontoise, 5th
Tel: 01 55 42 77 88
www.clubquartierlatin.com
Health club with squash courts and pool, a fully equipped gym and a variety of classes.

In-Line Skating

Roller-skating, in all its forms, is hugely popular in Paris: Friday night sees thousands gather outside Tour Montparnasse at 10pm for the weekly three-hour skate through town. Everybody's welcome as long as they can keep up (www.pari-roller.com).

Paris-Plage

From mid-July to mid-August nearly 3 km (2 miles) of the Right Bank from Pont de Sully to Pont des Arts are converted into a beach, with hammocks, deck chairs, showers and a small pool. www.paris.fr. *See page 111.*

Swimming

Aquaboulevard
4–6 rue Louis-Armand, 15th
Tel: 01 40 60 10 00
www.aquaboulevard.com
A massive water world offering an exciting choice of waves, flumes and indoor and outdoor pools. Ideal fun for the kids.

Piscine Armand-Massard
66 boulevard du Montparnasse, 15th
Tel: 01 45 38 65 19
An underground sports centre with three pools.

Piscine Georges-Vallery
148 avenue Gambetta, 20th
Tel: 01 40 31 15 20
Built for the 1924 Olympics, when Johnny Weissmuller (aka Tarzan in films of old) won the gold medal.

Piscine des Halles
Centre Suzanne-Berlioux,
10 place de la Rotonde, 1st
Tel: 01 42 36 98 44
Part of the Forum des Halles, with a 50-metre/yd pool.

Piscine Joséphine-Baker
Quai François-Mauriac, 13th
Tel: 01 56 61 96 50
Modern floating 25-metre/yd pool moored on the Seine next to the Bibliothèque Nationale-François Mitterrand with a kid's pool, a sundeck, a sauna and a jacuzzi.
Piscine Jean-Taris
66 rue Thouin, 5th
Tel: 01 55 42 81 90
A very pleasant 25-metre/yd pool with a view of the Panthéon.
Piscine du Marché St-Germain
12 rue Lobineau, 6th
Tel: 01 56 31 25 40
Underground 25-metre/yd pool.

Tennis

Jardin du Luxembourg
6th, tel: 01 43 25 79 18.
Anyone can play tennis here, and it's not expensive. Summer, daily 8am–9pm; winter, 8am–sunset.
Centre Sportif d'Orléans
7 avenue Paul-Appell, 14th
Tel: 01 45 40 55 88
A variety of sports are on offer (athletics, football, basketball) in addition to nine tennis courts.
Courcelles
209 rue de Courcelles, 17th
Tel: 01 48 88 00 17
Tennis lessons at all levels.

Spectator

Football fans should pay homage at the massive **Stade de France**, designed by architects Zubléna, Macary, Regembal and Constantini for the 1998 World Cup. The stadium is also used for concerts, seating around 100,000. Located at Rue Francis-de-Pressensé, in St-Denis, tel: 01 55 93 00 00, www.stadefrance.fr (Métro Porte de Paris; RER B to La Plaine-Stade de France, or RER D to Stade de France-St-Denis). Guided tours are available; daily 10am–5pm, except during events; charge.

The huge **Palais Omnisports de Bercy** (8 boulevard de Bercy, 12th, tel: 01 40 02 60 60, www.bercy.fr) offers a vast range of events including football, ice sports, motor sports and horse riding.

Major sports events include the **Six Nations** rugby in Feb–Mar, the Marathon in April, and the **French Tennis Open** in May–June at Stade Roland-Garros. For racing fans, the **Grand Prix de l'Arc de Triomphe** is run at Hippodrome de Longchamp, Bois de Boulogne, in October. **Parc des Princes** (16th *arrondissement)* is home to Paris's premier football team, Paris St-Germain.

BELOW: cooling off in the Piscine Joséphine-Baker.

COURSES

Paris hosts numerous schools and courses for people of all ages. **Le Centre d'Information et de Documentation Jeunesse (CIDJ)** has information sheets on education in France, available from 101 quai Branly, 15th, tel: 01 44 49 12 00, www.cidj.com. Schools may also help with travel and accommodation.

French Language

A good reference site for locating course centres is www.fle.fr.
Alliance Française
101 boulevard Raspail, 6th. Tel: 01 42 84 90 00, www.alliancefr.org
Institut de Langue et de Culture Françaises (ILCF)
12 rue Casette, 6th
Tel: 01 44 39 52 00, www.icp.fr
Ecole de Langue Française pour Etrangers (ELFE)
8 villa Ballu, 9th
Tel: 01 48 78 73 00
www.elfe-paris.com
Eurocentres
13 passage Dauphine, 6th
Tel: 01 40 46 72 00
www.eurocentres.com

Cookery

Le Cordon Bleu
8 rue Léon-Delhomme, 15th
Tel: 01 53 68 22 50
www.lecordonbleuparis.com
Ritz Escoffier
15 place Vendôme, 1st
Tel: 01 43 16 30 30
www.ritzparis.com

History and Culture

Collège de France
11 place Marcelin Berthelot, 5th
www.college-de-france.fr
Admission to the lectures and seminars is free and open to all. About five thousand people attend the various lectures each year.
Institut Parisien de Langue et de Civilisation Françaises
9 rue de Lisbonne, 8th
Tel: 01 40 56 09 53
www.institut-parisien.com
Courses in language and culture.

SHOPPING

BEST BUYS

Each of the city's different *quartiers* has its own mood and atmosphere, and shops often reflect local history and the type of people who live there. Expect conventional, classic BCBG wear ("bon chic, bon genre", the Paris equivalent of a Sloane or Preppy) with a dose of St-Tropez gilt in Passy; boho designers on the steep streets of Montmartre; designer couture and an international clientele along Avenue Montaigne and Rue du Faubourg St-Honoré; and street-wise garb around Les Halles and Rue Etienne-Marcel.

SHOPPING

What to Buy

Paris is the designer city of the world. Alongside France's chains such as Naf Naf and Kookaï, all the top-name couturiers have boutiques. The top couture houses are in the Avenue Montaigne area and around the Faubourg St-Honoré, with more individual boutiques clustering around the Marais and St-Germain-des-Prés.

Other main shopping areas include Rue de Rivoli, which runs from the Marais to the Louvre, the streets around the Opéra and Boulevard Haussmann. For smaller boutiques and more individual designs you're best advised to visit the appealing narrow alleys of the Marais. For quirky boutiques, young cutting-edge design and exotic food shops, visit the backstreets of Montmartre (around Rue des Abbesses), the Bastille (around Rue Keller) and Oberkampf.

SALES

Traditionally the sales *(soldes)* are held in July, just after Christmas and throughout January. However, many shops have mid-season reductions so you may pick up bargains all year round.

Where to Buy

Department Stores

Bazar de l'Hôtel de Ville (BHV)
55 rue de Verrerie, 4th
Tel: 01 42 74 90 00
www.bhv.fr
This sizeable department store caters for all things domestic with a strong emphasis on DIY.

Le Bon Marché Rive Gauche
24 rue de Sèvres, 7th
Tel: 01 44 39 80 00
www.lebonmarche.fr
One of Paris's most stylish *grands magasins*, housed in a building designed by the architect Gustave Eiffel. Once called "*une cathédrale du commerce*", it sells haute couture fashions and make-up. Highlights of the ground floor are the Theatre of Beauty, devoted to the hottest make-up artist brands, and the men's section, Balthazar, with polished wood floors and designer boutiques.

Galeries Lafayette
40 boulevard Haussmann, 9th
Tel: 01 42 82 34 56
www.galerieslafayette.com
An entire floor devoted to lingerie, and the largest perfume department in the world, beneath a breathtakingly beautiful Art Nouveau steel-and-glass dome – just some of the delights of this massive department store that carries over 75,000 brand names.

La Grande Epicerie de Paris
38 rue de Sèvres, 7th
tel: 01 44 39 81 00
www.lagrandeepicerie.fr
Le Bon Marché's gourmet grocery store sells every delicacy under the sun.

Au Printemps
64 boulevard Haussmann, 9th
Tel: 01 42 82 57 87
www.printemps.com
The store is situated in three separate buildings – each devoted to a theme: L'Homme (men's fashion), La Maison (home) and La Mode (women's fashion). There is an excellent selection of new designer collections, plus large departments specialising in china, kitchenware and stationery.

TAX

Most prices include TVA (value-added tax, or VAT). The base rate in France is currently 19.6 per cent (2010) but it can be as high as 35 per cent on some luxury items.

Foreign visitors can claim back TVA, and this is worth doing if you spend over €650 (€175 for non-EU residents) in one place. Ask the store for a *bordereau de vente à l'exportation* (export sales invoice). This must be completed and presented with the goods to customs officers on leaving France. Pack items separately for ease of access. The form is mailed back to the retailer, which refunds the TVA in a month or two. Certain goods (such as antiques) may need special clearance. For more information, contact the Centre de Renseignements des Douanes, tel: 03 11 20 44 44.

Designer Names

Agnès b
2, 3, and 6 rue du Jour (the street nos. refer to stores for children's, men's and women's fashions, respectively), 1st
Tel: 01 45 08 56 56
www.agnesb.fr
The quintessential French designer clothes that are relatively affordable.

Emporio Armani
149 boulevard St-Germain, 6th
Tel: 01 53 63 33 50
www.emporioarmani.com.
Classic, chic Italian design.

Azzedine Alaïa
7 rue de Moussy, 4th
Tel: 01 42 72 19 19
Slinky couture.

Balenciaga
10 avenue George V, 8th
Tel: 01 47 20 21 11
www.balenciaga.com
Vintage couture house now back at the top of the fashion tree thanks to Nicolas Ghesquière.

Chanel
31 rue Cambon, 1st
Tel: 01 42 86 26 00
www.chanel.fr
You can still find that quilted bag and tailored suit, or Chanel No. 5 perfume, but the classics are displayed alongside Karl Lagerfeld's take on leisurewear.

Chloé
54–6 rue du Faubourg St-Honoré, 8th
Tel: 01 44 94 33 00
www.chloe.com
Delicate, hip fashions, now created under Swedish designer Paulo Melim Andersson.

Christian Lacroix
73 rue du Faubourg St-Honoré, 8th
Tel: 01 42 68 79 04
www.christian-lacroix.fr
Christian Lacroix's exuberant colours evoke the vibrant palettes of Provençal artists.

Christian Dior
30 avenue Montaigne, 8th
Tel: 01 40 73 54 44
www.dior.com
Flimsy, bias-cut outfits, teetering talons and gilded cosmetics.

Colette
213 rue St-Honoré, 8th
Tel: 01 55 35 33 90
www.colette.fr
The "lifestyle boutique" for the new millennium generation.

BELOW: head to Antoine & Lili for colourful designs.

Comme des Garçons (RED)
54 rue du Faubourg St-Honoré, 8th
Tel: 01 53 30 27 27
Trends from Rei Kawakubo displayed in chilli-pepper-red interiors.

Givenchy
3 avenue George V, 8th
Tel: 01 44 31 50 00
www.givenchy.com
French couture by British designer Julien MacDonald, who replaced Alexander McQueen.

Gucci
60 avenue Montaigne, 8th
Tel: 01 56 69 80 80
www.gucci.com
Italian-style house for diehard fashionistas.

Hermès
24 rue du Faubourg St-Honoré, 8th
Tel: 01 40 17 47 17
www.hermes.com
For that perfect silk scarf.

Isabelle Marant
16 rue de Charonne, 11th
Tel: 01 49 29 71 55
Boho designs, for those who like their clothes effortlessly fashionable and discreetly sexy.

Jean-Paul Gaultier
6 rue Vivienne, 2nd
Tel: 01 42 86 05 05
Outlandish tailoring for men and women, plus accessories.

Jil Sander
56 avenue Montaigne, 8th
Tel: 01 44 95 06 70
Trend-setting German fashion.

COIFFURE

If you need a haircut while in Paris, you could head for the ubiquitous Toni and Guy (try 248 rue St-Honoré, 75001, tel: 01 40 20 98 20) or one of Jean-Claude Biguine's many salons (check www.biguine.com for the addresses).

Kenzo
3 place des Victoires, 1st
Tel: 01 40 39 72 03
www.kenzo.com
Flamboyant colours from the celebrated Japanese designer.

Louis Vuitton
101 avenue des Champs-Elysées, 8th
Tel: 01 53 57 52 00
www.vuitton.com
Trademark leather goods.

Patrick Cox
62 rue Tiquetonne, 2nd
Tel: 01 40 26 66 55
www.patrickcox.com
The shoes to be seen in, from the British designer.

Plein Sud
29 rue du Dragon, 6th
Tel: 01 45 48 79 29
Sexy fashion for women by top Moroccan designer Fayçal Amor.

Prada
10 avenue Montaigne, 8th
Tel: 01 53 23 99 40
www.prada.com
For a pair of the mules all Parisian women seem to favour in warm weather.

Sonia Rykiel
175 boulevard St-Germain, 6th
Tel: 01 49 54 60 60
www.soniarykiel.fr
Witty, wearable and beautifully cut designs. Menswear is across the road. Also at 70 rue du Faubourg St-Honoré.

Vanessa Bruno
25 rue St-Sulpice, 6th
Tel: 01 43 54 41 04
www.vanessabruno.com
Vanessa Bruno's individual clothes have a quiet femininity.

Yohji Yamamoto
4 rue Cambon, 1st
Tel: 01 40 20 00 71
www.yohjiyamamoto.co.jp
New fashion that draws its inspiration from traditional Japanese and Tibetan costumes.

Boutiques

Abou D'Abi Bazar
125 rue Vieille du Temple, 3rd
Tel: 01 42 71 13 26
This stylish shop sells a range of pretty women's wear by up-and-coming young designers.

Barbara Bui
23 rue Etienne-Marcel, 1st
Tel: 01 40 26 43 65
www.barbarabui.com
Super-smart garments for the woman about town.

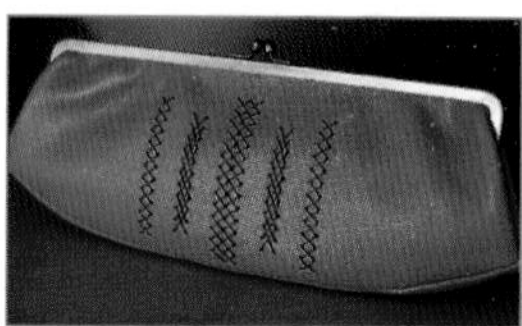

Antoine & Lili
Le Village, 95 quai de Valmy, 10th
Tel: 01 40 37 58 14
www.antoineetlili.com
Top quality women's and children's clothes. Very fashionable.

Cartier
13 rue la Paix, 1st
Tel: 01 58 18 23 00
www.cartier.com
The place for glittery diamond sparklers. There is also a

Brocantes

If you are interested in buying antiques and bric-a-brac, look out for the *brocantes* held in various parts of Paris, usually at weekends, publicised by posters and banners in the streets. They sell ceramics, jewellery, tools and furniture, and, because many of the traders come from outside Paris and are keen to sell their goods, they are often as cheap as the flea markets.

selection of vintage pieces.

Corinne Sarrut
40 rue des Francs-Bourgeois, 4th
Tel: 01 42 74 67 21
Very Parisian fashion label. Feminine silhouettes in an original mix of materials and colours.

Editions de Parfums Frédéric Malle
37 rue de Grenelle, 7th
Tel: 01 42 22 76 40
www.editionsdeparfums.com
The grandson of Parfums Christian Dior's founder, Frédéric Malle, gave seven of the world's leading "noses" carte blanche to create a fragrance under their own names. Judge the results for yourself in his elegant boutique.

L'Habilleur
44 rue de Poitou, 3rd
Tel: 01 48 87 77 12
End-of-line and ex-catwalk clothes from some of the top designers.

Loft Design By
20 rue Yvonne le Tac, 18th
Tel: 01 42 51 39 10
www.loftdesignby.com
Gap, French-style.

Maria Luisa
7 rue Rouget de Lisle, 1st
Tel: 01 47 03 96 15
One of the hottest multi-label stores in Paris.

Paul et Joe
62 rue des Saints-Pères, 7th
Tel: 01 42 22 98 98
www.paulandjoe.com
The fetish boutique of Parisian fashionistas filled with weathered-looking creations that emulate the continuing vintage craze.

Pronuptia
87 rue de Rivoli, 1st
Tel: 01 42 60 16 92
www.pronuptia.fr
Elegant wedding gowns and accessories.

Tara Jarmon
18 rue du Four, 6th
Tel: 01 46 33 26 60
www.tarajarmon.com
Elegant, pretty fashions from this Canadian designer.

High-Street Fashions

There is a growing number of high-street chains in France, many of which have branches across the capital – only one branch of each is listed for most of the following. This selection should start you off.

Cacharel
36 rue Tronchet, 9th
Tel: 01 42 68 38 88
www.cacharel.com
Delicate, feminine designer lingerie and perfume.

Etam
73 rue de Rivoli, 1st
Tel: 01 44 76 73 73
www.etam.com
The megastore branch of a chain selling women's and teens clothes and pretty, affordable lingerie.

Gap
102 rue de Rivoli, 1st
Tel: 01 44 88 28 28

BELOW: chic boutique on Avenue Montaigne.

www.gap.com
The US chain has gone down a storm in the French capital, and there seem to be branches of Gap everywhere. Practical urban wear for the family at good prices.

Kookaï
2 rue Gustave-Courbet, 16th
Tel: 01 47 55 18 00
www.kookai.fr
Inexpensive fashion for the young. Other branches can be found throughout Paris.

Morgan
165 rue de Rennes, 6th
Tel: 01 45 48 96 77
Familiar to the young UK market, this French chain offers groovy styles.

Promod
60 rue Caumartin, 9th
Tel: 01 45 26 01 11
www.promod.com
One of several branches in Paris. French fashions at reasonable prices. Good for jumpers, jewellery and coats.

Zara
44 avenue des Champs-Elysées, 8th
www.zara.com
Tel: 01 45 61 52 80
Expanding Spanish chain offering funky designs for men, women and children at high-street prices.

Shoes

The main shoe chains (which have branches across the city) include the following, all offering this season's styles at affordable prices:

André
106 and 138 rue de Rivoli, 1st

Tel: 01 53 40 96 84
www.andre.fr
France Arno
98 rue de Rivoli, 1st
Tel: 01 40 28 00 10.
Everyday shoes.
Mephisto
78 rue des Saints-Pères, 7th
Tel: 01 45 44 03 04
www.mephisto.com
French walking shoes for getting around Paris on foot.
Rodolphe Ménudier
14 rue de Castiglione, 1st
www.rodolphemenudier.com
Chic shoes for the well heeled.

Gifts and Gourmet

Androuet
134 rue Mouffetard, 5th
Tel: 01 47 64 39 20
www.androuet.com
This is an excellent cheese shop connected to the Androuet restaurant. Other branches include: 83 rue St-Dominique, 7th, tel: 01 45 50 45 75, and 19 rue Daguerre, 14th, tel: 01 43 21 19 09.
Bains Plus
51 rue des Francs-Bourgeois, 4th
Tel: 01 48 87 83 07
Everything you could possibly imagine for the bathroom.
Les Caves Taillevent
199 rue du Faubourg St-Honoré, 8th. Tel: 01 45 61 14 09
www.taillevent.com
Taillevent stores some 30,000 bottles in its underground cellar, but this excellent *cave* is not just for connoisseurs.
Debauve et Gallais
30 rue des Saints-Pères, 7th
Tel: 01 45 48 54 67
www.debauveetgallais.com
Chocolates fit for the kings of France.
E. Dehillerin
18 rue Coquillière,1st
Tel: 01 42 36 53 13
www.e-dehillerin.fr
Professional chefs have been coming to this Aladdin's cave for cooks since 1820. Packed to the rafters with traditional French cookware.
Diptyque Candles
34 boulevard St-Germain, 5th
Tel: 01 43 26 77 44
www.diptyqueparis.com
Heavenly scented candles.
Fauchon
26 place de la Madeleine, 8th
Tel: 01 70 39 38 00
www.fauchon.fr.
Luxury foodstore, celebrated for its gourmet buffets, a great in-house brasserie and Italian trattoria.
FNAC
74 avenue des Champs-Elysées, 8th
Tel: 0825 020 020
www.fnac.fr
Books, music, hi-fi and videos are all sold in this giant, long-established French chain. Concert tickets can also be bought here. Branches across the city. Late opening most nights.
Guerlain
68 avenue des Champs-Elysées, 8th
Tel: 01 45 62 52 57
www.guerlain.com
The French perfumier in a breath-takingly beautiful flagship store.
La Maison du Chocolat
8 boulevard de la Madeleine, 9th
Tel: 01 47 42 86 52
www.lamaisonduchocolat.com
Mouth-watering chocolate emporium.

BELOW: books, record and audiovisual empire, FNAC.

Maître Parfumeur et Gantier
84bis rue de Grenelle, 7th
Tel: 01 45 44 61 57
www.maitre-parfumeur-et-gantier.com.
Natural, hand-crafted perfumes not found on the mass market, and beautiful leather gloves.

Marie Papier
26 rue Vavin, 6th
Tel: 01 43 26 46 44
www.mariepapier.fr
Paper products, including hand-made stationery and albums.

Pétrossian
18 boulevard La Tour-Maubourg, 7th
Tel: 01 44 11 32 22
www.petrossian.fr
Caviar specialists who are also renowned for their smoked salmon and foie gras.

QuatreHomme Fromagerie
62 rue de Sèvres, 7th
Tel: 01 47 34 33 45
Cheeses and more.

Sennelier
3 quai Voltaire, 7th
Tel: 01 42 60 72 15
www.magasinsennelier.com
One of the capital's oldest art supplies shops.

Séphora
70 avenue des Champs-Elysées, 8th
Tel: 01 53 93 22 50
www.sephora.com
Perfume chain with branches across Paris. This one is huge (see www.sephora.com for other branches).

Children

Apache
Forum des Halles, Porte Berger, Niveau 2
Tel: 01 44 88 52 00
www.apache.fr
Colourful toy store with an activities studio and cyber-café.

Chantelivre
13 rue de Sévres, 6th
Tel: 01 45 48 87 90
Children's bookshop with a small English-language section, plus CDs, videos and stationery.

Les Cousins d'Alice
36 rue Daguerre, 14th
Tel: 01 43 20 24 86
Stuffed animals, books, construction games and much more.

ABOVE: treats for the kids at bright and buzzy Apache.

Les Deux Tisserins
36 rue des Bernardins, 5th
Tel: 01 46 33 88 68
A large collection of wooden toys, plus clothing and accessories.

FNAC Junior
19 rue Vavin, 6th
Tel: 08 92 35 06 66
www.eveiletjeux.com
Educational and fun games, toys, videos and CDs for young kids.

Pain d'Epices
29 passage Jouffroy, 9th
Tel: 01 47 70 08 68
www.paindepices.fr
A doll enthusiast's paradise.

Du Pareil au Même
1 rue St-Denis, 1st
Tel: 01 40 13 07 43
www.dpam.com
Affordable French children's clothes.

Petit Bateau
26 rue Vavin, 6th
Tel: 01 55 42 02 53
www.petit-bateau.com
Children and women's underwear, T-shirts and sleepwear in the softest cotton.

Markets

Le Marché d'Aligre
Rue and Place d'Aligre, 12th
General. Good for cheap fruit and veg. Tue–Sun 7.30am–1.30pm.

Le Marché Biologique
Organic produce markets at Boulevard Raspail, 14th, on Sun, and Boulevard des Batignolles, 17th, Sat morning.

Ile de la Cité
Place Louis-Lépine, 4th
Flowers. Daily 8am–7.30pm. Birds. Sun 8am–7pm. The adjacent **Quai de la Mégisserie** sells birds, fish and small animals.

Le Marché Maubert
Place Maubert, 5th
Produce and flowers. Tue, Thur and Sat 7am–2.30pm.

Place de la Madeleine
East side of the church, 8th
Flowers. Mon–Sat 8am–7.30pm.

Le Marché Place Monge
Place Monge, 5th
Produce, flowers, cheese and home-made comestibles. Wed, Fri and Sun 7am–2.30pm.

Le Marché St-Germain
Rue Lobineau, 6th
Produce, cheese, wine and flowers. Tue–Sat 8.30am–1pm, 4–7.30pm, Sun 8am–1.30pm.

Le Marché Aux Puces de St-Ouen (Clignancourt)
Avenue de Clignancourt, 18th
The flea market giant in the north of Paris. Sat–Mon, 8am–6.30pm.

Le Marché Aux Puces de Vanves
Avenue Marc Sagnier, 14th.

A–Z

AN ALPHABETICAL SUMMARY OF PRACTICAL INFORMATION

Addresses

Paris is divided into numbered districts – *arrondissements* – and people refer to them by number, saying, for example, that they live "in the 5th". Street names are followed by a five-digit postcode, in which the last digits are the *arrondissement* number, so an address with a 75008 code will be in the 8th *arrondissement*, and 75012 in the 12th.

Budgeting for Your Trip

The price of accommodation ranges across the spectrum. You can get a double room in a small pension for under €50 a night, or you can pay €300 in a luxury hotel. An average price, however, for an en suite double room in a centrally located, comfortable hotel is around €100–150.

Meals also cover a wide price range, but on average expect to pay €30–40 for a three-course meal with a half-bottle of house wine. In French restaurants the most economical (and most usual) way to order food is from a *prix fixe* set menu (also called a *menu* or a *formule*), which gives two, three or four courses, and coffee, for a set price. Drinks are not usually included. *Menus* are a real bargain, with many for €20–30 or less. Ordering *à la carte* is always more expensive. Note too, that many restaurants only offer bargain menus for lunch, so it will be more economical to eat at midday than in the evening.

The average entrance price to a national museum or gallery is €7–8 (municipal ones are free), but a *Paris Museum Pass* or *Paris Visite* travelcard can give great savings *(see pages 282, 295)*.

A taxi from the airport will cost around €45–60, depending on traffic, plus €1 per bag and a tip of about 5 percent. Single Métro and bus fares cost €1.60, or €11.60 for a *carnet* of 10 tickets, but, again, it's much more economical to take advantage of the various travelcards available on Paris's transport system. For details, *see page 282*.

Business Hours

Office workers normally start early (8.30am is not uncommon) and often stay at their desks until 6pm or later. This is partly to make up for the long lunch hours (two hours, from around noon) traditional in public offices. Many companies are changing to shorter lunch breaks, as employees appreciate the advantages of getting home earlier in the evening.

Traditionally **banks** open from Monday to Friday 9am to 5.30pm and are closed on Saturday and Sunday. However, many banks now close on Monday instead, and open on Saturday morning.

Food shops, especially bakers, tend to open early. Most boutiques and department stores open about 9am, but some do not open until 10am. Traditionally most French shops close from around noon to 2.30pm, but in Paris many remain open until 7 or 7.30pm. Big department stores do not close at lunchtime, and open until 9 or 10pm on Thursday. Most shops close on Sunday, but bakers and patisseries are usually open in the morning.

Suburban hypermarkets are usually all day until 8 or 9pm. Most shops are closed on Monday morning, some all day Monday. If you want to buy a picnic lunch, remember to get everything you need before midday.

Business Visitors

Business travel accounts for about a third of French tourism revenue. This important market has led to the creation of a spe-

cial Conference and Incentive Department at French tourist offices in London and New York. This department deals with business travel enquiries, and helps organise hotels, conference centres and incentive deals.

Conferences and Exhibitions

Paris is a world leader for conferences, exhibitions and trade fairs, and La Défense is the largest business district in Europe. For further information, call Info-Défense, tel: 01 47 74 84 24, or visit www.ladefense.fr.

For lists of exhibitions and details on participating, contact **Promo Salons** agency, via www.promosalons.com, with many offices around the world.

Many châteaux and hotels offer luxurious accommodation for smaller gatherings, and it's even possible to organise a congress at Disneyland Paris.

Trade Fair Venues

Palais des Congrès, Porte Maillot, 17th, tel: 01 40 68 22 50, www.palais-congres-paris.fr.
Paris-Expo, Porte de Versailles, 15th, tel: 01 40 68 22 22, www.parisexpo.fr; Paris's biggest trade fair complex.
Parc des Expositions de Paris-Nord, Villepinte, near Roissy-Charles de Gaulle airport, tel: 01 40 68 22 22, www.expoparisnord.com.
CNIT, La Défense, tel: 01 40 68 22 22, www.cnit.fr; has links to other salons at Porte de Champerret and Carrousel du Louvre.

Chambers of Commerce

An excellent source of information on local companies, export and import technicalities, translation agencies and conference centres is the **Chambre de Commerce et d'Industrie de Paris**, 27 avenue de Friedland, 8th, tel: 0820 012 112, www.ccip.fr. The **Franco-British Chamber of Commerce** is at 31 rue Boissy-d'Anglas, 8th, tel: 01 53 30 81 30, www.francobritishchambers.com. There are also French Chambers of Commerce in key cities around the world. In London, the Chamber is at 21 Dartmouth Street, London SW1H 9BP, tel: 020 7092 6600, www.ccfgb.co.uk.

Climate

France is the only European country that is both North European and Mediterranean. In Paris, the climate is similar to that of southern England, but less changeable, and temperatures can be higher in mid-summer. The average maximum in July and August is 25°C (76°F), the average minimum 15°C (58°F), but 27°C (80°F) is not unusual. In January, expect a maximum of 6°C (43°F), a minimum of 1°C (43°F). To check the weather for your visit, see www.weather.com.

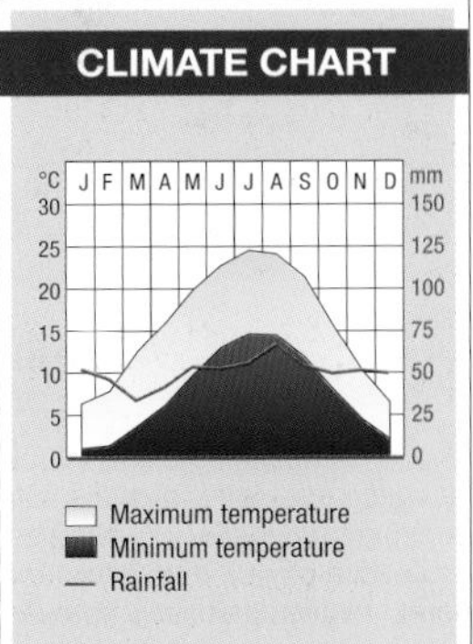

When to Visit

Spring, when the temperature is ideal for sightseeing, is probably the best time to visit Paris, although you should be prepared for showers. Autumn mornings can be sharp, but by midday the skies are usually clear and bright. Some believe that winter light shows Paris at its best.

What to Wear

Paris is a great city to explore on foot, so comfortable walking shoes are essential. Bring warm clothes if you're coming to Paris in winter, as the weather can be very chilly, and remember to have something waterproof (or at the least an umbrella) with you in spring or autumn, as showers are quite common.

Most Parisians are very style-conscious, and won't brave even the corner shop without displaying a fair amount of sartorial élan. Casual tourists might therefore consider taking a smart change of clothes – in case, for example, you might want to try a night out at one of the city's many upmarket restaurants, where smart dress is de rigueur.

Complaints

To complain about a purchase, return it to the shop as soon as possible. In a serious dispute, contact the local Direction Départementale de la Concurrence, de la Consommation et de la Répression des Fraudes (consult the telephone directory for details).

Crime and Safety

Police

In the event of loss or theft, a report must be made in person at the nearest police station *(commissariat)* as soon as possible after the event. This will also be required if you wish to claim from your insurance company. Visit www.prefecture-police-paris.interieur.gouv.fr for station locations, or for emergency help tel: 17.

Security

If you take sensible precautions with your possessions, you should be safe in Paris. There is a problem with pickpockets in some of the Métro stations. Obvious centres of prostitution (such as Les Halles and parts of the Bois de Boulogne) are best avoided at night. As anywhere else, use care when withdrawing money with debit or credit cards at a bank, currency exchange office or ATM machine, and make sure others cannot see your PIN. It's always a good idea to keep a photocopy of your passport in case of theft *(see also Emergencies).*

Customs Regulations

There are no official restrictions on the movement of goods within the European Union, provided that the goods were purchased within the EU. However, people of all nationalities must declare, upon arrival or departure, sums of cash exceeding €7,600.

Duty-paid goods If you are an EU resident and buy goods in France on which you pay tax, there are no longer any restrictions on the amounts you may take home with you. However, EU law has set "guidance levels" on the amounts that are acceptable of the following:

- **Tobacco** 3,200 cigarettes, or 400 cigarillos, or 200 cigars, or 1 kg of tobacco
- **Spirits** 10 litres
- **Fortified wine/wine** 90 litres (not more than 60 litres may be sparkling wine)
- **Beer** 110 litres

If you exceed these amounts you must be able to show that the goods are for personal use, for example a family wedding.

Duty-free goods If you are from outside the EU and buy goods duty-free in France, the following limits still apply (these quantities may be doubled if you live outside Europe):

- **Tobacco** 200 cigarettes, or 100 cigarillos, or 50 cigars, or 250 g of tobacco
- **Alcohol** 1 litre of spirits or liqueurs over 22 percent volume, or 2 litres of fortified, sparkling wine or other liqueurs.
- **Perfume** 50 g of perfume, plus 250 ml of eau de toilette.

There are no restrictions on the amount of currency you can take into France.

For more information contact Centre de Renseignements des Douanes, tel: 08 11 20 44 44, or check www.douane.gouv.fr.

Disabled Travellers

Travellers with mobility problems are advised to book accommodation in advance. Official hotel lists use a symbol to denote wheelchair access, but it's a good idea to check with the hotel regarding the exact facilities available. Information on hotels with good access facilities can be found on the Paris Tourist Office website, www.parisinfo.com.

Budget hotels in the Campanile chain have at least one room for disabled guests.
Contact Hôtel Première Classe, 18 rue du Pont-des-Halles, 94656 Rungis Cedex, tel: 01 49 78 01 45, www.premiereclasse.fr.
Maison des Clubs UNESCO, 43 rue de la Glacière, 13th, tel: 01 43 36 00 63, has accommodation for disabled young people.

Wheelchairs to rent

CRF Matériel Médical, 153 boulevard Voltaire, 11th, tel: 01 43 73 98 98, www.cap-vital-sante.com.

French Organisations

Association des Paralysés de France, 17 boulevard Auguste-Blanqui, 13th, tel: 01 40 78 69 00, www.apf.asso.fr.
The association may be able to answer specific enquiries and can provide branch addresses.
CIDJ *(see page 316, Study in France)* youth information service has extensive information on services for less able young travellers. It publishes *Vacances pour Personnes Handicapées* and leaflets on activity and sports holidays for young disabled people.
Union Nationale des Associations de Parents d'Enfants Inadaptés (UNAPEI), 15 rue Coysevox, 18th, tel: 01 44 85 50 50, www.unapei.org. Parents may wish to contact this organisation for information about facilities for children with disabilities.
Comité de Liaison pour le Transport des Personnes Handicapées, Conseil National des Transports, 34 avenue Marceau, 9th, tel: 01 53 23 85 85, www.coliac.cnt.fr. Gives brief information on accessibility and arrangements for less able passengers on public transport, and contacts for special transport schemes in France.
Ptitcar, 01 42 24 70 73, www.ptitcar.com, is an excellent transport company that operates a fleet of wheelchair-accessible vehicles for transport and tours. They also prepare vacation itineraries for wheelchair users, and offer other helpful services.

UK Organisations

RADAR, The Royal Association for Disability and Rehabilitation, 12 City Forum, 250 City Road, London EC1V 8AF, tel: 020 7250 3222, www.radar.org.uk. Provides helpful and friendly advice.
Mobilise (Disabled Drivers' Association and Disabled Drivers' Motor Club), tel: 01508 489449, www.mobilise.info.

US Organisations

Society for Accessible Travel and Hospitality (SATH), 347 Fifth Avenue, Suite 605, New York, tel: 212-447 7284, www.sath.org. A non-profit organisation that represents travellers with disabilities, and can also provide information.
MossRehab Resource Net www.mossresourcenet.org. A website with a very wide range of information on travelling and other disability-related issues.

USEFUL INFORMATION

The following guides are useful for people with disabilities:
- **Access in Paris** A guidebook that provides essential information for anyone with a mobility problem, including the elderly or parents travelling with young children. It can be obtained from Access Project, 39 Bradley Gardens, West Ealing, London W13 8HE, www.accessinparis.org.
- **Door to Door** The UK government's online guide to travel for disabled people, with a section on travelling abroad. www.dptac.gov.uk/door-to-door.
- **Michelin Red Guides** Both the *France* and *Camping-Caravanning* guides indicate hotels that have facilities for guests with disabilities.
- **Rick Steves' Easy Access Europe** A guide for travellers with mobility problems covering several European countries, including France. Available in bookshops.

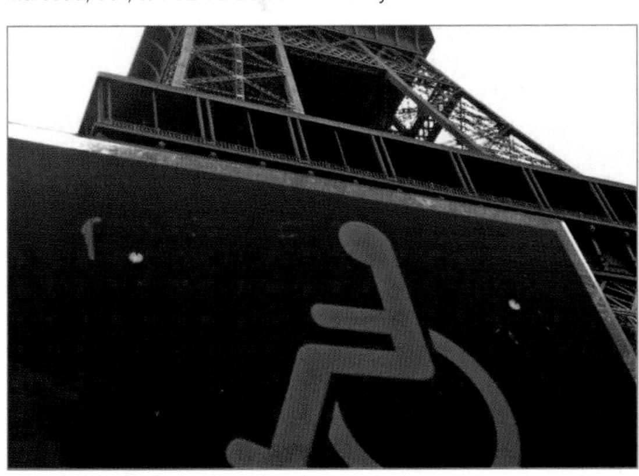

Embassies and Consulates

• Australia
4 rue Jean-Rey, 15th
Tel: 01 40 59 33 00
www.france.embassy.gov.au

• Canada
35 avenue Montaigne, 8th
Tel: 01 44 43 29 00
www.international.gc.ca/canada-europa/france

• New Zealand
7ter rue Léonard-de-Vinci, 16th
Tel: 01 45 01 43 43
www.nzembassy.com/france

• Republic of Ireland
12 avenue Foch, 16th
Tel: 01 44 17 67 00
www.embassyofireland.fr

• South Africa
59 quai d'Orsay, 7th
Tel: 01 53 59 23 23
www.afriquesud.net

• UK
35 rue du Faubourg-St-Honoré, 8th, tel: 01 44 51 31 00
Consular services: 18bis rue d'Anjou, 8th, tel: 01 44 51 31 01
http://ukinfrance.fco.gov.uk

• US
2 avenue Gabriel, 8th
Tel: 01 43 12 22 22
http://france.usembassy.gov
Office of American Services (consular services for US travellers or residents): 2 rue St-Florentin, 1st

Electricity

The standard voltage is 220 volts. Round-pin plugs are used, so pack an adaptor (available at airports as well as any store selling travel-related items). Visitors from North America with 110v equipment will also need a transformer for the higher voltage.

Entry Requirements

Visas and Passports

All visitors to France require a valid passport. No visa is required by visitors from European Union (EU) member states, the US, Australia, Canada or Japan. Nationals of other countries may need a visa; if in doubt, check with the French Consulate in your home country. For anyone (including EU nationals) who wants to stay longer than 90 days, it is no longer obligatory to obtain a *carte de séjour*, but it is still advisable to get one, from French Consulates or the Préfecture de Police, 9 boulevard du Palais, 4th, Paris.

Gay Travellers

The Marais (the 4th *arrondissement*) is the most gay-friendly district in Paris, with gay-oriented restaurants, wine bars, boutiques, bookstores, beauty salons, hotels, bars and discos. For more information check out the websites www.legayparis.fr, www.paris-gay.com and www.gay-paris.net (all in French and English). There are various free magazines you can pick up in most gay bars in the 3rd and 4th *arrondissements*. The gay magazine *Têtu* is a useful source of information, and can be bought at most news kiosks in the city.

Health & Medical Care

If you are an EU national and you fall ill in France, you can receive emergency medical treatment from doctors, dentists and hospitals. You will have to pay the cost of this treatment, but are entitled to claim from the French *Sécurité Sociale*, which refunds up to 70 percent of your medical expenses. To receive a refund you must have a **European Health Insurance Card** (**EHIC**). These are available online at www.dh.gov.uk or can be ordered through post offices and health centres. While travelling, keep the card safe.

If you need to see a doctor, expect to pay at least €45 per consultation, with prescription charges on top. The doctor will provide a statement of treatment *(feuille de soins)*. With this, EU citizens can reclaim around 70 percent of the cost of treatment. If you buy any medicines on prescription, check that the price stamp *(vignette)* is attached to the *feuille de soins* by the chemist, so that you can reclaim this cost too. When complete, the *feuille de soins* and prescription should be sent as soon as possible to the local *Caisse Primaire d'Assurance Maladie* (the doctor or chemist will have the address, or see the phone book under *Sécurité Sociale*) for your refund. It can also be a good idea

Emergencies

Ambulance:	15
Police:	17
Fire service:	18
Emergency calls from a mobile phone:	112

SOS Help English-language helpline (daily 3–11pm):
01 46 21 46 46

to include a photocopy of your EHIC, and keep copies yourself of the other documents. The refund will be sent to your home, which will take about a month. If you have any difficulties, contact the **Caisse Primaire d'Assurance Maladie de Paris**, 27 rue Georges Auric, 75019 Paris, tel: 01 53 38 70 00, or in the UK call tel: 0191 218 1999.

For more information, consult the leaflet **Health Advice for Travellers** (available from post offices, online at www.dh.gov.uk or by tel: 020 7210 4850). Reciprocal EU health agreements do not cover all medical expenses, such as the cost of bringing a sick person back to the UK, so the Department of Health advises travellers also to take out private insurance. If you plan to drive in France, you should check that your motor insurance covers you for accidents abroad.

For travellers from North America, a comprehensive travel insurance policy with full medical cover is essential. You can also contact the **International Association for Medical Assistance to Travellers (IAMAT),** based in Guelph, Ontario, tel: 519 836 0102, www.iamat.org. This non-profit-making group offers members fixed rates for treatment from participating physicians. Members receive a passport-sized medical record and a directory of English-speaking IAMAT doctors in France. Membership is free, but a donation is requested.

In Paris, you can find English-speaking health services at the private **American Hospital** (Hôpital Américain de Paris, tel: 01 46 41 25 25, www.american-hospital.org), which is highly regarded and very expensive, or the **British Hospital** (Hôpital Franco-Britannique, tel: 01 46 39 22 22, www.british-hospital.org), which is covered by the French social security system. However, not all the staff are bilingual, and the hospital is mainly known for its maternity unit.

Pharmacies

Most pharmacies display flashing green neon crosses, and are open from 9 or 10am to 7 or 8pm. At night, they all post the addresses of the nearest late-opening pharmacies in their windows. Staff can provide basic medical advice and services. The following pharmacies also open late every night:

Dhéry, 84 avenue des Champs-Elysées, 8th (Métro George V), tel: 01 45 62 02 41. Open 24 hours.

Pharmacie Européenne de la Place de Clichy, 6 place de Clichy, 9th (Métro Place de Clichy), tel: 01 48 74 65 18. Open 24 hours.

Pharmacie des Halles, 10 boulevard de Sébastopol, 4th (Métro Châtelet), tel: 01 42 72 03 23, fax: 01 42 72 52 10. Mon–Sat 9am–midnight and Sun 9am–10pm.

Publicis Drugstore, 133 avenue des Champs-Elysées, 8th (Métro Etoile), tel: 01 47 20 39 25. Mon–Fri 9am–2am, Sat–Sun from 10am.

Internet

There is an enormous wealth of information available over the web, from pages telling you how to get to your destination, to how to speak the language when you get there. The following entries are only the tip of the iceberg:

www.parisinfo.com official site of the Paris Tourist Office, with information on hotels, sites, events, exhibitions, transport, weather and more

www.franceguide.com official site of the French Tourist Office, Maison de la France, for general information on France

www.cestsoparis.com new tourist office site highlighting the hip side of Paris

www.paris.org *The Paris Pages*, a private site with general information on Paris

HOSPITALS

All state hospitals have casualty departments *(urgences)*. A complete list is available on www.aphp.fr. The following are some of the larger ones:

- **Hôpital Bichat**
46 rue Henri-Huchard, 18th
Tel: 01 40 25 80 80
- **Hôpital Fernaud-Widal**
(poisons control centre)
200 rue du Faubourg St-Denis, 10th
Tel: 01 40 05 45 45
- **Hôpital Hôtel-Dieu**
1 place du Parvis-Notre-Dame, 4th
Tel: 01 42 34 82 34
- **Hôpital Necker**
(children's hospital)
149 rue de Sèvres, 15th
Tel: 01 44 49 40 00
- **Hôpital de la Pitié-Salpêtrière**
47 boulevard de l'Hôpital, 13th
Tel: 01 42 16 00 00
- **Hôpital St-Louis**
1 avenue Claude-Vellefaux, 10th
Tel: 01 42 49 49 49

Lost Property

If your documents, cash, credit cards or other belongings are lost or stolen, go to the *commissariat de police* closest to the scene of the incident as soon as possible – even before contacting your credit card company or your consulate.

If you lose your passport, report it to your consulate immediately after notifying the police. There is a complete list of consulates in the local Yellow Pages *(Pages Jaunes)*.

If credit cards are lost or stolen, local numbers are:

- **American Express**, tel: 0800 908 600
- **Diners Club**, tel: 01 47 62 75 50
- **MasterCard**, tel: 08 00 90 13 87
- **Visa**, tel: 08 36 69 08 80

To reclaim anything else lost in Paris, go (with ID) to the **Bureau des Objets Trouvés**, 36 rue des Morillons, 15th, tel: 08 21 00 25 25 (Métro Convention); Mon–Thur 8.30am–5pm, Fri 8.30am–4.30pm. You must go in person: don't expect to sort out any enquiry by phone.

www.magicparis.com travel, shops, hotels, events and more
www.paris.fr site of the Mairie de Paris, the Town Hall
www.ratp.fr the Paris transport system site
www.culture.fr official site of the Ministry of Culture
www.monuments-nationaux.fr official site of France's Department of National Monuments
www.rmn.fr guide to national museum exhibitions
www.centrepompidou.fr Pompidou Centre
www.louvre.fr Musée du Louvre
www.tour-eiffel.fr Eiffel Tower
www.musee-orsay.fr Musée d'Orsay
www.musee-rodin.fr Musée Rodin
www.invalides.org Les Invalides
www.chateauversailles.fr Château de Versailles
www.meteo.fr weather online
www.pagesjaunes.fr the French Yellow Pages
www.opera-de-paris.fr Opéras Palais Garnier and Bastille
www.lemonde.fr France's most respected newspaper

www.mondediplo.com *Le Monde*'s supplement *Le Monde Diplomatique* in English
www.figaroscope.fr online edition of *Le Figaro*'s weekly Paris arts and restaurant supplement
www.ttc.org French news and analysis from *The Tocqueville Connection*, published in the US
www.timeout.com/paris *Time Out* city guide for Paris
www.disneylandparis.com everything about the resort

Maps

Plan de Paris par Arrondissement is the most useful map for visitors. It can be bought for €6.50 at any of the ubiquitous newsstands and kiosks around the city. You may also be able to get by on the tourist office maps.

Media

Newspapers

The two main national dailies are *Le Monde*, the most influential paper in the country, which has a rather dry and leftish slant on politics and economic news, and sells about 300,000 copies daily. The more conservative *Le Figaro* sells about 525,000 copies.

The paper representing the Communist Party is *L'Humanité*, and not veering so heavily left is Jean-Paul Sartre's brainchild, *Libération*. France's biggest-selling daily is *France-Soir*, with a circulation of around 1.3 million. The major weekly news magazines are *Le Point* (right), *L'Express* (centre) and *Le Nouvel Observateur* (left), which each sell around 350,000–500,000 copies. British, American and other European dailies are available on the same day at city-centre kiosks and shops showing *journaux* or *presse* signs.

The *International Herald Tribune*, published in Paris, has listings for the city. To find out what is going on in Paris, try *L'Officiel des Spectacles or Pariscope* (both out on Wednesday), which give listings of movies, clubs, exhibitions, concerts, theatres and more.

Radio

France Inter (87.8 MHz) is the biggest station, offering something to suit all tastes. Radio Classique (101.1 MHz) plays non-stop lightweight classical music.

For something a bit less mainstream, France Musiques (91.7 and 92.1 MHz). RTL (104.3 MHz), a popular station throughout France, plays music from the charts interspersed with chat.

Europe 1 (104.7 FM) is the best for morning news coverage, while France Info (105.5 FM) is a non-stop French news channel.

Television

TF1, France 2, France 3, France 5/Arte and M6 are the five main television stations. There is also a huge choice of cable channels, which are often available in larger hotels.

Canal+ is a subscription channel, which shows big-name films. CNN and BBC World are also available in many hotels.

Money

Currency

The euro (€) is the official French currency and is available in 500, 200, 100, 50, 20, 10 and 5 euro notes, and 2 euro, 1 euro, 50 cent, 20 cent, 10 cent, 5 cent, 2 cent and 1 cent coins. There are 100 cents to 1 euro.

Credit Cards

Most large shops and restaurants and almost all hotels accept credit cards. The most common in France are Visa, MasterCard and Carte Bleue (often called "CB"). American Express (Amex) and Diner's Club (DC) are widely recognised, and many places also accept Maestro and Cirrus, but if you don't see a card's sticker in a hotel or restaurant window, it's advisable to double-check.

Exchange

Bureaux de change at train stations vary their hours in high or low seasons, but most are open Monday to Friday 7am–7pm. In banks, separate exchange counters are increasingly rare.

Exchange offices at **Roissy-Charles de Gaulle** (terminals 2A, 2B and 2D) and **Orly Sud** airports are open daily until 11pm. **Travelex** at 194 rue de Rivoli, 1st, tel: 01 47 03 49 52, or for other locations visit: www.travelex.com. **American Express** at 11 rue Scribe, 9th, tel: 01 47 77 72 30, www.americanexpress.com. Mon–Sat 9am–6.30pm. Take your passport if you want to cash travellers' cheques.

PUBLIC HOLIDAYS

New Year's Day, Easter Monday, 1 May (Labour Day), 8 May (end of World War II in Europe), Ascension Day – mid/late May, Whit Monday – late May, 14 July (Bastille Day), 15 August (Feast of the Assumption), 1 November (All Saints' Day), 11 November (Armistice Day, 1918), 25 December (Christmas).

Boîtes aux lettres.....

Dernières levées:
- Province et Etranger à 18h00
- Paris et Banlieue à 20h00
- Le samedi (toutes destinations) à 13h00
- Le dimanche (Paris et Banlieue) à 16h00

Cash Machines

You can draw cash from bank dispensing machines (ATMs) using a credit card or European bank cashpoint card, using your PIN if your card is one of the following: Visa, MasterCard, Maestro or Cirrus. Be sure to confirm with your home bank that both your card and PIN can be used abroad.

Tipping

Restaurants By law, restaurant bills must include a service charge, which is usually 12 or 15 percent. Nevertheless, it is common to leave a small additional tip (not more than 5 percent) for the waiter if the service has been especially good. Address waiters as *Monsieur* (never *garçon*) and waitresses as *Mademoiselle*, if they are young, or *Madame*, if they are older.
Taxis Rounding up to the nearest euro is the norm.

Postal Services

The French post office is run by the PTT (*Poste et Télécommunications*). The main branches are open Mon–Fri 8am–7pm and Sat 8am–noon. The central post office at 52 rue du Louvre, 1st, tel: 01 40 28 76 00, www.laposte.fr, operates a daily 24-hour service. Another large post office is at Place de la Bourse, 1st, tel: 01 44 88 23 00, fax: 01 42 33 38 49, Mon–Fri 8.15am–6.30pm, Sat 8am–noon. Fax and photocopying facilities and limited Internet access are available in all larger post offices.

Stamps *(timbres)* are available at most *tabacs* (tobacconists) and other shops selling postcards or greetings cards. For postcards and letters weighing up to 20 grams, postage costs €0.54 within France and €0.60 to the rest of the EU. Sending a letter airmail to Australia, the US and Canada costs €0.90.

Religious Services

Most religious believers in France are Catholic, and Paris's many churches, including Notre-Dame, are open to the public. For a list of all denominational churches, temples and synagogues, look out for the guide *Plan de Paris par Arrondissement* from a kiosk or bookshop. For information on catholic services contact the **Service d'Information Religieuse**, http://catholique-paris-cef.fr.

There are services in English around Paris, notably in the **American Church**, 65 quai d'Orsay, 7th, tel: 01 40 62 05 00, or visit www.acparis.org.

Student Travellers

Students and young people under the age of 26 can get cut-price travel to Paris *(see page 280)*. For a prolonged stay, it may be worth finding out about an exchange visit or study holiday. The following organisations provide information or arrange visits.

UK Services

The **British Council** provides opportunities for international youth experience, exchange and other projects. Contact the **Education and Training Group**, British Council, 10 Spring Gardens, London SW1A 2BN, tel: 020 7930 8466, www.britishcouncil.org/new/learning.

Those who can speak French could approach UK-based camping holiday operators, such as **Holidaybreak** (Hartford Manor, Greenbank Lane, Northwich, Cheshire CW8 1HW, tel: 01606 787 522, www.holidaybreakjobs.com, which often employ students as site attendants in France and other European countries in summer.

US Services

American Council for International Studies (ACIS), Boston Regional Office, 343 Congress Street, Suite 3100, Boston, MA, 02210, tel: 800 888 ACIS or 617 236 2051, www.acis.com.
Council on International Educational Exchange (CIEE), 7 Custom House Street, 3rd Floor, Portland, ME 04101, tel: 1 800 407 8839 or 207 553 7600, fax: 207 553 4299, www.ciee.org. Work and study programmes overseas.
Youth for Understanding, 6400 Goldsboro Road, Suite 100, Bethesda, MD 20817, tel: 240 235 2100, fax: 240 235 2104, www.yfu.org. One of the world's oldest and largest international exchange organisations.

Study in France

Several French tour operators can organise study tours and language courses.
Office National de Garantie des Séjours Linguistiques, 8 rue César-Franck, 15th, tel: 01 42 73 36 70, www.loffice.org, is a national association that quality-checks all its members that offer language courses. Write for a list of schools, or try the following organisations:
Centre d'Information et de Documentation Jeunesse (CIDJ), 101 quai Branly, 15th, tel: 01 44 49 12 00 (from Monday to Friday 1–6pm), www.cidj.com. A national organisation that disseminates information on youth and student activities.
CROUS, 39 avenue Georges-Bernanos, 5th, tel: 01 40 51 36 00, www.crous-paris.fr. Provides information on student accommodation, Resto-U canteens and courses and enrolment for British students studying in France.

For further suggestions about courses in Paris, *see page 301*.

OPERATOR SERVICES

Directory Enquiries
118 218
International Directory Enquiries
32 12
International Operator
32 12 + country code
Reverse charges/ collect calls: You cannot normally make reverse-charge calls within France, but you can to other countries where such calls are accepted. Go through the international operator and ask to make a PCV (pay-say-vay) call.

Telephones

All telephone numbers in France have 10 digits. Paris and Ile de France numbers begin with 01, while the rest of France is divided into four zones: Northwest 02; Northeast 03; Southeast and Corsica 04; and Southwest 05. Toll-free phone numbers begin with 0800; all other numbers beginning with 08 are charged at variable rates; and 06 numbers are mobile phones. You get 50 percent more call-time for your money if you ring between 10.30pm and 8am on weekdays, and from 2pm at weekends.

Most public phone boxes in Paris are now operated with a card *(télécarte)*. A *télécarte* can be bought from kiosks, *tabacs* and post offices for 50 or 120 units (currently €7.50 or €15). Insert the card and follow the instructions on the screen. You can only receive calls at phone boxes displaying a blue bell sign.

You can also phone from post offices. To call long-distance, ask at the counter and you will be assigned a booth – you pay when the call is over. Cafés and *tabacs* often also have public phones, which usually take coins or *jetons*, coin-like discs bought at the bar.

To dial Paris from the UK: 00 (international code) + 33 (France) + 1 (Paris) + an eight-figure number. To call other countries from France, first dial the international code (00), then the country code: Australia 61, UK 44, US and Canada 1. If using a US credit phonecard, call the company's access number:
Sprint, tel: 08 00 99 00 87;
AT&T, tel: 08 00 99 00 11;
MCI, tel: 08 00 99 00 19.

Time Zone

France is one hour ahead of Greenwich Mean Time (GMT) and six ahead of Eastern Standard Time. Most French people use the 24-hour clock, so 1pm appears as 13h00 on timetables and is referred to as *treize heures*.

Tour Operators

By Boat

Cruises on the Seine last an hour, with commentaries in several languages. In high season, boats leave about every half-hour between 10am and 10pm.

Batobus, a very enjoyable eight-stop "riverbus" service, based at Port de la Bourdonnais by the Eiffel Tower, tel: 08 25 05 01 01, www.batobus.com.

Bateaux Mouches depart from Pont de l'Alma, tel: 01 42 25 96 10, www.bateaux-mouches.fr.

Bateaux Parisiens from Quai Montebello, evening cruises from the Eiffel Tower, tel: 0825 01 01 01, www.bateauxparisiens.com.

Vedettes de Paris depart from Port de Suffren, tel: 01 44 18 19 50, www.vedettesdeparis.com.

Vedettes du Pont Neuf from Pont Neuf, tel: 01 46 33 98 38, www.vedettesdupontneuf.com.

There are interesting trips along Canal St-Martin, starting at Port de l'Arsenal (Bastille) and continuing almost to the *Périphérique*. Lasting three hours, they are worth the money, but take warm clothes, as you spend a lot of time in locks and under bridges.

Canauxrama, 13 quai de la Loire, 19th, tel: 01 42 39 15 00, www.canauxrama.com.

Paris Canal, 19–21 quai de la Loire, 19th, tel: 01 42 40 96 97, www.pariscanal.com.

By Coach

Coach trips allow you to see Paris with minimum effort. Most companies provide a cassette commentary in several languages and will pass the major sights but do not stop along the way.

Les Cars Rouges runs double-decker buses to the main tourist sites. You can hop off, sightsee, then catch a later bus. A commentary runs in both English and French. Tel: 01 53 95 39 53, www.carsrouges.com.

Cityrama leaves from 4 place des Pyramides, 1st, tel: 01 44 55 61 00 (www.cityrama.com).

Paris Vision leaves from 214 rue de Rivoli, 1st, tel: 01 42 60 30 01, www.parisvision.com.

Paris L'Open Tour, operated by RATP, runs a similar service, also with open-topped double-decker buses, tel: 01 42 66 56 56, www.paris-opentour.com.

By Bicycle

Fat Tire Bike Tours – Paris, 24 rue Edgar-Faure, 15th, tel/fax: 01 56 58 10 54, www.fattirebiketoursparis.com, offers popular guided bike tours. The same company also runs segway tours, a novel way to see the city.

Tourist Offices

The French Tourist Board Lincoln House, 300 High Holborn, London WC1V 7JH, tel: 0906 824 4123 (calls 60p per minute), http://uk.franceguide.com. Mon–Fri 10am–4pm. Useful source of information before you travel.

Tourist Offices in Paris

All provide ample information and can book hotels. Most are closed 1 May and 25 Dec.

- **Carrousel du Louvre**, 99 rue de Rivoli, 1st, Métro: Palais Royal-Musée du Louvre. Daily 10am–6pm.
- **25 rue des Pyramides**, 1st, Métro: Pyramides. June–Oct daily 9am–7pm, Nov–May Mon–Sat 10am–7pm, Sun 11am–7pm.
- **Champs-Elysées**, corner of avenue Marigny, 8th, Métro: Champs Elysées-Clémenceau. Apr–Sept daily 9am–7pm.
- **Gare de Lyon**, 20 boulevard Diderot, 12th, Métro: Gare de Lyon. Mon–Sat 8am–6pm.
- **Gare du Nord**, 18 rue de Dunkerque, 10th, Métro: Gare du Nord. Daily 8am–6pm.
- **Anvers**, outside 72 boulevard Rochechouart, 18th, Métro: Anvers. Daily 10am–6pm.
- **Montmartre**, 21 place du Tertre, 18th. Métro: Abbesses. Daily 10am–7pm.

Useful Addresses

Information Service about Paris, in English, tel: 08 92 68 30 00.

RATP information, in English, tel: 08 92 69 32 46, www.ratp.fr.

SNCF, tel: 08 92 35 35 35, www.sncf.fr, for train information.

Weights & Measures

Metric measurements are always used in France. For a quick conversion: 1 metre is about a yard, 100 grams is just under 4 oz, 1 kg is 2 lbs 2 oz. Distance is in kilometres: 1 km equals five-eighths of a mile, so 80 km is 50 miles.

Tourist Information

- **www.parisinfo.com** has details of all services.
- To call the Paris Tourist Office, tel: 08 29 68 30 00; calls cost €0.34 per minute.

LANGUAGE

UNDERSTANDING THE LANGUAGE

General

French is the native language of more than 90 million people and the acquired language of 180 million. It is a Romance language descended from the Vulgar Latin spoken by the Roman conquerors of Gaul. It still carries the reputation of being the most cultured language in the world and the most beautiful. People often tell stories about the impatience of the French towards foreigners who do not attempt to speak their language. In general, however, if you attempt to communicate with them in French, they will appreciate it and may even overcome their reluctance to respond in English.

Since much of the English vocabulary is related to French, thanks to the Norman Conquest in 1066, travellers will often recognise many helpful cognates: words such as *hôtel, café* and *bagages* hardly need to be translated. You should be aware, however, of some misleading "false friends" *(faux amis)*, words that look like English words but mean something different.

le car coach, also railway carriage
le conducteur bus driver
personne can mean either person or nobody, depending on the context.

BASIC RULES

If you speak no French at all, it is worth trying to master a few simple phrases. The fact that you have made an effort is likely to break the ice. More and more French people like practising their English on visitors, especially waiters and the younger generation. Pronunciation is the key; they really will not understand if you get it very wrong. Remember to **emphasise each syllable**, but not to pronounce the last consonant of a word as a rule, unless it is followed by a vowel. Also bear in mind "er", "et" and "ez" endings are pronounced "ay" (this includes the plural "s") and "h"s are silent.

Whether to use "**vous**" or "**tu**" is a vexed question; increasingly the familiar form of "tu" is used, but it is safer to be formal, and use "vous". It is very important to be courteous; always address people as **Mademoiselle**, **Madame** or **Monsieur**, and address them by their surnames until you are confident first names are acceptable. When entering a shop always say, *"Bonjour Monsieur/Madame/ Mademoiselle,"* and *"Merci, au revoir,"* when leaving.

Garçon is the word for waiter but is never used directly; say *Monsieur*, *Madame* or *Mademoiselle*, to attract a waiter's attention.

The Alphabet

Learning the pronunciation of the French alphabet is a good idea. In particular, learn how to spell out your name.
a = ah, **b** = bay, **c** = say, **d** = day, **e** = uh, **f** = ef, **g** = zhay, **h** = ash, **i** = ee, **j** = zhee, **k** = ka, **l** = el, **m** = em, **n** = en, **o** = oh, **p** = pay, **q** = kew, **r** = ehr, **s** = ess, **t** = tay, **u** = ew, **v** = vay, **w** = dooblah vay, **x** = eex, **y** = ee grek, **z** = zed.

Useful Words & Phrases

How much is it? *C'est combien?*
What is your name? *Comment vous appelez-vous?*
My name is... *Je m'appelle...*
Do you speak English? *Parlez-vous anglais?*
I am English/American *Je suis anglais(e)/américain(e)*
I don't understand *Je ne comprends pas*
Please speak more slowly *Parlez plus lentement, s'il vous plaît*
Can you help me? *Pouvez-vous m'aider?*
I'm looking for... *Je cherche...*
Where is...? *Où est...?*
I'm sorry *Excusez-moi/Pardon*
I don't know *Je ne sais pas*
No problem *Pas de problème*
Have a good day! *Bonne journée!*
That's it *C'est ça*
Here it is *Voici*
There it is *Voilà*
Let's go *On y va/Allons-y*
See you tomorrow *A demain*
See you soon *A bientôt*
Show me the word in the book *Montrez-moi le mot dans le livre*
At what time? *A quelle heure?*
When? *Quand?*
What time is it? *Quelle heure est-il?*
yes *oui*
no *non*
please *s'il vous plaît*
thank you *merci*
(very much) *(beaucoup)*
you're welcome *de rien*
excuse me *excusez-moi*
hello *bonjour*
hi/bye *salut*
OK *d'accord*
goodbye *au revoir*
good evening *bonsoir*
here *ici*
there *là*
left *gauche*
right *droite*
straight on *tout droit*
far *loin*
near *près d'ici*
opposite *en face*
beside *à côté de*
over there *là-bas*
today *aujourd'hui*
yesterday *hier*
tomorrow *demain*
now *maintenant*
later *plus tard*
right away *tout de suite*
this morning *ce matin*
this afternoon *cet après-midi*
this evening ce soir

On Arrival

I want to get off at... *Je voudrais descendre à...*
Is there a bus to the Louvre? *Est-ce qu'il y a un bus pour le Louvre?*
What street is this? *Sur quelle rue sommes-nous?*
Which line do I take for...? *Quelle ligne dois-je prendre pour...?*
How far is...? *A quelle distance se trouve...?*
Validate your ticket *Compostez votre billet*
airport *l'aéroport*
railway station *la gare*
bus station *la gare routière*
Métro stop *la station de Métro*
bus *l'autobus, le car*
bus stop *l'arrêt*
platform *le quai*
ticket *le billet*
return ticket *aller-retour*
hitch hiking *l'autostop*
toilets *les toilettes*
This is the hotel address *C'est l'adresse de l'hôtel*
I'd like a (single/double) room... *Je voudrais une chambre (pour une/deux personnes)...*
...with shower *avec douche*
...with bath *avec salle de bain*
Is breakfast included? *Le prix comprend-il le petit-déjeuner?*
May I see the room? *Puis-je voir la chambre?*
washbasin *le lavabo*
bed *le lit*
key *la clé*
elevator *l'ascenseur*
air-conditioned *climatisé*

Emergencies

Help! *Au secours!*
Stop! *Arrêtez!*
Call a doctor *Appelez un médecin*
Call an ambulance *Appelez une ambulance*
Call the police *Appelez la police*
Call the fire brigade *Appelez les pompiers*
Where is the nearest telephone? *Où est le téléphone le plus proche?*
Where is the nearest hospital? *Où est l'hôpital le plus proche?*
I am sick *Je suis malade*
I have lost my passport/purse *J'ai perdu mon passeport/porte-monnaie*

Shopping

Where is the nearest bank (post office)? *Où se trouve la banque (Poste) la plus proche?*
I'd like to buy *Je voudrais acheter*
How much is it? *C'est combien?*
Do you take credit cards? *Est-ce que vous acceptez les cartes de crédit?*
I'm just looking *Je regarde seulement*
Have you got? *Avez-vous...?*
I'll take it *Je le prends*
I'll take this one/that one *Je prends celui-ci/celui-là*
What size is it? *C'est quelle taille ?*
Anything else? *Avec ceci?*
size (clothes) *la taille*
size (shoes) *la pointure*
cheap *bon marché*
expensive *cher*
enough *assez*
too much *trop*
a piece of *un morceau de*
each *la pièce (eg ananas, €2 la pièce)*
receipt *le reçu*
chemist *la pharmacie*
bakery *la boulangerie*
bookshop *la librairie*
library *la bibliothèque*
department store *le grand magasin*
delicatessen *la charcuterie/le traiteur*
fishmonger *la poissonnerie*
grocery *l'alimentation/l'épicerie*
tobacconist *le tabac* (also sells stamps and newspapers)

market *le marché*
supermarket *le supermarché*
junk shop *la brocante*

Sightseeing

town *la ville*
old town *la vieille ville*
street *la rue*
square *la place*
abbey *l'abbaye*
cathedral *la cathédrale*
church *l'église*
keep *le donjon*
mansion *l'hôtel*
hospital *l'hôpital*
town hall *l'hôtel de ville/la mairie*
nave *la nef*
stained glass *le vitrail*
staircase *l'escalier*
tower *la tour (La Tour Eiffel)*
walk *le tour*
country house/castle *le château*
Gothic *gothique*
Roman *romain*
Romanesque *roman*
museum *le musée*
art gallery *la galerie*
exhibition *l'exposition*
tourist information office *l'office du tourisme/le syndicat d'initiative*
free *gratuit*
open *ouvert*
closed *fermé*
every day *tous les jours*
all year *toute l'année*
all day *toute la journée*
swimming pool *la piscine*
to book *réserver*
town map *le plan*
road map *la carte*

Dining Out

Table d'hôte (the "host's table") is one set menu served at a set price. *Prix fixe* is a fixed-price menu. *A la carte* means differently priced dishes chosen from the menu.
breakfast *le petit-déjeuner*
lunch *le déjeuner*
dinner *le dîner*
meal *le repas*
first course *l'entrée/les hors d'œuvre*
main course *le plat principal*
made to order *sur commande*
drink included *boisson comprise*
wine list *la carte des vins*
the bill *l'addition*
fork *la fourchette*
knife *le couteau*
spoon *la cuillère*
plate *l'assiette*
glass *le verre*
napkin *la serviette*
ashtray *le cendrier*
I am a vegetarian *Je suis végétarien(ne)*
I am on a diet *Je suis au régime*
What do you recommend? *Qu'est-ce que vous recommandez?*
Do you have local specialities? *Avez-vous des spécialités locales?*
I'd like to order *Je voudrais commander*
That is not what I ordered *Ce n'est pas ce que j'ai commandé*
Is service included? *Est-ce que le service est compris?*
May I have more wine? *Encore du vin, s'il vous plaît*
Enjoy your meal *Bon appétit!*

Breakfast and Snacks

baguette **long thin loaf**
pain **bread**
petits pains **rolls**
beurre **butter**
poivre **pepper**
sel **salt**
sucre **sugar**
confiture **jam**
miel **honey**
œufs **eggs**
...à la coque **boiled eggs**
...au bacon **bacon and eggs**
...au jambon **ham and eggs**
...sur le plat **fried eggs**
...brouillés **scrambled eggs**
tartine **bread with butter**
yaourt **yoghurt**
crêpe **pancake**
croque-monsieur **ham and cheese toasted sandwich**
croque-madame **...with a fried egg on top**
galette **type of cake**
pan bagna **bread roll stuffed with salade niçoise**
quiche **tart of eggs and cream with various fillings**
quiche lorraine **quiche with bacon**

First Course

An *amuse-bouche, amuse-gueule* or appetiser is something to "amuse the mouth", before the first course
anchoïade **sauce of olive oil, anchovies and garlic, served with raw vegetables**
assiette anglaise **cold meats**
potage **soup**
rillettes **rich fatty paste of shredded duck, rabbit or pork**
tapenade **spread of olives and anchovies**
pissaladière **Provençal pizza with onions, olives and anchovies**

Main Courses

***Viande* Meat**
bleu saignant **rare**
à point **medium**
bien cuit **well done**
grillé **grilled**
agneau **lamb**
andouille/andouillette **tripe sausage**
bifteck **steak**
boudin **sausage**
boudin noir **black pudding**
boudin blanc **white pudding (chicken or veal)**
blanquette **stew of veal, lamb or chicken with creamy egg sauce**
bœuf à la mode **beef in red wine with carrots, onions, mushroom and onions**
à la bordelaise **beef with red wine and shallots**
bourguignon **cooked in red wine, onions and mushrooms**
brochette **kebab**
caille **quail**
canard **duck**
carbonnade **casserole of beef, beer and onions**
carré d'agneau **rack of lamb**
cassoulet **stew of beans, sausages, pork and duck from southwest France**
cervelle **brains (food)**
châteaubriand **thick steak**
choucroute **Alsace dish of**

sauerkraut, bacon and sausages
confit **duck or goose preserved in its own fat**
contre-filet **cut of sirloin steak**
coq au vin **chicken in red wine**
côte d'agneau **lamb chop**
daube **beef stew with red wine, onions and tomatoes**
dinde **turkey**
entrecôte **beef rib steak**
escargot **snail**
faisan **pheasant**
farci **stuffed**
faux-filet **sirloin**
feuilleté **puff pastry**
foie **liver**
foie de veau **calf's liver**
foie gras **goose or duck liver pâté**
gardian **rich beef stew with olives and garlic from the Camargue**
cuisses de grenouille **frogs' legs**
grillade **grilled meat**
hachis **minced meat**
jambon **ham**
langue **tongue**
lapin **rabbit**
lardons **small pieces of bacon, often added to salads**
magret de canard **breast of duck**
médaillon **round piece of meat**
moelle **beef bone marrow**
mouton navarin **stew of lamb with onions, carrots and turnips**
oie **goose**
perdrix **partridge**
petit-gris **small snail**
pieds de cochon **pig's trotters**
pintade **guinea fowl**
Pipérade **Basque dish of eggs, ham, peppers and onion**
porc **pork**
pot-au-feu **casserole of beef and vegetables**
poulet **chicken**
poussin **young chicken**
rognons **kidneys**
rôti **roast**
sanglier **wild boar**
saucisse **fresh sausage**
saucisson **salami**
veau **veal**

***Poissons* Fish**
à l'américaine **made with white wine, tomatoes, butter and cognac**
anchois **anchovies**
anguille **eel**
bar/loup **sea bass**
barbue **brill**
belon **Brittany oyster**
bigorneau **sea snail**
Bercy **sauce of fish stock, butter, white wine and shallots**
bouillabaisse **fish soup, served with grated cheese, garlic croutons and spicy rouille sauce**
brandade **salt cod purée**
cabillaud **cod**
calamars **squid**
colin **hake**
coquillage **shellfish**
coquilles Saint-Jacques **scallops**
crevette **shrimp**
daurade **sea bream**
flétan **halibut**
fruits de mer **seafood**
hareng **herring**
homard **lobster**
huître **oyster**
langoustine **large prawn**
limande **lemon sole**
lotte **monkfish**
morue **salt cod**
moule **mussel**
moules marinières **mussels in white wine and onions**
oursin **sea urchin**
raie **skate**
saumon **salmon**
thon **tuna**
truite **trout**

***Légumes* Vegetables**
ail **garlic**
artichaut **artichoke**
asperge **asparagus**
aubergine **eggplant, aubergine**
avocat **avocado**
bolets **boletus mushrooms**
céleri rémoulade **grated celery with mayonnaise**
cèpes **boletus mushrooms**
champignon **mushroom**
chanterelle **wild mushroom**
chips **potato crisps**
chou **cabbage**
chou-fleur **cauliflower**
concombre **cucumber**
cornichon **gherkin**
courgette **zucchini, courgette**
cru **raw**
crudités **raw vegetables**
épinards **spinach**
frites **chips, French fries**
gratin dauphinois **sliced potatoes baked with cream**
haricot **dried bean**
haricots verts **green beans**
lentilles **lentils**
maïs **corn**
mange-tout **snow pea**
mesclun **mixed-leaf salad**
navet **turnip**
noisette **hazelnut**
noix **nut, walnut**
oignon **onion**
panais **parsnip**
persil **parsley**
pignon **pine nut**
poireau **leek**
pois **pea**
poivron **bell pepper**
pomme de terre **potato**
pommes frites **chips, French fries**
primeurs **early fruit and vegetables**
radis **radis**
roquette **arugula, rocket**
ratatouille **Provençal vegetable stew of aubergines, courgettes, tomatoes, peppers and olive oil**
riz **rice**
salade niçoise **egg, tuna, olives, onions and tomato salad**
salade verte **green salad**
truffe **truffle**

***Fruit* Fruit**
ananas **pineapple**
cerise **cherry**
citron **lemon**
citron vert **lime**
figue **fig**
fraise **strawberry**
framboise **raspberry**
groseille **redcurrant**
mangue **mango**
mirabelle **yellow plum**
pamplemousse **grapefruit**
pêche **peach**
poire **pear**
pomme **apple**
raisin **grape**
prune **plum**
pruneau **prune**
reine claude **greengage**

***Sauces* Sauces**
aïoli **garlic mayonnaise**
béarnaise **sauce of egg, butter, wine and herbs**

forestière **with mushrooms and bacon**
hollandaise **egg and butter**
lyonnaise **with onions**
meunière **fried fish with butter, lemon and parsley sauce**
meurette **red wine sauce**
Mornay **sauce of cream, egg and cheese**
Parmentier **served with potatoes**
paysan **rustic-style, ingredients depend on the region**
pistou **Provençal sauce of basil, garlic and olive oil; vegetable soup with the sauce**
provençale **sauce of tomatoes, garlic and olive oil**
papillotte **cooked in paper**

Dessert **Pudding, dessert**
chèvre **goat's cheese**
clafoutis **baked pudding of batter and cherries**
coulis **purée of fruit or vegetables**
crème anglaise **custard**
crème caramel **caramelised egg custard**
crème Chantilly **whipped cream**
fromage **cheese**
gâteau **cake**
île flottante **whisked egg whites floating in custard sauce**
pêche melba **peaches with ice cream and raspberry sauce**
poire Belle-Hélène **pear with ice cream and chocolate sauce**
tarte tatin **upside-down tart of caramelised apples**

In the Café

les boissons **drinks**
café **coffee**
...au lait or *crème* **...with milk or cream**
...déca/décaféiné **...decaffeinated**
...espresso/noir **...black espresso**
...filtre **...filtered coffee**
thé **tea**
tisane **herb infusion**
verveine **verbena tea**
chocolat chaud **hot chocolate**
lait **milk**
eau minérale **mineral water**
gazeux **fizzy**
non-gazeux **non-fizzy**
limonade **fizzy lemonade**
citron pressé **fresh lemon juice served with sugar**
orange pressée **fresh squeezed orange juice**
entier **full (eg full cream milk)**
frais, fraîche **fresh or cold**
bière **beer**
...en bouteille **...bottled**
...à la pression **...on tap**
apéritif **pre-dinner drink**
kir **white wine with cassis, blackcurrant liqueur**
kir royale **kir with champagne**
avec des glaçons **with ice**
sec **neat**
rouge **red**
blanc **white**
rosé **rosé**
brut **dry**
doux **sweet**
crémant **sparkling wine**
vin de maison **house wine**
vin de pays **local wine**
carafe/pichet **pitcher**
...d'eau/de vin **...of water/wine**
demi-carafe **half-litre**
quart **quarter-litre**
panaché **shandy**
digestif **after-dinner drink**
armagnac **brandy from the Armagnac region of France**
calvados **Normandy apple brandy**

Where is this wine from?
De quelle région vient ce vin?
cheers! *santé!*
hangover *gueule de bois*

Days of the Week

Days of the week, seasons and months are not capitalised in French.

Monday *lundi*
Tuesday *mardi*
Wednesday *mercredi*
Thursday *jeudi*
Friday *vendredi*
Saturday *samedi*
Sunday *dimanche*

Seasons

spring *le printemps*
summer *l'été*
autumn *l'automne*
winter *l'hiver*

Months

January *janvier*
February *février*
March *mars*
April *avril*
May *mai*
June *juin*
July *juillet*
August *août*
September *septembre*
October *octobre*
November *novembre*
December *décembre*

Saying the date
20 October 2010 *le vingt octobre, deux mille dix*

Numbers

0 *zéro*
1 *un, une*
2 *deux*
3 *trois*
4 *quatre*
5 *cinq*
6 *six*
7 *sept*
8 *huit*
9 *neuf*
10 *dix*
11 *onze*
12 *douze*
13 *treize*
14 *quatorze*
15 *quinze*
16 *seize*
17 *dix-sept*
18 *dix-huit*
19 *dix-neuf*
20 *vingt*
21 *vingt-et-un*
30 *trente*
40 *quarante*
50 *cinquante*
60 *soixante*
70 *soixante-dix*
80 *quatre-vingts*
90 *quatre-vingt-dix*
100 *cent*
200 *deux cents*
500 *cinq cents*
1000 *mille*
1,000,000 *un million*

• Note that the number 1 is often written like an upside down V, and the number 7 is always crossed.

Further Reading

History

A Concise History of France, by Roger Price. Cambridge University Press, 1993. Excellent historical overview.
The Eiffel Tower: And Other Mythologies, by Roland Barthes. University of California Press, 1997. A collection of essays by this influential French critic.
Foreign Correspondents: Paris in the Sixties, by Peter Lennon. Picador/McClelland & Stewart, 1994. Journalist Lennon spent the decade in Paris where he witnessed the 1968 student riots.
The Illustrated History of Paris and the Parisians, by Robert Laffont. New York: Doubleday & Co., 1958.
A Woman's Life in the Court of the Sun King, by Duchesse d'Orléans. Trans. Elborg Forster. Baltimore: John Hopkins University Press, 1984. The Duchesse's letters reveal court life in the 17th century.

Art and Architecture

Guide to Modern Architecture in Paris, by Hervé Martin. Editions Syos-Alternatives, 1990. For descriptions and locations of buildings by *arrondissement*.
Paris: A City in the Making, by Le Pavillon de l'Arsenal. Babylone, 1992. A catalogue of the architectural evolution of Paris.
A Propos de Paris, by Henri Cartier-Bresson. Bulfinch Press, 1998. Some 130 stunning black-and-white photographs of the capital, spanning 50 years.
Brassai: The Eye of Paris, by Richard Howard. Abrams, 1999. Part biography, part catalogue of a photography exhibition of Brassai's pictures of Paris.
The Cathedral Builders, by Jean Gimpel. New York: Harper & Row, 1984. The story of the hands and minds behind the cathedrals of France.
Paris: An Architectural History, by Anthony Sutcliffe. Yale University Press, 1993. A great book on the architecture of the capital across the ages.
Three Seconds of Eternity, by Robert Doisneau. Neues Publishing Company, 1997. Gorgeous photographs of 1940s and 1950s Paris, chosen by the champion of black-and-white photography himself.

Feedback

We do our best to ensure the information in our books is as accurate and up-to-date as possible. However, some mistakes and omissions are inevitable and we are reliant on our readers to put us in the picture. We would welcome your feedback on any details related to your experiences using the book "on the road". The more details you can give us (particularly with regard to addresses, emails and telephone numbers), the better. We will acknowledge all contributions, and we'll offer an Insight Guide to the best letters received.

Please write to us at:
Insight Guides
PO Box 7910
London SE1 1WE
United Kingdom
Or send email to:
insight@apaguide.co.uk

Food

Paris Bistro Cooking, by Linda Dannenberg. Clarkson Potter, 1991. Tasty dishes from a wealth of Paris brasseries.
The Paris Café Cookbook, by Daniel Young. William Morrow & Co, 1998. Recipes and excerpts on recommended cafés in the capital.

Other Insight Guides

Insight Guide: France is the major book in the French series covering the whole country, with features on food and drink, culture and the arts. Other titles include *Southwest France* and *The French Riviera*.

Insight Fleximaps

Insight Fleximaps have a tough, laminated rainproof finish and feature a list of the top 10 sites in a city or area, and an in-depth index. Fleximaps in the French series include *Paris* and *Nice, Cannes & Monaco*.

Insight Step by Step

Insight's Step by Step guides provide a series of timed itineraries, with recommended stops for lunch. The itineraries are plotted on an accompanying pull-out map. Titles incude *Paris* and *Nice & the French Riviera*.

Insight Smart Guides

Smart Guide: Paris puts the city at your fingertips. The best of Paris is listed by district, with detailed maps to provide orientation. Paris A–Z lists over 400 amazing thigs to see and do, from architecture and bars to restaurants and shopping, and much more.

Art and Photo Credits

4Corners Images 251B, 255T, 256B
akg-images 26TL & TR, 27B, 35TL, 130BL
Alamy 10C
Art Archive 10T, 28B, 138, 149BL
Bruno Barbey/Magnum Photos 35TR
Pete Bennett/Apa 8C, 77T, 285
Sebastien Bouthillette 269
The Bridgeman Art Library 24, 26B, 27TR, 28TL, 30TL, TR & CR, 31 (all), 33 (all), 38 (all), 39 (all), 40C, 92B, 123B, 139T, 164BR, 230BL, 237T & B, 271 (all)
Robert Capa/Magnum Photos 34TL
Henri Cartier-Bresson/Magnum Photos 205BL
Elodie Chapuis 296B
Corbis 30B, 32, 34TR, 40B, 41R, 79BL, 96B, 161BL, 215B, 259B, 276, 313
Kevin Cummins/Apa 7T, 11TL, 14/15, 16/17, 18, 19, 46, 64/65, 88, 93BR, 100, 104BL, 107C, 113, 121B, 126L, 126T, 130T, 149BR, 152B, 153B, 153T, 163T, 164T, 171T, 176, 185T, 186, 192B, 203T, 218, 223B, 224, 248T, 251T, 262, 263, 264B, 268TR, 281all, 282B, 283BL & BR, 300
Jerry Dennis/Apa 1, 9CTL, CTR, CB & CBR, 27TL, 45, 47B, 48B, 54TR & CR, 70T, 71CT, C & CB, 78C, 79BR, 81T, 83T & BR, 106B, 107T, 110B, 118, 121T, 122B, 124 (all), 128BL, 131T, 133BL, 136, 139B, 144B, 145T & BL, 158, 162, 163BR, 165T & BL, 166BR, 167TR, BL & BR, 169T & BL, 182T, 183B, 192T, 194T & C, 196TL, 200B, 202B, 203BL, 211T, 212TL & TR, 214T, 221T, 223T, 226T & C, 227B, 228L, 240/241, 243, 265T, 268TL & B, 278, 279, 280, 294, 295, 296T, 299B, 315, 317
Annabel Elston/Apa 9TL, 12BR, 25, 28TR, 70C, 91T, 137, 152T, 227T, 264T
Everynight 296B
Ronald Grant Archive 37T, 181B
Getty Images 3, 35R, 36L, 36R, 42/43
John Heseltine 6T, 270T
Ho visto nina volare 260/261
iStockphoto.com 221B, 225T, 235T
Timo Jaakonaho/Rex Features 254, 257
Britta Jaschinski/Apa 8B, 10B, 11TR & B, 12T & BL, 13C & B, 48C, 50, 51, 52 (all), 53 (all), 54TL, 55 (all), 66/67, 70CB, 85, 90T & BL, 91B, 93BL, 94T, 95BL, 98BL, 99 (all), 101 (all), 102, 108 (all), 109 (all), 110T, 111T, 112, 119, 120C, 129 (all), 131BL & BR, 132B, 133CL & BR, 134, 135 (all), 143, 144C, 145BR, 147T, 148T & C, 149T, 151T, 154, 155, 160T, 161T & BR, 168T & B, 169BR, 170 (all), 171B, 172, 173, 177, 178BL, 179T, 180B, 182BR, 183T, 184TR, 188, 189, 195B, 200C, 201T, 202T, 203BR, 205T & BR, 206, 211B, 213BL, 214B, 215T, 216, 217, 219, 222B, 225BL, 227TL, 228R, 229T & B, 230T, 231R, 232, 233, 283T, 284, 286, 288, 290, 291, 293, 297T, 298, 302 (all), 303, 304 (all), 305 (all), 306 (all), 307, 310B, 314T, 316
The Kobal Collection 37B
Daquella Manera 311
Luigi Morante 312
Musée Association Les Amis d'Edith Piaf 181T
Musée de la Mode et du Costume 222T
Musée de la Ville de Paris 29, 95T
Ilpo Musto/Apa 8T, 9TR, CBL & B, 20 (all), 21, 22, 23 (all), 44, 47TL & TR, 48T, 49, 70CT & B, 71T & B, 74, 75, 77B, 78B, 79T, 80 (all), 81B, 82 (all), 83BL, 84 (all), 89, 90BR, 91C, 92T, 93T & CL, 94BL & BR, 95BR, 96C, 97 (all), 98BR, 103, 120B, 122T, 123C, 125 (all), 126BR, 127 (all), 128T, C & BR, 130BR, 132T, 142, 150T & B, 151C & B, 159, 163BL, 164BL, 165BR, 166T & BL, 167TL, 178T & BR, 180T, 185B, 193B, 194B, 195T, 196TR & B, 197 (all), 198 (all), 199 (all), 201B, 204, 207, 225BR, 226B, 230BR, 231L, 236, 242, 244, 245, 246CR, 247 (all), 248B, 263, 266 (all), 267 (all), 270B, 282T, 283C, 292, 299T, 308, 309, 310T, 314B, 318
Paris Tourist Office/Angélique Clément 148B
Paris Tourist Office/Fabian Charaffi 13T, 147B, 297B
Paris Tourist Office/Amélie Dupont 111B, 146
Clare Peel 269T
Flore Pellerin 106T
Photo Bibliothèque Nationale, Paris 182BL
Press Association Images 105, 203CL
David Robertson/PYMCA 61ML
Sophie Robichon/Mairie de Paris 212B, 213BR
Arnaud Terrier/Mairie de Paris 301
Topfoto 34B, 41L, 184TL
©Walt Disney Company 255B, 256T, 258, 259T
Bill Wassman 107B

Photo Features

56/57: all **Britta Jaschinski/Apa**
58/59: all **Britta Jaschinski/Apa**
60/61: Alamy 60CL& CR; **Kevin Cummins/Apa** 60BR; **Everynight** 60BL, 60C; **Bus Palladium** 61CBR; **Jerry Dennis/Apa** 60TL; **La Flèche d'Or** 60/61C; **Philippe Levy** 61BR
62/63: The Ronald Grant Archive 62/63C, 62CR & BR, 63TR & BR; **The Kobal Collection** 62BL, 63CL; **Time & Life Pictures/Getty Images** 63CR
86/87: Corbis 86CR; **Jerry Dennis/Apa** 87CR; **Getty Images** 87TR; **Monique Jacob/Apa** 87BL; **Ilpo Musto/Apa** 86/87C, 86TL, 87BR
114/115: Corbis 114/115; **Jerry Dennis/Apa** 114CL & CR; **Britta Jaschinski/Apa** 115TR; **Ilpo Musto/Apa** 114BR, 115CL; **Superstock** 115B
140/141: The Art Archive 140TL; **The Bridgeman Art Library** 140/141, 141CR; **Jerry Dennis/Apa** 140BL; **Ilpo Musto/Apa** 140/141B, 141TR & BL
156/157: AFP/Getty Images 157BL; **Kevin Cummins/Apa** 156/157T; **Jerry Dennis/Apa** 157TR; **iStockphoto.com** 156CL; **Britta Jaschinski/Apa** 156BR, 157BR
174/175: The Bridgeman Art Library 174BL, 175TR & BL; **Corbis** 174TL & TR, 175TL; **Jerry Dennis/Apa** 174BR; **Getty Images** 175BR
208/209: Jerry Dennis/Apa 208BR; **Britta Jaschinski/Apa** 209BR; **Ilpo Musto/Apa** 208/209C, 208CL & CR, 209TR, CL & BL
234/235: Corbis 235T, CR & BR; **Getty Images** 234TR; **iStockphoto.com** 234TL; **Ilpo Musto/Apa** 234BR, 235L
238/239: The Art Archive 239BR; **The Bridgeman Art Library** 238TL & BL; **Getty Images** 239TR; **Ilpo Musto/Apa** 238/239C, 238BR, 239BL
252/253: Jerry Dennis/Apa 252/253C, 253BL; **The Kobal Collection** 253TR; **Ilpo Musto/Apa** 252CL, CR & BR, 253BR
272/275: The Bridgeman Art Library 273TR, 274TL; **Jerry Dennis/Apa** 272/273CT & B, 272BR, 274BR, 275BL; **Ilpo Musto/Apa** 272TL, 273BR, 274/275C, 275CR & BR; **Clare Peel** 273CR, 274CL

Map Production: Mike Adams, Neal Jordan-Caws, James Macdonald and Stephen Ramsay

Book Production: Linton Donaldson, Mary Pickles

Paris Street Atlas

The key map shows the area of Paris covered by the atlas section. An index of street names and places of interest shown on the maps can be found on the following pages. For each entry there is a page number and grid reference.

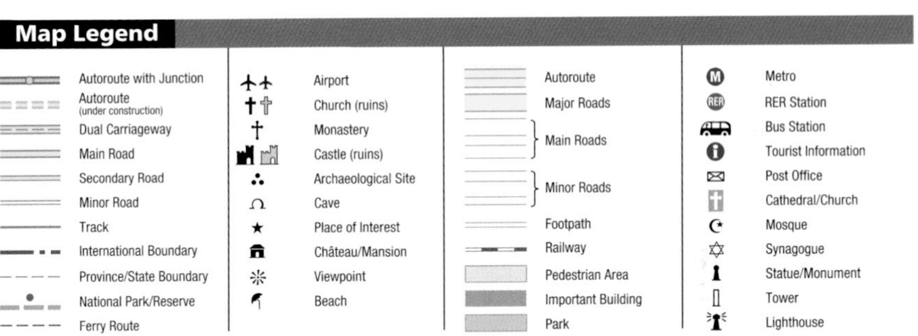

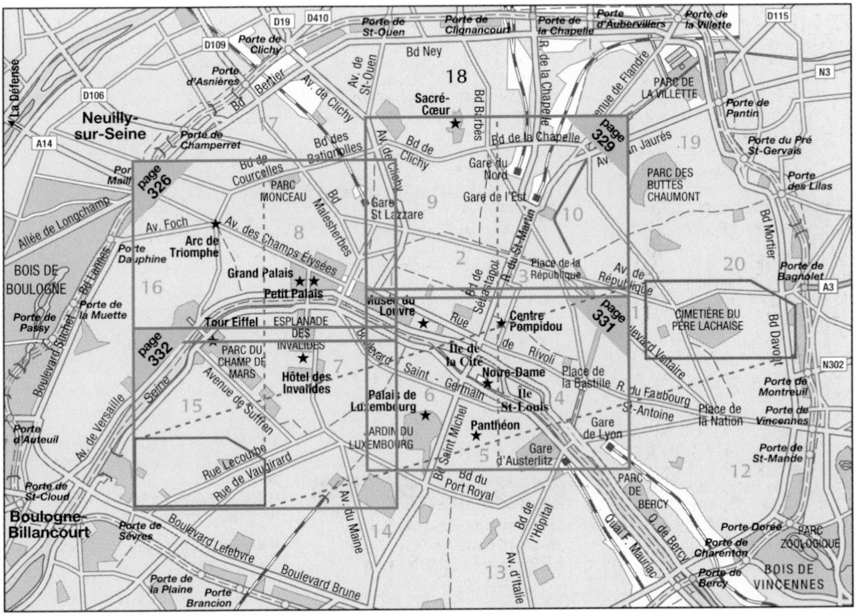

A
B
1
2
3
4
0 100 200 300 400 500 m
0 100 200 300 400 500 yds
TERNES
CHAILLOT
Palais des Congrès
Pl. de la Porte Maillot
Porte Maillot
Neuilly Porte Maillot
Sq. de l'Amiral Bruix
Pl. du Gal. Koenig
Blvd. Pershing
Pl. de Verdun
Boulevard Pereire (Nord)
Boulevard Pereire (Sud)
Avenue de la Grande Armée
St-Ferdinand Ste-Thérèse
Pl. St-Ferdinand
Argentine
Pl. Y. et C. Morandat
Pl. du Gal. Patton
Espace Wagram
Pl. des Ternes
Ternes
St-Alexandre-Nevsky
Avenue de Wagram
Avenue Niel
Avenue Mac Mahon
Avenue Carnot
St-Joseph
Ch. de Gaulle Étoile
Arc de Triomphe
Pl. Charles-de-Gaulle
Chambre de Commerce et d'Industrie de Paris
St-Sacrement
Avenue Foch
Musée Arménien/ Musée d'Ennery
Pl. du Venezuela
Avenue Victor Hugo
Victor Hugo
Pl. Victor Hugo
Kléber
George V
St-George's
Réservoirs de Passy
St-Honoré d'Eylau
Nouvelle Église St-Honoré d'Eylau
Pl. Jean Monnet
Avenue d'Iéna
Avenue Marceau
Pl. des États-Unis
Pl. Amiral de Grasse
St-Pierre de Chaillot
American Cathedral in Paris
Boissière
St-Etienne
Musée Guimet
Musée Galliera
Musée de la Mode et du Costume
Th. des Champs-Élysées
Pl. de Mexico
Iéna
Pl. d'Iéna
Président Wilson
Palais de Tokyo
Musée d'Art Moderne de Paris
Site de Création Contemporaine
Pl. de l'Alma
Alma Marceau
Trocadéro
Ministère de l'Environnement
Union de l'Europe Occidentale
Av. Georges-Mandel
Pl. du Trocadéro et du 11 Novembre
Cité de l'Architecture et du Patrimoine
CIMETIÈRE DE PASSY
Musée de l'Homme (reopens 2012)
Palais de Chaillot
JARDIN DU TROCADÉRO
Musée de la Marine
Pl. de Varsovie
Port Debilly
Pont de l'Alma
Pl. de la Résistance
Port de la Bourdonnais
Musée du Quai Branly
Tour Eiffel
Avenue Rapp
Av. Paul-Doumer
Rue de Passy
Avenue Kléber
Avenue Raymond Poincaré
Avenue d'Eylau
Rue de Longchamp
Rue de la Pompe
Avenue de New York
Pont d'Iéna

332

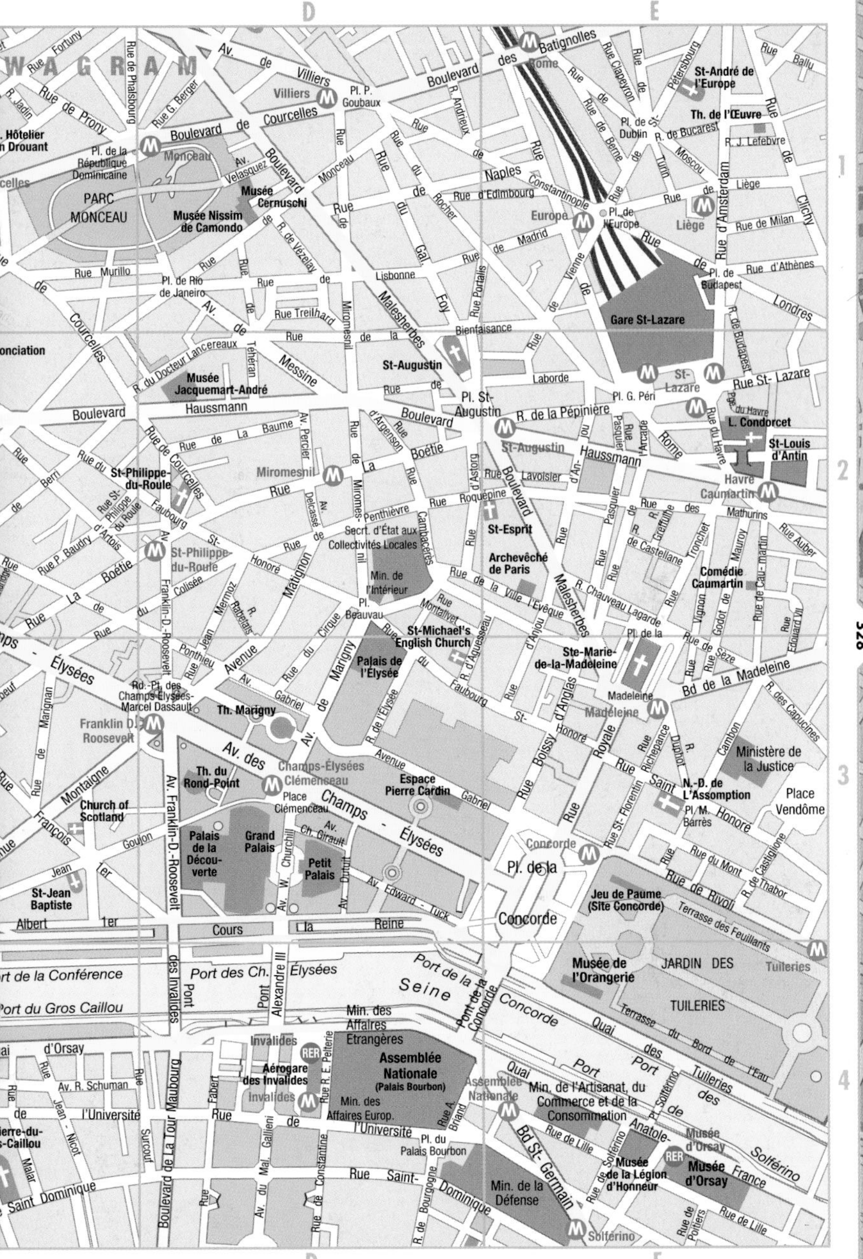
D
E
1
2
3
4
WAGRAM
Rue Fortuny
R. Jadin
Rue de Prony
Rue de Phalsbourg
Rue G. Berger
Av. de Villiers
Villiers
Pl. P. Goubaux
Boulevard de Courcelles
Boulevard des Batignolles
Rome
R. Andrieux
Rue Clapeyron
Rue de St-Pétersbourg
St-André de l'Europe
Th. de l'Œuvre
Rue Ballu
Hôtelier
Drouant
Pl. de la République Dominicaine
Monceau
Av. Velasquez
Musée Cernuschi
PARC MONCEAU
Musée Nissim de Camondo
Rue de Monceau
Rue du Rocher
Rue de Naples
Rue de Constantinople
Rue d'Edimbourg
Rue de Berne
Pl. de Dublin
R. de Bucarest
Rue de Turin
Rue de Moscou
R. J. Lefebvre
Rue de Clichy
Liège
Rue de Liège
Rue d'Amsterdam
Rue de Milan
Europe
Pl. de l'Europe
Rue de Madrid
Rue de Vienne
R. de Vézelay
Rue Murillo
Pl. de Rio de Janeiro
Rue de Lisbonne
Rue du Gal. Foy
Rue Portalis
Pl. de Budapest
Rue d'Athènes
Rue de Londres
Gare St-Lazare
Rue Treilhard
Rue de Miromesnil
Boulevard Malesherbes
Av. de Messine
Rue de la Bienfaisance
R. de Budapest
Av. de Courcelles
R. du Docteur Lancereaux
Rue de Téhéran
Musée Jacquemart-André
St-Augustin
Rue Laborde
St-Lazare
Rue St-Lazare
Pl. G. Péri
Boulevard Haussmann
Pl. St-Augustin
R. de la Pépinière
Pge. du Havre
L. Condorcet
St-Louis d'Antin
Rue de La Baume
Av. Percier
Rue d'Argenson
Rue La Boétie
Rue d'Astorg
Rue Lavoisier
Rue d'Anjou
Rue Pasquier
Rue de l'Arcade
Rue de Rome
Rue du Havre
Havre Caumartin
St-Philippe-du-Roule
Rue de Courcelles
Rue du Berri
Rue St-Philippe du Roule
Miromesnil
Av. Delcassé
Rue de Penthièvre
Rue Roquépine
St-Esprit
Rue des Mathurins
R. Greffulhe
Rue Auber
Rue P. Baudry
Rue d'Artois
Rue du Faubourg St-Honoré
Secrt. d'État aux Collectivités Locales
Rue Cambacérès
Archevêché de Paris
R. de Castellane
Rue Tronchet
Comédie Caumartin
Rue de Caumartin
Rue Matignon
Rue Mermoz
R. Rabelais
Rue du Colisée
Min. de l'Intérieur
Rue de la Ville l'Évêque
R. Chauveau Lagarde
Rue Vignon
Rue Godot de Mauroy
Rue Edouard VII
Av. Franklin-D.-Roosevelt
Rue de Ponthieu
Rue Jean Mermoz
Rue du Cirque
Pl. Beauvau
Rue Montalivet
St-Michael's English Church
Rue de Surène
R. d'Aguesseau
Pl. de la Madeleine
Ste-Marie-de-la-Madeleine
Rue de Sèze
Av. des Champs-Élysées
Avenue de Marigny
Palais de l'Élysée
Bd de la Madeleine
Rd.-Pt. des Champs Élysées-Marcel Dassault
Av. Gabriel
Th. Marigny
R. de l'Élysée
Rue Boissy d'Anglas
Rue Royale
Madeleine
R. des Capucines
Franklin D. Roosevelt
Rue de Marignan
Champs-Élysées Clémenceau
Th. du Rond-Point
Place Clémenceau
Espace Pierre Cardin
Rue Richepance
R. Duphot
Rue Cambon
Ministère de la Justice
Rue Montaigne
Rue François 1er
Church of Scotland
Av. W. Churchill
Av. Ch. Girault
Rue Saint Honoré
N.-D. de L'Assomption
Pl. M. Barrès
Place Vendôme
Rue Goujon
Palais de la Découverte
Grand Palais
Petit Palais
Av. Dutuit
Concorde
Rue St-Florentin
Rue du Mont Thabor
Rue de Castiglione
Pl. de la Concorde
Rue Jean Goujon
St-Jean Baptiste
Av. Edward Tuck
Rue de Rivoli
Jeu de Paume (Site Concorde)
Terrasse des Feuillants
Cours Albert 1er
Cours la Reine
Tuileries
Port de la Conférence
Port des Ch. Élysées
Pont des Invalides
Pont Alexandre III
Port de la Concorde
Pont de la Concorde
Seine
Musée de l'Orangerie
JARDIN DES TUILERIES
Port du Gros Caillou
Quai de la Concorde
Terrasse du Bord de l'Eau
Quai d'Orsay
Min. des Affaires Etrangères
Invalides
Aérogare des Invalides
Rue R. E. Pelterie
Assemblée Nationale (Palais Bourbon)
Port des Tuileries
Quai des Tuileries
Av. R. Schuman
Boulevard de La Tour Maubourg
Rue Fabert
Min. des Affaires Europ.
Rue A. Briand
Assemblée Nationale
Min. de l'Artisanat, du Commerce et de la Consommation
Passerelle Solférino
Quai Anatole-France
Port de Solférino
Rue de l'Université
Rue Jean Nicot
Rue Surcouf
Rue de Lille
Musée d'Orsay
Pierre-du-Caillou
Rue Malar
Av. du Mal. Gallieni
Rue de Constantine
Pl. du Palais Bourbon
Rue de Solférino
Musée de la Légion d'Honneur
Rue Saint Dominique
Rue Saint-Dominique
R. de Bourgogne
Min. de la Défense
Bd St-Germain
Rue de Poitiers
Solférino

328

A
B
1
2
3
4
MONTMARTRE
La Fourche
Cimetière de Montmartre
Moulin de la Galette
Moulin du Radet
Musée de Montmartre
Parc de la Turlure
Château Rouge
St-Pierre
Basilique du Sacré-Cœur
Espace Montmartre S.Dali
Pl. du Tertre
Funiculaire
Sq. Willette
Halle St-Pierre
Abbesses
Moulin Rouge
Blanche
Pl. Blanche
St-Jean Montmartre
Pl. de Clichy
Pl. Clichy
Pigalle
Pl. Pigalle
Anvers
Barbès Rochechouart
Boulevard de Clichy
Boulevard Rochechouart
St-André de l'Europe
Musée de la Vie Romantique
Th. de l'Œuvre
Rue Victor - Massé
Av. Trudaine
Rue de Liège
Liège
Dt. Evang. Christuskirche
Th. de Paris
Casino de Paris
Musée Gustave-Moreau
St-Georges
St-Constantin/ Ste-Hélène
Gare St-Lazare
Ste-Trinité
Trinité
N.-D. de Lorette
Cadet
Poissonnière
Sq. de Montholon
Rue Lafayette
Rue de Maubeuge
St-Lazare
L. Condorcet
St-Louis d'Antin
Au Printemps
Galeries Lafayette
Chaussée d'Antin
Havre Caumartin
Le Peletier
Folies Bergère
Auber
RER
Palais Garnier
Boulevard Haussmann
Richelieu Drouot
Grévin
Comédie Caumartin
Musée du Parfum
Olympia
Opéra
Pl. de l'Opéra
Bd des Capucines
Bd des Italiens
Bd Montmartre
Grands Boulevards
Bd Poissonnière
Bonne Nouvelle
Bd de la Madeleine
Crédit Foncier de France
Ministère de la Justice
Place Vendôme
N.-D. de L'Assomption
Cour des Comptes
Quatre Septembre
Rue du Quatre - Septembre
Palais Brongniart
Bourse
Rue Réaumur
Sentier
Bibliothèque Nationale-Richelieu
Basilique N.-D. des Victoires
St-Roch
Pyramides
Rue Saint-Honoré
Rue de Rivoli
Terrasse des Feuillants
Tuileries
Jardin du Palais Royal
Banque de France
Pl. des Victoires
Hôtel des Postes
Rue Montmartre
Avenue de l'Opéra

327

330

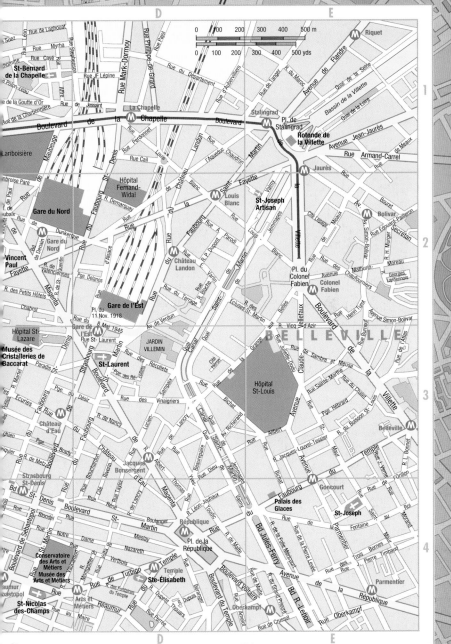

328

333

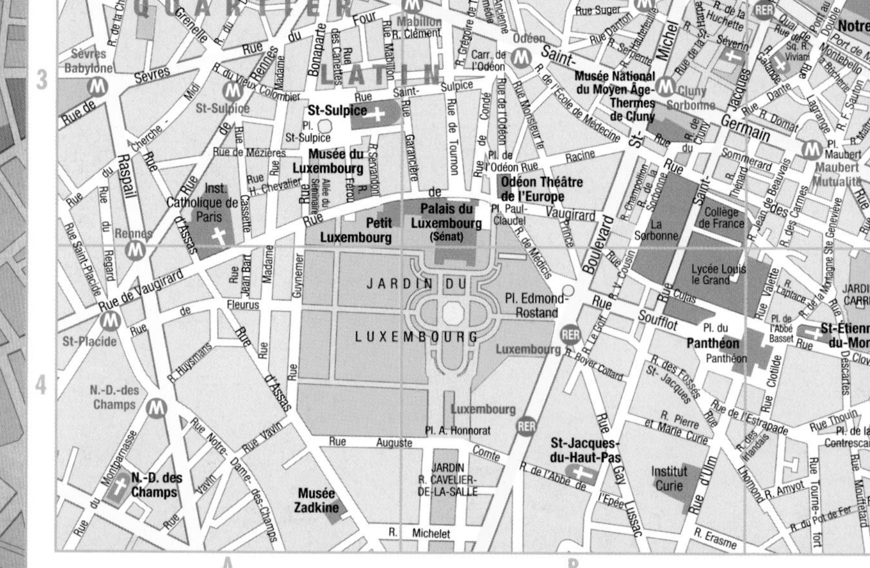
A
B
1
2
3
4
JARDIN DES TUILERIES
Rue de Rivoli
Tuileries
St-Roch
Pyramides
Musée des Arts Décoratifs
Comédie Française
Palais Royal
JARDIN DU PALAIS ROYAL
Banque de France
Hôtel des Postes
St-Eustache
Bourse de Commerce
Étienne Marcel
Les Halles
Forum des Halles
Châtelet Les Halles
JARDIN DU CARROUSEL
Arc de Triomphe du Carrousel
Pl. du Carrousel
Cour Napoléon
Pyramide
Musée du Louvre
JARDIN DE L'INFANTE
Palais Royal Musée du Louvre
Louvre Rivoli
St-Germain-l'Auxerrois
Pont Neuf
Châtelet
Tour St Jacques
Musée d'Orsay
Quai des Tuileries
Port des Tuileries
Port de Solférino
Quai Voltaire
Quai Malaquais
Quai François-Mitterrand
Institut de France
Hôtel des Monnaies
École Nationale Supérieure des Beaux-Arts
Th. du Châtelet
Th. de la Ville
Conciergerie Palais de Justice
Ste-Chapelle
ÎLE DE LA CITÉ
Préfecture de Police
Hôtel Dieu
Cité
St-Thomas d'Aquin
Rue du Bac
Bd St-Germain
St-Germain-des-Prés
Mabillon
QUARTIER LATIN
Odéon
St-Michel
Notre-Dame
Sèvres Babylone
St-Sulpice
Musée National du Moyen Âge-Thermes de Cluny
Cluny Sorbonne
Maubert Mutualité
Musée du Luxembourg
Inst. Catholique de Paris
Odéon Théâtre de l'Europe
Palais du Luxembourg (Sénat)
Petit Luxembourg
La Sorbonne
Collège de France
Lycée Louis le Grand
Rennes
JARDIN DU LUXEMBOURG
Pl. Edmond-Rostand
Luxembourg
Panthéon
St-Étienne-du-Mont
JARDIN CARRÉ
St-Placide
N.-D.-des Champs
N.-D. des Champs
Musée Zadkine
JARDIN R. CAVELIER-DE-LA-SALLE
St-Jacques-du-Haut-Pas
Institut Curie
Rue de Vaugirard
Boulevard Raspail
Boulevard St-Michel
Rue St-Jacques
Rue Soufflot
Rue d'Assas
Rue Gay Lussac
Rue d'Ulm
Rue Mouffetard
Pl. de la Contrescarpe

329
D
E
1
2
3
4
Musée des Arts et Métiers
Ste Élisabeth
Arts et Métiers
St-Nicolas-des-Champs
Sq. du Temple
Parmentier
Oberkampf
Cirque d'Hiver
Filles du Calvaire
MARAIS
JARDIN ST-AIGNAN
Musée d'Art et d'Histoire du Judaïsme
Musée de la Chasse et de la Nature
Archives Nat.
Musée de l'Histoire de France
Hôtel de Rohan
Musée National Picasso
St-Sébastien-Froissart
St-Ambroise
Richard Lenoir
St-Denys du St-Sacrement
Musée Bricard
Musée Cognacq-Jay
Musée Carnavalet
Chemin Vert
Bréguet-Sabin
Biblio-thèque Hist.
Pl. des Vosges
Maison de Victor Hugo
St-Gervais-St-Protais
St-Paul/St-Louis
Mémorial de la Shoah
Hôtel de Sully (Centre des Monuments Nationaux)
Théâtre de la Bastille
Hôtel de Sens
Pont Marie
Pl. de la Bastille
ÎLE ST-LOUIS
Mémorial de la Déportation
St-Louis-en-l'Île
Sully Morland
Opéra National de Paris Bastille
Ledru-Rollin
Bibliothèque de l'Arsenal
Institut du Monde Arabe
Viaduc des Arts
Universités Paris VI-Paris VII Pierre et Marie Curie
JARDIN TINO ROSSI
Jussieu
Arènes de Lutèce
Ménagerie
Quai de la Rapée
Pl. Mazas
Gare de Lyon
RER
JARDIN DES PLANTES
Place Valhubert
Gare d'Austerlitz
Muséum National d'Histoire Naturelle
Mosquée de Paris (Institut Musulman)
Grande Galerie de l'Evolution
0 100 200 300 400 500 m
0 100 200 300 400 500 yds

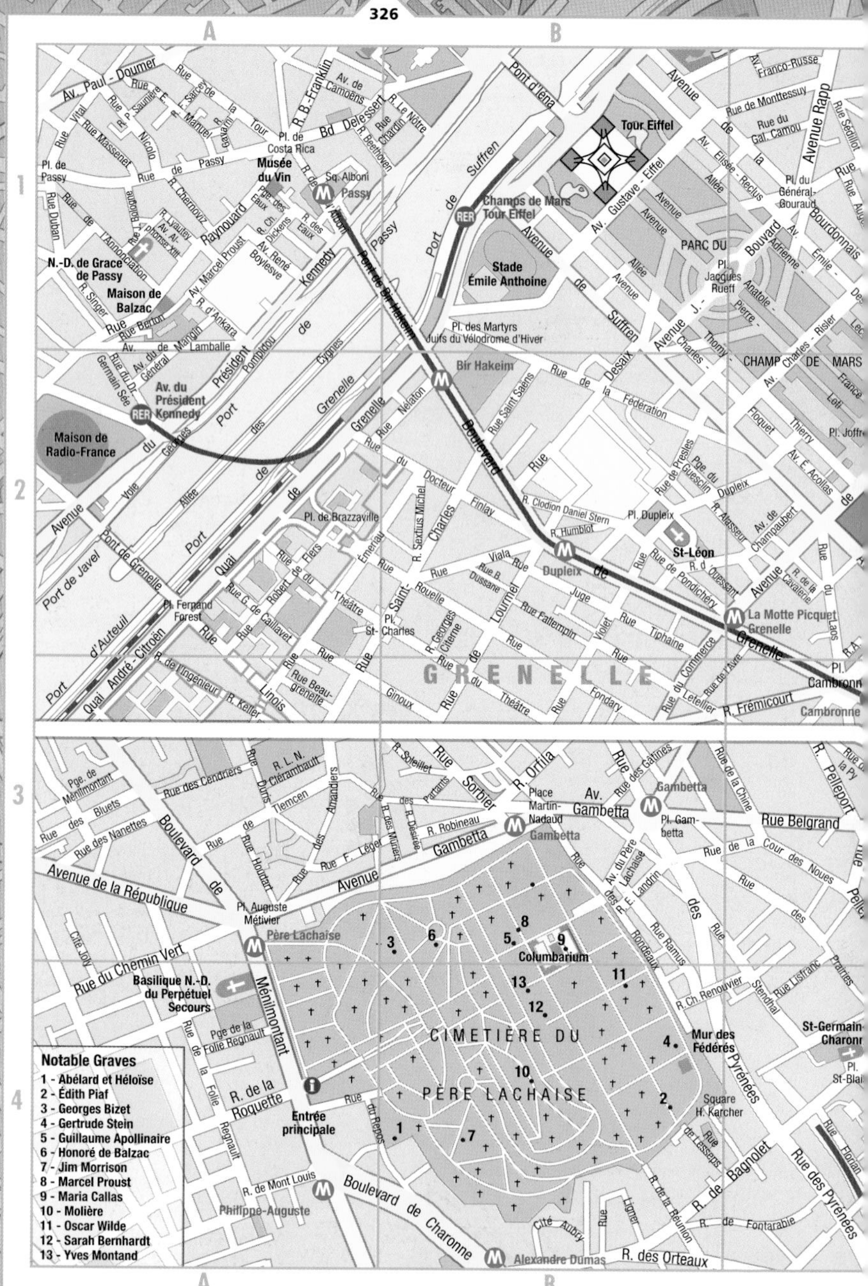

326

Notable Graves

1 - Abélard et Héloïse
2 - Édith Piaf
3 - Georges Bizet
4 - Gertrude Stein
5 - Guillaume Apollinaire
6 - Honoré de Balzac
7 - Jim Morrison
8 - Marcel Proust
9 - Maria Callas
10 - Molière
11 - Oscar Wilde
12 - Sarah Bernhardt
13 - Yves Montand

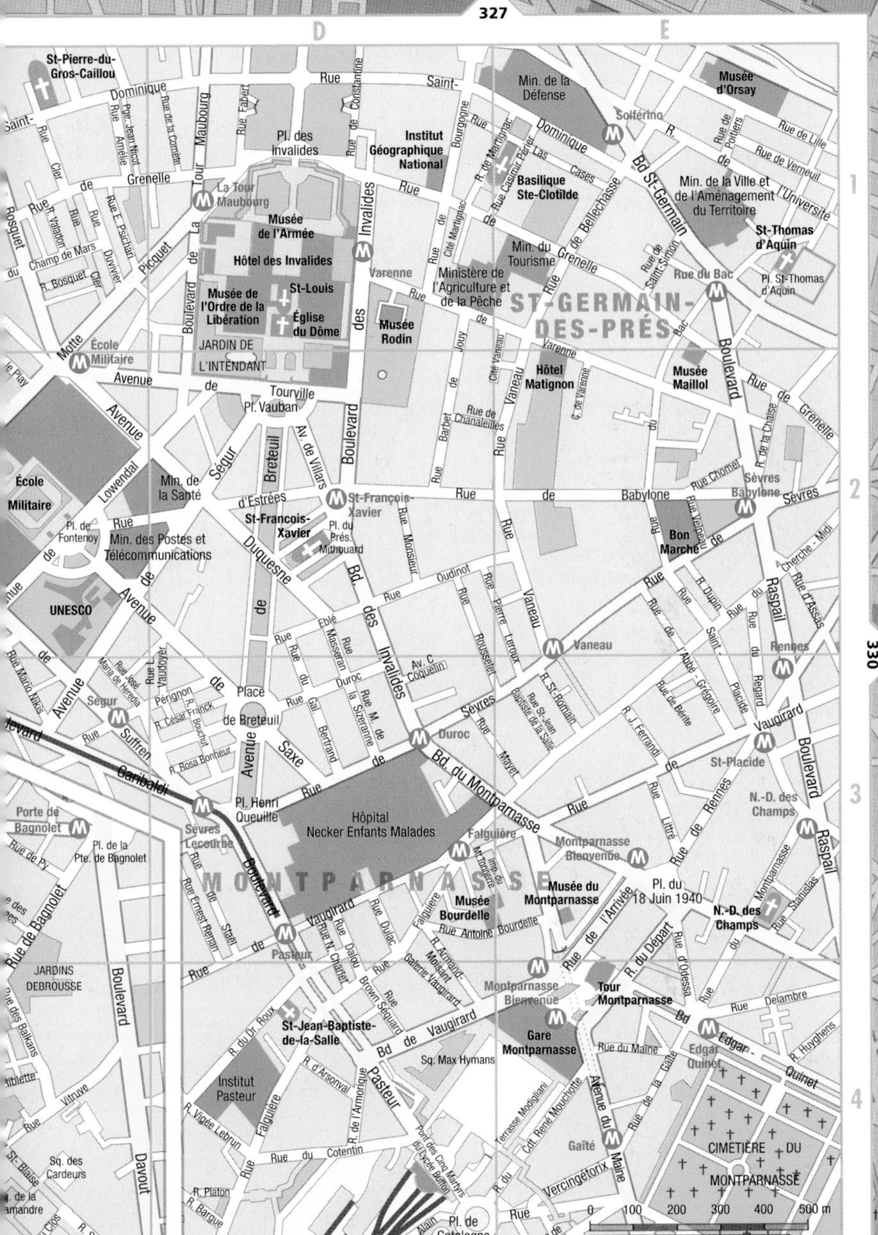

D
E
1
2
3
4
330

St-Pierre-du-Gros-Caillou
Rue Saint-Dominique
Rue de Grenelle
Rue Cler
Rue Amélie
Pge. Jean Nicot
Rue de la Comète
Boulevard de La Tour Maubourg
Rue Fabert
Rue de Constantine
Pl. des Invalides
Institut Géographique National
Min. de la Défense
Musée d'Orsay
Solférino
Rue de Lille
Rue de Verneuil
Rue de Poitiers
Rue de l'Université
Bd St-Germain
Rue de Bourgogne
R. de Martignac
Rue Casimir Périer
Rue Las Cases
Basilique Ste-Clotilde
Rue de Bellechasse
Min. de la Ville et de l'Aménagement du Territoire
St-Thomas d'Aquin
Pl. St-Thomas d'Aquin
Rue du Bac
Rue de Saint-Simon
La Tour Maubourg
Rue R. Valadon
Rue E. Psichari
Rue Duvivier
Champ de Mars
R. Bosquet
Rue Cler
Avenue Bosquet
Avenue de La Motte Picquet
Musée de l'Armée
Hôtel des Invalides
St-Louis
Église du Dôme
Musée de l'Ordre de la Libération
JARDIN DE L'INTENDANT
Boulevard des Invalides
Varenne
Musée Rodin
Cité Martignac
Ministère de l'Agriculture et de la Pêche
Min. du Tourisme
ST-GERMAIN-DES-PRÉS
Rue de Varenne
Cité Vaneau
Hôtel Matignon
C. de Varenne
Musée Maillol
Boulevard Raspail
Rue de la Chaise
École Militaire
Avenue de Tourville
Pl. Vauban
Avenue de Ségur
Avenue de Breteuil
Av. de Villars
Rue Barbet de Jouy
Rue de Chanaleilles
Rue Vaneau
Rue de Babylone
Rue Chomel
Sèvres Babylone
Rue de Sèvres
Rue Velpeau
Bon Marché
École Militaire
Avenue de Lowendal
Min. de la Santé
Rue d'Estrées
St-François-Xavier
Pl. du Prés. Mithouard
Pl. de Fontenoy
Min. des Postes et Télécommunications
Rue Duquesne
Rue Monsieur
Rue Oudinot
Rue Pierre Leroux
Rue Rousselet
Cherche-Midi
Rue d'Assas
Rue R. Dupin
Rue de l'Abbé-Grégoire
Rue Saint-Placide
Rue du Regard
Rennes
UNESCO
Avenue de Suffren
Rue Eblé
Rue Masseran
Rue Duroc
Av. C Coquelin
Vaneau
R. St-Romain
Rue St-Jean Baptiste de la Salle
Rue de Bérite
R. J. Ferrandi
Rue Mario Nikis
Rue José Maria de Heredia
Rue L. Vaudoyer
Pérignon
R. César Franck
R. Bouchut
R. Rosa Bonheur
Place de Breteuil
Avenue de Saxe
Rue du Gal. Bertrand
Rue de la Sizeranne
Rue M. de
Duroc
Rue Mayet
Ségur
Boulevard Garibaldi
Pl. Henri Queuille
Sèvres Lecourbe
Hôpital Necker Enfants Malades
Bd. du Montparnasse
Rue de Vaugirard
St-Placide
Boulevard Raspail
N.-D. des Champs
Rue Littré
Rue de Rennes
Porte de Bagnolet
Pl. de la Pte. de Bagnolet
Rue de Py
MONTPARNASSE
Falguière
Rue Mt Tonnerre
Imp. du
Montparnasse Bienvenüe
Musée du Montparnasse
Pl. du 18 Juin 1940
Rue de l'Arrivée
N.-D. des Champs
Rue Stanislas
Rue Notre-Dame-des-Champs
Rue du Montparnasse
Rue de Bagnolet
Rue Ernest Renan
Rue de Staël
Boulevard de Vaugirard
Rue Falguière
Rue N. Charlet
Rue Dalou
Rue Dulac
Musée Bourdelle
Rue Antoine Bourdelle
R. Armand-Moisant
Galerie Vaugirard
R. du Départ
Rue d'Odessa
JARDINS DEBROUSSE
Boulevard Davout
Rue des Balkans
Pasteur
Rue Brown Séquard
Montparnasse Bienvenüe
Tour Montparnasse
Rue Delambre
Bd Edgar Quinet
R. Huyghens
St-Jean-Baptiste-de-la-Salle
R. du Dr. Roux
Bd de Vaugirard
Gare Montparnasse
Rue du Maine
Edgar Quinet
Riblette
Rue Vitruve
R. d'Arsonval
Boulevard Pasteur
Sq. Max Hymans
Institut Pasteur
R. Vigée Lebrun
Rue Falguière
R. de l'Armorique
Pont des Cinq Martyrs du Lycée Buffon
Terrasse Modigliani
Cdt. René Mouchotte
Avenue du Maine
Rue de la Gaîté
Gaîté
CIMETIÈRE DU MONTPARNASSE
St-Blaise
Sq. des Cardeurs
Rue du Cotentin
R. Platon
R. Bargue
R. de la Mandre
Rue du Clos
R. St-Blaise
Rue Vercingétorix
Pl. de Catalogne
Rue Alain
Rue de l'Ouest
0 100 200 300 400 500 m
0 100 200 300 400 500 yds

A
B
1
2
3
4
Hôtel Banville
Hôtel Andrea
Av. du Roule
Av. de la Porte des Ternes
Pl. du Gal. Koenig
Av. de Verzy
Rue de Montrosier
Rue de Sablonville
Rue du Midi
Rue de Chartres
Blvd. Pershing
Palais des Congrès
R. Belidor
Boulevard Pereire (Nord)
Boulevard Pereire (Sud)
Pl. de Verdun
Pl. de la Porte Maillot
Porte Maillot
Sq. de l'Amiral Bruix
RER
Neuilly Porte Maillot
R. du Débarcadère
Avenue de la Grande Armée
R. D. Poisson
Rue Brunel
Pl. St-Ferdinand
Rue St-Ferdinand
Rue du Colonel Moll
R. d'Armaillé
St-Ferdinand Ste-Thérèse
Rue Labie
Avenue des Ternes
Rue Guersant
R. Torricelli
Rue Lebon
Rue Pierre Demours
R. Faraday
R. de St-Senoch
Rue Laugier
Avenue Niel
Rue Rennequin
Rue Fourcroy
R. Villebois Mareuil
Rue Bayen
Rue Saussier Leroy
Rue Laugier
Rue Poncelet
R. Th. de Banville
Avenue de Wagram
R. Théodule Ribot
Rue de Courcelles
Rue Léon
Rue Marguerite
Rue Renaudes
Pl. de République de l'Équateur
Sven Kyrk
TERNES
Pl. des Ternes
Ternes
Espace Wagram
St-Alexandre-Nevsky
Rue du Faubourg St-Honoré
Rue Daru
Avenue Hoche
Sq. du Roule
Rue des Acacias
R. de l'Arc de Triomphe
Avenue Mac Mahon
Rue de l'Étoile
Guy Savoy
St-Joseph
Rue Beaujon
Argentine
Pl. du Gal. Patton
Pl. Y. et C. Morandat
R. Anatole de la Forge
Avenue Carnot
Rue Weber
Villa Dupont
Rue Marbeau
Rue Lalo
Rue Pergolèse
Av. de Malakoff
Rue Duret
Rue Piccini
Rue Le Sueur
Rue Chalgrin
R. Rude
Ch. de Gaulle Étoile
Arc de Triomphe
Pl. Charles-de-Gaulle
Ch. de Gaulle-Étoile
Av. de Tilsit
Villa Saïd
Sq. de l'Av. Foch
Avenue Foch
Av. de Friedland
St-Sacrement
Taillevent
Rue Lord Byron
Rue Balzac
Rue Washington
Avenue des Champs
Musée Arménien/ Musée d'Ennery
R. Crevaux
Rue Picot
Rue de la Pompe
Avenue Victor-Hugo
Pl. du Venezuela
Rue Leroux
Rue Paul Valéry
Rue Lauriston
Rue de Presbourg
Kléber
Avenue Kléber
Rue La Pérouse
Rue Dumont d'Urville
R. Newton
Rue Galilée
George V
Rue Vernet
Fouquet's Barrière
Ladurée Salon de Thé
R. Euler
Rue Spontini
Rue E. Ménier
Rue Dosne
Rue Bugeaud
Victor Hugo
Pl. Victor Hugo
Réservoirs de Passy
Rue Copernic
Hôtel Keppler
Rue Keppler
Rue Bassano
Rue Magellan
Hôtel François 1er
Pl. H. Dunant
Rue Bauchart
Rue Lincoln
Rue Quentin Bauchart
Rue Pierre Charron
St-Honoré d'Eylau
Rue Mérimée
Pl. Jean Monnet
Nouvelle Église St-Honoré d'Eylau
Rue Boissière
Rue Cimarosa
Rue de Belloy
CHAILLOT
Avenue d'Iéna
Pl. des États-Unis
Rue Giraudoux
Four Seasons George V
Av. George V
Hôtel de Serbie
Pl. Amiral de Grasse
R. G. Bizet
Rue de l'Amiral d'Estaing
Rue de Lübeck
St-Pierre de Chaillot
American Cathedral in Paris
Rue Pierre 1er de Serbie
Rue du Boccador
Avenue Marceau
Boissière
Rue Belles Feuilles
Rue St-Didier
Rue Raymond Poincaré
R. Léo Delibes
Rue Hamelin
Rue Boissière
Rue de Longchamp
Pl. de Mexico
St-Etienne
Musée Guimet
Musée Galliera
Musée de la Mode et du Costume
R. Goethe
R. de Galliera
Hôtel de la Trémoille
Th. des Champs-Élysées
Rue Decamps
Avenue d'Eylau
Iéna
Pl. d'Iéna
Président Wilson
Rue de Magdebourg
Palais de Tokyo
Pl. de l'Alma
Alma Marceau
Av. Georges-Mandel
Ministère de l'Environnement
Rue Greuze
R. du Pasteur M. Boegner
Union de l'Europe Occidentale
Av. du Président Wilson
R. de la Manutention
Tokyo Eat
Musée d'Art Moderne de Paris
Site de Création Contemporaine
Trocadéro
Pl. du Trocadéro et du 11 Novembre
Palais de Chaillot
Av. Albert de Mun
Rue Fresnel
Pont de l'Alma
CIMETIÈRE DE PASSY
Rue Cortambert
Rue Pétrarque
R. du Cdt. Schloesing
Rue Scheffer
Rue Louis David
Av. Paul-Doumer
JARDIN DU TROCADÉRO
Av. des Nations-Unies
Av. de New York
Passerelle Debilly
RER
Pl. de la Résistance
Rue Cognacq-Jay
Rue Vineuse
R. B.-Franklin
Pl. de Varsovie
Pont d'Iéna
Musée du Quai Branly
Rue de l'Université
Av. de la Bourdonnais
Rue Franco-Russe
Au Bon Accueil
Avenue Rapp
Avenue Bosquet
Rue de Monttessuy
Rue du Gal. Camou
Rue Sédillot
Hotel
Restaurant
0 100 200 300 400 500 m
0 100 200 300 400 500 yds
Bd. Delessert
Rue Chardin
R. Le Nôtre
Av. des
Avenue
Tour Eiffel
Fontaine de Mars
340

D
E
1
2
3
4
336
341
WAGRAM
Rue de Phalsbourg
Av. de Villiers
Boulevard des Batignolles
Villiers
Pl. P. Goubaux
Rome
Rue de Rome
Rue Clapeyron
Rue de St-Pétersbourg
St-André de l'Europe
Rue Ballu
Rue Jadin
Rue de Prony
Rue G. Berger
Boulevard de Courcelles
R. Andrieux
Berne Opéra
Pl. de Dublin
R. de Bucarest
Th. de l'Œuvre
R. J. Lefebvre
Hôtelier Drouant
Pl. de la République Dominicaine
Monceau
Av. Velasquez
Rue Monceau
Rue de Naples
Rue de Berne
Rue de Turin
Rue de Moscou
Rue d'Amsterdam
Rue de Liège
Rue de Clichy
PARC DE MONCEAU
Musée Cernuschi
Musée Nissim de Camondo
Boulevard Malesherbes
Rue d'Edimbourg
Rue de Constantinople
Europe
Pl. de l'Europe
Rue de Milan
Liège
R. de Vézelay
Rue du Gal. Foy
Rue de Madrid
Rue de Vienne
Rue Murillo
Pl. de Rio de Janeiro
Rue de Lisbonne
Rue de Rocher
Rue Portalis
Pl. de Budapest
Rue d'Athènes
Rue de Londres
Rue de Courcelles
Rue de Téhéran
Rue Treilhard
Rue Miromesnil
Gare St-Lazare
Rue de la Bienfaisance
R. de Budapest
R. du Docteur Lancereaux
Av. de Messine
Musée Jacquemart-André
Café Jacquemart-André
St-Augustin
Laborde
St-Lazare
Rue St-Lazare
Boulevard Haussmann
Pl. St-Augustin
Pl. G. Péri
R. de la Pépinière
Rue du Havre
Rue de Rome
L. Condorcet
St-Louis d'Antin
Rue de La Baume
Av. Percier
Rue d'Argenson
Rue La Boétie
Miromesnil
Rue de Miromesnil
Rue d'Astorg
Rue Lavoisier
Rue d'Anjou
Rue Pasquier
Havre Caumartin
Rue du Berri
St-Philippe-du-Roule
Bradford Elysées
Hôtel Daniel
Rue du Faubourg St-Honoré
Av. Delcasse
Rue de Penthièvre
Rue Cambacérès
Rue Roquépine
St-Esprit
Rue des Mathurins
R. Greffulhe
Hôtel Madeleine Opéra
Rue de Castellane
Rue Auber
Rue P. Baudry
R. d'Artois
St-Philippe-du-Roule
Le Bristol
Archevêché de Paris
Rue Tronchet
Comédie Caumartin
Rue de la Ville l'Évêque
Rue Montalivet
R. Chauveau Lagarde
Rue Vignon
Rue Godot de Mauroy
Rue de Caumartin
Rue Edouard VII
Rue du Colisée
Rue Jean Mermoz
Rue Rabelais
Av. Matignon
Pl. Beauvau
Rue du Cirque
Rue de Ponthieu
Sens
Market
Avenue de Marigny
Palais de l'Élysée
R. d'Aguesseau
Rue Boissy d'Anglas
Ste-Marie-de-la-Madeleine
Pl. de la Madeleine
Rue de Sèze
Bd de la Madeleine
R. des Capucines
Rd.-Pt. des Champs-Élysées Marcel Dassault
Av. Gabriel
Rue de Marignan
Spoon, Food & Wine
Franklin D. Roosevelt
Café Le Nôtre
Th. Marigny
R. de l'Élysée
Madeleine
Lavinia
Rue Cambon
Hôtel Mansart
Ministère de la Justice
Hôtel Ritz
Av. des Champs-Élysées
Th. du Rond-Point
Champs-Élysées Clémenceau
Espace Pierre Cardin
Avenue Gabriel
L'Estaminet Gaya
Rue Duphot
Rue Royale
Hôtel de Crillon
N.-D. de L'Assomption
Place Vendôme
Ave Montaigne
Alain Ducasse Plaza Athénée
Savy
Church of Scotland
Place Clémenceau
Av. Ch. Girault
Pl. M. Barrès
Rue St-Florentin
Rue St-Honoré
L'Ardoise
Rue du Mont Thabor
R. de Castiglione
Rue François 1er
Hôtel Plaza-Athénée
Av. Franklin-D.-Roosevelt
Palais de la Découverte
Grand Palais
Av. W. Churchill
Petit Palais
Av. Dutuit
Av. Edward - Tuck
Concorde
Pl. de la Concorde
Rue de Rivoli
Jeu de Paume (Site Concorde)
Terrasse des Feuillants
Hôtel Meurice
Kinugawa
Rue Jean Goujon
St-Jean Baptiste
Cours Albert 1er
Cours la Reine
Hôtel Brighton
Musée de l'Orangerie
JARDIN DES TUILERIES
Tuileries
Pont des Invalides
Pont Alexandre III
Seine
Pont de la Concorde
Terrasse du Bord de l'Eau
Quai des Tuileries
Min. des Affaires Etrangères
Invalides
RER
Rue R. E. Pelterie
Assemblée Nationale (Palais Bourbon)
Quai d'Orsay
Aérogare des Invalides
Av. R. Schuman
Rue Jean-Nicot
L'Esplanade
Min. des Affaires Europ.
Rue A. Briand
Assemblée Nationale
Min. de l'Artisanat, du Commerce et de la Consommation
Rue Solférino
Musée d'Orsay
Rue de l'Université
Rue Surcouf
Boulevard de La Tour Maubourg
Rue Fabert
Av. du Mal. Gallieni
Rue de Constantine
Pl. du Palais Bourbon
Rue de Lille
Quai Anatole-France
L'Affriolé
Bellota-Bellota
L'Ami Jean
Rue Malar
Rue Saint-Dominique
Rue de Bourgogne
Min. de la Défense
Bd St-Germain
Musée de la Légion d'Honneur
Le 20 de Bellchasse
Rue de Poitiers
St-Pierre-du-Gros-Caillou
Chez les Anges
Solférino

A
B
1
2
3
4
335
L'Etoile de Montmartre
Musée de Montmartre
Terrass
Le Bouclard
Timhôtel Montmartre
La Famille
Regyn's Montmartre
Le Sancerre
Au Grain de Folie
Chez Toinette
Le Relais Gascon
La Fourmi
Hôtel Royal Fromentin
Moulin Rouge
Basilique du Sacré-Cœur
Halle St-Pierre
L'Auberge du Clou
Pétrelle
Hôtel Amour
Musée de la Vie Romantique
Musée Gustave-Moreau
Casa Olympe
Chez Jean
Dok's Café
Gare St-Lazare
Printemps
Galeries Lafayette
Palais Garnier
Hôtel Madeleine Opéra
Hôtel Chopin
Grévin
Folies Bergère
Aux Lyonnais
Hôtel Vivienne
Café de la Ville
Lavinia
Harry's Bar
Hôtel Mansart
Ministère de la Justice
Hôtel Ritz
L'Estaminet Gaya
Place Vendôme
Drouant
La Ferme Opéra
Hôtel Edouard VII
L'Absinthe
L'Ardoise
Juvéniles
Bibliothèque Nationale-Richelieu
Basilique N.-D. des Victoires
1. Le Grand Véfour
2. Willi's Wine Bar
Kinugawa
Hôtel Meurice
Hôtel Brighton
Hôtel Normandy
Takara
Banque de France
Restaurant du Palais Royal
Hôtel de Rouen
Le Tambour
Hôtel Tiquetonne
L'Escargot Montorgueil
A
B

338

D
E
1
2
3
4
0 100 200 300 400 500 m
0 100 200 300 400 500 yds
Hotel
Restaurant
Le Bouclard
Kube Rooms & Bars
Rotonde de la Villette
St-Joseph Artisan
Chez Michel
Hôtel Apollo
Holiday Inn Paris-Gare de l'Est
Le Jemmapes
Hôtel Garden St Martin
Chez Prune
Palais des Glaces
Auberge Pyrénées-Cévennes
Astier
Au P'tit Garage
Plein Soleil
L'Abreuvoir
Café Charbon, La Maizon
Hôtel Saint-Louis Bastille
Rosso
Guillaume
Au Bascou
Andy Wahloo
Gare du Nord
Gare de l'Est
Hôpital Fernand Widal
Hôpital St-Louis
Hôpital St-Lazare
BELLEVILLE
Bassin de la Villette
Pl. de Stalingrad
Pl. du Colonel Fabien
Pl. de la République
Conservatoire des Arts et Métiers
Musée des Arts et Métiers
Jardin Villemin
Boulevard de la Chapelle
Boulevard de Magenta
Boulevard de Sébastopol
Boulevard Voltaire
Boulevard du Temple
Avenue de la République
Avenue Jean-Jaurès
Avenue de Flandre
Boulevard de la Villette
Quai de Valmy
Quai de Jemmapes

339

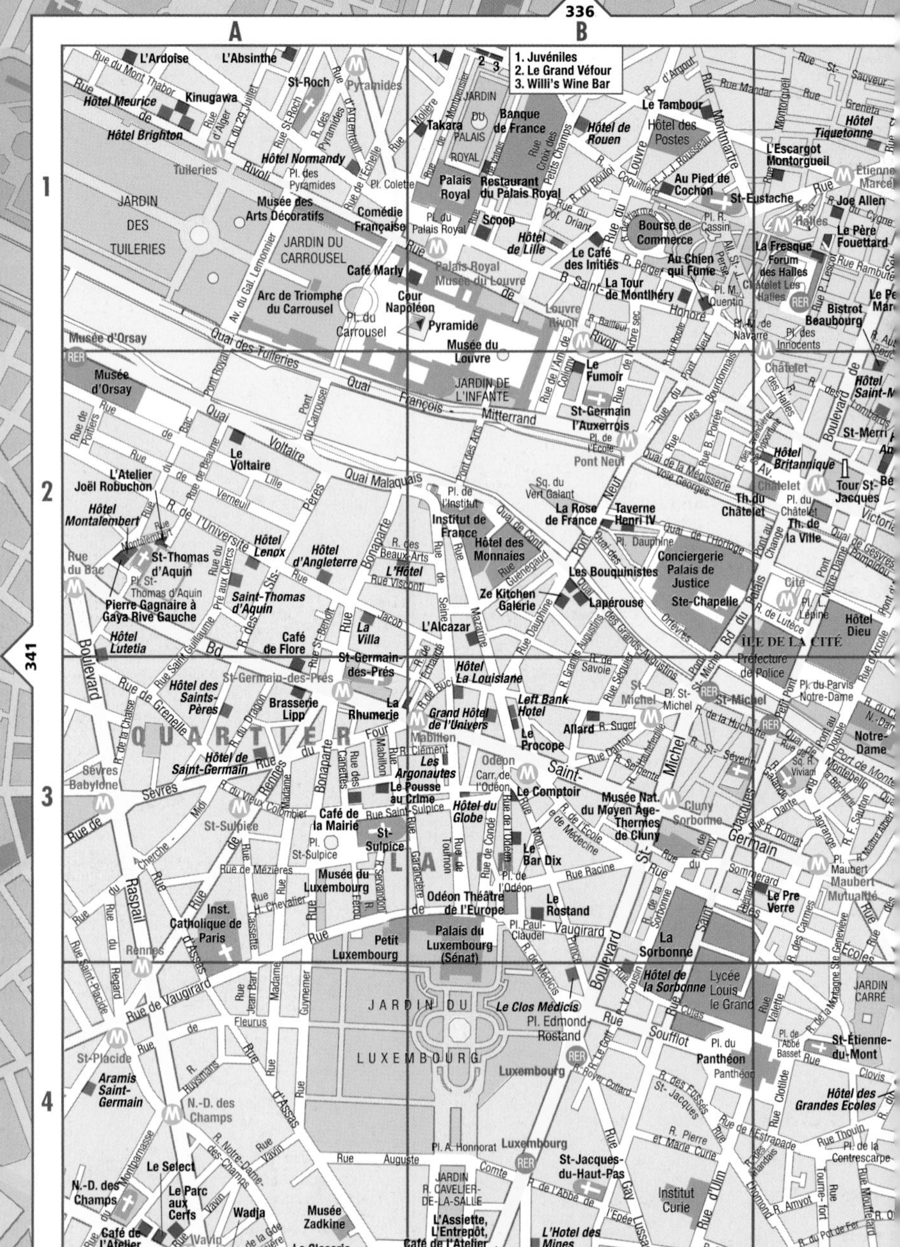

336

341

A B

1. Juvéniles
2. Le Grand Véfour
3. Willi's Wine Bar

1

L'Ardoise
L'Absinthe
St-Roch
Pyramides
Hôtel Meurice
Kinugawa
Hôtel Brighton
Tuileries
Hôtel Normandy
Pl. des Pyramides
Pl. Colette
JARDIN DES TUILERIES
Musée des Arts Décoratifs
Comédie Française
JARDIN DU CARROUSEL
Café Marly
Arc de Triomphe du Carrousel
Pl. du Carrousel
Cour Napoléon
Pyramide
Musée d'Orsay
Takara
JARDIN DU PALAIS ROYAL
Banque de France
Palais Royal
Restaurant du Palais Royal
Pl. du Palais Royal
Scoop
Hôtel de Lille
Palais Royal Musée du Louvre
Musée du Louvre
Hôtel de Rouen
Le Tambour
Hôtel des Postes
Au Pied de Cochon
St-Eustache
Bourse de Commerce
Pl. R. Cassin
Le Café des Initiés
Au Chien qui Fume
La Tour de Montlhéry
Pl. M. Quentin
Louvre Rivoli
Hôtel Tiquetonne
L'Escargot Montorgueil
Étienne Marcel
Joe Allen
Le Père Fouettard
La Fresque
Forum des Halles
Châtelet Les Halles
Bistrot Beaubourg
Pl. M. de Navarre
Pl. des Innocents

2

Musée d'Orsay
JARDIN DE L'INFANTE
Le Fumoir
St-Germain l'Auxerrois
Pl. de l'École
Pont Neuf
Le Voltaire
L'Atelier Joël Robuchon
Hôtel Montalembert
Rue du Bac
St-Thomas d'Aquin
Pl. St-Thomas d'Aquin
Hôtel Lenox
Hôtel d'Angleterre
Saint-Thomas d'Aquin
Pierre Gagnaire à Gaya Rive Gauche
Hôtel Lutetia
Café de Flore
La Villa
Pl. de l'Institut
Institut de France
Hôtel des Monnaies
L'Hôtel
L'Alcazar
Sq. du Vert Galant
La Rose de France
Taverne Henri IV
Pl. Dauphine
Les Bouquinistes
Ze Kitchen Galerie
Lapérouse
Conciergerie Palais de Justice
Ste-Chapelle
Châtelet
Hôtel Saint-Merri
St-Merri
Hôtel Britannique
Th. du Châtelet
Th. de la Ville
Tour St-Jacques
Pl. du Châtelet
Cité
Pl. L. Lépine
Hôtel Dieu
ÎLE DE LA CITÉ

3

St-Germain-des-Prés
Hôtel des Saints-Pères
Brasserie Lipp
La Rhumerie
QUARTIER LATIN
Hôtel de Saint-Germain
Sèvres Babylone
St-Sulpice
Mabillon
Les Argonautes
Le Pousse au Crime
Café de la Mairie
St-Sulpice
Pl. St-Sulpice
Musée du Luxembourg
Hôtel La Louisiane
Grand Hôtel de l'Univers
Left Bank Hôtel
Le Procope
Allard
Odéon
Carr. de l'Odéon
Le Comptoir
Hôtel du Globe
Le Bar Dix
Pl. de l'Odéon
Odéon Théâtre de l'Europe
Le Rostand
Pl. Paul-Claudel
Inst. Catholique de Paris
Petit Luxembourg
Palais du Luxembourg (Sénat)
St-Michel
Pl. St-Michel
Musée Nat. du Moyen Âge-Thermes de Cluny
Cluny Sorbonne
Préfecture de Police
Pl. du Parvis Notre-Dame
Notre-Dame
Sq. R. Viviani
Le Pre Verre
Maubert Mutualité
Pl. Maubert
La Sorbonne

4

Rennes
St-Placide
Aramis Saint-Germain
N.-D. des Champs
JARDIN DU LUXEMBOURG
Le Clos Médicis
Pl. Edmond-Rostand
Luxembourg
Hôtel de la Sorbonne
Lycée Louis le Grand
Panthéon
Pl. du Panthéon
JARDIN CARRÉ
Pl. de l'Abbé Basset
St-Étienne-du-Mont
Hôtel des Grandes Écoles
Pl. de la Contrescarpe
Le Select
N.-D. des Champs
Le Parc aux Cerfs
Wadja
Café de l'Atelier
Les Tontons
Vavin
Musée Zadkine
La Closerie des Lilas
Pl. A. Honnorat
JARDIN R. CAVELIER-DE-LA-SALLE
L'Assiette, L'Entrepôt, Café de l'Atelier
St-Jacques-du-Haut-Pas
L'Hotel des Mines
L'Ourcine
Institut Curie

A B

337
D
E
1
2
3
4
MARAIS
Musée des Arts et Métiers
Au Bascou
Guillaume
Chez Omar
Murano Urban Resort
Cirque d'Hiver
Hôtel Beaumarchais
Astier
L'Abreuvoir
Hôtel Saint-Louis Bastille
Rosso
Café Charbon
Le Pamphlet
Hôtel du Petit Moulin
L'Apparemment Café
Musée de la Chasse et de la Nature
Archives Nat.
Musée d'Art et d'Histoire du Judaïsme
Musée de l'Histoire de France
La Perle
Musée Nat. Picasso
St-Denys du St-Sacrement
Le Dôme du Marais
Musée Bricard
Hôtel de la Bretonnerie
Au Petit Fer à Cheval
Le Petit Marché
Musée Carnavalet
Café de la Gare
Curieux Spaghetti Bar
Le Duo
Stolly's
Pavillon de la Reine
Grand Hôtel Jeanne d'Arc
Maison de Victor Hugo
L'Ambroisie
Hôtel de la Place des Vosges
St-Gervais-St-Protais
Mémorial de la Shoah
Hôtel de Sully (Centre des Monuments Nationaux)
Hôtel de Sens
Bofinger
Bar à Nénette
Bistrot à Vins Mélac, Crêperie Bretonne Fleurie
Mon Vieil Ami
Hôtel Lutèce
Hôtel du Jeu de Paume
Aux Vins des Pyrénées
Hôtel St-Louis Marais
Opéra National de Paris Bastille
Hôtel des Deux-Iles
Isami
L'Escale
ÎLE ST-LOUIS
Le Pavillon Bastille
Paris Main d'Or
Chez René
Institut du Monde Arabe
L'Encrier
Moissonnier
Universités Paris VI-Paris VII Pierre et Marie Curie
Viaduc des Arts
Comme Cochons
Arènes de Lutèce
Ménagerie
JARDIN DES PLANTES
Muséum National d'Histoire Naturelle
Grande Galerie de l'Evolution
Gare d'Austerlitz
Gare de Lyon
Le Train Bleu
Paradis Thaï, Chez Paul, L'Avant-Goût
L'Oulette
Hotel
Restaurant
0 100 200 300 400 500 m
0 100 200 300 400 500 yds

334
A
B
1
2
3
4
0 100 200 300 400 500 m
0 100 200 300 400 500 yds
Hotel
Restaurant
Musée du Vin
Passy
Le Sezz
N.-D. de Grace de Passy
Maison de Balzac
Tour Eiffel
Au Bon Accueil
Le Café Constant
Champs de Mars Tour Eiffel
Stade Émile Anthoine
PARC DU
CHAMP DE MARS
Pl. des Martyrs Juifs du Vélodrome d'Hiver
Bir Hakeim
Av. du Président Kennedy
Maison de Radio-France
Pl. de Brazzaville
Pl. Dupleix
St-Léon
Dupleix
La Motte Picquet Grenelle
Pl. Fernand Forest
Pl. St-Charles
GRENELLE
Pl. Cambronne
Cambronne
Quai André-Citroën
Pont de Grenelle
Pont d'Iéna
Avenue de la Bourdonnais
Avenue Rapp
Boulevard de Grenelle
Avenue de Suffren
Gambetta
Place Martin-Nadaud
Pl. Gambetta
Rue Belgrand
Avenue de la République
Boulevard de Ménilmontant
Rue du Chemin Vert
Pl. Auguste Métivier
Père Lachaise
Basilique N.-D. du Perpétuel Secours
Columbarium
CIMETIÈRE DU PÈRE LACHAISE
Mur des Fédérés
Square H. Karcher
Entrée principale
Philippe-Auguste
Boulevard de Charonne
Alexandre Dumas
R. des Orteaux
Rue des Pyrénées
R. de Bagnolet
St-Germain Charonne
Notebale Graves
1 - Abélard et Héloïse
2 - Édith Piaf
3 - Georges Bizet
4 - Gertrude Stein
5 - Guillaume Apollinaire
6 - Honoré de Balzac
7 - Jim Morrison
8 - Marcel Proust
9 - Maria Callas
10 - Molière
11 - Oscar Wilde
12 - Sarah Bernhardt
13 - Yves Montand

335
D
E
L'Affriolé
Bellota-Bellota
L'Ami Jean
Chez les Anges
Grand Hôtel Lévêque
Café du Marché
Le Walt
L'Arpège
Le Vin de Bellechasse
Hôtel Duc de Saint-Simon
Hôtel Montalambert
L'Atelier Joël Robuchon
Pierre Gagnaire à Gaya Rive Gauche
Hôtel Lutetia
Hôtel Mayet
Hôtel Aviatic
Le Parc aux Cerfs
Café de l'Atelier
Le Select
La Coupole
Hôtel Istria St-Germain
La Cagouille
ST-GERMAIN-DES-PRÉS
MONTPARNASSE
Musée d'Orsay
Hôtel des Invalides
Musée Rodin
Bon Marché
Tour Montparnasse
Gare Montparnasse
Hôpital Necker Enfants Malades
Institut Pasteur
CIMETIÈRE DU MONTPARNASSE
UNESCO
1
2
3
4
338
D
E

STREET INDEX

A

B

C

T

U

V

W–Z

General Index

A page reference in **bold** indicates the main entry in the book. A page reference in *italics* indicates a photograph.

A

B

C

N

O

P

Q

R

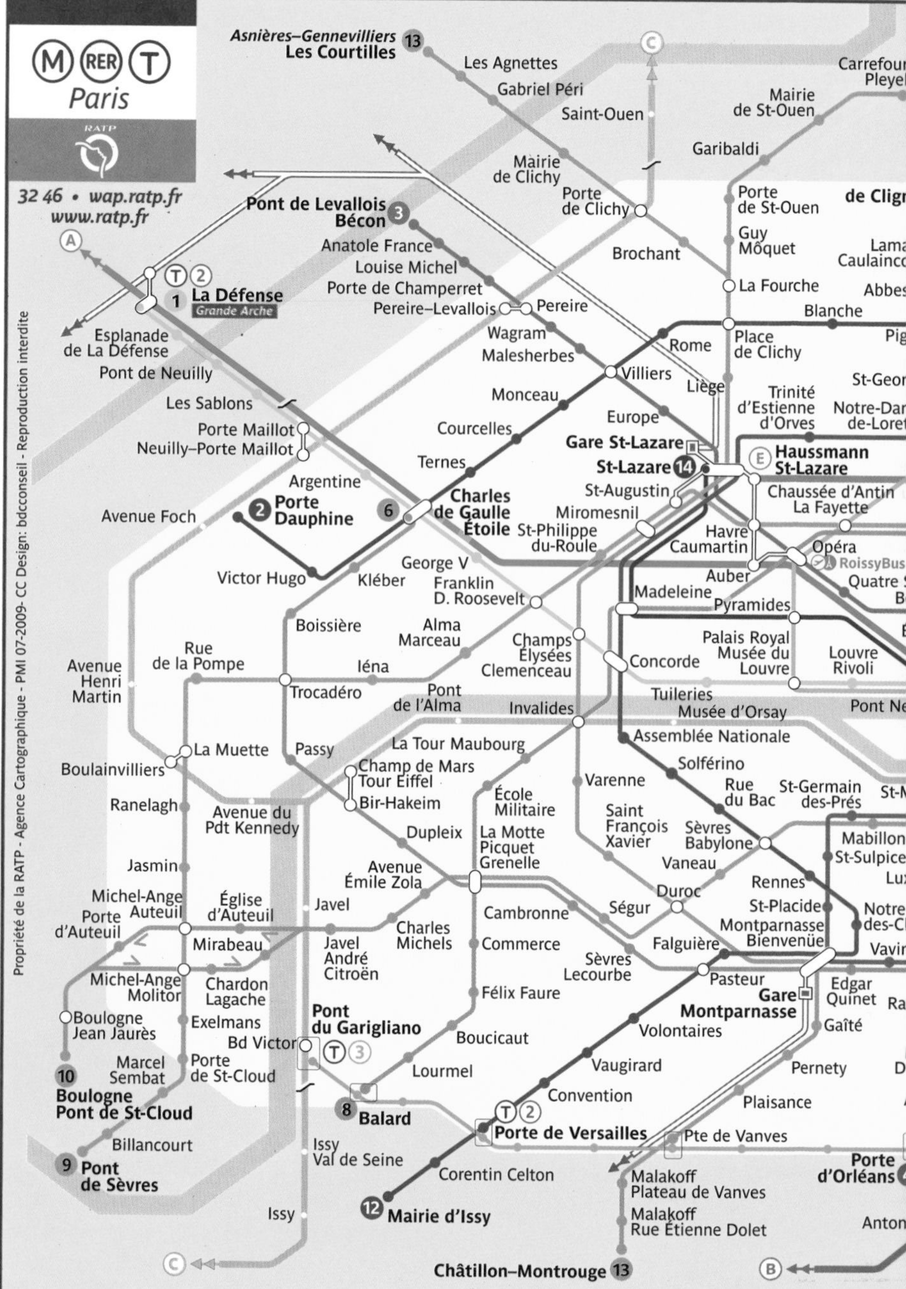
M RER T
Paris
RATP
32 46 • wap.ratp.fr
www.ratp.fr
Propriété de la RATP - Agence Cartographique - PMI 07-2009- CC Design: bdcconseil - Reproduction interdite
Asnières–Gennevilliers
Les Courtilles
13
Les Agnettes
Gabriel Péri
Saint-Ouen
Mairie de Clichy
Porte de Clichy
Carrefour Pleyel
Mairie de St-Ouen
Garibaldi
Porte de St-Ouen
Guy Môquet
La Fourche
Brochant
Pont de Levallois Bécon
3
Anatole France
Louise Michel
Porte de Champerret
Pereire–Levallois
Pereire
Wagram
Malesherbes
Monceau
Villiers
Rome
Place de Clichy
Blanche
Liège
Europe
Courcelles
Ternes
Gare St-Lazare
St-Lazare
14
Haussmann St-Lazare
E
St-Augustin
Miromesnil
Chaussée d'Antin La Fayette
Havre Caumartin
Opéra
RoissyBus
Auber
Madeleine
Pyramides
Trinité d'Estienne d'Orves
Notre-Dame-de-Lorette
St-Georges
Abbesses
Lamarck Caulaincourt
de Clignancourt
A
La Défense
Grande Arche
1
T 2
Esplanade de La Défense
Pont de Neuilly
Les Sablons
Porte Maillot
Neuilly–Porte Maillot
Argentine
2
Porte Dauphine
6
Charles de Gaulle Étoile
Avenue Foch
St-Philippe du-Roule
George V
Victor Hugo
Kléber
Franklin D. Roosevelt
Boissière
Alma Marceau
Champs Élysées Clemenceau
Concorde
Palais Royal Musée du Louvre
Louvre Rivoli
Tuileries
Rue de la Pompe
Avenue Henri Martin
Iéna
Trocadéro
Pont de l'Alma
Invalides
Musée d'Orsay
Pont Neuf
Passy
La Tour Maubourg
Assemblée Nationale
La Muette
Boulainvilliers
Champ de Mars Tour Eiffel
Bir-Hakeim
Solférino
Varenne
École Militaire
Rue du Bac
St-Germain des-Prés
Ranelagh
Avenue du Pdt Kennedy
Dupleix
La Motte Picquet Grenelle
Saint François Xavier
Sèvres Babylone
Vaneau
Mabillon
St-Sulpice
Jasmin
Avenue Émile Zola
Duroc
Rennes
St-Placide
Notre-Dame-des-Champs
Michel-Ange Auteuil
Porte d'Auteuil
Église d'Auteuil
Javel
Cambronne
Ségur
Montparnasse Bienvenüe
Charles Michels
Mirabeau
Javel André Citroën
Commerce
Falguière
Vavin
Michel-Ange Molitor
Chardon Lagache
Sèvres Lecourbe
Pasteur
Edgar Quinet
Gare Montparnasse
Boulogne Jean Jaurès
Exelmans
Félix Faure
Volontaires
Gaîté
Pont du Garigliano
Bd Victor
T 3
Boucicault
Marcel Sembat
Porte de St-Cloud
Vaugirard
Pernety
10
Boulogne Pont de St-Cloud
Lourmel
Convention
Plaisance
8
Balard
T 2
Porte de Versailles
Pte de Vanves
Billancourt
9
Pont de Sèvres
Issy Val de Seine
Corentin Celton
Malakoff Plateau de Vanves
Porte d'Orléans
Issy
12
Mairie d'Issy
Malakoff Rue Étienne Dolet
C
Châtillon–Montrouge
13
B